EIGHT DRAMAS

OF

CALDERÓN

EIGHT DRAMAS

OF

CALDERÓN

PEDRO CALDERÓN DE LA BARCA

Translated from the Spanish by
EDWARD FITZGERALD

Foreword by
MARGARET R. GREER

UNIVERSITY OF ILLINOIS PRESS
Urbana and Chicago

Foreword © 2000 by the Board of Trustees
of the University of Illinois
All rights reserved
Manufactured in the United States of America
∞ This book is printed on acid-free paper.

Library of Congress Cataloging-in-Publication Data
Calderón de la Barca, Pedro, 1600–1681.
Eight dramas of Pedro Calderón de la Barca /
translated from the Spanish by Edward FitzGerald ;
foreword by Margaret R. Greer.
p.   cm.
ISBN 0-252-06903-X (pbk. : alk paper)
1. Calderón de la Barca, Pedro, 1600–1681—
Translations into English. I. Title: 8 dramas of
Pedro Calderón de la Barca. II. FitzGerald, Edward,
1809–1883. III. Title.
PQ6292.A1F513   2000
862'.3—dc21   99-087264

P 5 4 3 2 1

CONTENTS

FOREWORD

Margaret R. Greer

Edward FitzGerald's translations of Pedro Calderón de la Barca's plays have won an enduring popularity with theater lovers, a popularity that shows no signs of diminishing. Since their first publication between 1853 and 1865, at least twelve editions or reprints of his collected Calderón translations have appeared, and individual plays—particularly *"Such Stuff as Dreams Are Made Of"*—have also been included in anthologized translations of classic drama. They have earned a place on the stage as well as the page. Witness William Poel's nineteenth-century promptbook of *"Such Stuff as Dreams Are Made Of,"* with prompt notes, deletions, additions, and a cast list with actors' addresses, preserved in the Victoria and Albert Museum in London and a typewritten copy of the same play used by the National Broadcasting Company in New York in 1938. As recently as 1997, FitzGerald's version of that play was performed by the Logos Theatre Company at the Grace Theatre in London.[1]

Like the Spanish *comedia* form itself, FitzGerald's renditions made their mark in spite of, not thanks to, their reception by literary critics. FitzGerald frankly acknowledged in the "Advertisement" that prefaced the 1853 edition of his *Six Dramas of Calderón* that he had "sunk, reduced, altered and replaced" much that he deemed not suited to English tastes. The anonymous critic who reviewed the volume for *The Athenaeum* in September of that year took advantage of that admission to dismiss his efforts as worthless, without so much as comparing FitzGerald's translations with Calderón's originals.[2] Lope de Vega, who at the turn of the seventeenth century developed the model for Spanish popular theater that Calderón would perfect, faced analogous discredit from defenders of classical dramatic precepts. But Lope and Calderón were dramatic poets who understood their public better than did their critics and shaped their dramas accordingly.

FitzGerald (1809–83) was an early Victorian poet and translator who understood the sort of dramatic reconstruction that could open up the vitality of Spanish Baroque drama for the English public of his day. Apart from his renderings of Calderón, he is best known as translator of the *Rubáiyát of Omar Khayyám* and as a superb letter-writer whose personal and literary friendships have been preserved in several volumes of letters. It is not surprising, therefore, that one of the Calderonian plays he chose to translate is *Keep Your Own Secret*, in which the reliability of friendship is a key issue.

FitzGerald was born and lived most of his life in Suffolk, attended King Edward the Sixth's Grammar School at Bury St. Edwards, then entered Trinity College, Cambridge, in 1826 and completed his degree in 1830. Having inherited wealth, he thereafter dedicated his life to reading, writing, boating, and the letter-writing that sustained his many friendships. His more famous friends included the three Tennyson brothers and Carlyle, but the most significant for his translations of Calderón was E. B. Cowell, professor of Sanskrit at Cambridge. From a shared interest in Latin and Greek classics, they went on to read Spanish and Persian literature together. In August 1850, he wrote to Frederick Tennyson that he had "begun to nibble at Spanish: at their old Ballads; which are fine things . . . I have also bounced through a play of Calderón."

He also corresponded with James Russell Lowell, Longfellow's successor as Smith Professor of Modern Languages at Harvard and appointed American ambassador to Spain in 1877. When FitzGerald received a Calderón medal from the Spanish ambassador for his translations, he gave Lowell credit for his receipt of that honor when he wrote to Charles Eliot Norton on January 18, 1882. He told Norton he thought the award should really have gone to his friend Cowell, "always reading, and teaching, Calderón at Cambridge now (as he did to me thirty years ago), in spite of all his Sanskrit Duties."

Calderón (1600–1681), whom FitzGerald would call "one of the Great Men of the world," was born and raised in Madrid in a family of the lower nobility, educated in the Jesuit Colegio Imperial, and enrolled in the University of Alcalá in 1614. He left Alcalá in 1615 when his apparently despotic father died, stipulating in his will that Pedro should continue his studies toward the priesthood and assume a chaplaincy endowed by his maternal aunt. Pedro did study canon law at the University of Salamanca between 1615 and 1619 but then turned toward a literary career, writing plays and poetry for literary competitions and entering the service of the constable of

Castile in Madrid in 1621, the same year the theater-loving Philip IV ascended the throne.

Just two years later, one of the plays performed at court during the 1623 visit of Prince Charles of Wales to Spain was Calderón's *Love, Honor and Power.* That play's title marks preoccupations that would persist throughout his career: the conflicting claims of personal desires, the public exigencies of the honor code, and the demands—and limits—of royal and paternal power. The clash frequently involves a father-son conflict and a double plot, as in his most famous work, *Life Is a Dream* (FitzGerald's *"Such Stuff as Dreams Are Made Of "*), a philosophical drama questioning knowledge, faith, freedom, and political power. A variant of that father-son conflict also animates *Three Judgments at a Blow.*

Calderón wrote approximately 120 three-act plays, most of his most famous by 1642. In delightful comedies such as *Beware of Smooth Water,* his intellectual, self-conscious art laughs at its own dramatic conventions as well as social customs. "Wife-murder" tragedies like *The Painter of His Own Dishonor* invite audiences to judge the lethal effects of the honor code. Calderón dramatizes the power of Catholic faith in religious dramas such as *The Constant Prince* (which FitzGerald did not like) and his Faustian story of two Christian martyrs, *The Mighty Magician. The Mayor of Zalamea* pits civilian justice and honor as classless moral integrity against military law and aristocratic privilege.

Calderón was made a Knight of the Military Order of Santiago by Philip IV in 1637, and between 1640 and 1642 he served in two campaigns during the Catalonian Revolt. During that dark decade his two brothers died, and war and royal mourning closed the theaters (1644–49). In 1651 Calderón chose to become a priest and take up the endowed family chaplaincy. Thereafter, he wrote less for public theaters but composed numerous court productions. In elaborate court spectacle plays he wrote tragicomedies on mythological themes, making lavish and effective use of music, dance, scenery, and stage effects that simultaneously entertained, exalted, and instructed the reigning monarch. From 1648 until his death, Calderón was the exclusive author of the Madrid *autos sacramentales* (allegorical religious dramas), one-act, open-air performances for the annual Corpus Christi festival. Neither the court spectacle plays nor the *autos* drew FitzGerald's interest. He did, however, translate lengthy descriptions that Calderón included in one version of *Beware of Smooth Water* and that give some sense of Baroque court ceremonies in the progression of Philip IV's second wife, Mariana of Austria, from Vienna to Madrid.

Within decades of their composition, translations of Calderón's works or adaptation of his plots spread his influence to Italy, France, England, the Spanish Netherlands, Holland, and Germany. In Germany and England they would become central in the Romantic renewal of appreciation of the genius of Spanish golden age drama and its master craftsman, Calderón. By FitzGerald's day, his reputation as a dramatist had declined, as the English poet commented in a letter to W. B. Donne on August 10 1852: "I have begun again to read Calderón with Cowell: the *Mágico* we have just read, a very grand thing. I suppose Calderón was over-praised some twenty years ago: for the last twenty it has been the fashion to underpraise him, I am sure. His Drama may not be the finest in the world: one sees how often too he wrote in the fashion of his time and country: but he is a wonderful fellow: One of the Great Men of the world."

Although it was the *Magician* and *Life Is a Dream* that first captured FitzGerald's admiration, he chose to translate first "less famous plays as still seemed to me suited to English taste," as he says in his "Advertisement." The collection of the first six plays in the present volume, published in 1653 as *Six Dramas of Calderón,* was the only publication FitzGerald allowed to bear his name. He did so to distinguish them from those of Dennis Florence MacCarthy, whose translations appeared in almost the same month of 1853 as FitzGerald's and to whom he refers as his "literal rival" in Calderón. A decade later, after he had translated from Persian *Salámán and Absál* by Jámi and the *Rubáiyát,* he returned to Calderón. "I have caught up a long ago begun Version of my dear old *Mágico,* and have so recast it that scarce a Plank remains of the original!" he wrote to Cowell on August 31, 1864. Telling Cowell that he would treat *La vida es sueño* the same way, he also said that those two plays were causing him more difficulty than all the others put together. FitzGerald's renderings of the two plays, privately printed in 1865, are in fact considerably more radical reconstructions of Calderón's original than the first six published.

Significantly, FitzGerald did not refer to his version of *Mágico* as a "translation," which implies carrying meaning with relative fidelity from one language to another. Rather, he called it a "recasting," thus selecting the Spanish term for a dramatic adaptation, *refundición,* a word borrowed from metallurgy that literally means melting down an object and recasting it in a significantly different form. Such recasting was not contrary to Calderón's own practice. The last of the triad of great Spanish dramatists, Calderón perfected the three-act polymetric *comedia* form developed by Lope de Vega and furthered by Tirso de Molina. Often rewriting his own plays and those of others, he excised extraneous elements and made plot, character, theme, and poetic imagery a synergistic unity. Calderón turned the sensual brilliance and dense syntax of Gongoristic poetry into dramatic conceits that enact in language the tensions of Baroque aesthetics and Counter-Reformation court life.

FitzGerald performed a similar refashioning of Calderón's play as he tailored them to dramatic conventions more familiar to a public accustomed to Elizabethan theater and the poetry of British Romanticism. This involved further streamlining the plots, eliminating or drastically simplifying the double plot structure common in Calderonian plays, and diminishing the significance of the comic subplot in most plays. He rearranged scenes and added or subtracted elements to make the action and psychological development of characters smoother and more plausible for a public unaccustomed to the conventions of the Spanish *comedia,* in which character development occurs with a few swift strokes, in movement, and in social interaction rather than inward-focused analysis. For example, in *Painter,* to smooth the shock of loss and recovery for Alvaro's father, sister, and beloved Serafina, he added, "The gleam of hope, ... / A little piece of wreck / That floated to the coast of Spain, and thence / Sent to my hands, with these words scratcht upon't— / 'Escaped alive, Alvaro.'" In *The Mighty Magician,* he removed the subplot of two servants who share the same woman on alternate days and rewrote the mountain-opening scene so that it could be rationalized as an effect of Cipriano's fantasy.

Where FitzGerald cut whole scenes (e.g., between Ana and her brother Felix in *Keep Your Own Secret*), however, he found a way to include the excised plot information in subsequent dialogue so that no dramatic holes remain. He played up similarities with Shakespearean equivalents, adopting Prospero's words in *The Tempest* for his title for *"Such Stuff as Dreams Are Made Of"* and in recasting the comic roles, sometimes pointing out in footnotes their kinship to those of Shakespeare. Guided by his judgment of artistic decorum, he rendered their parts in prose, which he used for most of *The Mayor of Zalamea*. Yet with occasional self-conscious rhyming such as that of Fife in the opening scene of *"Such Stuff,"* he retained some shadow of the metatheatrical play Calderón often assigned to such characters.[3]

FitzGerald described his poetics of translation in a letter to Cowell of April 17, 1859: "I suppose very few People have ever taken such Pains in Translation as I have: though certainly not to be literal. But at all Cost, a Thing must live: with a transfusion of one's own worse Life if one can't retain the Original's better. Better a live Sparrow than a stuffed Eagle." As an experiment, I read FitzGerald's *Three Judgments at a Blow* without first rereading the Spanish version and found that his English rendering did indeed take flight with a velocity and dramatic impact akin to that of Calderón's original. In that play, as in *Gil Perez, the Gallician,* FitzGerald keeps most of the action-packed complexity and rapid pace of Calderón's creation. The opening of *Keep Your Own Secret* similarly preserves in lovely solar imagery the lightning-bolt swiftness with which love arrives in many *comedias*.

At the same time, as FitzGerald admitted, there are losses in his translations. Although his modified blank verse regularly achieves a sonority and poetic beauty all its own, it cannot produce the subtle changes of mood and characterization afforded by the polymetric structure of the Spanish *comedias*. Nor does FitzGerald retain the repeated, interlacing webs of poetic imagery that weave great depth and complexity of meaning into Calderón's greatest dramas. Yet his recastings continue to extend to English-speaking readers a bridge by which to enter the bounteous dramatic world crafted four centuries ago by Pedro Calderón de la Barca.

NOTES

1. My thanks to Susan Fischer for supplying this information from her inventory of performances.

2. Iran B. Hassani Jewett, *Edward FitzGerald* (Boston: Twayne Publishers, 1977), p. 62.

3. For a thoughtful and thorough analysis of FitzGerald's recasting of this play, see Frederick A. De Armas, "The Apocalyptic Vision of *La vida es sueño:* Calderón and Edward FitzGerald," *Comparative Literature Studies* 23 (Summer 1986): 119–40; and De Armas, "Rosaura Subdued: Victorian Readings of Calderón's *La vida es sueño," South Central Review* 4 (Spring 1987): 43–62.

The first appearance of Calderon plays in a FitzGerald translation was in 1853 when the volume *Six Dramas of Calderon* was published by Pickering of London. A flippant notice of the book in *The Athenaeum* so hurt FitzGerald that he withdrew from the publishers all unsold copies and never again allowed his name to appear on the title page of any of his books. The remaining two Calderon plays *(The Mighty Magician* and *"Such Stuff as Dreams Are Made of")* were printed separately for private distribution sometime between November 1864 and February 1865. The setting copy for the Dolphin Master edition of *Eight Dramas of Calderon* has been *The Variorum and Definitive Edition of the Poetical and Prose Writings of Edward FitzGerald,* which was collected and arranged by George Bentham and published by Doubleday, Page and Company of New York in 1902. In every case where the text showed a variation it was FitzGerald's final choice that was selected for reproduction here.

ADVERTISEMENT

(to *Six Dramas of Calderón*, published in 1853)

In apologizing for the publication of so free translations of so famous a poet as Calderon, I must plead, first, that I have not meddled with any of his more famous plays; not one of those on my list being mentioned with any praise, or included in any selection that I know of, except the homely Mayor of Zalamea. Four of these six indeed, as many others in Calderon, may be lookt on as a better kind of what we call melodramas. Such plays as the *Magico Prodigioso* and the *Vida es Sueño* (I cannot rank the *Principe Constante* among them) require another translator, and, I think, form of translation.

Secondly, I do not believe an exact translation of this poet can be very successful; retaining so much that, whether real or dramatic Spanish passion, is still bombast to English ears, and confounds otherwise distinct outlines of character; Conceits that were a fashion of the day; or idioms that, true and intelligible to one nation, check the current of sympathy in others to which they are unfamiliar; violations of probable, nay *possible*, that shock even healthy romantic licence; repetitions of thoughts and images that Calderon used (and smiled at) as so much stage properties — so much, in short, that is not Calderon's own better self, but concession to private haste or public taste by one who so often relied upon some striking dramatic crisis for success with a not very accurate audience, and who, for whatever reason, was ever averse from any of his dramas being printed.

Choosing therefore such less famous plays as still seemed

to me suited to English taste, and to that form of verse in which our dramatic passion prefers to run, I have, while faithfully trying to retain what was fine and efficient, sunk, reduced, altered, and replaced much that seemed not; simplified some perplexities, and curtailed or omitted scenes that seemed to mar the breadth of general effect, supplying such omissions by some lines of after-narrative; and in some measure have tried to compensate for the fulness of sonorous Spanish, which Saxon English at least must forego, by a compression which has its own charm to Saxon ears.

That this, if proper to be done at all, might be better done by others, I do not doubt. Nay, on looking back over these pages, I see where in some cases the Spanish individuality might better have been retained, and northern idiom spared; and doubtless there are many inaccuracies I am not yet aware of. But if these plays prove interesting to the English reader, I and he may be very sure that, whatever of Spain and Calderon be lost, there must be a good deal retained; and I think he should excuse the licence of my version till some other interests him as well at less expense of fidelity.

I hope my *Graciosos* will not be blamed for occasional anachronisms not uncharacteristic of their vocation.

THE PAINTER

OF HIS OWN DISHONOUR

DRAMATIS PERSONÆ

FEDERIGO, *Prince of Orsino*
CELIO, *his Friend*
DON LUIS, *Governor of Naples*
PORCIA, *his Daughter*
ALVARO, *his Son*
FABIO,
BELARDO, } *their Servants*
JULIA,
DON JUAN ROCA
SERAFINA, *his Wife*
DON PEDRO, *his Father-in-law*
LEONELO, } *their Servants*
FLORA,

MASKERS, MUSICIANS, SAILORS, &C.

ACT I

Scene I. *A Room in* don luis' *palace at Naples.*
— *Enter* don luis *and* don juan *meeting.*

Luis Once more, a thousand times once more, Don Juan,
Come to my heart.
    Juan   And every fresh embrace
Rivet our ancient friendship faster yet!
    Luis Amen to that! Come, let me look at you —
Why, you seem well —
    Juan   So well, so young, so nimble,
I will not try to say how well, so much
My words and your conception must fall short
Of my full satisfaction.
    Luis   How glad am I
To have you back in Naples!
    Juan   Ah, Don Luis,
Happier so much than when I last was here,
Nay, than I ever thought that I could be.
    Luis How so?
    Juan   Why, when I came this way before,
I told you (do you not remember it?)
How teased I was by relatives and friends
To marry — little then disposed to love —
Marriage perhaps the last thing in my thoughts —
Liking to spend the spring time of my youth
In lonely study.
    Luis   Ay, ay, I remember:
Nothing but books, books, books — still day and night
Nothing but books; or, fairly drowsed by them,

By way of respite to that melancholy,
The palette and the pencil —
In which you got to such a mastery
As smote the senseless canvas into life.
O, I remember all — not only, Juan,
When you were here, but I with you in Spain,
What fights we had about it!
  Juan   So it was —
However, partly wearied, partly moved
By pity at my friends' anxieties,
Who press'd upon me what a shame it were
If such a title and estate as mine
Should lack a lineal inheritor,
At length I yielded —
Fanned from the embers of my later years
A passion which had slept in those of youth,
And took to wife my cousin Serafina,
The daughter of Don Pedro Castellano.
  Luis I know; you showed me when you last were here
The portrait of your wife that was to be,
And I congratulated you.
  Juan   Well now
Still more congratulate me — as much more
As she is fairer than the miniature
We both enamoured of. At the first glance
I knew myself no more myself, but hers,
Another (and how much a happier!) man.
  Luis Had I the thousand tongues, and those of brass,
That Homer wished for, they should utter all
Congratulation. Witty too, I hear,
As beautiful?
  Juan Yourself shall judge of all,
For even now my lady comes; awhile
To walk the Flora of your shores, and then
Over your seas float Venus-like away.
  Luis Not *that*, till she have graced our gardens long,
If once we get her here. But is she here?
  Juan Close by — she and her father, who would needs
See her abroad; and I push'd on before
To apprise you of our numbers — so much more

Than when I first proposed to be your guest,
That I entreat you —
 Luis   What?
 Juan   — to let us go,
And find our inn at once — not over-load
Your house.
 Luis Don Juan, you do me an affront —
What if all Naples came along with you? —
My heart — yes, and my house — should welcome them.
 Juan I know. But yet —
 Luis   But yet, no more "but yets" —
Come to my house, or else my heart shall close
Its doors upon you.
 Juan   Nay, I dare not peril
A friendship —
 Luis   Why, were 't not a great affront
To such a friendship — when you learn besides,
I have but held this government till now
Only to do you such a courtesy.
 Juan But how is this?
 Luis   Sickness and age on-coming,
I had determined to retire on what
Estate I had — no need of other wealth —
Beside, Alvaro's death — my only son —
 Juan Nay, you have so felicitated me,
I needs must *you*, Don Luis, whose last letter
Told of a gleam of hope in that dark quarter.
 Luis A sickly gleam — you know the ship he sail'd in
Was by another vessel, just escaped
The selfsame storm, seen to go down — it seem'd
With all her souls on board.
 Juan   But how assured
'T was your son's ship? —
 Luis   Alas, so many friends
Were on the watch for him at Barcelona,
Whither his ship was bound, but never came —
Beside the very messenger that brought
The gleam of hope, premised the tragedy —
A little piece of wreck,
That floated to the coast of Spain, and thence

Sent to my hands, with these words scratcht upon 't —
"*Escaped alive, Alvaro.*"
 Juan   When was this?
 Luis Oh, months ago, and since no tidings heard,
In spite of all inquiry. But we will hope.
Meanwhile, Serafina — when will she be here?
 Juan She must be close to Naples now.
 Luis   Go then,
Tell her from me —
I go not forth to bid her welcome, only
That I may make that welcome sure at home.
 Juan I'll tell her so. But —
 Luis   What! another "*But*"?
No more of that. Away with you. — Porcia!

            [*Exit* JUAN.

      Enter PORCIA

Daughter, you know (I have repeated it
A thousand times, I think) the obligation
I owe Don Juan Roca.
 Porcia   Sir, indeed
I've often heard you talk of him.
 Luis   Then listen.
He and his wife are coming here to-day —
Directly.
 Por. Serafina!
 Luis   Yes.
To be our guests, till they set sail for Spain;
I trust long first —
 Por.   And I. How glad I am!
 Luis You! what should make you glad?
 Por.   That Serafina,
So long my playmate, shall be now my guest.
 Luis Ay! I forgot — that's well, too —
Let us be rivals in their entertainment.
See that the servants, Porcia, dress their rooms
As speedily and handsomely as may be.
 Por. What haste can do (which brings its own excuse)
I'll do — 't is long a proverb hereabout

That you are Entertainer-general,
Rather than Governor, of Naples.

Luis   Ay,
I like to honour all who come this way.

Enter LEONELO

Leonelo Peace to this house! — and not only that, but
a story beside. — A company of soldiers coming to a certain
village, a fellow of the place calls out for *two* to be billeted
on him. "What!" says a neighbour, "you want a double share
of what every one else tries to shirk altogether?" "Yes," says
he, "for the more nuisance they are while they stay, the more
glad one is of their going." In illustration of which, and also
of my master's orders, I crave your Lordship's hand, and your
Ladyship's foot, to kiss.

Luis Welcome, good Leonelo. I was afraid I had over-
looked you in receiving your master.

Por.   And how does marriage agree with you, Leonelo?

Leon.   One gentleman asked another to dine: but such an
ill-ordered dinner that the capon was cold, and the wine hot.
Finding which, the guest dips a leg of the capon into the
wine. And when his host asks him what he's about — "Only
making the wine heat the capon, and the capon cool the
wine," says he. Now just this happened in my marriage.
My wife was rather too young, and I rather too old; so, as
it is hoped —

Por.   Foolery, foolery, always! — tell me how Serafina is —

Leon.   In a coach.

Por.   What answer is that?

Leon.   A very sufficient one — since a coach includes happiness, pride, and (a modern author says) respectability.

Por.   How so?

Leon.   Why, a certain lady died lately, and for some reason or other, they got leave to carry her to the grave in a
coach. Directly they got her in, — the body, I mean, — it
began to fidget — and when they called out to the coachman —
"Drive to St. Sepulchre's!" — "No!" screams she, — "I won't
go there yet. Drive to the Prado first; and when I have had a
turn there, they may bury me where they please."

Luis   How can you let your tongue run on so!

Leon.   I'll tell you. A certain man in Barcelona had five or six children: and he gave them each to eat —

(Voices within.) "Way there! way!"

Por.   They are coming.

Leon.   And in so doing, take that story out of my mouth.

Enter JULIA

Julia   Signor, your guests are just alighting.

Luis   Come, Porcia —

Leon.   (No, no, stop you and listen to me about those dear children.)

Por.   They are coming upstairs — at the door —

Enter DON JUAN *leading* SERAFINA, DON PEDRO, *and* FLORA — *all in travelling dress.*

Luis   Your hand, fair Serafina, whose bright eyes
Seem to have drawn his lustre from the sun,
To fill my house withal; — a poor receptacle
Of such a visitor.

Por.   Nay, 't is for me
To blush for that, in quality of hostess;
Yet, though you come to shame my house-keeping,
Thrice welcome, Serafina.

Serafina   How answer both,
Being too poor in compliment for either!
I'll not attempt it.

Ped.   I am vext, Don Luis,
My son-in-law should put this burden on you.

Luis   Nay, vex not me by saying so. — What burden?
The having such an honour as to be
Your servant? —

Leon.   Here's a dish of compliments!

Flora   Better than you can feed your mistress with.

                                    (Guns heard without.)

Juan   What guns are those?

Enter FABIO

Fabio   The citadel, my lord,

Makes signal of two galleys in full sail
Coming to port.

Luis   More guests! the more the merrier!

Ped.   The merrier for them, but scarce for you,
Don Luis.

Luis   Nay, good fortune comes like bad,
All of a heap.   What think you, should it be,
As I suspect it is, the Prince Orsino
Returning; whom, in love and duty bound,
I shall receive and welcome —

Juan   Once again,
Don Luis, give me leave —

Luis   And once again,
And once for all, I shall *not* give you leave.
Prithee, no more —
All will be easily arranged.   Porcia,
You know your guest's apartments — show her thither:
I'll soon be back with you.

Ped.   Permit us, sir,
To attend you to the port, and wait upon
His Highness.

Luis   I dare not refuse that trouble,
Seeing what honour in the prince's eyes
Your company will lend me.

Leon.   And methinks
I will go with you too.

Juan   What, for that purpose?

Leon.   Yes — and because perhaps among the crowd
I shall find some to whom I may relate
That story of the children and their meat.

[*Exeunt* DON LUIS, PEDRO, JUAN,
                    LEONELO, FABIO, &C.

Ser.   Porcia, are they gone?

Por.   They are.

Ser.   Then I may weep.

Por.   Tears, Serafina!

Ser.   Nay, they would not stay
Longer unshed.   I would not if I could
Hide them from you, Porcia.   Why should I,
Who know too well the fount from which they flow?

Por.   I only know you weep — no more than that.

Ser.   Yet 't is the seeing you again, again
Unlocks them — is it that you do resent
The discontinuance of our early love,
And that you *will* not understand me?
   Por.   Nay, —
What can I say!
   Ser.   Let us be *quite* alone.
   Por.   Julia, leave us.
   Ser.   Flora, go with her.
   Julia   Come, shall we go up to the gallery,
And see the ships come in?
   Flora   Madam, so please you.
                       [*Exeunt* FLORA *and* JULIA.
   Ser.   Well, are we *quite* alone?
   Por.   Yes, quite.
   Ser.   All gone.
And none to overhear us?
   Por.   None.
   Ser.   Porcia.
You knew me once when I was happy!
   Por.   Yes,
Or thought you so —
   Ser.   But now most miserable!
   Por.   How so, my Serafina?
   Ser.   You shall hear —
Yes, my Porcia, you remember it, —
That happy, happy time when you and I
Were so united that, our hearts attun'd
To perfect unison, one might believe
That but one soul within two bodies lodg'd.
This you remember?
   Por.   Oh, how could I forget!
   Ser.   Think it not strange that so far back I trace
The first beginnings of *another* love,
Whose last sigh having now to breathe, whose last
Farewell to sigh, and whose deceased hopes
In one last obsequy to commemorate,
I tell it over to you point by point
From first to last — by such full utterance
My pent up soul perchance may find relief.

Por.   Speak, Serafina.

Ser.   You have not forgot
Neither, how that close intimacy of ours
Brought with it of necessity some courtesies
Between me and your brother, Don Alvaro —
Whose very name, oh wretched that I am!
Makes memory, like a trodden viper, turn,
And fix a fang in me not sharp enough
To slay at once, but with a lingering death
Infect my life —

Por.   Nay, calm yourself.

Ser.   We met,
Porcia — and from those idle meetings love
Sprang up between us both — for though 't is true
That at the first I laugh'd at his advances,
And turn'd his boyish suit into disdain,
Yet true it also is that in my heart
There lurk'd a lingering feeling yet behind,
Which if not wholly love, at least was liking,
In the sweet twilight of whose unris'n sun
My soul as yet walk'd hesitatingly.
For, my Porcia, there is not a woman,
Say what she will, and virtuous as you please,
Who, being lov'd, resents it: and could he
Who most his mistress's disfavour mourns
Look deeply down enough into her heart,
He'd see, however high she carries it,
Some grateful recognition lurking there
Under the muffle of affected scorn.
You know how I repell'd your brother's suit:
How ever when he wrote to me I tore
His letters — would not listen when he spoke —
And when, relying on my love for you,
Through you he tried to whisper his for me,
I quarrell'd with yourself — quarrell'd the more
The more you spoke for him.   He wept — I laugh'd;
Knelt in my path — I turn'd another way;
Though who had seen deep down into my heart,
Had also seen love struggling hard with pride.
Enough — at last one evening as I sat

Beside a window looking on the sea,
Wrapt in the gathering night he stole unseen
Beside me.   After whispering all those vows
Of love which lovers use, and I pass by,
He press'd me to be his.   Touch'd by the hour,
The mask of scorn fell from my heart, and Love
Reveal'd himself, and from that very time
Grew unconceal'd between us — yet, Porcia,
Upon mine honour, (for I tell thee *all*,)
Always in honour bounded.   At that time
In an ill hour my father plann'd a marriage
Between me and Don Juan — yours, you know,
Came here to Naples, whence he sent your brother,
I know not on what business, into Spain;
And we agreed, I mean Alvaro and I,
Rather than vex two fathers at one time
By any declaration of our vows,
'T were best to keep them secret — at the least,
Till his return from Spain.   Ah, Porcia,
When yet did love not thrive by secrecy?
We parted — he relying on my promise,
I on his quick return.   Oh, mad are those
Who, knowing that a storm is up, will yet
Put out to sea.   Alvaro went — my father
Urged on this marriage with my cousin.   Oh! —
    Po:.   You are ill, Serafina!
    Ser.   Nothing — nothing —
I reason'd — wept — implor'd — excus'd — delay'd
In vain — O mercy, Heaven!
    Por.   Tell me no more:
It is too much for you.
    Ser.   Then suddenly
We heard that he was dead — your brother — drown'd —
They married me — and now perhaps he lives.
They say — Porcia, can it be? — I know not
Whether to hope or dread if that be true; —
And every wind that blows your father hope
Makes my blood cold; I know that I shall meet him,
Here or upon the seas — dead or alive —
Methinks I see him now! — Help! help!   [*Swoons.*

Por.   Serafina! —
She has fainted! — Julia! Flora! —

Enter ALVARO

Alv.   My Porcia!
Por.   Alvaro! *(They embrace.)*
Alv.   I have outrun the shower of compliment
On my escapes — which you shall hear anon —
To catch you to my heart.
Por.   Oh joy and terror!
Look there! —
Alv.   Serafina!
And sleeping too!
Por.   Oh, swooning! see to her
Till I get help.   [*Exit.*
Ser. (in her swoon).   Mercy, mercy!
Alvaro, slay me not! — I am not guilty —
Indeed I am not! —
Alv.   She dreams—and dreams of me—but very strangely—
Serafina! —
Ser. (waking).   Dead! — or return'd alive to curse and slay
        me! —
But I am innocent! — I could not help —
They told me you were dead — and are you not? —
And I must marry him —
Alv.   Must marry? — whom? —
Why, you are dreaming still —
Awake! — 't is your Alvaro — *(Offers to embrace her.)*
Ser.   No, no, no —
I dare not —
Alv.   Dare not!

Enter PORCIA, FLORA, JULIA

Por.   Quick, quick!
Flora   My lady!
Julia   My lord alive again!
Alv.   Porcia, come hither — I am not alive,
Till I have heard the truth — nay, if 't be true

That she has hinted and my heart forebodes,
I shall be worse than dead —

[*Retires with* PORCIA *to back of Stage.*

Enter JUAN *and* PEDRO

Juan   What is the matter?
My Serafina!
    Pedro   We have hurried back,
Told of your sudden seizure — What is it?
    Ser.   The very heart within me turn'd to ice.
    Juan   But you are better now? —
    Ser.   Yes — better — pray,
Be not uneasy for me.
    Alv. (to PORCIA *in the rear).* This is true then!
    Por.   Nay, nay, be not so desperate, Alvaro,
Hearing but half the story — no fault of hers —
I'll tell you all anon.   Come, Serafina,
I'll see you to your chamber.
    Pedro   She will be better soon —
    Juan   Lean upon me, my love — so — so.
    Alv.   Oh, fury!
    Ser.   Oh, would to heaven these steps should be my last,
Leading not to my chamber, but my grave!
    Por. (to ALVARO*).*   Wait here — compose yourself — I shall
       be back
Directly.   [*Exeunt* PORCIA, SERAFINA, *and* JUAN.
    Alv.   She is married — broke her troth —
And I escaped from death and slavery
To find her — but the prince! — Oh weariness!

Enter the PRINCE ORSINO, CELIO, DON LUIS, *and Train*

    Prince   Each day, Don Luis, I become your debtor
For some new courtesy.
    Luis   My lord, 't is I
Who by such small instalments of my duty
Strive to pay back in part the many favours
You shower upon your servant.   And this last,
Of bringing back Alvaro to my arms,

Not all my life, nor life itself, could pay.

 Prince Small thanks to me, Don Luis; but indeed
The strangest chance — two chances — two escapes —
First from the sinking ship upon a spar,
Then from the Algerine who pick'd him up,
Carried him captive off —
He first adroitly through their fingers slipping
That little harbinger of hope to you,
And then, at last, himself escaping back
To Barcelona, where you know I was —
If glad to welcome, house, and entertain
Any distrest Italian, how much more,
Both for his own sake and for yours, your son,
So making him, I trust, a friend for life.

 Alv. Rather a humble follower, my lord.

 Luis I have no words to thank you — we shall hear
The whole tale from Alvaro by and by —
To make us merry — once so sad to him.
Meanwhile, Alvaro, thou hast seen thy sister?

 Alv. Yes, sir —

 Luis   Oh what a joy 't is to see thee!

 Prince A day of general joy.

 Alv. (aside).   Indeed! —

 Prince   Especially
To her, Alvaro —

 Alv. Sir?

 Prince   I mean your sister.

 Alv. Yes, my lord — no — I am not sure, my lord —
A friend of hers is suddenly so ill,
My sister is uneasy —

 Luis   Serafina!
Indeed! — I know your Highness will forgive
My seeing to her straight.   [*Exit.*

 Alv.   And I, my lord,
Would fain see some old faces once again
As soon as may be.

 Prince   Nay, no more excuse —
Follow your pleasure.

 Alv. (aside). 'T is no friend I seek,
But my one deadliest enemy — myself.   [*Exit.*

Prince   Celio, I think we have well nigh exhausted
The world of compliment, and wasted it:
For I begin to doubt that word and deed
Are wasted all in vain.
    Celio   How so, my lord?
    Prince   Why, if I never am to see Porcia
Whom I have come so far and fast to see —
    Cel.   *Never*, my lord! her father's guest is ill,
And she for a few minutes —
    Prince   *Minutes*, Celio!
Knowest thou not minutes are years to lovers?
    Cel.   I know that lovers are strange animals.
    Prince   Ah, you have never loved.
    Cel.   No, good my lord,
I'm but a looker-on; or in the market
Just give and take the current coin of love —
Love her that loves me; and, if she forget,
Forget her too.
    Prince   Ah, then I cannot wonder
You wonder so at my impatience;
For he that cannot love, can be no judge
Of him that does.
    Cel.   How so?
    Prince   I'll tell thee, Celio.
He who far off beholds another dancing,
Even one who dances best, and all the time
Hears not the music that he dances to,
Thinks him a madman, apprehending not
The law that rules his else eccentric action.
So he that 's in himself insensible
Of love's sweet influence, misjudges him
Who moves according to love's melody:
And knowing not that all these sighs and tears,
Ejaculations, and impatiences,
Are necessary changes of a measure,
Which the divine musician plays, may call
The lover crazy; which he would not do
Did he within his own heart hear the tune
Play'd by the great musician of the world.
    Cel.   Well, I might answer, that, far off or near,

Hearing or not the melody you tell of,
The man is mad who dances to it.   But
Here is your music.

Enter PORCIA

Porcia   I left my brother here but now.
Prince   But now,
Sweet Porcia, you see he is not here —
By that so seeming earnest search for him
Scarce recognising me, if you would hint
At any seeming slight of mine toward you,
I plead not guilty —
    Por.   You mistake, my lord —
Did I believe my recognition
Of any moment to your Excellency,
I might perhaps evince it in complaint,
But not in slight.
        Prince   Complaint! —
        Por.   Yes, sir — complaint.
    Prince   Complaint of what?   I knowing, Porcia,
And you too knowing well, the constant love
That I have borne you since the happy day
When first we met in Naples —
    Por.   No, my lord —
You mean my love to you, not yours to me —
Unwearied through your long forgetful absence.
    Prince   How easily, Porcia, would my love
Prove to you its unchanged integrity,
Were it not that our friends —
    Por.   Your friends indeed,
Who stop a lame apology at the outset.

Enter SERAFINA

Serafina   I cannot rest, Porcia, and am come
To seek it in your arms — but who is this?
    Por.   The Prince Orsino.
    Ser.   Pardon me, my lord —
I knew you not — coming so hurriedly,
And in much perturbation.

Prince   Nay, lady,
I owe you thanks for an embarrassment
Which hides my own.
   Ser.   Let it excuse beside
What other courtesies I owe your Highness,
But scarce have words to pay. Heaven guard your Highness —
Suffer me to retire.   [*Exit.*
   Por. I needs must after her, my lord.   But tell me,
When shall I hear your vindication? —
To-night?
   Prince   Ay, my Porcia, if you will.
   Por.   Till night farewell, then.   [*Exit.*
   Prince   Farewell. — Celio,
Didst ever see so fair an apparition,
As her who came and went so suddenly?
   Cel.   Indeed, so sweetly mannered when surprised,
She must be exquisite in her composure.
   Prince   Who is she?
   Cel.   Nay, my lord, just come with you,
I know as little —
What! a new tune to dance to? —
   Prince   In good time,
Here comes Alvaro.

Enter ALVARO

   Alvaro   How restless is the sickness of the soul!
I scarce had got me from this fatal place,
And back again —
   Prince   Alvaro!
   Alv.   My lord —
   Prince   Who is the lady that was here anon?
   Alv.   Lady, my lord — what lady? —
   Prince   She that went
A moment hence — I mean your sister's guest.
   Alv. (This drop was wanting!)
My lord, the daughter of a nobleman
Of very ancient blood —
Don Pedro Castellano.

Prince   And her name?

Alv.   Serafina.

Prince   And a most seraphic lady!

Alv.   You never saw her, sir, before?

Prince   No, surely.

Alv. (aside).   Would I had never done so!

Prince   And in the hasty glimpse I had,
I guess her mistress of as fair a mind
As face.

Alv.   Yes, sir —

Prince   She lives in Naples, eh?

Alv.   No — on her way
To Spain, I think —

Prince   Indeed! — To Spain.   Why that?

Alv.   (How much more will he ask?)
My lord, her husband —

Prince   She is married then? —

Alv.   Torture!

Prince   And who so blest to call her his, Alvaro?

Alv.   Sir, Don Juan Roca, her cousin.

Prince   Roca?   Don Juan Roca?   Do I know him?

Alv.   I think you must; he came, sir, with my father
To wait upon your Grace.

Prince   Don Juan Roca!
No; I do not remember him — should not
Know him again.

Enter DON LUIS

Luis   My lord, if my old love
And service for your Highness may deserve
A favour at your hands —

Prince   They only wait
Until your tongue has named it.

Luis   This it is then —
The captain of the galleys, good my lord,
In which your Highness came,
Tells me that, having landed you, he lies
Under strict orders to return again
Within an hour.

Prince   'T is true.

Luis   Now, good my lord,
The ships, when they go back, must carry with them
Some friends who, long time look'd for, just are come,
And whom I fain —

Prince   Nay, utter not a wish
I know I must unwillingly deny.

   Alv.   Confusion on confusion!

Prince   I have pledg'd
My word to Don Garcia of Toledo,
The galleys should not pass an hour at Naples.
I feel for you, — and for myself, alas!
So sweet a freight they carry with them.   But
I dare not — and what folly to adore
A Beauty lost to me before I found it!

                       [*Exeunt* PRINCE *and* CELIO.

   Luis   And those I so had long'd for, to avenge
Their long estrangement by as long a welcome,
Snatcht from me almost ere we'd shaken hands! —
Is not this ill, Alvaro? —

   Alv.   Ill indeed.

   Luis   And, as they needs must go, my hospitality,
Foil'd in its spring, must turn to wound myself
By speeding their departure.   *(Going.)*

   Alv.   Sir, a moment.
Although his Highness would not, or could not,
Grant you the boon your services deserv'd,
Let not that, I beseech you, indispose you
From granting one to me.

   Luis   What is 't, Alvaro?
'T were strange could I refuse you anything.

   Alv.   You sent me, sir, on state affairs to Spain,
But being wreckt and captur'd, as you know,
All went undone.
Another opportunity now offers;
The ships are ready, let me go and do
That which perforce I left undone before.

   Luis   What else could'st thou have askt,
In all the category of my means,
Which I, methinks, had grudg'd thee!   No, Alvaro,

The treacherous sea must not again be trusted
With the dear promise of my only son.
    Alv.   Nay, for that very reason, I entreat you
To let me go, sir.   Let it not be thought
The blood that I inherited of you
Quail'd at a common danger.
    Luis   I admire
Your resolution, but you must not go,
At least not now.
Beside, the business you were sent upon
Is done by other hands, or let go by
For ever.
    Alv.   Nay, sir —
    Luis   Nay, Alvaro.   [*Exit.*
    Alv.   He is resolved.   And Serafina,
To whose divinity I offered up
My heart of hearts, a purer sacrifice
Than ever yet on pagan altar blaz'd,
Has play'd me false, is married to another,
And now will fly away on winds and seas,
As fleeting as herself.
Then what remains but that I die?   My death
The necessary shadow of that marriage!
Comfort! — what boots it looking after that
Which never can be found?   The worst is come,
Which 't were a blind and childish waste of hope
To front with any visage but despair.
Ev'n that one single solace, were there one,
Of ringing my despair into her ears,
Fails me.   Time presses; the accursed breeze
Blows foully fair.   The vessel flaps her sails
That is to bear her from me.   Look, she comes —
And from before her dawning beauty all
I had to say fades from my swimming brain,
And chokes upon my tongue.

       Enter SERAFINA, *drest as at first, and* PORCIA

    Porcia   And must we part so quickly? —
    Serafina   When does happiness
Last longer?

Alv.   Never! — who best can answer that?
I standing by, why ask it of another?
At least when speaking of such happiness
As, perjur'd woman, thy false presence brings!

　Ser.   Alvaro, for Heaven's sake spare me the pang
Of these unjust reproaches.

　Alv.   What! unjust!

　Ser.   Why, is it not unjust, condemning one
Without defence?

　Alv.   Without defence indeed!

　Ser.   Not that I have not a most just defence,
But that you will not listen.

　Alv.   Serafina,
I listen'd; but what wholly satisfies
The criminal may ill suffice the judge;
And in love's court especially, a word
Has quite a different meaning to the soul
Of speaker and of hearer.   Yet once more,
Speak.

　Ser.   To what purpose?   I can but repeat
What I have told your sister, and she you, —
What on the sudden waking from my swoon,
I, who had thought you dead so long, Alvaro,
Spoke in my terror, suddenly seeing you
Alive, before me.

　Alv.   I were better, then,
Dead than alive?

　Ser.   I know not — were you dead
I might in honour weep for you, Alvaro;
Living, I must not.

　Alv.   Nay then, whether you
Forswear me living or lament me dead,
Now you must hear me; if you strike the wound,
Is it not just that you should hear the cry?

　Ser.   I must not.

　Alv.   But I say you must.

　Ser.   Porcia,
Will you not help me when my life and honour
Are thus at stake?

　Alv.   Porcia's duty lies

In keeping watch that no one interrupt us.

Porcia   Between the two confus'd, I yield at last
To him, both as my brother, Serafina,
And for his love to you.   Compose yourself;
I shall be close at hand, no harm can happen.
And let him weep at least who has lost all.   [*Exit.*

Ser.   If I am forc'd to hear you then, Alvaro,
You shall hear me too, once more, once for all,
Freely confessing that I loved you once;
Ay, long and truly loved you.   When all hope
Of being yours with your reported death
Had died, then, yielding to my father's wish,
I wed another, and am — what I am.
So help me Heaven, Alvaro, this is all!

Alv.   How can I answer if you weep?
Ser.   No, no,
I do not weep, or, if I do, 't is but
My eyes, — no more, no deeper.

Alv.   Is 't possible you can so readily
Turn warm compassion into cold disdain!
And are your better pulses so controll'd
By a cold heart, that, to enhance the triumph
Over the wretched victim of your eyes,
You make the fount of tears to stop or flow
Just as you please?   If so, teach me the trick,
As the last courtesy you will vouchsafe me.

Ser.   Alvaro, when I think of what I was,
My tears will forth; but when of what I am,
My honour bids them cease.

Alv.   You *do* feel then —
Ser.   Nay, I'll deny it not.
Alv.   That, being another's —
Ser.   Nay, no argument —
Alv.   These tears —
Ser.   What tears?
Alv.   Are the relenting rain
On which the Iris of my hope may ride;
Or a sweet dew —
Ser.   Alvaro —
Alv.   That foretells

That better day when in these arms again —
 Ser. Those arms! Alvaro, when that day shall come
May heaven's thunder strike me dead at once!
(Cannon within.)

Mercy, what's that?

Enter PORCIA

 Por.   A signal from the ship,
'T is time: your father and Don Juan now
Are coming for you.
 Alv.   O heavens!
 Por.   Compose yourself,
And you, Alvaro — (*Motions him back.*)

Enter DON JUAN, LUIS, PEDRO, LEONELO, &C.

 Luis Lady, believe how sadly I am come
To do you this last office.
 Juan   Trembling still? —
But come, perhaps the sea-breeze, in requital
Of bearing us away from those we love,
May yet revive you.
 Luis Well, if it must be so,
Lady, your hand. Porcia, come with us.

[Exeunt all but ALVARO.

ACT II

SCENE I. *A room in* DON JUAN's *house at Barcelona: he is discovered painting* SERAFINA. *It gradually grows dusk.*

Juan   Are you not wearied sitting?
Serafina   Surely not
Till you be wearied painting.
    Juan   Oh, so much
As I have wish'd to have that divine face
Painted, and by myself, I now begin
To wish I had not wish'd it.
    Ser.   But why so?
    Juan   Because I must be worsted in the trial
I have brought on myself.
    Ser.   You to despair,
Who never are outdone but by yourself!
    Juan   Even so.
    Ser.   But *why* so?
    Juan   Shall I tell you why?
Painters, you know, (just turn your head a little,)
Are nature's apes, whose uglier semblances,
Made up of disproportion and excess,
Like apes, they easily can imitate:
But whose more gracious aspect, the result
Of subtlest symmetries, they only outrage,
Turning true beauty into caricature.
The perfecter her beauty, the more complex
And hard to follow; but her perfection
Impossible.
    Ser.   That I dare say is true,

But surely not in point with me, whose face
Is surely far from perfect.
    Juan   Far indeed
From what is perfect call'd, but far beyond,
Not short of it; so that indeed my reason
Was none at all.
    Ser.   Well now then the true reason
Of your disgust.
    Juan   Yet scarcely my disgust,
When you continue still the cause of it.
Well then, to take the matter up again —
The object of this act, (pray, look at me,
And do not laugh, Serafina,) is to seize
Those subtlest symmetries that, as I said,
Are subtlest in the loveliest; and though
It has been half the study of my life
To recognise and represent true beauty,
I had not dreamt of such excess of it
As yours; nor can I, when before my eyes,
Glass the clear image in my trembling soul;
And therefore if that face of yours exceed
Imagination, and imagination
(As it must do) the pencil; then my picture
Can be but the poor shadow of a shade.
Besides, —
    Ser. Can there be any thing besides?
    Juan 'T is said that fire and light, and air and snow,
Cannot be painted; how much less a face
Where they are so distinct, yet so compounded,
As needs must drive the artist to despair!
I'll give it up. — (*Throws away his brushes, &c.*)
       The light begins to fail too.
And, Serafina, pray remember this,
If, tempted ever by your loveliness,
And fresh presumption that forgets defeat,
I'd have you sit again, allow me not, —
It does but vex me.
    Ser.   Nay, if it do that
I will not, Juan, or let me die for it, —
Come, there's an oath upon 't.

Juan   A proper curse
On that rebellious face.

Enter LEONELO

Leonelo   And here comes in a story: —
A man got suddenly deaf, and seeing the people about him
moving their lips, quoth he, "What the devil makes you all
dumb?" never thinking for a moment the fault might be in
himself.   So it is with you, who lay the blame on a face that
all the world is praising, and not on your own want of skill
to paint it.

Juan   Not a very apt illustration, Leonelo, as you would
admit if you heard what I was saying before you came in.
But, whose soever the fault, I am the sufferer.   I will no
more of it, however.   Come, I will abroad.

Ser.   Whither, my Lord?

Juan   Down to the pier, with the sea and the fresh air, to
dispel my vexation.

Ser.   By quitting me?

Juan   I might indeed say so, since the sight of you is the
perpetual trophy of my defeat.   But what if I leave you in
order to return with a double zest?

Ser.   Nay, nay, with no such pretty speeches hope to delude me; I know what it is.   The carnival with its fair masks.

Juan   A mask abroad when I have that face at home!

Ser.   Nay, nay, I know you.

Juan   Better than I do myself?

Ser.   What wife does not?

Leon.   Just so.   A German and the priest of his village
coming to high words one day, because the man blew his
swine's horn under the priest's window, the priest calls out in
a rage, "I'll denounce your horns to the parish, I will!" which
the man's wife overhearing in the scullery, she cries out,
"Halloa, neighbour, here is the priest revealing my confession!"

Ser.   What impertinence, Leonelo.

Leon.   Very well then, listen to this: a certain man in
Barcelona had five or six children, and one day —

Juan   Peace, foolish fellow.

Leon. Those poor children will never get the meat well into their mouths.

Juan Farewell, my love, awhile.

[*Exeunt* JUAN *and* LEONELO.

Ser. Farewell, my lord.

Thou little wicked Cupid,
I am amused to find how by degrees
The wound your arrows in my bosom made,
And made to run so fast with tears, is healing.
Yea, how those very arrows and the bow
That did such mischief, being snapt asunder —
Thyself art tamed to a good household child.

Enter FLORA, *out of breath*

Flora O madam!

Ser. Well, Flora, what now?

Flora O madam, there is a man down-stairs!

Ser. Well?

Flora Drest sailor-like.

Ser. Well?

Flora He will not go away unless I give this letter into your hands.

Ser. Into my hands? from whom?

Flora From the lady Porcia he says, madam.

Ser. From Porcia, well, and what frightens you?

Flora Nothing, madam, and yet —

Ser. And yet there is something.

Flora O my lady, if this should be Don Alvaro!

Ser. Don Alvaro! what makes you think that?

Flora I am sure it is he.

Ser. But did you tell him you knew him?

Flora I could not help, madam, in my surprise.

Ser. And what said he then?

Flora That I must tell you he was here.

Ser. Alvaro! —

Flora, go back, tell him you dared not tell me,
Fearful of my rebuke, and say beside,
As of your own advice, that it is fit,
Both for himself and me,

That he depart immediately.
Flora   Yes, madam.

As she is going, enter ALVARO, *as a Sailor*

Alv.   No need.   Seeing Don Juan leave his house,
I have made bold to enter, and have heard
What Flora need not to repeat.
Ser.   Nay, sir,
Rather it seems as if you had not heard;
Seeing the most emphatic part of all
Forbad your entrance.
Alv.   So might it seem perhaps,
Inexorable beauty: but you know
How one delinquency another breeds;
And having come so far, and thus disguised,
Only to worship at your shrine, Serafina,
(I dare not talk of love,) I do beseech you
Do not so frown at my temerity,
As to reject the homage that it brings.
Ser.   Don Alvaro,
If thus far I have listen'd, think it not
Warrant of further importunity.
I could not help it — 't is with dread and terror
That I have heard thus much; I now beseech you,
Since you profess you came to honour me,
Show that you did so truly by an act
That shall become your honour well as mine.
Alv.   Speak, Serafina.
Ser.   Leave me so at once
And without further importunity
That I may be assured *you* are assured
That lapse of time, my duty as a wife,
My husband's love for me, and mine for him,
My station and my name, all have so changed me,
That winds and waves might sooner overturn
Not the oak only,
But the eternal rock on which it grows,
Than you my heart, though sea and sky themselves
Join'd in the tempest of your sighs and tears.

Alv.　But what if I remember other times
When Serafina was no stubborn oak,
Resisting wind and wave, but a fair flower
That open'd to the sun of early love,
And follow'd him along the golden day:
No barren heartless rock,
But a fair temple in whose sanctuary
Love was the idol, daily and nightly fed
With sacrifice of one whole human heart.
　Ser.　I do not say 't was not so;
But, sir, to carry back the metaphor
Your ingenuity has turn'd against me,
That tender flower, transplanted it may be
To other skies and soil, might in good time
Strike down such roots and strengthen such a stem
As were not to be shook: the temple, too,
Though seeming slight to look on, being yet
Of nature's fundamental marble built,
When once that foolish idol was dethroned,
And the true God set up into his place,
Might stand unscathed in sanctity and worship,
For ages and for ages.
　Alv.　　　　　Serafina,
Why talk to me of ages, when the account
Of my misfortune and your cruelty
Measures itself by hours, and not by years!
It was but yesterday you loved me, yes,
Loved me, and (let the metaphor run on)
I never will believe it ever was,
Or is, or ever can be possible
That the fair flower so soon forgot the sun
To which so long she owed and turn'd her beauty,
To love the baser mould in which she grew:
Or that the temple could so soon renounce
Her old god, true god too while he was there,
For any cold and sober deity
Which you may venerate, but cannot love,
Newly set up.
　Ser.　　　I must leave metaphor,
And take to sober sense; nor is it right,

Alvaro, that you strive
To choke the virtuous present with the past,
Which, when it was the past, was virtuous too,
But would be guilty if reiterate.
Nor is it right, nor courteous, certainly,
Doubting what I declare of my own heart;
Nay, you who do yourself affirm, Alvaro,
How well I loved you when such love was lawful,
Are bound to credit me when I declare
That love is now another's.

    Alv.   Serafina —
    Juan (speaking within).   Light, light, there!

Enter FLORA *hurriedly*

    Flora   Madam, my lord, my lord.
    Alv.   Confusion!
    Ser.   O ye heavens!
    Flora   The old lover's story,
Brother or husband sure to interrupt.
    Juan (within).   A light there, Flora! Serafina! night
Set in, and not a lamp lit in the house?
    Alv.   He comes.
    Ser.   And I am lost!
    Flora   Quick, Don Alvaro.
Into this closet, till my lord be gone
Into his chamber, in, in, in!
    Alv.   My fears
Are all for you, not for myself.   [*Hides in the closet.*
    Flora   In, in!
    Juan (entering).   How is it there's no light?
    Ser.   She had forgot —
But here it comes.

Enter FLORA *with lights*

              'T was kind of you, my lord, —
So quickly back again —
Sooner than I expected.
    Juan   Yes, a friend

Caught hold of me just as I reach'd the pier,
And told me to get home again.
   Ser. (aside).   My heart!
   Juan   And wherefore do you think?
   Ser.   Nay, I know not.
   Juan   To tell you of a festival, Serafina,
Preparing in your honour.
   Ser. (aside).   I breathe again.
   Juan   The story's this.   It is the carnival,
You know, and, by a very ancient usage,
To-morrow all the folk of Barcelona,
Highest as well as lowest, men and women,
Go abroad mask'd to dance and see the shows.
And you being newly come, they have devised
A dance and banquet for you, to be held
In Don Diego's palace, looking forth
So pleasantly (do you remember it?)
Upon the sea.   And therefore for their sakes,
And mine, my Serafina, you must for once
Eclipse that fair face with the ugly mask;
I'll find you fitting dress, — what say you?
   Ser.   Nay,
What should I say but that your will is mine,
In this as evermore?
And now you speak of dress, there are ev'n now
Some patterns brought me in the nick of time
To choose from, in my chamber; prithee come,
And help me judge.
   Juan   I would that not your robe
Only, but all the ground on which you walk
Were laced with diamond.
   Ser.   What not done yet
With compliment?   Come — come.   *(She takes a light.)*
   Juan   But wherefore this?
   Ser.   My duty is to wait upon you.
   Juan   No.
Take the lamp, Flora.
   Ser.   Flora waits on me,
And I on you.
   Juan   What humour's this?

But be it as you will.   [*Exeunt* JUAN *and* SERAFINA.

   Flora (letting out ALVARO).   Now is the time, Signor
       Alvaro! hist!
The coast is clear, but silently and swiftly —
Follow — but, hush! stop! wait!
   Alv.   What now?
   Flora   A moment!
Back, back, 't is Leonelo.
   Alv.   Put out the light, I can slip past him.
   Flora (falls putting out light).   No sooner said than done.
       O Lord, Lord, Lord.

Enter LEONELO

   Leon.   What is the matter?
   Flora   The matter is, I have fallen.
   Leon.   Into temptation?
   Flora   It is well, sir, if I have not broken my leg; here, sir,
cease your gibing, and get this lamp lighted directly.
   Leon. (stumbling over ALVARO).   Halloa!
   Flora   What now?
   Leon.   I've fallen now, and on your temptation I think,
for it has got a beard.
   Alv. (groping his way).   The fool! but I can find the door.
                                          [*Exit.*
   Leon.   There goes some one!
   Flora   The man's mad!
   Leon.   Am I! Halloa! halloa, there!

Enter JUAN *with light*

   Juan   What is the matter?
   Flora   Nothing, nothing, my lord.
   Leon.   Nothing?   I say it is something, a great —
   Flora   My lord, going to shut the door, I stumbled, fell,
and put out the light, that's all.
   Leon.   And I stumbled too.
   Juan   Well?
   Leon.   Over a man.
   Juan   In this chamber!

Leon. Yes, and —

Flora Nonsense! my lord, he stumbled against *me*, as we both floundered in the dark.

Leon. You! What have you done with your beard then?

Juan Are you mad? or is this some foolery?

Leon. My lord, I swear I stumbled over a fellow here.

Juan (aside). And she so anxious to light me to her chamber! What is all this? Take the lamp, Leonelo. Though partly I think you have been dreaming, I will yet search the house; come with me. I will draw the sting of suspicion at once, come what come may.

[*Draws sword and exit.*

Flora (to LEON.*).* All of your work. A murrain on your head,

Making this pother.

Leon. Minx! what is said, is said.

[*Exeunt severally.*

SCENE II. *The garden of* DON LUIS' *palace at Naples; a window with a balcony on one side, or in front: — night. Enter the* PRINCE *and* CELIO *muffled up.*

Celio Still sighing? pardon me, your Highness, but
This melancholy is a riddle to me.

Prince Ah, Celio, so strange a thing is love,
The sighs you think are melancholy sighs,
Yet are not so; I have indeed drunk poison,
But love the taste of it.

Cel. I used to think
'T was all of being away from your Porcia;
But now when better starr'd, her brother absent,
Her father unsuspicious, at her bidding
Night after night you come beneath her lattice,
And yet —

Prince If Porcia be not the cause
Of my complaint she cannot be the cure:
Yet (such is love's pathology) she serves
To soothe the wound another made.

Cel. Who then was she, my lord, for whose fair sake

You cannot either love this loving lady,
Nor leave her?
  Prince   I would tell you, Celio,
But you would laugh at me.
   Cel.   Tell me, however.
  Prince Rememberest not the lady whom we saw
For a few minutes, like some lovely vision,
In this same house, a little while ago?
Not Porcia, but her diviner guest.
  Cel. Oh, I remember, is it then to be
The specialty of your Highness' love,
That, whereas other men's dies off by absence,
Yours quickens — if it can be love at all
Caught from one transitory glance?
  Prince   Nay, Celio;
Because a cloud may cover up the sun
At his first step into the firmament,
Are we to say he never rose at all?
Are we to say the lightning did not flash
Because it did but flash, or that the fountain
Never ran fresh because it ran so fast
Into its briny cradle and its grave?
My love, if 't were but of one moment born,
And but a moment living, yet was love;
And love it *is*, now living with my life. *(A harp heard.)*
  Cel. O fine comparisons! but hark, I hear
The widow'd turtle in the leaves away
Calling her faithless mate.
  Prince   Yes, Celio, 't is
Porcia — if she sings to me of *love*,
I am to approach the window; but if *jealousy*,
I am to keep aloof. Listen!
  Porcia (singing within).

    Of all the shafts to Cupid's bow,
     The first is tipt with fire;
    All bare their bosoms to the blow,
     And call the wound Desire.

      (She appears at the window.)

Prince   Ah! I was waiting, lovely Porcia,
Till your voice drew me by the notes of love,
Or distanc'd me by those of jealousy.
   Por.   Which needs not music, prince, to signify,
Being love's plain, prose history.
   Prince   Not always;
For instance, I know one,
Who, to refute your theory, Porcia,
Attracts men by her jealousy as much
As she repels them by her love.
   Por.   Nay, then
Men must be stranger beings than I thought.
   Prince   I know not how that is, I only know
That in love's empire, as in other empires,
Rebellion sometimes prospers.
   Por.   That the night
Would give us leave to argue out their point!
Which yet I fear it will not.
   Prince   Why?
   Por.   My father,
Who frets about my brother's sudden absence,
Sits up enditing letters after him;
And therefore I have brought my harp, that while
We talk together I may touch the strings,
So as he, hearing me so occupied,
May not suspect or ask for me.   Besides,
We can talk under cover of the music.
   Prince   Not the first time that love has found himself
Fretted, Porcia.
   Por.   Oh, the wretched jest!
But listen —
The music is for him, the words for you,
For I have much to tell you underneath
This mask of music.   *(Plays on the harp.)*
You know my father has been long resolv'd
To quit this government, and to return
To his own country place — which resolution,
First taken on my brother's suppos'd death,
My brother's sudden absence has revived;
And brought to a head — so much so, that to-morrow,

To-morrow, he has settled to depart
To Bellaflor — I scarce can say the words —
But let my tears —
    Prince   'T is well that you should mask
Ill news under sweet music: though, indeed,
A treason to make sweet the poison'd cup.
    Por.   Who more than I —

Enter JULIA *within, hurried*

    Julia   Madam, madam, your father
Is gone into the garden — I hear his steps.
    Por.   Nay then — *(Sings)*

> *Love's second is a poison'd dart,*
>   *And Jealousy is nam'd:*
> *Which carries poison to the heart*
>   *Desire had first inflam'd.*

    Prince   She sings of jealousy — we must retire;
Hist, Celio!   [CELIO *and* PRINCE *retreat.*

Enter LUIS

    Julia   Who's there?
    Por.   Speak!
    Luis   Oh, I, Porcia,
Who writing in my study, and much troubled
About your brother, was seduc'd away
By your harp's pleasant sound and the cool night,
To take a turn in the garden.
    Por.   Yes, sir, here
I sit, enjoying the cool air that blows
Up from the shore among the whispering leaves.
    Luis   What better? but, Porcia, it grows late,
And chilly, I think: and though I'd have you here
Singing like a nightingale the whole night through,
It must not be. Will you come in?   [*Exit.*
    Por.   Directly —
I've but a moment.
    Prince (entering).   And you shall not need
Repeat the love call, for I heard —

Por. (playing as she speaks).   Nay, listen,
And that attentively.   To-morrow, then,
We go to Bellaflor, (you know the place,) —
There in the hill-top, hid among the trees,
Is an old castle; ours, but scarcely us'd,
And kept by an old man who loves me well,
And can be secret.   And if you should come
That way by chance, as hunting it may be,
I think we yet may meet.
   Luis (within).   Porcia!
   Por.   Sir!
   Luis (within).   It's time, indeed, to shut your window.
   Por.   Hark,
I dare no longer.
   Prince   Then farewell!
   Por.   Farewell!
Remember Bellaflor: while you retreat
Among the trees, I still shall sing to you
Of love; not that dark shape of jealousy,
But in the weeds of absence.
   Prince   A descant
That suits us both, — *(aside)*, but on a different theme.
   Por. (singing).

> *The last of Cupid's arrows all*
>   *With heavy lead is set;*
> *That vainly weeping lovers call*
>   *Repentance or Regret.*

   [*As she retires still singing from the window within,
the* PRINCE *and* CELIO *retire back into the garden.*

SCENE III.   *A street before* DON DIEGO's *house in Barcelona.
— Enter* ALVARO *and* FABIO, *masked: other Masks pass
across, and into* DIEGO's *house.*

   Alv.   This is the place; here will I wait till she comes by.
I know her dress, but I dared not follow her till myself
disguised.
   Fab.   And no doubt, sir, you will find good opportunity
of talking to her.   'T is the old and acknowledged usage of

this season, that any one may accost any one so long as both
are masked, and so neither supposed to know the other.

Alv.   Oh, a brave usage, and a brave invention, that of
the Carnival!   One may accost whom one pleases, and
whisper what one will, under the very ears of husband,
father, or duenna!

Fab.   So received a custom, that even among this hot-
headed jealous people of Spain, no mortal quarrel has yet
arisen on these occasions, though plenty to provoke it.

Alv.   Look! the Masks are coming; I hear the music
within.   She must soon be here.   Let us withdraw round
this corner till she come.   [*Exeunt.*

SCENE IV.   *A garden leading down to the sea; on one side
a Portico. — Masks singing and dancing; in the course of
which enter and mix with them,* JUAN, SERAFINA, LEO-
NELO, FLORA, *and afterwards* ALVARO; *all masked.*

CHORUS

> *Tantara, tantara, come follow me all,*
> *Carnival, Carnival, Carnival.*
> *Follow me, follow me, nobody ask;*
> *Crazy is Carnival under the mask.*
> *Follow me, follow me, nobody knows;*
> *Under the mask is under the rose.*
> *Tantara, tantara, &c.*

Juan   How like you all this uproar?
Ser.   O quite well.
Juan (aside).   And so should I,
Did not a shadow from that darken'd room
Trail after me.   But why torment myself!
   Leon.   My lord, the dancers wait.
   Juan (to the musicians).   Pardon me.   Strike up!
   Voices   Strike up! strike up!
   A Voice   The castanets!
   Voices   The castanets! the castanets!
   Musician   What will you have?
   Voices   The Tarazana! the Tarazana!
                  [*A dance, during which* ALVARO *observes* SERAFINA.

Fab.   You recognize her?

Alv.   Yes, Fabio, my heart
Would recognise her under any dress,
And under any mask.

Fab.   Now is your time.

Alv. (*to* SERAFINA).   Mask, will you dance with me?

Ser.   No, Cavalier;
You come too late.

Alv.   Too late?

Ser.   I am engag'd.

Alv.   Nevertheless —

Ser.   Nay, sir, I am not apt
To change my mind.

Alv.   I hop'd that in my favour
You might perhaps.

Ser.   'T was a delusion.

Alv.   But,
Fair Mask, didst never change thy mind before?

Ser.   Perhaps once — to such purpose that that *once*
Forbids all other.

Juan   Serafina, the Mask
Has askt your hand to dance.   On these occasions
You must permit him, whether known or not.
Unknown, the usage of the time allows;
If known, 't were more discourteous to refuse.

Ser.   My lord, 't was chiefly upon your account
That I refus'd to dance with him; if you
Desire it, I am ready.

Juan   How, my love,
On my account?

Ser.   Liking your company
Much better.

Juan   Nay, take the humour of the time,
And dance with him.   (*Aside.*) I marvel who it is
That follows Serafina, and to whom,
The very indisposition that she shows,
Argues a kind of secret inclination.

Alv.   Well, do you still reject me? —

Ser.   I am bidden
To dance with you; what measure will you call?

Alv.   Play "Love lies bleeding!"

Ser.   And why that —

Alv.   Because
The spirit of the tune and of the words
Moves with my heart, and gives me leave beside
Amid its soft and slow divisions
To gaze on you and whisper in your ear.

[*A minuet by the Masks: during which* ALVARO *constantly
whispers* SERAFINA, *who seems distrest; after some time,
they return in the figure to the front of the Stage.*]

Ser.   I've heard enough, sir; save for courtesy,
Too much.   No more.

Alv.   Brief as the happiness
That once was mine!   But —

Ser.   Stay, sir, I will hear
No more.   I had not danc'd with you at all,
But that I wish'd to tell you once for all
How hopeless is your passion — the great danger
Your coming hither put and puts me to,
And that not my honour only, but my life,
Depends upon your quitting me at once,
Now and for ever.

Alv.   Serafina!

Ser. (aloud).   I am tired;
Pardon me, friends, I cannot dance.

Juan   My love,
What is 't?   Unwell?

Ser.   I know not.

A Woman   Stop the ball!

Another   All in her honour too!

Another   What is the matter?

Juan   You are but tir'd with dancing.

Ser.   No, no, no,
Let us go home.

Juan   Pardon us, friends,
Continue you your revels; we will go
Into the house awhile, and rest; I think
The heat and dancing have distrest her much,
But she'll be better.   To your dance again.

Come, Serafina. *(Aside.)*   Leonelo! hither!
Find out the Mask that with your lady danc'd.
   Leon.   I'll watch him to the world's end — or beyond,
If need be.
   Juan   Good — Come, Serafina.
[Exeunt JUAN and SERAFINA.

   Alv.   So end my hopes for ever.   Fool! who seeking
For what once lost could never more be found,
Like to a child after a rainbow running —
Leaving my father, who had only just
Recover'd me to his old heart again,
Without adieu — equipp'd this Brigantine
(Down to the bottom may she go with me!)
In chase of this — not Serafina — no —
But this false Siren,
Who draws me with the music of her beauty,
To leave me in destruction.
   Leon. (watching him).   This must be some monk, who
knows of some better entertainment elsewhere.
   Alv.   And after all,
Not one kind word of welcome or of thanks,
But that her life depended on my leaving her,
Who would for her have sacrificed my own
In any way but that.   But it is done!
Henceforward I renounce all hope; henceforth —
And why not all despair? — the world is wide,
Eh, Fabio? and the good old saw says well
That fortune at the worst must surely mend.
Let us to sea, the ship is ready; come,
Away with all this foolery.   *(Throws off mask, &c.)*
   Leon.   Here is a harlequin sailor!
   Fabio   Well resolv'd.
   Alv.   Wear them what other fool may list,
I'll straight aboard, and if the wind and sea
Can rise as they were wont, I'll stretch all sail
Toward the perdition she consigns me to.
Halloa there!   *(Whistles.)*

Enter SAILORS

   Sail.   Captain?

Alv.   How is 't for a cruise?

Sail.   Oh, never better; just a breeze to keep
The ship from looking in her glass too long.

Alv.   Aboard, aboard then!   Farewell all my hopes;
My love, farewell for ever!

Voices (within).   Fire! fire! fire!

Alv.   What's this?

Voices   Fire! fire! in Don Diego's palace!
Help! help!

Alv.   She there! my life shall save the life
She said it jeopardied.

> [*As he is going out, enter* JUAN *with* SERAFINA *fainted*
> *in his arms.*

Juan   Friends! Gentlemen! if you would help in this ca-
lamity, take charge for a moment of this most precious thing
of all, till I return.

Alv. (taking SERAFINA *in his arms).*   Trust me, sir.

> [JUAN *rushes off.*

Leon.   Stop, my lord, stop a moment — he is gone, and
this man —

Alv.   Serafina in my arms! my ship at hand!
O love, O destiny! — aboard, aboard —
O 't is the merriest proverb of them all,
How one man rises by his neighbour's fall.

> [*Exit, carrying off* SERAFINA.

Leon.   Halloa! stop him! stop him! it is my mistress; Don
Juan! my lord! my lord! the rascal has carried her off! my
lord! my lord!   [*Runs after* ALVARO.

1st Voice in the crowd   The fire is getting under.

2nd Voice   No lives lost?

3rd Voice   Only, they say, one poor girl of the lady Serafina's.

Enter DON JUAN *hurriedly*

Juan   I thought I heard Leonelo calling me — But where
is Serafina?   This is the place — yes — Serafina!   I left them
here — taken her perhaps fainting as she was for help.   Gentlemen, have you seen any here with a lady, fainted, in their
charge — a sailor, I think?

1st Man   Not I, sir.

2nd Man   Nor I.

3rd Man   Stay.   I think there were some sailors with a lady in their arms.

Juan   And where —

Enter LEONELO *breathless*

Leon.   Oh, my lord, my lord!

Juan   Speak!

Leon.   The Mask who danced with my lady —

Juan   Where is she?

Leon.   Was the sailor you gave her in charge to — He has carried her off.

Juan   The Mask! the sailor!

Leon.   I saw him throw off his disguise, and now he has carried her off — to the shore — to sea — to the ship there now spreading her sails in the harbour.

Juan   Man! beware lest I blast thee!

Leon.   As if I were the sailor!   I tell you I ran after them, shouted, struggled, but was pushed aside, knocked down —

Juan   To the shore, to the shore! follow me!

Voices   What is the matter?

Juan   What I dare not name till it be avenged; Pirate! — Ruffian!   Oh fool, I might have guessed — but I will find them through water and fire too.   To the shore!

[*Exit* JUAN, LEONELO *after him; confusion, &c.*

ACT III

SCENE I. *A room in* DON LUIS' *country-house near Naples.*

Enter DON LUIS *reading a letter*

Luis "You bid me tell you why it is Don Juan Roca has
not written to you so long: and though it be pain to do so, I
dare no longer defer answering you. At a carnival dance
here, the palace of Don Diego de Cordona, in which the
festival was held, took fire so suddenly, as people had much
ado to escape with their lives. Don Juan's wife fainting
from terror, he carried her out, and gave her in charge to a
sailor standing near, while he himself returned to help at the
fire. No doubt this sailor was a pirate: for he carried her off
to his ship and set sail immediately. Don Juan returning
and finding her gone rushes madly after; casts himself into
the sea in his rage and desperation; is rescued half drowned,
and taken to his house, from which he was missed — he and
his servant Leonelo — some days ago, taking scarce any thing
with him, and leaving no hint of whither he is gone. And
since that hour we have heard nothing of him, or of Serafina."
My heart prevents my eyes from reading more.
O heavens! to what chance and danger is
The fortune of the happiest, and still more,
The honour of the noblest, liable!
Ill fortune we may bear, and, if we choose,
Sit folded in despair with dignity;
But honour needs must wince before a straw,
And never rest until it be avenged.
To know where Juan is, and by his side

To put myself, and run all risk with him
Till he were righted, and the offender too,
I'd give my life and all I'm worth; no corner
In the wide earth but we would ferret it,
Until — Porcia!

Enter PORCIA

 Por.   Pray, sir, pardon me,
But I would know what vexes you, you stand
Angrily talking to yourself alone:
This letter in your hand — What is it, sir?
 Luis   Nothing, nothing, Porcia; (for Juan's sake
I must dissemble) — Nay, I have received
A letter upon business that annoys me.
 Por.   I'm sorry, sir, for that, for I had come
To ask a favour of you.
 Luis   Well, why not?
 Por.   They say that those who ask unseasonably
Must be content with a refusal.
 Luis   Nay,
Between us two no season's out of season.
 Por.   So? then I'll ask.   Alvaro —
 Luis   All but that!
Ask me not that way.
 Por.   Then 't is *not* the season.
 Luis   The season for all else but that which never
Can be in season.   How often have I told you
Never to speak to me again of him!
 Por.   What has my brother done, sir, after all,
To make you so inveterate?
 Luis   What done!
To leave my house, to which I only just
Had welcom'd him as only a father can,
Without adieu, or word of when or where,
And then as suddenly come back, forsooth,
Knock at my door, as if he had but made
A morning call, and think to find it open —
It and my heart — open to him as ever.
 Por.   But may not, sir, the thoughtlessness of youth

Be some excuse?   Pray you remember, sir,
How on a sudden you yourself determin'd
To leave the cheerful city and come here,
Among dull woods and fields, and savage people;
And surely 't was no wonder that my brother
Should, ill advis'd, no doubt, but naturally,
Slip for a month back to the busy world
To which his very dangers had endear'd him.
And now to prove
How much he feels your anger and his fault,
Since his return he has lived quietly,
I might say almost *eremitically*,
Up in the mountain, yet more solitary
And still than this is, doing penance there.
Let me plead for him, sir; let him come down,
To kiss your hand and see you once again.

    Luis   He should be grateful to you, Porcia —
Well, let him come.

    Por.   Bless you for saying so!
I'll go myself to him this evening,
And tell him this good news.

    Luis   Do so.   Ah me!
That all were settled thus!   Did I but know
Where Juan is, and where his enemy!   [*Exit.*

    Julia (entering).   Well, madam, you have gain'd your
        point.

    Por.   Yes, Julia,
Two points; for, first, my brother will come back;
And, secondly, so doing, leave the old castle
At my disposal, where the Prince and I
May meet together in security.
I'll write to Alvaro now, and do you tell
The messenger who brought his letter hither,
I'll go this evening up the mountain.   So
Belardo, the old porter,
Who knows and loves me well, will look for me,
And understand the purpose of my going.

    Julia   Ah, now I see, beside his bow and arrows,
Love arms himself with trick and stratagem.

    Por.   And something else; give me my arquebuss;

So, Love and I perchance, as says the song,
May hit a hart, as we shall go along.

SCENE II.   *A room in* DON LUIS' *castle in the hills. —*
Enter ALVARO *and* FABIO.

Alv.   How is 't with Serafina?
Fab.   Nay, you know.
Ever the same.
Alv.   You mean still weeping?
Fab.   Ay.
Alv.   Yes, from the hour when, fainting in my arms,
She pass'd from raging flame to the wild seas,
And opening those heavenly eyes again,
Still with the hue of death upon her cheek,
She saw herself in my ship — in my power, —
She has not ceas'd to weep; all my caresses
Unable to console her.
I fondly hoped that she —

Enter SERAFINA

Ser.   Good Fabio,   [*Exit* FABIO.
Leave us awhile.   "You fondly hoped," Alvaro —
So much I heard, connected with my name;
And I perhaps have something on that text
Would clear the matter up to both of us.
"You fondly hoped" — was 't not that I might be
So frail, so lost to shame, and so inconstant,
That for the loss of husband, home, and honour,
Lost in one day, I might console myself
With being in his arms, who robb'd me of all!
Was 't this you hoped?
Alv.   No, Serafina, but —
Ser.   But what?
Alv.   And yet perhaps 't was that I hop'd —
The very desperation of my act
Bringing its pardon with it, soon or late,
Seeing, the very element of love
Is rashness, that he finds his best excuse
In having none at all.   Ah, Serafina,

How greatly must he love, who all for love
Perils the hope of being loved at all!

   Ser.   Poor argument!   I rather draw that he
Who ventures on such desperate acts can have
No true respect for her he outrages,
And therefore no true love.   No, daring traitor —
But I'll not strive to break the heart of flint,
But wear it with my tears.   Hear me, Alvaro,
In pity — in mercy — hear me.
This thing is done, there is no remedy,
Let us not waste the time in arguing
What better had been done; the stars so rul'd it —
Yea, providence that rules the stars.   Well then,
What next?   Alvaro, I would speak of this;
And if 't be right I owe you any thing,
Be it for this one boon, a patient hearing.
Listen to me —
I never draw a breath but 't is on fire
With Juan's vengeance; never move a step
But think I see his fierce eyes glaring at me
From some dark corner of this desolate house
In which my youth is buried.   And what gain *you*
By all this crime and misery?   My body,
But not my soul; without possessing which,
Beauty itself is but a breathing corpse,
But a cold marble statue, unsuffus'd
With the responsive hue of sympathy,
Possess'd, but not enjoy'd.
Oh, ill betide that villain love, not love,
That all its object and affection finds
In the mere contact of encircling arms!
But if this move you not — consider, Alvaro —
Don Juan is a nobleman — as such
Bound to avenge his honour; he must know
'T was you who did this monstrous act, for Flora
Would tell him all.   There is one remedy:
'T is this, that you, despairing of my love,
Which you can never gain — forego me quite,
And give me up to some cold convent's cloister,
Where buried I may wear away —

Alv.   No more,
Rather than give you up again, Serafina,
Pray heaven's thunder —   *(Shot within.)*
  Ser.   Again, this dreadful omen!
'T is for my death!
  Alv.   Fear not — Belardo! ho!
What shot was that?

Enter BELARDO

  Bel.   Your sister Porcia
Is coming up the mountain; nay, is now
At the very gate.
  Ser.   O, whither must I go!
  Alv.   Belardo, lead her hence.
  Bel.   Not that way, sir,
By which your sister enters.
  Alv.   In here then.
I'll go and meet Porcia.
  Ser.   Mercy, heaven!
      [*She goes in at one door, as* PORCIA *enters by another.*
  Alv.   How now, Porcia, you look pleased to-day!
  Por.   And well I may — for two reasons, Alvaro.
  Alv.   Well, what are they?
  Por.   First, I have got my father to relax in his humour
against you.
  Alv.   My good sister!
  Por.   So as he will see you at Bellaflor this very evening.
  Alv.   Good! and your second reason?
  Por.   That coming up the pass I made the crowning shot
of my life with this arquebuss — a hare at full speed — flying,
I might say.
  Alv.   Give you joy of both your hits, Porcia.
  Por.   I am so proud of the last (though glad of the first,
Alvaro) that I shall try my luck and skill a little longer about
the castle this evening.
  Alv.   ʹSo —
  Por.   You will not wait for me, but go down at once to
Bellaflor, and show my father you value his forgiveness by
your haste to acknowledge it.

Alv.   You say well; but you will go with me?

Por.   Fear not, I shall soon be after you.

Alv.   Well, if so, then — *(apart to* BELARDO,) Belardo, remember you get the lady to her room directly my sister is gone out.

Por.   Our roads lie together as far as the gate at least. *(Aside to* BELARDO.)   If the Prince happen to come hither, tell him to wait for me, Belardo; I shall be back directly. Come, brother.

[*Exeunt* ALVARO *and* PORCIA.

Bel.   They say a Pander is a good business; and yet here am I ministering both to brother and sister with very little profit at the year's end.

Ser. (entering cautiously).   Porcia's gone?

Bel.   Yes, she is gone.

Ser.   Had she resolv'd on going into the room where I was she could have done it; there was neither key nor bolt within.   But she is gone and I can get to my own.

Bel.   No.

Ser.   Belardo! why?

Bel.   Some one coming.

Ser.   Again!   [*She hides as before.*

Enter PRINCE

Prince   How now, Belardo, where is your mistress? she advised me her brother would be away, and she here this evening.

Bel.   Your Highness comes in good time.   She went with him, but will be back directly.   She is here.

Enter PORCIA

Por.   Not far behind, you see.   Scarce had he taken the turn to Bellaflor, when I turn'd back.

Prince   How shall I thank you for this favour?

Por.   My brother's living here has been the reason of our not meeting before; but that is remedied for the future.

Prince   And how?

Por.   He is at last reconciled to my father, and is even now gone home, to Bellaflor.

Prince (aside). My heart thanks you but little, being away with another; but if I cannot avenge memory, I will thus try and deceive or amuse it. My lovely Porcia!

Bel. (aside). She hears every word they say!

Por. Ah, you flatter still.

Prince Flatter!

Por. Do I not know there is a Siren at Naples —

Prince Porcia, to prove to you how unfounded that suspicion is, I have these many days wholly quitted Naples, and, out of a melancholy that has taken hold of me, now live retired in a little Villa hard by this: you may imagine at least one reason for my doing so. And so enchanted am I with my solitude, that till this evening (when you broke it as I could wish) I have not once stirred abroad; my only occupation being to watch some pictures that I am having done, by the best masters of Italy and of Spain too; one of which country I have happen'd on, who might compete with Apelles. As I told you, I have spent whole days in watching them at work.

Por. My jealousy whispered —

Enter BELARDO

Bel. Unlucky to be sure.

Por. What now?

Bel. What can make your brother return so suddenly?

Por. My brother!

Bel. He is now at the gate.

Por. He must suspect the Prince! O, my lord, hide yourself.

Prince Where?

Por. Any where! — quick! here.

> [*She puts him where* SERAFINA *is.*

Prince For your sake, Porcia.

Enter ALVARO

Alv. I cannot be easy till I am assured that Serafina —— Porcia here?

Por. Alvaro!

Alv. You left me on a sudden?

Por.   I was tired, and came back for rest.

Alv.   So —

Por.   But you?

Alv.   I bethought me that, considering my father's late indisposition toward me, it were better you were at my side when I went to him.

Por.   So —

Alv.   So that if he should relapse into ill-humour, you know how to direct him.

Por.   Well, shall we start again together?

Alv.   Is not that best?

Por.   As you please.

Alv. (aside).   She will not then stumble on Serafina.

Por. (aside).   I shall so get him out of the Prince's way.

[*Exeunt* PORCIA *and* ALVARO.

Bel.   Now then the two imprison'd ones get out.

Enter the PRINCE, *and* SERAFINA, *her hand before her face*

Ser.   In vain — you shall not know me.

Prince   Nay, in vain
You try to be unknown.

Ser.   Consider —

Prince   Nay,
Down with that little hand, too small a cloud
To hide the heaven of your beauty from me.
Lady, I know you — but one such.   And know
That love himself has wrought a miracle,
To this unlikeliest place, by means unlikeliest,
Bringing us here together.

Bel.   Only this was wanting to the plot!   The sister's gallant in love with the brother's mistress!

Ser.   Generous Orsino! if I try in vain
To hide me from you — wretched that I am
To have to hide at all — but the less wretched
Being unmaskt by your nobility —
I ask this mercy at your feet; betray not
The secret chance has now betray'd to you.
I am a wretch'd woman, you a Prince.
Grant me this boon; and yet one more, to leave me

To weep my miseries in solitude.

Prince Madam, your prayer is not in vain. Your name,
Upon the word and honour of a Prince,
Shall never pass my lips.
And for that second wish, hardest of all,
I yet will pay for one delicious glance
The greatest price I can, by leaving you.
Farewell — you owe me more anxiety
Than you believe.

Ser. I shall not be asham'd
To own the debt, though hopeless to repay it.
But heav'n shall do that for me. Farewell, my lord.

Prince Farewell. [*Exeunt* PRINCE *and* SERAFINA.

Bel. I wonder if they know the ancient line,
"I'll keep your secret, only you keep mine." [*Exit.*

SCENE III. *The* PRINCE'S *Villa.* — *Enter* DON JUAN *in poor
apparel; and* CELIO.

Cel. Your business with the Prince, sir?

Juan Only to speak
About a picture I have finish'd for him.

Cel. He is not here at present; not, I think,
Return'd from hunting.

Juan Will he soon be home?

Cel. I cannot speak to that, sir. [*Exit* CELIO.

Juan Why, what a fate is mine!
All of a sudden — but I dare not say it;
Scarce could I of myself believe it, if
I told it to myself; so with some things
'T is easier to bear, than hear of them;
And how much happens daily in this strange world,
Far easier to be done than be believed.
Who could have thought that I, being what I was
A few days back, am what I am; to this
Reduc'd by that name *Honour;* whose nice laws,
Accurst be he who framed!
Little he knew the essence of the thing
He legislated for, who put my honour
Into another's hand; made my free right

Another's slave, for others to abuse,
And then myself before the world arraign'd,
To answer for a crime against myself!
And one being vain enough to make the law,
How came the silly world to follow it,
Like sheep to their own slaughter!   And in all
This silly world is there a greater victim
To its accursed custom than myself!

Enter LEONELO, *poorly drest*

Leon.   Yes, one,
Who follows your misfortunes, and picks up
The crumbs of misery that fall from you;
My chief subsistence now.
  Juan   And I have left
Country and home to chase this enemy,
Of whom as yet no vestige —
  Leon.   And no wonder,
Seeing he travels with you.
  Juan   In these rags —
  Leon.   And very hungry; and so we come at last
To Naples; for what purpose?
  Juan   Why, if 't be
Some former lover; would he not return
To his own country, and hers?
  Leon.   In which meanwhile
We starve without a stiver in our pockets,
While friends swarm round us, if you would, my lord,
Reveal yourself.
  Juan   Shorn of my honour?   No!
  Leon.   And I, not being shorn of appetite,
Would publish my disgraceful want of food
To all the world.   There is Don Luis now,
Your ancient friend.
  Juan   What friend but, if he be
True to himself and me, must be my enemy,
And either wholly turn his face away,
Or look at me with pity and contempt?
I will reveal myself to no one, nay,

Reveal *myself* I cannot, — not myself
Until I be aveng'd.
 Leon.   And so you make
The painter's trade your stalking-horse,
To track your enemy, and in these rags
Come to the Prince.
 Juan   Oh let me die in rags,
Rather than he should recognise me! Once
He saw me —
 Leon. O, my lord, fear not for that;
Hunger, and rags, and sleeplessness, and anguish,
Have chang'd you so your oldest friend would pass you.
 Juan They have that merit then. But see — the Prince.

     Enter PRINCE

I kiss your Highness' hand.
 Prince   Well, Spaniard,
What would you with me?
 Juan   I waited on your Highness,
To tell you of a picture I had finisht.
Thinking your Grace might like —
 Prince   I thank you, sir,
What is the subject?
 Juan   Hercules, my lord;
Wherein (unless I do deceive myself)
I think the fair and terrible are join'd
With some success.
 Prince As how?
 Juan   As thus, my lord.
The point I have chosen in that history
Is where the faithless Centaur carries off
Deijanira, while beyond the river
Stands Hercules with such a face and gesture
As not a man, I think, who looks on it,
But would exclaim, "Jealousy and Revenge!"
 Prince I long to see it.
 Juan   That is the main group;
But far away, among the tangled thicks
Of a dark mountain gap, this Hercules

Fires his own funeral pile to the smoky clouds.
And I would have this motto for the whole,
"So Jealousy in its own flames expires."
    Prince   Not only do I like the subject well,
But now especially, being deeply scorcht,
Not with the flame that burn'd up Hercules,
But that for which the unlucky Centaur died.
    Juan   Indeed, my lord.
    Prince   Indeed — and, having done
This picture for me, you shall set about
One other.
    Juan   At your pleasure.
    Prince   You shall know then,
That of a certain lady, whom but once
I saw, and for a moment, I became
Infatuated so, her memory
Every where and for ever, day and night,
Pursues me.   Hopeless of obtaining her,
And ev'n of ever seeing her again,
Chance has discover'd to me where she lives
Conceal'd — I know not why, but so it is —
And 't would at least console my hopeless love,
To have her picture.   You are a foreigner
Who know not nor are known by any here,
So I can better trust you with a secret
I dare not even to herself reveal.
    Juan   I'll do my best to serve you; but I fear,
If she be such a creature as you say,
That I shall fail to satisfy myself
Or you.
    Prince   Why so?
    Juan   I tried at such a face
Once.
    Prince   Nay, I know that beauty's subtlest essence
Is most impossible to seize.   But yet
I shall commit this business to your hands
Most confidently.
    Juan   I'll do my best.
    Prince   Come then,
Remembering this business must be done

With all despatch and secrecy.   Yourself
Must not be seen by her, nor I, who know not
(I told you) how or why she should be there;
But my authority, and a little gold,
(At least, I hope,) shall set the door ajar,
That you may catch a sight of her.   Myself
Will be at hand, and ready to protect you
Against all danger.

Juan   I will trust your Highness,
And also (let me say so) trust myself,
Although but a poor painter.

Prince   I believe it;
And each of us shall play his part, I think,
That neither shall depart unsatisfied.   [*Exit* PRINCE.

Juan   Perhaps, but not as you suppose.   Leonelo,
Put up my brushes and my colours, and —
My pistols with them.

Leon.   Pistols!   Is 't to paint
In body colour?

Juan   Put them up.

Leon.   And whither
Are we to carry them?

Juan   I do not know.
Whither the Prince shall carry me, I go.

                                          [*Exeunt.*

SCENE IV.   *A room in* DON LUIS' *Villa.* — *Enter* LUIS
                and ALVARO.

Alv.   Now, sir, that (thanks to Porcia) you have open'd
Your arms to me once more, I cannot rest
(So favour ever calls for favour) till
You tell me what the inward trouble is
That mars your outward feature.   I was cause
Of so much trouble to you, that I dread
Lest of this also, which with troubled looks
You still keep speaking to yourself apart,
Like people in a play.

Luis   Alvaro, no.
Thank God, this trouble lies not at your door.

Let that suffice.

Alv.   You will not trust me, sir?

Luis   Why will you press me? since you must be told,
It is about my friend — Don Juan Roca.

Alv.   Don Juan!

Luis   Yes, Don Juan.

Alv.   What of him?
(I'll drink the cup at once!) *(aside).*

Luis   What evil star
Made him my friend!

Alv.   Too true! *(aside).*   But what has
      happen'd?

Luis   Why will you know? and should I dare to tell
My friend's dishonour?   Well, no more than this —
Some wretch — some villain — some accurs'd — but
Be there bad name enough to brand him by,
I have not breath for it — nor is it well
For you or for myself — has ravisht from him
His wife, his Serafina.
And I, O God! not able to avenge him!

Alv. (aside).   Does he know all? and knowing whose the
      crime
Cannot, he says, avenge it on his son?
Shall I then tell, and gain at least the grace
Of a confession?   Hear me, sir.

Luis   Nay, nay,
I know what you would say, how vain it is
To vex myself who cannot help my friend —
We neither knowing who the villain is,
Nor whither both are fled: heaven! if we did,
I should not now be idly moaning here.

Alv.   All's safe! *(aside).*   Nor I, sir; give me but a clue,
(Not only for Don Juan's sake, but yours,)
I'll track the villain through the world.

Luis   Alvaro,
Your words are music to me.

Alv.   Still, my father,
I will say what to say you said was vain.
Until some clue be found, let not this grief
Consume you so.

Luis   Such wounds are hard to heal.
Yet, quicken'd by your courage, and to show
How well I like your counsel — come, Alvaro,
I will with you to your hill castle there;
That which has been your banishment so long,
Shall witness now our reconciliation.
We'll go this evening — now — together.
    Alv.   Good, sir.
But pardon me, let me go on before
To apprize Belardo of your going thither —
And also Serafina! *(apart).*   [*Exit.*
    Luis   Be it so!
    Julia (entering).   My lord, Don Pedro is without, and fain
Would speak to you.
    Luis   Admit him, Julia.
The wound re-opens — Serafina's father!
No doubt upon what errand.

Enter DON PEDRO

    Ped.   Ah, Don Luis,
Your arms! *(they embrace).*
    Luis   Don Pedro, I must surely thank
The cause to which my poor retirement owes
This honour.
    Ped.   Yet a thankless cause, Don Luis.
These many days I have heard nothing of
Don Juan and my daughter; they neither write
Themselves, nor any one to whom I write
To ask about them answers to the purpose.
What may this mean?   I have come hither thinking
That you, who are the model of all friends,
May deal more clearly with me.   You may think
What I endure from this suspense.   In mercy
Relieve me from it quickly.
    Luis (aside).   Poor old man;
What shall I say? tell his grey hairs at once
The ruin of his honour and his love?
    Ped.   You pause, my lord!
    Luis   And yet I need not wonder,

I nothing hear of them if you do not.

    Ped.   And you know nothing of them?

Enter PORCIA *hurriedly*

    Por.   Sir, I hear
You are going (are you not?) this evening
To the castle, with my brother.
But who is this?

    Ped.   Ever your slave, sweet lady.

    Por.   Oh, pardon me, my lord.

    Luis   Nay, pardon *me*
That I cut short your compliments, Porcia.
(This interruption, come so opportune,
Shall carry what ill news I have to tell
Into the open air at least.)   Don Pedro,
I am going to the mountain, as she says;
You to the city; for some way at least
Our roads are one, and I would talk with you
About this business without interruption.
Will 't please you come?

    Ped.   Your pleasure's mine.   Adieu,
Fair lady.

    Por.   Farewell, sir.

    Luis   Porcia, you
Will follow in the carriage.

                         [*Exeunt* LUIS *and* PEDRO.

    Por.   And should go
More gladly, were my lover there to meet me.   [*Exit.*

SCENE V. *The garden under* ALVARO's *castle. — A large grated door in the centre. — Enter* PRINCE, JUAN, LEONELO, *and* BELARDO.

    Prince (to BELARDO*).* You know your office; take this diamond by way of thanks.

    Bel. I know little of diamonds but that they sell for less than you give for them. But this [*to* JUAN] is to be your post.

    Juan I am ready.

    Prince Remember, Spaniard, it is for *me* you run this hazard, if there be any; I shall be close at hand to protect you. Be not frightened.

Juan   Your Highness does not know me: were it otherwise, danger cannot well appal him whom sorrows like mine
have left alive.

Bel.   And, another time — doubloons, not diamonds.

[*Exeunt* PRINCE *and* LEONELO.

Here she mostly comes of an evening, poor lady, to soothe
herself, walking and sitting here by the hour together. This
is where you are to be.   Go in; and mind you make no noise.

[*Puts* JUAN *into the grated door, and locks it.*

Juan (through the grated window).   But what are you
about?

Bel.   Locking the door to make all sure.

Juan   But had it not better be unlockt in case —

Bel.   Hush! she comes.

Juan   My palette then.

Enter SERAFINA

Ser.   How often and how often do I draw
My resolution out upon one side,
And all my armed sorrows on the other,
To fight the self-same battle o'er again!

Juan   He stands in the way; I cannot see her face.

Bel.   Still weeping, madam?

Ser.   Wonder not, Belardo:
The only balm I have.   You pity me:
Leave me alone then for a while, Belardo;
The breeze that creeps along the whispering trees
Makes me feel drowsy.

Juan (to BELARDO) *whispering.*   She turns her head away,
I cannot see her still.

Ser.   What noise was that?

Bel.   Madam?

Ser.   I thought I heard a whisper.

Bel.   Only
The breeze, I think.   If you would turn this way,
I think 't would blow upon you cooler.

Ser.   Perhaps it will.
Thank you.   I am very miserable and very weary.

Bel.   She sleeps: that is the lady.
Make most of time.   [*Exit.*
    Juan   Yes.   Now then for my pencil.
Serafina! found at last!   Whose place is this?
The Prince? no!   But the stray'd lamb being here,
The wolf is not far off.   She sleeps!   I thought
The guilty never slept: and look, some tears
Still lingering on the white rose of her cheek.
Be those the drops, I wonder,
Of guilty anguish, or of chaste despair?
This death-like image is the sculptor's task,
Not mine.
Or is it I who sleep, and dream all this,
And dream beside, that once before I tried
To paint that face — the daylight drawing in
As now — and when somehow the lamp was out,
A man — I fail'd: and what love fail'd to do,
Shall hate accomplish?   She said then, if ever
She suffer'd me to draw her face again,
Might she die for it.   Into its inmost depth
Heav'n drew that idle word, and it returns
In thunder.
    Ser. (dreaming).   Juan!   Husband! on my knees.
Oh Juan — slay me not!

        Enter ALVARO; *she wakes and rushes to him*

                       Alvaro,
Save me, oh save me from him!
    Alv.   So the wretch
Thrives by another's wretchedness.   My love!
    Juan   Alvaro, by the heavens!
    Alv.   Calm yourself;
You must withdraw awhile.   Come in with me.
    Juan   Villain!
    Ser. (clinging to ALVARO).   What's that!
    Juan (shaking at the door).   The door is fast;
Open it, I say! —
Then die — thou and thy paramour!
    [*Shoots a pistol at each through the grating. — Both fall:*

SERAFINA *into the arms of* BELARDO, *who has come in during the noise.— Then directly enter* DON LUIS, PEDRO, PORCIA.

Luis   What noise is this?

Ser.   My father! — in your arms
To die; — not by your hand — Forgive me — Oh!   [*Dies.*

Ped. (taking her in his arms).   My Serafina!

Luis   And Alvaro!

Alv.   Ay,
But do not curse me now!   [*Dies.*

Enter the PRINCE *and* LEONELO

Leon.   They must have found him out.

Prince   Whoever dares
Molest him, answers it to me.   Open the door.
But what is this?   [BELARDO *unlocks the door.*

Juan (coming out).   A picture —
Done by the Painter of his own Dishonour
In blood.
I am Don Juan Roca.   Such revenge
As each would have of me, now let him take,
As far as one life holds.   Don Pedro, who
Gave me that lovely creature for a bride,
And I return to him a bloody corpse;
Don Luis, who beholds his bosom's son
Slain by his bosom friend; and you, my lord,
Who, for your favours, might expect a piece
In some far other style of art than this:
Deal with me as you list; 't will be a mercy
To swell this complement of death with mine;
For all I had to do is done, and life
Is worse than nothing now.

Prince   Get you to horse,
And leave the wind behind you.

Luis   Nay, my lord,
Whom should he fly from? not from me at least,
Who lov'd his honour as my own, and would
Myself have help'd him in a just revenge,
Ev'n on an only son.

Ped.   I cannot speak,
But I bow down these miserable gray hairs
To other arbitration than the sword;
Ev'n to your Highness' justice.

Prince   Be it so.
Meanwhile —

Juan   Meanwhile, my lord, let me depart;
Free, if you will, or not.   But let me go,
Nor wound these fathers with the sight of one
Who has cut off the blossom of their age:
Yea, and his own, more miserable than all.
They know me; that I am a gentleman,
Not cruel, nor without what seem'd due cause
Put on this bloody business of my honour;
Which having done, I will be answerable
Here and elsewhere, to all for all.

Prince   Depart
In peace.

Juan   In peace!   Come, Leonelo.

[*He goes out slowly, followed by* LEONELO: *and the curtain
falls.*

Some alterations of this play were made with a view to the
English stage, where, spite of the slightness of many parts, I still
think it might be tried.

Its companion play, the *Medico de su Honra*, is far more
famous; has some more terrible, perhaps some finer, situations; but
inferior, I think, in variety of scene, character, and incident.

It may add a little to the reader's interest, as it did to mine, to
learn from Mr. Ticknor, that Calderon wrote a *"Tratado defendi-
endo la nobleza de la Pintura."*

KEEP YOUR OWN SECRET

DRAMATIS PERSONÆ

ALEXANDER, *Prince of Parma*
NISIDA, *his Sister*
DON CESAR, *his Secretary*
DON ARIAS
DON FELIX   *Gentlemen of the Court*
DONNA ANNA, *Sister to Don Felix*
ELVIRA, *her Maid*
LAZARO, *Don Cesar's Servant*

ACT I

Scene I. *A Room in the Palace.* — *Enter the* Prince
Alexander *and* Don Arias.

Prince I saw her from her carriage, Arias,
As from her East, alight, another sun
New ris'n, or doubling him whose envious ray
Seem'd as I watch'd her down the corridor,
To swoon about her as she mov'd along;
Until, descending tow'rd my sister's room,
She set, and left me hesitating like
Some traveller who with the setting sun
Doth fear to lose his way; her image still,
Lost from without, dazzling my inner eye —
Can this be love, Don Arias? if not,
What is it? something much akin to love.
   Ar.   But had you not, my lord, often before
Seen Donna Anna?
   Prince   Often.
   Ar.   Yet till now
Never thus smitten! how comes that, my lord?
   Prince Well askt — though ignorantly.   Know you not
That not an atom in the universe
Moves without some particular impulse
Of heaven?   What yesterday I might abhor,
To-day I may delight in: what to-day
Delight in, may as much to-morrow hate.
All changes; 't is the element the world,
And we who live there, move in.   Thus with me;
This lady I have often seen before,
And, as you say, was ne'er a sigh the worse,

Until to-day; when, whether she more fair,
Or I less blind, I know not — only know
That she has slain me; though to you alone
Of all my friends I would my passion own.

Ar.   Much thanks; yet I must wonder, good my lord,
First, that in all your commerce with Don Cupid
You never, I think, dealt seriously till now.

Prince   Perhaps: but if Don Cupid, Arias,
Never yet tempted me with such an offer?
Besides, men alter; princes who are born
To greater things than love, nevertheless
May at his feet their sovereignty lay down
Once in their lives; as said the ancient sage —
"He were a fool who had not done so once,
Though he who does so twice is twice a fool."

Ar.   So much for that.   My second wonder is,
That you commit this secret to *my* keeping;
An honour that, surpassing my desert,
Yea, and ambition, frights me.   Good my lord,
Your secretary, Don Cesar, —
To whom you almost trust the government
Of your dominions, — whom you wholly love,
I also love, and would not steal from him
A confidence that is by right his own;
Call him, my lord: into his trusty heart
Pour out your own; let not my loyalty
To you endanger what I owe to him;
For if you lay 't on me —

Prince   Don Arias,
I love Don Cesar with as whole a heart
As ever.   He and I from infancy
Have grown together; as one single soul
Our joys and sorrows shar'd; till finding him
So wise and true, as to another self
Myself, and my dominion to boot,
I did intrust: you are his friend, and surely
In honouring you I honour him as well.
Besides, Arias, I know not how it is,
For some while past a change has come on him;
I know not what the cause: he is grown sad,

Neglects his business — if I call to him,
He hears me not, or answers from the purpose,
Or in mid answer stops. And, by the way,
We being on this subject, I would fain,
Being so much his friend, for both our sakes,
You would find out what ails and occupies him;
Tell him from me to use my power as ever,
Absolute still: that, loving him so well,
I'd know what makes him so unlike himself;
That, knowing what it is, I may at least,
If not relieve his sorrow, share with him.

    Ar.   Oh, not unjustly do you bear the name
Of Alexander, greater than the great
In true deserts!

Enter LAZARO *(with a letter)*

    Laz.   Not here? my usual luck; had I bad news to tell my master, such as would earn me a broken head, I should find him fast enough; but now when I have such a letter for him as must bring me a handsome largess, oh, to be sure he's no where to be found.   But I'll find him if I go to —

    Prince   How now?   Who's there?

    Laz.   The Prince! — Mum! *(hides the letter and turns to go)*.

    Prince   Who is it, I say?

    Ar.   A servant, my lord, of Don Cesar's, looking for his master, I suppose.

    Prince   Call him back; perhaps he can tell us something of his master's melancholy.

    Ar.   True, my lord.   Lazaro!

    Laz.   Eh?

    Ar.   His Highness would speak with you.

    Prince   Come hither, sir.

    Laz.   Oh, my lord, I do well enough here: if I were once to kiss your Highness' feet, I could not endure common shoe-leather for a month to come.

    Ar.   His humour must excuse him.

    Prince   You are Don Cesar's servant, are you?

    Laz.   Yes, one of your trinity; so please you.

    Prince   Of my trinity, how so?

Laz. As thus; your Highness is one with Don Cesar; I am one with him; ergo —

Prince Well, you are a droll knave. But stop, stop: Whither away so fast?

Laz. Oh, my lord, I am sure you will have none of so poor an article as myself, who am already the property of another too.

Prince Nay, I like your humour, so it be in season. But there is a time for all things. I want you now to answer me seriously and not in jest: and tell me the secret of your master's melancholy, which I feel as my own. But perhaps he is foolish who looks for truth in the well of a jester's mouth.

Laz. But not so foolish as he who should throw it there. And therefore since my master is no fool, it is unlikely he should have committed his mystery to me. However, in my capacity of *Criado*, whose first commandment it is, "Thou shalt reveal thy master's weakness as thy own," I will tell you what I have gathered from stray sighs and interjections of his on the subject. There has lately come over from Spain a certain game of great fashion and credit called Ombre. This game Don Cesar learned; and, playing at it one day, and happening to hold Basto, Malilla, Spadille, and Ace of Trumps in his hand, stood for the game; and lost. On which he calls out "foul play," leaves the party, and goes home. Well, at night, I being fast asleep in my room, comes he to me in his shirt, wakes me up, and, dealing cards as it were with his hands, says, "If I let this trick go, I am embeasted for that, and besides put the lead into the enemy's hand; therefore I trump with one of my matadores, and then I have four hearts, of which the ten-ace *must* make, or else let them give me back my nine cards as I had them before discarding." And this I take it is the cause of his dejection.[1]

---

[1] I will not answer for the accuracy of my version of this dilemma at Ombre: neither perhaps could Lazaro for his: which, together with the indifference (I presume) of all present readers on the subject, has made me indifferent about it. Cesar, I see, starts with almost the same fine hand Belinda had, who also was
"Just in the jaws of ruin and Codille,"
as he was, but, unlike him, saved by that unseen king of hearts that
"Lurk'd in her hand and mourn'd his captive queen."

Prince   The folly of asking you has been properly chastised by the folly of your answer.   You are right; Don Cesar would never have intrusted with a grave secret one only fit for idle jest.

Laz.   Ah, they are always importing some nonsense or other from Spain.   God keep your Highness; I will take warning not to intrude my folly upon you any more (until you try again to worm some truth out of me).

[*Aside and exit.*

Prince   A droll fellow!   Were one in the humour, he might amuse.

Ar.   Oh, you will always find him in the same, whenever you are in the mood.   He cannot be sad.

Prince   He cannot be very wise then.

Ar.   He is as God made him.   Did you never hear any of his stories?

Prince   I think not.

Ar.   He will hardly tell you one of himself that yet might amuse you.   He was one day playing at dice with me; lost all his money; and at last pawned his very sword, which I would not return him, wishing to see how he got on without. What does he but finds him up an old hilt, and clapping on a piece of lath to that, sticks it in the scabbard.   And so wears it now.

Prince   We will have some amusement of him by and by. Alas! in vain I hope with idle jest
To cool the flame that rages in my breast.
Go to Don Cesar: get him to reveal
The sorrows that he feeling I too feel.
I'll to my sister; since, whether away,
Or present, Donna Anna needs must slay,
I will not starve with absence, but e'en die
Burn'd in the sovereign splendour of her eye.

[*Exeunt severally.*

SCENE II.   *A Room in* DON CESAR'S *House.* — *Enter*
DON CESAR *and* LAZARO *meeting.*

Laz.   A letter, sir, Elvira just gave me.

Ces. A letter! Give it me. How long have you had it?

Laz. I looked for you first at the Prince's.

Ces. Where I was not?

Laz. You know it! I am always looking for what cannot be found in time. But if you like the letter I shall claim my largess for all that.

Ces. Ah! what does she say?

Laz. The folly, now, of a man with his watch in his hand asking other people for the time of day!

Ces. My heart fails me. Even if your news be good it comes late. [*He reads the letter.*

Laz. So let my reward then — only let it come at last.

Ces. O Lazaro, half drunk with my success,
I lose my wits when most I've need of them.
She writes to me, my lady writes to me
So sweetly, yea, so lovingly;
Methinks I want to tear my bosom open,
And lay this darling letter on my heart.
Where shall I shrine it?

Laz.   O, if that be all,
Keep it to patch your shoe with; I did so once
When some such loving lady writ to me,
And it did excellently; keeping tight
Her reputation, and my shoe together.

Ces. O Lazaro! good Lazaro! take for this
The dress I wore at Florence.

Laz.   Bless you, sir.

Ces. My letter! oh my lady!

Laz.   I bethink me
Upon remembrance, sir, as I may say,
The pockets of that dress were very large
And empty.

Ces.   They shall be well lined. Don Arias!

Enter DON ARIAS

Ar. Ay, Cesar, Arias coming to complain
On his own score, and that of one far greater.

Ces. A solemn preamble. But for the charge,
And him who heads it.

Ar.   The Prince, our common Lord,
Who much perplext and troubled too, Don Cesar,
About the melancholy that of late
(No need say more of that which best you know)
Has clouded over you, has askt of me
Whom he will have to be your bosom friend,
The cause of it. — Alas, 't is very plain
I am not what he thinks. — Well, I am come,
Say not as friend, but simple messenger,
To ask it of yourself.

Ces.   You do yourself
And me wrong, Arias; perchance the Prince —
But yet say on.

Ar.   His Highness bids me say
That if your sadness rise from any sense
Of straiten'd power, whatever residue
Of princely rule he hitherto reserved,
He gives into your hands; as sov'reign lord
To govern his dominions as your own.
Thus far his Highness.   For myself, Don Cesar,
Having no other realm to lord you of
Than a true heart, I'd have you think betimes,
That, deep as you are rooted in his love,
Nay, may be all the more for that, he feels
Your distaste to his service, and himself:
I'd have you think that all a subject's merits,
However highly heap'd, however long,
Still are but heaps of sand, that some new tide
Of royal favour may wash clean away,
One little error cancelling perhaps
The whole account of life-long services.
Be warn'd by me; clear up your heavy brow,
And meet his kind looks with a look as kind,
Whatever cloud be on the heart within:
If not your friend, Don Cesar, as your servant
Let me implore you.

Ces.   Oh, Don Arias,
I kiss his Highness' feet, and your kind hands
That bring his favours to me: and to each
Will answer separately.   First to him; —

Tell him I daily pray that Heav'n so keep
His life, that Time, on which his years are strung,
Forget the running count; and, secondly,
Assure him, Arias, the melancholy
He speaks of not a jot abates my love
Of him, nor my alacrity in his service;
Nay, that 't is nothing but a little cloud
In which my books have wrapt me so of late
That, duty done, I scarce had time or spirit
Left to enjoy his gracious company:
Perhaps too, lest he surfeit of my love,
I might desire by timely abstinence
To whet his liking to a newer edge.
Thus much for him.   For you, Don Arias,
Whose equal friendship claims to be repaid
In other coin, I will reveal to you
A secret scarcely to myself confest,
Which yet scarce needs your thanks, come at a moment
When my brimm'd heart had overflow'd in words,
Whether I would or no.   Oh, Arias,
Wonder not then to see me in a moment
Flying from melancholy to mere joy,
Between whose poles he ever oscillates,
Whose heart is set in the same sphere with mine:
Which saying, all is said.   I love, my friend;
How deeply, let this very reticence,
That dare not tell what most I feel, declare.
Yes, I have fixt my eyes upon a star;
Toward which to spread my wings ev'n against hope,
Argues a kind of honour.   I aspir'd,
And (let not such a boast offend the ears,
That of themselves have open'd to my story,)
Not hopelessly: the heav'n to which I pray'd
Answer'd in only listening to my vows;
Such daring not defeated not disdain'd.
Two years I worshipp'd at a shrine of beauty,
That modesty's cold hand kept stainless still;
Till wearied, if not mov'd by endless prayers,
She grants them; yea, on this most blessed day,
With this thrice blessed letter.   You must see it,

That your felicitations by rebound
Double my own; the first victorious trophy
That proud ambition has so humbly won.
Oh, Arias, 't is much I have to tell,
And tell you too at once; being none of those
Who overmuch entreaty make the price
Of their unbosoming; who would, if they knew
In what the honour of their lady lies,
Name her at once, or seal their lips for ever.
But you are trusty and discreet: to you
I may commit my heart; beseeching you
To keep this love-song to yourself alone,
Assigning to the Prince, remember this,
My books sole cause of my abstraction.
Donna Anna de Castelvi
(I can go on more freely now the name
Of her I worship bars my lips no more,)
Is she who so divides me from myself
That what I say I scarcely know, although
I say but what I feel: the melancholy
You ask about, no gloomy sequestration
Out of the common world into a darker,
But into one a thousand times more bright;
And let no man believe he truly loves,
Who lives, or moves, or thinks, or hath his being
In any other atmosphere than Love's,
Who is our absolute master; to recount
The endless bead-roll of whose smiles and tears
I'd have each sleepless night a century.
Much have I said — have much more yet to say!
But read her letter, Arias, the first seal
Of my success, the final one, I think,
Of my sure trust in you; come, share with me
My joy, my glory, my anxiety;
And above all things, once more, Arias,
Down to your secret'st heart this secret slip;
    For every secret hangs in greater fear
    Between the speaker's mouth and hearer's ear,
Than any peril between cup and lip.
    Ar.   You have good cause for joy.

Ces. You will say so
When you have read the letter.

Ar. You desire it. *(Reads.)*
"To confess that one is loved is to confess that one loves too;
for there is no woman but loves to be loved. But alas, there
is yet more. If to cover my love I have pretended disdain,
let the shame of now confessing it excuse me. Come to me
this evening and I will tell you what I can scarce understand
myself. Adieu, my love, adieu!" Your hands are full indeed
of happy business.

Ces. Enough: you know what you shall tell the Prince
In my behalf: if he be satisfied
I'll wait on him directly.

Ar. Trust to me.

Ces. Let my sighs help thee forward, O thou sun,
What of thy race in heaven remains to run:
Oh do but think that Dafne in the west
Awaits thee, and anticipate thy rest!

[Exeunt CESAR *and* LAZARO.

Ar. Charg'd with two secrets,
One from my Prince, the other from my friend,
Each binding equally to silence, each
Equally the other's revelation needing,
How shall I act, luckless embosomer
Of others' bosoms! how decide between
Loyalty and love with least expense to both!
The Prince's love is but this morning's flower,
As yet unsunn'd on by his lady's favour;
Cesar's of two years' growth, expanded now
Into full blossom by her smiles and tears;
The Prince too loves him whom his lady loves,
And were he told, might uncontested leave
The prize that one he loves already owns;
And so both reap the fruit, and make the excuse
Of broken silence, if it needs must break.
And yet I grope about, afraid to fall
Where ill-advised good-will may ruin all. *[Exit.*

SCENE III.   *A Corridor in the Palace. — Enter* PRINCE,
DON FELIX, DONNA ANNA, *and train.*

Prince   I must show you the way.

Anna   Your Highness must not do yourself so great indignity.

Prince   To the bounds at least of my sister's territory.

Anna   Nay, my lord, that were undue courtesy.

Prince   What courtesy, madam, can be undue from any
man to any lady?

Anna   When that lady is your subject, whom your very
condescension dazzles to her own discomfiture.

Prince   What, as the morning star dazzles the sun whom
he precedes as petty harbinger?   If I obey you 't is that I
fear my own extinction in your rays.   Adieu.

Anna   God keep your Highness.   [*Exit.*

Prince   Don Felix, will you attend your sister?

Felix   I only stay to thank your Highness, (both as subject
and as servant,) for all the honour that you do us; may Heaven
so prolong your life that even oblivion herself —

Prince   Nay, truce to compliment: your sister will not of
my company, unless under your proxy.   So farewell.   [*Exit*
FELIX.]   Is there a greater nuisance than to have such windy
nonsense stuff'd into one's ears, when delight is vanished
from the eyes!

Enter ARIAS

But, Don Arias!   You have seen Cesar?

Ar.   Yes, my lord; but ere I tell you about him, would
know how far this last interview with Donna Anna has ad-
vanced your love.

Prince   Oh Arias, Arias, my love for her
So blends with my solicitude for him,
I scarce can hold me clear between the two.
Yet let me tell you.   In my sister's room,
Whither I went, you know, upon our parting,
I saw my lady like a sovereign rose
Among the common flowers; or, if you will,
A star among the roses; or the star
Of stars, the morning star: yea, say at once
The sun himself among the host of heaven!
My eyes and ears were rapt with her; her lips

Not fairer than the words that parted them.
At length she rose to go: like the ev'ning star
Went with the ev'ning; which, how short, say love
Who'd spin each golden moment to a year,
Which year would then seem than a moment less.
    Ar. Is then, my lord, this passion so deep fixt?
    Prince Nay, but of one day's growth —
    Ar.   I come in time then,
My lord, in one word, if you love Don Cesar,
Cease to love Donna Anna.
    Prince   Arias,
He who begins to hint at evil news
Is bound to tell it out — nothing or all.
Why do you hesitate?
    Ar.   Because, my lord,
But hinting this to you, I break the seal
Of secrecy to him.
    Prince   But it is broken;
And so —
    Ar.   Oh, Cesar, pardon him who fails
His pledge to you to serve his Prince! My lord,
The cloud you long have seen on Cesar's brow
Is not, as he would have you think it, born
Of bookish studies only, but a cloud,
All bright within, though dark to all without,
Of love for one he has for two long years
Silently worshipt.
    Prince   Donna Anna!
    Ar.   Ay.
    Prince Cesar loves Donna Anna! be it so —
I love him, as you say, and would forego
Much for his sake. But tell me, Arias,
Knows Anna of his passion?
    Ar.   Yes, my lord,
And answers it with hers.
    Prince   Oh wretched fate!
Desperate ere jealous — jealous ere in love!
If Cesar but lov'd her, I could, methinks,
Have pardon'd, even have advanc'd his suit
By yielding up my own. But that *she* loves,

Blows rivalry into full blaze again.
And yet I will not be so poor a thing
To whine for what is now beyond my reach,
Nor must the princely blood of Parma
Run jealous of a subject's happiness.
They love each other then?
  Ar.   I even now
Have seen a letter —
  Prince   Well?
  Ar.   That Donna Anna
Has written him, and in such honey'd words —
  Prince Why, is it not enough to know she loves him?
You told me so: my mind made up to that,
Why should a foolish letter fright it back?
And yet — yet, what last spark of mortal love
But must flame up before it dies for ever
To learn but what that foolish letter said!
Know you?
  Ar. I saw it.
  Prince   You saw it! and what said it?
  Ar. After a chaste confession of her love,
Bidding him be to-night under her lattice.
  Prince Under her lattice, while his Prince is left
Abroad; they two to whisper love together,
While he gnaws hopeless jealousy alone.
But why, forsooth, am I to be the victim?
If I can quench my love for Cesar's sake,
Why not he his for me? Tell me, Don Arias,
Does Cesar know my passion?
  Ar.   How should he,
You having told the secret but to me?
  Prince By the same means that I know his.
  Ar.   My lord,
My loyalty might well be spar'd that taunt.
  Prince Ah, Arias, pardon me, I am put out,
But not with you, into whose faithful charge
I vest my love and honour confidently,
Enough, in what I am about to do
I mean no malice or ill play to Cesar:
'T is but an idle curiosity:

And surely 't is but fair, that if his Prince
Leave him the lists to triumph in at leisure,
I may at least look on the game he wins.
You shall keep close to him, and tell me all
That passes between him and her I love.
    Ar.   But having taunted me with my first step
In your behalf, my lord —
    Prince   Nay, sir, my will
At once absolves and authorises you,
For what is told and what remains to tell.
    Ar.   But, sir —
    Prince   No more —
    Ar.   I must obey your bidding,
But yet —
    Prince   I may divert my jealousy,
If not avenge it.
    Ar.   Ah! what straits do those
Who cannot keep their counsel fall into!
    Prince   All say so, and all blab, like me and you!
Look where he comes; let us retire awhile.
                          [PRINCE *and* ARIAS *retire.*

Enter CESAR *and* LAZARO

    Ces.   O Phœbus, swift across the skies
           Thy blazing carriage post away;
           Oh, drag with thee benighted day,
           And let the dawning night arise!
           Another sun shall mount the throne
               When thou art sunk beneath the sea;
           From whose effulgence, as thine own,
               The affrighted host of stars shall flee.
    Laz.   A pretty deal about your cares
           Does that same Phœbus care or know;
           He has to mind his own affairs,
               Whether you shake your head or no.
           You talk of hastening on the day?
               Why, heaven's coachman is the Sun,
           Who can't be put out of his way
               For you, sir, or for any one.

Ces. The Prince! and something in my bosom tells me
All is not well. My lord, though my repentance
Does not, I trust, lag far behind my fault,
I scarce had dar'd to approach your Highness' feet,
Had not my friend, Don Arias, been before
As harbinger of my apology.
    Prince Cesar, indeed Don Arias has told me
The story of your sadness: and so well,
I feel it, and excuse it, as my own;
From like experience. I do not resent,
But would divert you from it. Books, my friend,
Truly are so seductive company,
We are apt to sit too long and late with them,
And drowse our minds in their society;
This must not be; the cause of the disease
Once known, the cure is easy; if 't is books
Have hurt you, lay them by awhile, and try
Other society — less learn'd perhaps,
But cheerfuller — exchange the pent-up air
Of a close study for the breathing world.
Come, we'll begin to-night;
Visit in disguise (as I have wish'd to do)
The city, its taverns, theatres, and streets,
Where music, masque, and dancing may divert
Your melancholy: what say you to this?
    Ces. Oh, my kind lord, whose single word of pardon
Has turn'd all leaden grief to golden joy,
Made me another man, or, if you will,
The better self I was —
    Prince   Why this is well;
To-night together then —
    Ces.   Yet pardon me.
    Prince How now?
    Ces.   It almost would revive my pain
That you should spend yourself upon a cure
Your mere forgiveness has already wrought.
Let this day's happiness suffice the day,
And its night also: 't will be doubly sweet,
Unbought by your annoyance.
    Prince   Nay, my Cesar,

Fear not for that: after so long estrangement,
My pain would be the losing sight of you
On this first night of your recovery.
Lazaro!

   Laz. My lord?

   Prince   You too shall go with us.

   Laz. And not a trustier shall your Highness find
To guard your steps.

   Prince   What! you are valiant?

   Laz. As ever girded sword.

   Prince   Your weapon good too?

   Laz. He touches on the quick *(aside).* Yes, good enough,
My lord, for all my poor occasions.
Although when waiting on your Grace, indeed,
A sword like yours were better.

   Prince   You depreciate
Your own to enhance its value. Sharp is 't?

   Laz.   Ay,
Not a steel buckler but at the first blow
'T would splinter it in two. (The sword I mean.) *Aside.*

   Prince Well temper'd?

   Laz.   As you bid it.

   Prince   And the device
Inscrib'd upon it?

   Laz.   "Thou shalt do no murder" —
Having no love for homicide, *per se,*
Save on occasion.

   Prince   Your description
Makes me desire to see that sword.

   Laz.   My lord!

   Prince Indeed it does. Show it me.

   Laz.   Oh, my lord,
I have a vow.

   Ces. (aside). Oh weariness!

   Prince   A vow?

   Laz. Ay, register'd in heaven!
Never to draw this weapon from her sheath
Except on mortal quarrel. If in such
Your Highness' service challenge her, why, then
She shall declare herself.

Ces.   I'm desperate!
But yet one effort more.   My lord, you see
(You cannot fail) how your mere word of grace
Has of itself brighten'd me up again;
I do beseech you —
    Prince   Pardon me, my Cesar,
Rather I see the cloud that 'gins to break
Is not entirely gone; nay, will return
If you be left alone — which must not be:
If not for your sake, Cesar, yet for mine,
Who feel for your disquiet as my own;
And since our hearts are knit so close together,
Yours cannot suffer but mine straightway feels
A common pain; seek we a common cure.
To-night I shall expect you.   Until then,
Farewell.   [*Exit.*

    Ces.   Fortune! to see a fair occasion
So patiently pursued, so fairly won,
Lost at the very moment of success!
O Lazaro — what will my lady say!
    Laz.   That I can't guess.
    Ces.   What will she do!
    Laz.   Oh that
Is answer'd far more easily.   She'll stand
All night beside the window to no purpose.
    Ces.   Why she must say my love was all pretence,
And her offended dignity vindicate,
Rejecting me for ever!   Misery!
    Laz.   Dear me, sir, what is now become of all
About, "Thou dawning night, benighted day,"
"Thou coachman sun!" etceteretera?
    Ces.   Wilt thou be ever fool!
    Laz.   If thou be not,
Listen — fools' bolts, they say, are quickly shot —
Who secrets have and cannot hold 'em,
Shall surely rue the day they told 'em.

ACT II

SCENE I. *A Public Square in Parma. — Night. — Enter*
PRINCE, CESAR, FELIX, ARIAS, *and* LAZARO, *disguised.*

Ar. A LOVELY night!
Prince   As Night we choose to call,
When Day's whole sun is but distributed
Into ten thousand stars.
Fel.   Beside the moon,
Who lightly muffled like ourselves reveals
Her trembling silver.
Laz.   What! by way, you mean,
Of making up the account?
Ces. (aside).   To think, alas!
The first sweet vintage of my love thus lost,
And, as my lady must too surely think,
By my forgetfulness. *(Aloud.)*   My lord, indeed
The night wears on.   May not the chiller air
That blows from the returning tide of day
Affect you?
Prince   Nay, my state forbidding me
Much to be seen about the streets by day,
The night must serve my purpose.
Ces. (aside).   Patience then!
And I must try and draw my thoughts from her
I cannot reach.   *(Aloud.)*   How does the lady Flora
Please you, my lord?
Prince   The lady Flora?   Oh,
What, she of Milan?   Such a distance off

Must cool one's love.

Laz.   Ah, very true, my lord;
What use the finest mistress in the moon,
Unless one were the man there?

Ar.   Signora Laura
Has a fair figure.

Laz.   Yes, and asks a high one.

Felix   A handsome hand.

Laz.   At scolding, yes.

Ar.   I think
She lives close by.

Laz.   But don't you bid for her
Without fair trial first, my lord.   Your women
Are like new plays, which self-complacent authors
Offer at some eight hundred royals each,
But which, when once they're tried, you purchase dear
Eight hundred for a royal.

Ces. (aside).   Now, methinks,
Ev'n now my lady at the lattice stands
Looking for me in vain and murmuring
"Why comes he not?   I doubted I was late,
But he comes not at all!"   And then — Ah me,
I have forgotten to forget! —
(Aloud.)   Celia sings well, my lord?

Laz.   A pretty woman
Can no more sing amiss than a good horse
Be a bad colour.

Ces.   The old Roman law
To all the ugly women us'd to assign
The fortunes of the handsome, thinking those
Sufficiently endow'd with their good looks.

Laz.   Ah! and there Laura lives, the lass who said
She'd sell her house and buy a coach withal;
And when they ask'd her, where she'd live, quoth she,
"Why, *in* my coach!"   "But when night comes," say they,
"Where then?" — "Why in the coach-house to be sure!"[1]

---

[1] The ambition for a coach so frequently laughed at by Calderon, is said to be in full force now; not for the novelty of the invention, then, nor perhaps the dignity, so much as for the real comfort of easy and sheltered carriage in such a climate.

Ces.   Indeed, indeed, my lord, the night wears on,
And sure your sister lies awake foreboding
Some danger to your person.
Consider her anxiety!
Prince (aside).   Nay, *yours*
Lies nearer to my heart.
Ces.   My lord?
Prince   I said
No matter for my sister, that was all;
She knows not I'm abroad.
Ces.   My hope is gone!
Laz.   There, yonder in that little house, there lives
A girl with whom it were impossible
To deal straightforwardly.
Prince   But why?
Laz.   She's crooked.
Ar.   And there a pretty girl enough, but guarded
By an old dragon aunt.
Laz.   O Lord, defend me
From all old women!
Prince   How so, Lazaro?
Laz.   Oh, ever since the day I had to rue
The conjurer's old woman.
Prince   Who was she?
Laz.   Why, my lord, once upon a time
I fell in love with one who would not have me
Either for love or money; so at last
I go to a certain witch — tell him my story:
Whereon he bids me cut a lock of hair
From my love's head and bring it to him.   Well,
I watch'd my opportunity, and one day,
When she was fast asleep, adroitly lopp'd
A lovely forelock from what seem'd her hair,
But was an hair-loom rather from her wig
Descended from a head that once was young
As I thought her.   For, giving it the witch,
To work his charm with, in the dead of night,
When I was waiting for my love to come,
Into my bed-room the dead woman stalk'd
To whom the lock of hair had once belong'd,

And claim'd me for her own.   O Lord, how soon
"Sweetheart" and "Deary" chang'd to "Apage!"
And flesh and blood to ice.

     Ces. (aside).   Alas! what boots it trying to forget
That which the very effort makes remember!
Ev'n now, ev'n now, methinks once more I see her
Turn to the window, not expecting me,
But to abjure all expectation,
And, as she moves away, saying, (methinks
I hear her,) "Cesar, come when come you may,
You shall not find me here."   "Nay, but my love,
Anna! my lady! hear me!"   Oh confusion,
Did they observe?

     Prince (aside to ARIAS).   How ill, Don Arias,
Poor Cesar hides his heart —

     Ar.   Ev'n now he tries
The mask again.

     Prince   Indeed I pity him,
Losing one golden opportunity;
But may not I be pitied too, who never
Shall have so much as one to lose?

     Ar.   Speak low;
You know her brother's by.

     Prince   No matter; true
Nobility is slowest to suspect.

     Musician (sings within).

> *Ah happy bird, who can fly with the wind,*
> *Leaving all anguish of absence behind;*
>   *Like thee could I fly,*
>   *Leaving others to sigh,*
> *The lover I sigh for how soon would I find!*[1]

     Ces.   Not an ill voice!
     Fel.   Nay, very good.
     Prince   How sweetly
Sweet words, sweet air, sweet voice, atone together!
Arias, might we not on this sweet singer
Try Lazaro's metal and mettle? you shall see.
Lazaro!

   [1] This little song is from the *Desdicha de la Voz.*

Laz. My lord!
Prince   I never go abroad
But this musician dogs me.
Laz.   Shall I tell him
Upon your Highness's request, politely,
To move away?
Prince   I doubt me, Lazaro,
He will not go for that, he's obstinate.
Laz. How then, my lord?
Prince Go up and strike him with your sword.
Laz. But were it brave in me, back'd as I am,
To draw my sword on one poor piping bird?
If I must do it, let me challenge him
Alone to-morrow.
But let me warn him first.
Prince   Do as I bid you,
Or I shall call you coward.
Ces.   Lazaro,
Obey his Highness.
Laz.   O good providence,
Temper the wind to a shorn lamb!
Musician (within).

> *Ah happy bird, whom the wind and the rain,*
> *And snare of the fowler, beset but in vain;*
> *Oh, had I thy wing,*
> *Leaving others to sing,*
> *How soon would I be with my lover again!*

Laz. (aloud within).   Pray God, poor man, if thou be
        innocent
Of any ill intention in thy chirping,
The blade I draw upon thee turn to wood!
A miracle! A miracle!   *(Rushing in).*
Prince   How now?
Laz. The sword I lifted on an innocent man
Has turn'd to wood at his assailant's prayer!
Take it, my lord, lay 't in your armoury
Among the chiefest relics of our time.
I freely give it you, upon condition

You give me any plain but solid weapon
To wear instead.
    Prince   You are well out of it.
It shall be so.
    Ces.   My lord, indeed the dawn
Is almost breaking.
    Prince   Let it find us here.
But, my dear Cesar, tell me, are you the better
For this diversion!
    Ces.   Oh, far cheerfuller.
Though with some little effort.
    Prince   And I too.
So love is like all other evils known;
With others' sorrow we beguile our own.   [*Exeunt.*

        SCENE II.   *The garden of* DONNA ANNA's *House:*
        DONNA ANNA *and* ELVIRA *at a window.* — *Dawn.*

    Elv.   Yet once more to the window?
    Anna   Oh Elvira,
For the last time! now undeceiv'd to know
How much deceiv'd I was!
Alas, until I find myself despis'd,
Methought I was desir'd, till hated, lov'd;
Was 't not enough to know himself belov'd,
Without insulting her who told him so!
Was 't not enough —
Oh wonder not, Elvira, at my passion;
Of all these men's enchantments, none more potent
Than what might seem unlikeliest — their disdain.
    Elv.   Indeed you have good cause for anger, madam:
But yet one trial more.
    Anna   And to what end?
I'll not play Tantalus again for him.
Oh shameful insult! had I dream'd of it,
Would I have written him so tenderly?
Told my whole heart? — But, once in love, what woman
Can trust herself, alas, with pen and ink?
    Elv.   Were he to come now after all, how then?
Would you reproach, or turn your back on him,
Or —

Anna   Nay, I know not.   Is 't not possible,
He is detain'd, Elvira, by the Prince
Upon state business?
   Elv.   You excuse him then!
   Anna   Oh, any thing to soothe me!
   Elv.   Who excuses
Will quickly pardon.
   Anna   Ay, if he came now,
Now, as you say, Elvira,
And made excuses which I knew were false,
I *would* believe them still.   Would he were come
Only to try.   Could I be so deceiv'd!

Enter CESAR *and* LAZARO, *below*

   Laz.   See you not day has dawn'd, sir?
   Ces.   Mine, I doubt,
Is set for ever.   Yet, in sheer despair,
I come to gaze upon the empty east!
But look!
   Laz.   Well, sir?
   Ces.   See you not through the twilight?
   Laz.   Yes, sir; a woman: and when I say a woman,
I mean two women.
   Ces.   Oh see if it be she.
   Laz.   'T would make Elvira jealous, sir.
   Ces.   Oh lady,
Is it you?
   Anna   Yes, I, Don Cesar: who all night
Have waited on your pleasure, unsuspecting
What now too well I know.
My foolish passion, sir, is well reveng'd
By shamed repentance.   Oh, you come at last,
Thinking belike, sir, with the morning star
Retrieve the waste of night; oh, you lov'd me, sir,
Or seem'd to do, till having won from me
Confession of a love I feel no more,
You turn it to disdain.   Oh think not, sir,
That by one little deed in love, like law,
You gain the full possession of my heart
For ever; and for this idle interview,

Do you so profit by it as to learn
Courtesy to a lady; which when learn'd
Come and repeat to me.   [*Retires from window.*
    Ces.   And having now
Arraign'd me of the crime, why do you leave me
To plead my exculpation to the winds?
O Donna Anna, I call Heav'n to witness
'T was not my negligence, but my ill star
That envied me such ill-deserv'd delight.
If it be otherwise,
Or even you *suspect* it otherwise,
Spurn me, not only now, but ever, from you.
Since better were it with a conscience clear
Rejected, than suspiciously receiv'd.
The Prince has kept me all the night with him
About the city streets: your brother, who
Was with us, can bear witness.   Yet if still
You think me guilty, but come back to say so,
And let me plead once more, and you once more
Condemn, and yet once more, and all in vain,
If you will only but come back again!
    Anna (returning to the window).   And this is true?
    Ces.   So help me Heav'n, it is!
Why, could you, Anna, in your heart believe
I could forget you?
    Anna   And, Don Cesar, you
That, were it so, I could forget my love?
But see, the sun above the mountain-tops
Begins to peep, and morn to welcome him
With all her smiles and tears.   We must begone.
I shall another quick occasion find,
When I shall call, and you — not lag behind?
    Ces.   Oh once more taken to your heart again,
My shame turns glory, and delight my pain.
Yet tell me —
    Anna   Well?
    Ces.   Of your suspicions *one*
Lingers within you?
    Anna   Ay, a legion,
That at your presence to their mistress' pride

Turn traitors, and all fight on Cesar's side!

Ces.   Farewell then, my divine implacable!

Anna   Victim and idol of my eyes, farewell!

[*Exeunt severally.*

Laz.   Well, and what has *my* mistress to say to me?
Does she also play the scornful lady?

Elv.   I?   why?

Laz.   Because my mistress' mistress does so to my master,
whose love I follow in shadow.

Elv.   Oh, I did not understand.

Laz.   When he's happy then I'm jolly;
When he's sad I'm melancholy:
When he's love-infected, I
    With the self-same fever fretted,
Either am bound like him to fry,
    Or if he chooses to forget it,
I must even take his cue,
And, Elvira, forget you.
Do you enact your lady.   Now,
Begin.   Be angry first —

Elv.   But how?

Laz.   Hide up, no matter how or why,
Behind the window-blind, while I
    Underneath it caterwaul; —

Elv.   What are the odds I don't reply?

Laz.   Just the odds that I don't call.

SCENE III.   *A Room in the Palace. — The* PRINCE *and* DON
FELIX, *discovered at the back of the stage.*

Fel.   Why is your Highness sad?

Prince   Not sad, Don Felix:
Oh would it were some certain shape of sorrow
That I might grapple with, not a vague host
Of undefin'd emotions! Oh how oft
The patching up of but a single seam
Opens a hundred others!   Lucky he
Who can to disenchantment bare his eyes
Once and for all, and in oblivion
Shut up vain hope for ever!

Enter CESAR, ARIAS, *and* LAZARO, *in front*

Ces. (to ARIAS *as they enter).* And so at last was satisfied.

Ar. His Highness and Don Felix.

Ces. I am sure that he who profits not by opportunity scarce covets it enough. Taking advantage of the cleared heaven, I have here written my lady, asking her when she will give me the meeting she promised; Lazaro, take the letter: Don Felix here, you can easily deliver it.

Laz. I'll feign an errand, and so get into the house.

[*Exit.*

Fel. (to PRINCE). Cesar and Arias, my lord.

Prince I know their business. Oh what a tempest does every breeze from that quarter raise in my bosom! Well, gentlemen?

Ar. Cesar, my lord, was telling me —

Prince About his melancholy studies still? Pray tell me.

Ces. Nay, my lord, all melancholy flies from the sunshine of your presence.

Prince What then?

Ces. I still distrust myself; Don Arias must, my lord, answer for me.

Prince Don Arias, then?

Ar. (aside). Fresh confidence should bind me his anew. But comes too late.

Ces. (aside to ARIAS). Be careful what you say.

Ar. Trust me. (CESAR *retires.*)

Prince (to ARIAS *apart).* Well now, Don Arias.

Ar. At first much enraged against him, at last she yielded to his amorous excuses; and, finding Don Felix here, he has sent her a letter beseeching another meeting.

Prince When?

Ar. This moment.

Prince Who can doubt the upshot! I must contrive to thwart them. *(Aloud.)* But ere I hear your story, Arias, I must tell Don Felix what I was about to do as these gentlemen came in and interrupted me: that his sister was ill — had fainted — from some vexation or fright, as I think.

Fel. Anna?

Prince So my sister told me. Had you not better see to her?

Fel. With your leave, my lord. [*Exit.*

Prince (aside). And so, as I wished, prevent her answering, if not getting, the letter. *(Aloud.)* I will ask Nisida how it was. [*Exit.*

Ces. What did you tell the Prince to draw this new trouble on me?

Ar. Ay, even so. Blame him who has been even lying in your service. Look you now, the Prince told me he had overheard the names "Don Felix" and "Donna Anna" between us as we came in talking; and, tethered to that, I was obliged to drag this fainting fit into the service.

Ces. Oh, if Felix find Lazaro at his house!

Ar. Fear not, anxiety will carry him home faster than a letter Lazaro.

Ces. Alas that the revival of my joy
Is the revival of a fresh annoy;
And that the remedy I long'd to seize
Must slay me faster than the old disease.

[*Exeunt.*

SCENE IV.   *An Apartment in* DON FELIX's *house.* —
DONNA ANNA *and* ELVIRA.

Elv. Well, have you finisht writing?
Anna   I have written,
Not finisht writing.   That could never be;
Each sentence, yea, each letter, as I write it,
Suggesting others still.   I had hop'd, Elvira,
To sum my story up in a few words;
Took pen and paper, both at the wrong end: —
Tried to begin, my mind so full I knew not
What to begin with; till, as one has seen
The fullest vessel hardly run, until
Some inner air should loose the lingering liquid,
So my charg'd heart waited till one long sigh
Set it a flowing.   I wrote, eras'd, re-wrote,
Then, pregnant love still doubling thought on thought,
Doubled the page too hastily, and blotted
All that was writ before; until my letter,
Blotted, eras'd, re-written, and perplext,
At least is a fair transcript of my heart.

Well, the sum is, he is to come, Elvira,
To-night, when Felix, as I heard him say,
Goes to our country house on business;
And all will be more quiet.   But here, read it.
   Elv.   My lord! my lord! — the letter!

Enter FELIX

   Anna (hiding the letter).   Heavens!
   Fel.   Too well
The traitorous colour flying from your cheeks
Betrays your illness and my cause of sorrow.
What is the matter?
   Anna   Nothing, brother.
   Fel.   Nothing!
Your changing face and your solicitude
To assure me there is nothing, but assure me
How much there is.   I have been told in fact,
And hurried home thus suddenly,
To hear it all.
   Anna (aside).   Alas! he knows my secret!
Felix, indeed, indeed, my love
Shall not dishonour you.
   Fel.   Your love?
I'm more at loss than ever.   But perhaps
You feign this to divert me from the truth.
What is the matter, truly?
   Anna   Be assur'd
I never will disgrace you.
   Fel.   Ah, she rambles,
Quite unrecover'd yet.
   Anna (apart to ELVIRA*).*   What shall I do?
   Elv. (apart).   Deny it all, there's many a step between
Suspicion and assurance.
   Fel.   You, Elvira,
(My sister cannot,) tell me what has happen'd?
   Elv.   Oh, nothing but a swoon, sir:
My mistress fainted: that is all: accounts
For all her paleness and discomfiture.
   Fel.   'T was that I heard.
   Elv.   I do assure you, sir,

We thought her dead — however she dissemble
Out of her love for you.

Fel.   'T was kind of her;
But yet not kindness, Anna, to delude me
Into a selfish ignorance of your pain.
Enough, you are better now?

Anna   Indeed.

Fel.   That's well.
But, by the way, what meant you by "*your love,*"
And "*not dishonouring me*"?

Anna   "*My love,*" and "*not
Dishonouring!*" did I say so?   I must mean,
My senses still half-drown'd, my love for you
That would not have you pain'd.   A true love, Felix,
Though a mistaken, may be, as you say,
Yet no dishonour.

Fel.   Still I have not heard
What caus'd this illness.

Anna (aside).   He presses hard upon me,
But I'll out-double him.   (*Aloud.*)   The cause of it?
Why — sitting in this room,
I heard a noise in the street there: went to the window,
And saw a crowd of people, their swords out, fighting
Before the door; and (what will foolish fear
Not conjure up?) methought that one of them
Was you — and suddenly a mortal chill
Came over me, and — you must ask Elvira
For all the rest.

Elv. (aside).   Why ever have the trouble
Of coining lies when truth will pass as well!

Enter LAZARO

Laz.   So far so good.

Fel.   Lazaro?

Laz. (seeing FELIX). Is 't his ghost? for certainly I left his
body at the palace.

Anna   My evil stars bear hard upon me!

Laz.   I'm done for, unless a good lie — (*Aloud.*)
Ruffian, rascal, scamp!

Fel.   How now?

Laz.   Murderer! villain!

Fel.   Softly, softly, breathe awhile! what's the matter?

Laz.   Nothing, nothing, yet had I not exploded incidentally, or as it were superficially, I had altogether burst. Oh the rascal! the slave!

Fel.   But tell me the matter.

Laz.   Oh the matter — indeed the matter — you may well ask it — indeed you may — Oh the murderer!

Fel.   Come, come, tell us.

Laz.   Ay, well, look here, my lords and ladies, lend me your ears: I was at cards: yes: for you must know, my lord, I sometimes like a bout as my betters do: you understand this?

Fel.   Yes — well?

Laz.   Well, being at cards, as I say: ay, and playing pretty high too: for I must confess that sometimes, like my betters — you understand?

Fel.   Go on — go on.

Laz.   Well, being, as I said, at cards,
And playing pretty high too — mark me that —
I get into discussion or dispute
(Whichever you will call it) with a man,
If man he may be call'd who man was none —
Ye gods! to prostitute the name of man
On such as that! — call him a manikin,
A madarin, a mandrake,
Rather than man — I mean in *soul*, mark you;
For in his outward man he was a man,
Ay, and a man of might.   Nay, more than man,
A giant, one may say.   Well, as I said,
This wretch and I got to high words, and then
(Whither high words so often lead) to blows;
Out came our swords.   The rascal having seen
What a desperate fellow at my tool I was,
Takes him eleven others of his kidney,
Worse than himself, and all twelve set on me.
I seeing them come on, ejaculate,
"From all such rascals, single or in league,
Good Lord, deliver us," set upon all twelve
With that same sword, mark me, our gracious Prince

Gave me but yesternight, and, God be praised,
Disgrac'd not in the giving —
Beat the whole twelve of them back to a porch,
Where, after bandying a blow with each,
Each getting something to remember me by,
Back in a phalanx all came down on me,
And then dividing, sir, into two parties,
Twelve upon this side — do you see? and nine
On this — and three in front —
 Fel.   But, Lazaro,
Why, twelve and nine are twenty-one — and three —
Why, your twelve men are grown to twenty-four!
How's this?
 Laz. How's this? why, counting in the shadows —
You see I count the shadows — twenty-four,
Shadows and all — you see![1]
 Fel.   I see.
 Laz.   Well, sir,
Had not that good sword which our gracious Prince
Gave me but yesterday broke in my hand,
I should have had to pay for mass, I promise you,
For every mother's son of them!
 Fel.   Indeed?
But, Lazaro, I see your sword's entire:
How's that?
 Laz. The most extraordinary part
Of all —
 Fel. Well, tell us.
 Laz.   Why, I had first us'd
My dagger upon one: and when my sword
Snapt, with its stump, sir, daggerwise I fought,
As thus; and that with such tremendous fury,
That, smiting a steel buckler, I struck out
Such sparks from it, that, by the light of them,
Snatching up the fallen fragment of my sword,
I pieced the two together.

---

[1] One cannot fail to be reminded of the multiplication of Falstaff's men in buckram, not the only odd coincidence between the two poets. Lazaro's solution of the difficulty seems to me quite worthy of Falstaff.

Fel.   But the dagger
You fought with first, and lost, you say — why, Lazaro,
'T is in your girdle.

Laz.   I account for that
Easily.   Look, sir, I drew it, as I said,
And struck amain.   The man I drew it on,
Seeing the coming blow, caught hold of it,
And struck it back on me; I, yet more skilful,
With God's good help did so present myself
That, when he struck at me, my own dagger's point
Return'd into its sheath, as here you see it.
Enough, I heard the cry of "Alguazils!"
Ran off, and, entering the first open door,
Now ask for sanctuary at your feet.

Fel.   I think it is your trepidation
Makes you talk nonsense.

Anna   Surely, my brother, this was the riot that so frighted
me.

Fel.   And was I then the man, "if man it could be called
who man was none," that Lazaro fought with?

Anna   I know not, I only know 't was some one of a handsome presence like yours.

Fel. (aside).   Perhaps his master — I much suspect it was
Cesar that was dicing, and afterward fighting; and his servant,
to cover him, invents this foolish story — *(Aloud.)*   I will
look into the street and see if it be clear.   [*Exit.*

Elv.   Now say your say.

Anna (giving LAZARO *her letter).*   And quickly, Lazaro;
taking this letter —

Laz. (giving CESAR's*).*   And you this premium upon it.

Anna   Bid him be sure to come to me this evening; I have
much to say.   And thus much to you, Lazaro; your quarrel
came in the nick of time to account for a swoon I had occasion
to feign.

Elv.   Quick! quick! he's coming back.

Laz.   Madam, farewell.

Anna   And if my plot succeed,
Feign'd quarrel shall to true love-making lead.   [*Exeunt.*

Scene V. *A Room in the Palace;* cesar *and* arias *talking: to whom after a time enter* lazaro.

Laz. Oh, I have had rare work.

Ces. The letter! *(takes it from* lazaro.*)*

Ar. And how did all end?

Laz. Well — as I am home at last safe and sound.

Ces. Arias, you share my heart; even read my letter with me. *(They read.)*

Laz. (aside). That my master should trust that babbler who let out about my wooden sword to the Prince! my life upon 't, he'll do the same to him; for he who sucks in gossip is the first to leak it.

Ar. Sweetly she writes!

Ces. How should it be but sweet, Where modesty and wit and true love meet?

Ar. And expects you this evening!

Ces. Till which each minute is an hour, each hour A day, a year, a century!

Laz. And then In sæcula sæculorum. Amen.

Ar. The Prince!

Ces. I dread his seeing me.

Ar. But how?

Ces. Lest, as already twice, he thwart me now.

Enter prince

Prince Cesar here, when I am on fire to know the upshot of my plot upon his letter! I must get quit of him.

Ces. Good day, my lord.

Prince Well, any news abroad?

Ar. Not that I know of, my lord.

Prince Cesar, there are despatches in my closet, have been lying there since yesterday, should they not be seen to at once?

Ces. My lord! *(aside.)* I foresaw it.

Prince Yes! I would have you look to them and report them to me directly.

Ces. (aside). Ah, this is better! *(Aloud.)* I'll see to them. *(Aside.)*

And then, I trust, day's work with daylight o'er,
Man, nor malicious star, shall cross me more.

[Exeunt CESAR and LAZARO.

Prince   And now about the letter?

Ar.   I only know, my lord, that though Felix got home first, Lazaro got there somehow, somehow gave her the letter, and somehow got an answer.

Prince   Hast seen it?

Ar.   Yes, my lord.

Prince   And —

Ar.   She appoints another meeting this evening.

Prince   And I must myself despatch his work, so as to leave him free to-night!   Oh, Arias, what can I do more?

Ar.   Cannot your Highness go there yourself, and so at least stop further advancement?

Prince   True, true; and yet I know not; it might be too suspicious.   I must consider what shall be done;

And what more subtle engine I may try
Against these lovers' ingenuity.   [*Exeunt.*

ACT III

SCENE I. *A Room in the Palace.* — PRINCE *and* DON ARIAS.

Ar.   How well the night went off! did not the music,
The lights, the dances, and the ladies' eyes,
Divert your Grace's sadness?
    Prince   Rather, Arias,
Doubled it.
Whithersoever Donna Anna mov'd,
My eyes, that ever followed hers along,
Saw them pursue Don Cesar through the crowd
And only rest on him; I curs'd him then,
And then excus'd him, as the judge should do
Whose heart is yearning with the guilt he damns.
    Ar.   Where will this passion end?
    Prince   I think in death,
Led by the fatal secret you have told me.
    Ar.   I err'd, my lord; but all shall yet be well.
But hush!   Don Cesar comes.
    Prince   Make out of him
How sits the wind of love.   Behind this screen
I'll listen. *(Hides.)*

Enter CESAR

    Ar.   Well, Don Cesar?
    Ces.   Nay, *ill*, Don Cesar!
Misfortune on misfortune! ev'n good fortune
Forswears her nature but to scowl on me!
Led by her letter, as the shades of night

Were drawing in, I went — not now to stand
Under her lattice with the cold, cold moon
For company, but in the very room
My lady warms and lightens with her presence!
There when we two had just begun to whisper
The first sweet words of love, upon a sudden,
As by some evil spirit prompted, her brother
Comes in, and on some frivolous pretext
Carries her to the palace.   I suspect
He knows my purpose.

    Ar.   Nay —

    Prince (listening).   He little thinks
His evil spirit is so near him now.

    Ces.   Ay, and dead weary of these sicken'd hopes
And lost occasions, I have resolv'd to break
Through disappointment and impediment,
And turning secret love to open suit,
Secure at once her honour, and her brother's,
And my own everlasting happiness,
By asking her fair hand, 'fore all the world!   *[Exit.*

    Ar.   You heard, my lord?

    Prince (advancing).   And if he ask her hand,
Felix will grant it as assuredly
As I would my own sister's!   Oh, Don Arias,
What now?

    Ar.   Don Felix comes.

    Prince   There's yet one way,
He comes in time — Felix!

Enter FELIX

    Fel.   My lord!

    Prince   Come hither.
You came in time — were present in my thoughts
Before your coming.   Hark you.   I have long
Long'd to requite your many services,
By more substantial meed than empty breath,
Too oft, they say, the end of princes' favour.
Much I design for you; but in mean time,
As some foretaste and earnest of my love,

A kinsman, a near kinsman of my own,
Has set his heart upon the lady Anna,
Your sister; fain would have her hand in marriage:
And I, with your good liking,
Have promis'd it to him.
    Fel.   Oh, my good lord,
Your favour overpowers me!
    Prince   Much content
Both for his sake, so near of my own blood,
(His letters show how deep his passion is,)
And yours, if you approve it.
    Fel.   Did I not,
Your will would be my law.
    Prince   Why this is well then.
We'll talk it over at our leisure; meanwhile,
For certain reasons, let this contract be
Between ourselves alone — you taking care
To pledge your sister's hand no other way.
    Fel.   O, trust to me, my lord — Heav'n watch above
Your Highness!
    Prince (aside). Oh mad end of foolish love!   [*Exit.*
    Fel. I'll straight away,
And tell my sister of the happiness
Awaits her. And may be shall learn of her
How my own suit prospers with Nisida,
The Prince's sister, which his present favour
Now blows upon so fairly. Cesar!

Enter CESAR

    Ces. Well found at last. Oh, Felix!
    Fel.   What is 't now?
Your heart seems labouring.
    Ces.   Yours must lighten it.
You know, Don Felix, how by blood and birth
I am a gentleman — not less, I trust,
In breeding and attainment; my estate
Sufficient for my birth — nurst by the Prince
In his own palace from my earliest years,
Until, howe'er unworthy of such honour,

Receiv'd into his inmost heart and counsel:
So far at least fitted for state affairs,
As ever given from my earliest youth
Rather to letters than to arms.   Enough:
You know all this, and know, or ought to know,
How much I am your friend?

    Fel.   I do believe it.

    Ces.   Yea, Felix, and would fain that friendship knit
By one still closer tie — Have you not guess'd,
By many a sign more unmistakable
Than formal declaration, that I love —
Presumptuously perhaps — but that I love
One of your house.   Which saying all is said:
For she is all your house who calls you "Brother."

    Fel.   Cesar, Heav'n knows how faithfully my heart
Answers to yours in all; how much I prize
The honour you would do me.   Would to God
That I had seen the signs of love you talk of,
Pointing this way; there is, I do assure you,
No man in all the world to whom more gladly
I would ally my sister and myself;
But I did not.   I grieve that it is so,
But dare not cancel what is now, too late,
Irrevocably agreed on with another.

    Ces.   By this "too late," I think you only mean
To tantalize my too late declaration.
If that be your intent, I am well punisht
Already; be content with my contrition.
You say you love me; and would well desire
To see me wed your sister; seal at once
My happiness, nor chill the opening day,
Nor my love's blossom, by a lingering "*Yea*."

    Fel.   Indeed, indeed, my Cesar, not to revenge
Delay of speech, or insufficient token,
But with repeated sorrow I repeat,
My sister's hand is pledg'd beyond recall,
And to another; whom, for certain reasons,
I dare not name, not even to herself,
As yet —

    Ces.   If I survive, 't is that fate knows

How much more terrible is life than death!
Don Felix, you have well reveng'd yourself
Upon my vain ambition, speech delay'd,
And signs that you would not articulate;
But let my fate be as it will, may hers,
Hers, yea, and his whose life you link to hers,
Be so indissolubly prosperous,
That only death forget to envy them!
Farewell.
    Fel.   Farewell then: and remember, Cesar,
Let not this luckless business interrupt
Our long and loving intimacy.
    Ces.   Nay,
It shall not, cannot, Felix, come what may.
                                    [*Exeunt severally.*

Enter PRINCE

    Prince   When in my love's confusion and excess
    I fancy many a fond unlikely chance,
Desire grows stronger, resolution less,
    I linger more the more I would advance.
False to my nobler self, I madly seize
    Upon a medicine alien to my ill;
And feeding still with that should cure disease,
    At once my peace and reputation kill
By turns; as the conflicting passions fire,
    And chase each other madly through my breast,
I worship and despise, blame and admire,
    Weep and rejoice, and covet and detest.
Alas! a bitter bargain he must choose,
Who love with life, or life with love, must lose!

Enter LAZARO

    Laz.   Where can my master be?   I shall go crazy, I think,
running from room to room, and house to house, after him and
his distracted wits.
    Prince   Lazaro!   Well, what news abroad?
    Laz.   Ah, my lord, there has been little of that under the
sun this long while, they say.   For instance, the slasht doublets

just come into fashion, and which they call new; why 't was I invented them years ago.

Prince   You? how?

Laz.   Why, look you; once on a time when I was not so well off as now, and my coat was out at elbows, the shirt came through: many saw and admired — and so it has grown into a fashion.

Prince   Who listens to you but carries away food for reflection!   [*Exit.*

Laz.   Aha! you are somewhat surfeited with that already, I take it.

So while the world her wonted journey keeps,
Lazarus chuckles while poor Dives weeps.

Enter CESAR

Ces.   Lazaro, I waited till the Prince was gone.
Listen to me.   Don Felix has betroth'd
His sister to another, not to me;
He will not tell me whom, nor does it matter:
All ill alike.   But out of this despair
I'll pluck the crown that hope could never reach.
There is no time to lose; this very night
I'll carry her away.

Laz.   Only beware
Telling Don Arias what you mean to do.
Is 't possible you see not all along
Your secret playing on his faithless lips?
Here's one last chance.

Ces.   True, true.

Laz.   You cannot lose
By secrecy — what gain by telling him?

Ces.   You may be right: and to clear up the cause
Of past mischance, and make the future safe,
I'll take your counsel.

Laz.   Then hey for victory!
Meanwhile, sir, talk with all and trust in none,
And least of all in him is coming hither.
And then in ocean when the weary sun
Washes his swollen face, "there shall be done
A deed of dreadful note."

Enter ARIAS

Ar.   How now, Don Cesar?
Laz. (aside).   Here are you, be sure,
When aught is stirring.
Ar.   How speeds Love with you?
Laz. (aside).   The lighter, sir, now you are left behind.
Ces.   Arias, my friend!   All's lost!
The love I grew deep in my heart of hearts
Is wither'd at the moment of its blossom.
I went to Felix, ask'd his sister's hand:
It was betroth'd, he told me, to another:
I was too late.   All's lost! It were in vain
Weeping for that I never can attain:
I will forget what I must needs forego,
And turn to other —
Laz. (to ARIAS).   Pray, sir, pardon me;
But pri'thee say no more to him just now;
It brings on such a giddiness.
Ar.   Alas!
But can I be of service?
Laz.   Only, sir,
By saying nothing more.
Ar.   I am truly sorry.   [*Exit.*
Laz.   That you can lie no longer in the matter.
Oh, the Lord speed you!
Ces.   O Love, if mortal anguish ever move thee,
At this last hour requite me with one smile
For all thy sorrows! let what I have suffer'd
Appease thy jealous godhead!   I complain not
That you condemn my merits as too poor
For the great glory they aspire unto;
Yet who could brook to see a rival bear
The wreath that neither can deserve to wear!

Enter PRINCE *and* ARIAS

Prince (to ARIAS).   Even so?
Good.   That he may not think 't was out of malice,
I made my business trench upon his love,
Now that his love's but Love-in-idleness,

I'll occupy him still.   Cesar!

Ces.   My lord?

Prince   I had like to have forgot.   'T is Monday, is 't not?
I have despatches both for Rome and Naples.
We must see to them to-night.

Ces.   My lord!

Prince   Bring hither
Your writing.

Ces. (apart).   Oh! the cup-full at my lips,
And dasht down, and for ever!
[*To* LAZARO.]   Villain, the victory you told me of!

Laz.   What fault of mine, sir?

Ces.   What fault! said you not
All now was well?

Laz.   Is 't I who make it wrong?

Ces.   You meddled.

Prince   Are you ready?

Ces.   Immediately.
Alas, alas! how shall my pen run clear
Of the thick fountain that is welling here!

Prince (aside).   And I shall learn from you how that dark
        pair
Contrive to smile, Jealousy and Despair.
        [*Desk and papers brought in: exeunt* ARIAS *and* LAZARO.
Now, are you ready?   (CESAR *sits at the desk.*)

Ces.   Ay, my lord.

Prince   Begin then.
"I am secretly" —

Ces.   "Secretly" — driven to madness!

Prince   "About the marriage" —

Ces.   "Marriage" — that never shall take place!

Prince   "All is fair for you" —

Ces.   "For you" — though perdition to me!

Prince   "Believe me" —

Ces.   I shall not survive it!

Prince   "That Donna Anna of Castelvi" —

Ces.   "That Donna Anna" — I can write no more!

Prince   "Is such in birth, beauty, and wit" —

Ces.   Oh, my lord, pardon me; but may I know
This letter's destination!

Prince   Eh? to Flanders!
Why do you ask?
Ces.   To Flanders!   But, my lord,
Surely no Flemish courier leaves to-day.
Might not to-morrow —
Prince (aside).   At the name of Anna
His colour chang'd.   *(Aloud.)*   No matter. 'T is begun,
And we'll ev'n finish it.   Where left I off?
Ces. (reading).   "Can write no more" —
Prince   Eh?   "Write no more?"   Did I
Say that?
Ces.   My lord?
Prince   The letter.   Give me it.
Ces. (aside).   Come what come may then, what is writ is
          writ!
Prince (reading).   "I am secretly driven to madness about
the marriage that never shall take place.   All is fair for you,
though perdition to me.   Believe me I shall not survive it,
that Donna Anna — I can write no more."
Was this what I dictated?
Ces. (throwing himself at the PRINCE's *feet).*   O my lord,
O noble Alexander! if the service
You have so often prais'd beyond desert
Deserve of you at all, snatch not from me
The only crown I ever ask'd for it,
To gild a less familiar brow withal.
This lady, Donna Anna,
Whom you are now devoting to another,
Is mine, my lord; mine, if a two years' suit
Of unremitted love not unreturn'd
Should make her mine; which mine beyond dispute
Would long ere this have made her, had not I
How many a golden opportunity
Lost, from my love to spend it on my Prince!
And this is my reward!   Oh, knew I not
How the ill star that rules my destiny
Might of itself dispose the gracious Prince,
Who call'd me for his friend from infancy,
To act my bitterest enemy unawares,
I might believe some babbler —

Prince   Nay, Don Cesar,
If in all these cross purposes of love
You recognise the secret hand of fate,
Accuse no mortal tongue, which could not reach
The stars that rule us all, wag as it would.
Enough.   I am aggriev'd, and not, I think,
Unjustly, that without my pleasure, nay,
Without my knowledge even, you, my subject,
And servant, (leaving the dear name of friend,)
Dispos'd so of yourself, and of a lady
Whose grace my court considers as its own.
Give me the pen: and, as you write so laxly,
I must myself report —
     Ces.   My lord!
     Prince   The pen. (*He writes.*)
     Ces.   If in misfortune's quiver there be left
One arrow, let it come!
     Prince   You could not write,
Don Cesar; but perhaps can seal this letter:
'T is for Don Felix; send it to him straight.
Or stay — I'd have it go by a sure hand:
Take it yourself directly.
     Ces.   At one blow
My love and friendship laid for ever low!   [*Exit.*

                    Enter FELIX *and* ARIAS

     Ar.   The letter must be written.
     Prince   Oh, Don Felix,
I have this moment sent to you.   No matter:
'T was but to say I have this instant heard
Your sister's bridegroom is in Parma; nay,
Perhaps already at your house.
     Fel.   Oh, my lord,
How shall I thank you for this gracious news?
     Prince   Nay, we will hear them from your sister's lips.
To her at once.
                                   [*Exit* FELIX.
                    And now, Don Arias,
You have to swear upon the holy cross

That hilts this sword, that neither Donna Anna
Know that I ever lov'd her, nor Don Cesar
I ever cross'd his love.
    Ar.   Upon this cross
I swear it; and beseech you in return
Never, my lord, to tell Don Cesar who
Reveal'd his secret.
    Prince   Be it so. I promise.
And now to see whether indeed I dare
The laurel claim with him whose name I wear.

                                  [*Exeunt.*

SCENE II.   *A Room in* FELIX's *House.* — ANNA *and* ELVIRA.

    Anna   Beside the charge of my own love, Elvira,
Whose crosses, I believe, will slay me soon,
My brother has confided to me at last,
His passion for the Princess Nisida;
And, for he knows that I am near her heart,
Would have me whisper it into her ears;
Which, were it such a passion as *I* feel,
His eyes would have reveal'd her long ago.
However, I have told her, and have got
An answer such — But look! he comes.

Enter FELIX

    Fel.   Oh, sister,
Might but your news be half as good as mine!
A largess for it, come.   You are betroth'd,
By me, and by the Prince himself, to one
In all ways worthy of you, and who long
Has silently ador'd.
    Anna (aside).   Is it possible?
Cesar!   *(Aloud.)*   Well, ask the largess that you will.
    Fel.   The Princess —
    Anna   Well?
    Fel.   What says she?
    Anna   All she could
At the first blush — nothing — and that means all:

Go to her, and press out the lingering Yes
That lives, they say, in silence.

Fel.   Oh, my sister!
But who comes here?

Enter CESAR *and* LAZARO

Ces. (giving the letter).   I, Felix.   This must be
My warrant — from the Prince.   Oh, misery!

Fel.   I thank you, Cesar.   *(Reads.)*
"Because happiness is the less welcome when anticipated, I
have hitherto withheld from you, that he to whom I have engaged your sister's hand, is — Don Cesar! in whom unites all
that man or woman can desire.   If the man lives who can
deserve such glory it is he.   Farewell."

Ces.   Great Heav'n!

Fel.   Nay, read the letter.

Enter PRINCE, NISIDA, ARIAS, *and Train*

Prince   He shall not need,
Myself am here to speak it.

Ces. (kneeling).   Oh, my lord!

Prince   Rise, Cesar.   If your service, as it did,
Ask'd for reward, I think you have it now;
Such as not my dominion alone,
But all the world beside, could not supply.
Madam, your hand; Don Cesar, yours.   I come
To give away the bride:
And after must immediately away
To Flanders, where, by Philip's trumpet led,
I will wear Maestricht's laurel round my brows;
Leaving meanwhile Don Felix Governor
Till my return — by this sign manual.

                              (Puts NISIDA's *hand in* FELIX's.*)*

Fel.   My lord, my lord!

Laz.   Elvira?

Elv.   Lazaro?

Laz.   I must be off.   Our betters if we ape,
And they ape marriage, how shall we escape?

Ar.   And learn this moral.   None commend

A secret ev'n to trustiest friend:
Which secret still in peril lies
Even in the breast of the most wise;
And at his babbling who should groan
Who could not even keep his own?

There are three other plays by Calderon, on this subject of keeping one's love secret; a policy whose neglect is punisht by a policy characteristically Spanish. 1. *Amigo, Amante, y Leal;* which has the same Prince and Arias, only the Prince confides his love to his rival. 2. *El Secreto a Voces;* where it is the ladies who shuffle the secret about the men. And 3. *Basta Callar,* a more complicated intrigue than any.

GIL PEREZ, THE GALLICIAN

DRAMATIS PERSONÆ

GIL PEREZ
ISABEL, *his sister*

DON ALONSO
MANUEL MENDEZ } *his two Friends*

PEDRO
CASILDA } *Servants in his house*

DONNA JUANA, *a Portuguese lady*
JUAN BAPTISTA, *a Lover of Isabel*
THE LORD HIGH ADMIRAL OF PORTUGAL
DONNA LEONOR, *his Cousin*
A SHERIFF
A JUDGE
LEONARDO, *a Traveller*

ALGUAZILS, OFFICERS, ATTENDANTS, FARMERS, &c.

ACT I

Scene I. *Outside* GIL PEREZ's *House. — Enter* PEDRO *running;* GIL PEREZ *after him with a drawn dagger; and* ISABEL *and* CASILDA *interceding.*

Isab.   FLY, Pedro, fly!
Gil   And what the use his flying
If I be after him?
Ped.   Hold him! hold him back,
Both of you!
Gil   By the Lord! I'll do for him.
Isab.   But why so savage with him?
Gil   He must pay
The long arrear of mischief you've run up.
Isab.   I understand you not.
Gil   I'll kill him first,
And then explain.
Isab.   I, who dread not bodily violence,
Dread your injurious words.   What have I done
That you should use me thus? — my enemy,
And not my brother.
Gil   You say well your enemy,
Who, if you do as you have done so long,
Will one day bathe his sword in your heart's blood,
And after in his own, and so wipe out
One scandal from the world.
Ped.   As the good soul
Who meddles to make peace between two brawlers
Oft gets the bloody nose, I'll take the hint.
Farewell, fair Spain! for evermore farewell!

Gil   Here! hark you, sir;
Before you go; you have escap'd this time
By luck, not by desert.   I give you warning,
Keep from my sight: for if I see your face
Fifty years hence, among the antipodes,
I'll pay you off.
         Ped.   Pray don't disturb yourself;
I'll take you at your word, and straight be off
To some old friends of mine — indeed relations —
In central Africa — the Ourang Outangs:
A colony so distant as I trust
Will satisfy us both.   And so, good bye.
                              [*Exit;* CASILDA *after him.*

         Isab.   He's gone, poor fellow.
And now perhaps, sir, as we are alone,
You'll tell me why you do affront me thus.
         Gil   Sister — oh, would to God that I had none
To call by such a name at such expense!
And can you think that I have been so blind,
As well as dumb, not to be ware the tricks
Of the sly gentleman who follows you
So constantly, and who, if this goes on,
Will one day filch away, not your own only,
But the long garner'd honour of our house?
Why, I have seen it all from first to last,
But would not show my teeth till I could bite;
Because, in points like this, a man of honour
Speaks once, and once for all.
This once is now.   I'll speak my mind to you;
Which, if you cannot understand, to-morrow
I must repeat in quite another language.
I know your man — Juan Baptista — one
Not man enough for me, and so, I tell you,
Not for my sister.   This should be enough,
Without his being, as he is, a Jew.
To get you from his reach I brought you here
To Salvatierra, deep amid the mountains,
And safe enough I thought; but even here
His cursed letters reach you through the hands
Of that fine rascal I have just pack'd off.

There; I have told my story; take 't to heart;
Dismiss your man at once, or, by the Lord,
If you and he persist, I'll fire his house,
And save the Inquisition that much trouble.

Isab. Your anger makes you blind — accusing me
Of things I never did.

Gil You never did!

Isab. But so it is, poor women must submit
To such insinuations.

Gil Pray, was 't I
Insinuated that letter then?

Isab. Peace, peace!
I can explain it all, and shall, when fit.
What would you have of me? You are my brother,
And not my husband, sir; consider that:
And therefore, in fraternal kindness bound,
Should even take my word without ado.
You talk of honour: is not honour then
Slow to suspect — would rather be deceived
Itself than prematurely to accuse?
I am your sister, Perez, and I know
My duty towards you and myself. Enough —
Which, if you cannot understand, to-morrow
I must repeat in quite another language. [*Exit.*

Gil She says not ill; it better were indeed
Had I kept on the mask a little longer,
Till they had dropt theirs beyond all denial.
She's right, and I was wrong; but from this time
I'll steer another course.

Enter CASILDA

Cas. A gentleman
(Of Portugal, he says) is at the door,
And asks for you.

Gil Bid him come in. Away,
My troubles for a while! [*Exit* CASILDA.

Enter MANUEL MENDEZ

Man. 'T was well, Gil Perez,

You sent so quickly, or my impetuosity
Had overrun your leave.

 Gil   What, Manuel Mendez!
Come to my arms. What! you in Salvatierra?

 Man. And, I assure you, at no small expense
Of risk and heart-ache.

 Gil   That's unwelcome news.

 Man. Not when 't is all forgotten in the joy
Of seeing you again.

 Gil   I shall not rest
Till I have heard; ill-manner'd though it be
To tax a man scarce winded from a journey
With such expense of breath.

 Man.   Then listen, Gil.
You, I am sure, remember (time and absence
Cannot have washt so much from memory)
The pleasant time when you were last at Lisbon,
And grac'd my house by making it your home.
I need not tell of all we did and talk'd,
Save what concerns me now; of the fair lady
You knew me then enamour'd of, (how deeply
I need not say — being a Portuguese,
Which saying, all is said) — Donna Juana,
At whose mere name I tremble, as some seer
Smit with the sudden presence of his God.
Two years we lived in the security
Of mutual love, with so much jealousy
(Without which love is scarcely love at all)
As serv'd to freshen up its sleeping surface,
But not to stir its depths. Ah, dangerous
To warm the viper, or, for idle sport,
Trust to the treacherous sea — sooner or later
They turn upon us; so these jealousies
I lik'd to toy with first turn'd upon me;
When suddenly a rich young cavalier,
Well grac'd with all that does and ought to please,
(For I would not revenge me with my tongue
Upon his name, but with my sword in 's blood,)
Demanded her in marriage of her father;
Who being poor, and bargains quickly made

'Twixt avarice and wealth, quickly agreed.
The wedding day drew nigh that was to be
The day of funeral too — mixt dance and dirge,
And grave and bridal chamber both in one.
The guests were met; already night began
Loose the full tide of noisy merriment,
When I strode in; straight through the wedding throng
Up to the bride and bridegroom where they were,
And, seizing her with one hand, with the other
Struck him a corpse; and daring all, to die
Fighting, or fighting carry off my prize,
Carried her off; lifted her on a horse
I had outside; struck spur; and lightning-like
Away, until we reach'd the boundary
Of Portugal, and, safe on Spanish ground,
At last drew breath and bridle.   Then on hither,
Where I was sure of refuge in the arms
Of my old friend Gil Perez; whom I pray
Not so much on the score of an old friendship,
So long and warm, but as a fugitive
Asking protection at his generous hands —
A plea the noble never hear in vain.
Nor for myself alone, but for my lady
Who comes with me, and whom I just have left
Under the poplars by the river-side,
Till I had told my news, and heard your answer.
A servant whom we met with on the way,
Pointed your house out — whither, travel-tir'd,
Press'd for my life, and deep in love with her
I bring, as curst by those I left behind,
And trusting him I come to —
    Gil   Tut, tut, tut!
Go on so, I'll not answer you at all;
All this fine talk to me! from Manuel Mendez!
As if 't were not enough to say, "Friend Gil,
I've left a gentleman I slew behind,
And got a living lady with me, so
Am come to visit you."   Why go about
With phrases and fine speeches?   I shall answer
Quite unpolitely thus, "Friend Manuel,

This house of mine is yours — for months, for years,
For all your life, with all the service in 't
That I or mine can do for you." So back,
And bring your lady, telling her from me
I stay behind because I am unapt
At such fine speeches as her lover makes.
 Man. Oh, let me thank you —
 Gil   Nay, 't were better far
Go to your lady; who may be ill at ease
Alone in a strange place.   [*Exit* MANUEL.
      What, Isabel!   *(She enters.)*
Isabel, if my former love and care
Deserve of you at all, forget awhile
All difference, (for there's a time for all,)
And help me now to honour an old friend
To whom I owe great hospitalities;
Manuel Mendez, who with his bride is come
To be my guest.
 Isab. I'll do my best for you.
But hark! what noise?   *(Shouts and fighting within.)*
 Gil   A quarrel's up somewhere.
 Voice within Take him alive or dead.
 Another voice   He'll slip us yet!
 Isab. Some one on horseback flying at full speed
From his pursuers.
 Voices within Fire upon him! fire! *(Shots within.)*
 Isab. Mercy, he's dead!
 Gil   Not he; only his horse;
And see he's up again, and gallantly
Flashing his sword around on his pursuers
Keeps them at bay, and fighting, fighting, still
Retreats —
 Isab. And to our house too —

     Enter DON ALONZO

 Alon.   Shelter! shelter!
In pity to a wretched man at last
Foredone!
 Gil What, Don Alonzo!

Alon.   But a moment,
To ask you cover my retreat, Gil Perez;
My life depends on reaching Portugal.

 Gil Away then to the bridge you see below there.
God speed you.

 Alon.   And keep you!   [*Exit.*

 Voices without   This way! this way!

 Gil But just in time!

Enter SHERIFF *with Officers*

 Officer   I'm sure he pass'd by here.

 Gil Well, gentlemen, your business?

 Sher.   Don Alonso —
Came he this way?

 Gil   He did, and he went that,
And must almost, unless I much mistake,
Be got to Portugal. For, by the Lord, sir,
His feet seem'd feather'd with the wind!

 Sher.   Away then!
After him!

 Gil   Stop a moment!

 Sher.   Stop! what mean you?

 Gil Just what I say. Come, Mr. Sheriff, come,
You've done your duty; be content with that;
And don't hunt gentlemen like wolves to death;
Justice is one thing, and fair play's another,
All the world over.

 Sher.   When I've got my man
I'll answer you.

 Gil   Perhaps before.

 Sher.   Why, sir,
Would you detain me?

 Gil   Why, if logic fails,
I must try other argument.

 Sher.   As what, sir?

 Gil Why, mathematical. As how? Look here.
You see me draw this line. Well then, 'fore God,
The man who passes it — dies. Q. E. D.

 Sher. Down with him!

Gil   Back, I advise you.
Voices   Down with him!
Gil Chicken-hearts! Curs! Oh, you will down with me,
Will you indeed? and this the way you do it?
                                   (*He fights with them.*)
One Oh, I am slain.
Sher.   I'm wounded.
Gil   Back with you!
                                   [*Exit, driving them in.*

SCENE II.   *The River-side. — Enter* JUANA *and* MANUEL.

Jua.   Oh never did I owe more to your love,
Than for this quick return.
   Man.   O my Juana,
The love such beauty as your own inspires,
Surmounts impossibilities.   However,
I needed not go on to Salvatierra,
Lighting on what I look'd for by the way,
Among the mountains; where my friend Gil Perez
(Whose honour I insult if I declare it)
Has pitcht his tent, with hospitality
Prophetic of our coming;
So peaceably our love may fold its wings
Under the shadow of my friend's.
   Jua.   Oh, Manuel,
She who has left home, country, friends, and fame,
And would contentedly leave life, for you,
Desires no other temple of her love
Than a bleak rock, whose unchang'd stedfastness
Shall not out-wear her own.
   Alon. (*within*).   I can no more!
   Jua. Listen!   What noise is that?
   Man.   A cavalier
Still with his sword in his exhausted hand.
He falls!

          Enter ALONSO, *who falls at the side*

   Alon.   They e'en must have me.
   Man.   Courage, sir.

Wounded? *(Voices within.)*

Alon.   Hark! the bloodhounds are close by;
And worse, they must have slain Gil Perez first,
Who else —

Enter GIL

Gil   Confound the rogues, they've got the bridge
And the way to 't, and heav'n itself, I think,
To fight upon their side.

  Man.   Gil, what is this?

Gil   Trying to help a friend out of a ditch,
I've tumbled in myself.

  Man.   Come, we are two
In hand, and one in heart; at least can fight
And die together.

  Alon.   Nay, add me;
The cause —

  Gil   There's but a moment.   Manuel,
I charge you by your friendship,
Draw not your sword to-day.

  Man.   Not I my sword
When theirs are on you?

  Jua. (clinging to MANUEL*).*   Heav'ns!

  Voices (within).   This way! this way!

  Man.   They're coming.

  Gil (to ALONZO*).* Listen! you can swim?

  Alon.   Alas —

  Gil   I mean upon my shoulders.   Manuel,
We two shall cross to Portugal,
Where follow us they may, but cannot seize us.
Meanwhile I leave you master of my house
And honour, centred (no time to say more)
In Isabel, my sister.   Swear to me
That you will see to this.

  Man.   I swear it, Gil.

  Gil   Enough, your hand!   Adieu!   Now, courage, sir!
(Takes ALONZO *on his shoulders and plunges into the river.)*

  Jua.   The man swims like a dolphin.

  Gil (within).   Manuel,
Remember!

Man.   How he wrestles with the flood!
And now is half-way over.
   Gil (within).   Manuel,
Remember!   I have trusted all to you.
   Man.   Waste not your breath.   I'll do 't.
   Gil (within).   Adieu!
   Man.   Adieu!
                    [*Exit* MANUEL *with* JUANA.

SCENE III.   *The Portuguese bank of the River. — Enter the*
ADMIRAL *of Portugal and* DONNA LEONOR *as from hunting.*

   Adm.   Since summer's fiery Sirius, fair cousin,
Neither from place nor power in heaven declines,
Will you not rest?
   Leonor   Ah, what a noble sport
Is hunting! who so abject-spirited
As not to love its generous cruelty?
   Adm.   It is indeed a noble imitation
Of noblest war.   As when a white-tuskt boar
Holds out alone against the yelling pack,
Gores one, o'erthrows another, all the while
Bristling his back like to some ridge of spears:
While many a gallant hound, foil'd in his onset,
Tears his own flesh in disappointed rage,
Then to the charge again — he and his foe,
Each with redoubled fury firing up:
A chivalry that nature has implanted
Ev'n in the heart of beasts.
   Leonor   So in falconry
That I love even better; when the heron
Mounts to the wandering spheres of air and fire,
Pois'd between which alternately she burns
And freezes, while two falcons, wheeling round,
Strive to out-mount her, tilting all along
The fair blue field of heaven for their lists;
Until out-ris'n and stricken, drencht in blood,
Plumb down she falls like to some crimson star;
A rivalry that nature has implanted
Ev'n in the breast of birds.

Enter PEDRO

Ped. Which is the way, I wonder? What with fright and weariness, I must rest awhile. Well, this is Portugal, where to be sure a poor Spanish pimp may hope to escape ferocious honour. That I should lose a post where others make their thousands at my first function! But who are these? Fine folks too! Pray Heaven they be in want of an officer.

Adm. A horse will soon carry you to the villa. Hark you, sir! *(To* PEDRO.*)*

Ped. My lord!

Adm. Who are you?

Ped. Nay, how should I know?

Adm. But are you one of my people?

Ped. Yes, if you like it. As said Lord Somebody, who neither serv'd king, man, or God, but who, entering the palace one day at supper-time, and seeing all the chamberlains at work without their coats, whips off his, and begins carrying up dishes. Suddenly in comes the major-domo, who, perceiving a stranger, asks if he be sworn of the service. "Not yet," says he, "but if swearing is all that's wanted, I'll swear to what you please." So 't is with me. Make me your servant, and I'll swear and forswear anything.

Adm. You are liberal of your humour.

Ped. 'T is all I have to be liberal of; and it would not be right to spare that.

Gil (within). Hold on, hold on!

Leonor Who's that?

Adm. Look, some one with erect head and vigorous arms, buffeting the wave before him.

Leonor With another on his shoulders too.

Adm. (to PEDRO). Now, would you win an earnest of future favour, plunge in to his assistance.

Ped. I would, sir, but I'm a wretched swimmer.

Leonor They have reacht the shore at last.

Enter GIL PEREZ *and* ALONSO, *drencht*

Alon. Thank Heaven for our escape!

Gil Ah, we're well quit of it.

Ped. Now, sir, if I can help. But Lord ha' mercy! *(Sees* GIL.)

Adm. What! going just when you are wanted?

Ped. I was born, my lord, with a tender heart; that seeing these poor fellows so drencht, bleeds for them. That he should pursue me even to Portugal! *(Is creeping away.)*

Adm. What! only just come, and going?

Ped. Oh, my lord, a sudden call. Excuse me. [*Exit.*

Adm. 'T is an idiot. But let me help you.

Alon. My life is in your hand.

Adm. In my hand? How is that?

Alon. You shall hear, if I may first know to whom I tell my story. Misfortune forces me to be cautious.

Adm. You are right; but need fear nothing from the Lord High Admiral of Portugal, who now speaks to you, and pledges himself to protect you so long as you stand on his estate.

Alon. Enough, my lord,
My name is Don Alonso de Tordoya,
Not un-illustrious in Spain. I love
A noble lady; whom going to visit,
When this same westering sun was young in heav'n,
I found a rival with her. I rush'd out,
Bidding him follow with his sword; he follow'd;
We fought, and with two passes in his side
I left him dead; the cry was after us;
The officers of justice at my heels.
No time to lose; I leap'd upon a horse,
And rode, until a shot, aim'd at his rider,
Kill'd him; then, taking to my feet, fled on,
Till, coming to a country house, I saw,
To my great joy, my friend —
　　Gil　　　　　　　　　　　Here enter I;
Who, seeing Don Alonso so hard set,
Offer'd my services to keep them back
Till he was safe in Portugal.
That country house of mine — a pleasure house
Some call it, though I've found but little there —
Stands in a narrow mountain gorge, through which
He and the bloodhounds after him must pass

To reach the river; as he says, he came,
And saw, and fled; had scarce got fifty yards,
Up comes the Sheriff with his yelling pack
Panting and blowing.   First most courteously
I begg'd them spare themselves as well as him
Further pursuit, but all in vain; push on
They would; whereon I was oblig'd to draw;
Disabled four or five, Heav'n help their souls!
Till, having done as much as he to figure
In justice's black book, like him I fled
After him to the river; where on finding
The bridge occupied by the enemy,
Catching my sword between my teeth, and him
Upon my shoulders, I so dash'd in,
And, at last, over; where now, thanks to Heav'n,
We meet your Excellency, who vouchsafes
Your shelter and protection.

    Adm.   'T was my word,
And I'll abide by 't.

    Alon.   I have need
Of all assurance, for the man I slew
Was of great note.

    Adm.   His name?

    Alon.   Prefacing that he was a cavalier
Of wholly noble parts and estimation,
And that 't is no disparagement to valour
To be unfortunate, I may repeat it, —
Don Diego d'Alvarado.

    Adm.   Wretched man!
My cousin! you have slain him!

    Leonor   You have slain
My brother, traitor!

    Gil   Oh, I see my sword
Must e'en be out again.

    Alon.   Your Excellency
Will pause before he draws his sword on one
Surrender'd at his feet.   My lord, remember
I slew Don Diego in the face of day,
In fair and open duel.   And, beside,

Is not your Excellency's honour pledg'd
To my security?

   Gil   Beside all which,
I say that if all Portugal, and all
Within it, admiralty and army too,
Combine, you shall not touch him while I live.

   Adm.   I know not what to do; upon one side
My promise, on the other the just call
Of retribution for my kinsman's death.
I must adjudge between them.   Don Alonso,
The word of Honour is inviolable,
But not less so her universal law.
So long as you stand upon ground of mine
I hold your person sacred: for so far
My promise holds; but set your foot beyond
E'en but an inch — remember, death awaits you.
And so farewell.

   Leonor   Nay, hold! though you have pledged
Your promise —

   Adm.   What I pledge is pledg'd for you,
As for myself; content you.   [*Exeunt* ADMIRAL *and* LEONOR.

   Alon.   Well, friend Gil,
What say you to all this?

   Gil   Why then, I say,
At least 't is better than it was.   To-day
The mouse, shut in the cupboard, there must stay:
But will jump out to-morrow — if she may.

ACT II

SCENE I. *A Wood near San Lucar in Andalusia.* — *Enter* MANUEL *and* JUANA *as travelling.*

Man.   MISFORTUNE on misfortune!
Jua.   Ay, they call
One to another.
Man.   Ah, my love!
That you should wander thus about with me
And find no home!   Gallicia, that I thought
Should be our port, unkindly storm'd us out
To Salvatierra, whence before the gale
We drive to Andalusia.
Jua.   Manuel,
My home is ever where you are.
Man.   Oh how
Requite such love! but you shall rest awhile
Till I and the poor fellow we pick'd up
Have found fit resting-place in San Lucar.
Pedro!

Enter PEDRO

Ped.   Sir!
Man.   Come you with me;
While you, Juana, underneath those trees —
Jua.   Weep your departure.   [*Exit* JUANA.
Man.   It shall not be long.
Although her grief blindly anticipates
A longer separation than she knows!

Ped. Alas, and how is that? and how can you
Foredoom such pain to one who loves you so?
Pardon me who am but your servant, sir,
And that but these two days, for saying it.

Man. Ah, Pedro, 't is not I who wills all this,
But fate; that, stronger than all human will,
Drove me from Portugal to Gallicia,
Thence hither; where my fate still urging on,
I must to sea, joining the armament
That sails to plant the banner of the church
Over the golden turrets of the north:
Leaving my lady — not, as you surmise,
Deserted and dishonour'd here behind,
But in some holy house at San Lucar,
With all the little substance I possess,
Till I return.   For to a soldier
His sword is property enough.   *(Drums within.)*

Ped.   And hark
The drum that answers you —

Man.   No doubt a troop
Recruiting for this war.

Ped.   See, they are coming.

Man. I'll take occasion by the forelock then.
Pedro, go, tell the Ensign of the troop
Two men would join his ranks.   I'll to Juana.   [*Exit.*

Enter GIL PEREZ *with soldiers*

Ped. This one looks affable.   *(To a Soldier.)*   Pray, sir,
can you courteously inform me which is the Ensign?

Soldier There — he with the red sash.

Ped. What, he with the lofty presence and broad shoulders?

Soldier Ay!

Gil (to the soldiers). Well, then, my lads, we shall agree
together very well, eh?

Soldiers Long live our noble Ensign!   [*Exeunt soldiers.*

Ped. Now's the time!

Gil (to himself). 'Fore heaven, this soldiering would be
pleasant enough did not that trouble follow and plague me.

Ped. Sir!

Gil   Leaving Isabel at such a risk —

Ped.   Sir Ensign!

Gil   That as fast as I gain honour here I run the chance of losing more at home.

Ped.   Noble Sir Ensign!

Gil   One good thing, however, my good Manuel keeps guard for me.

Ped.   He must surely be deaf this side — I'll try the other. Noble Ensign!

Gil (turning round).   Who is that?

Ped. (recognising him gradually).   A soldier — no, I only mean one who would be — no soldier.   If I said I wish'd to be a soldier, sir, I lied.

Gil   Rascal! you here? did I not warn you whenever and wherever —

Ped.   Oh, yes, yes, but how should I ever expect to find you here a soldiering?

Gil (setting upon him).   I'll teach you I *am* here, scoundrel, to whom I owe half my trouble.

Ped.   Help! murder! help!

Enter MANUEL

Man.   A soldier set upon my servant! stop, sir! how do you dare — Gil Perez!

Gil   Manuel!

Man.   Why, did I not leave you in Portugal?

Gil   And I you in Salvatierra, engaged to me by solemn promise and old love to guard my honour there?

Man.   We both have cause for wonder.   I will tell you all; but first we must be alone.

Gil   Ay, another wonder; this fellow yours?

Man.   In travelling hither we found him by the way, and took him.

Gil (to PEDRO).   Well, this saves your life for this time, sir; but, remember, you will not always have a friend at hand to do so much for you.

Ped.   I know that; I only wish you would be so gracious as to tell me where you are next bound, that I may take good care not to go thither.   But I know one place at least to

which you cannot follow me — your own estate — and thither
I set off immediately. *[Exit.*

    Gil   We are alone.   Come, I will tell you first
My story.   As you say you saw us last,
Alonso and myself, in Portugal;
Such an escape as (so the wise men say)
Is from the frying-pan into the fire.
We landing from the river on the estate
Of that great potentate the High Admiral,
Whose cousin, it turn'd out, was the very man
Alonso slew; whereat the Admiral,
Who had, before he knew this, promis'd us
Protection, gave us truly such protection
As the cat gives the mouse that she thinks safe
Under her paw.   But we escap'd from her,
And after much adventure came at last
To San Lucar here, where the Duke, who now
Is general of the war that our good king
Wages with England, courteously receiv'd us;
Gave Don Alonso a regiment; made me
An Ensign in it as you see; enough —
I know you will not wish a longer story
From one whose heart, until you tell him yours,
Hangs from a hair.
    Man.   To take the story up then
Where you did, Perez — scarcely had you plung'd
Into the river, than the sheriff's rout
Came after you; but, seeing all was lost,
Went angry to their homes, and I to yours;
Where I receiv'd such hospitality
As our old friendship — But I falter here,
Scarce knowing how to tell —
Nay, almost doubting if to tell at all,
Or to conceal, what to conceal and tell
At once were best.   You made me promise, Gil,
At parting — yea, with those last parting words
Wrung from your breathless struggle with the flood —
To watch the honour of your house.
I did so; and it is because I did so
That I was forc'd to leave it.

Gil   Manuel,
Your tongue is slaying me by syllables.
But tell me all. — How was 't?
    Man.   One Juan Baptista
Courted your sister.
    Gil   Well?
    Man.   And came at last
To such a boldness, that one night he stole
Into the house.
    Gil   Manuel!
    Man.   I, who was watching,
Ran from my chamber, found a muffled man;
Threw myself on him; he, alerter yet,
Leap'd from the window, and I after him
Into the street, where two he'd posted there
Came to his rescue; one of them I slew,
The other wounded, while the rogue himself
Fled and escap'd.   What could I do, my friend,
A foreigner, charg'd with a homicide
In a strange country, with Juana too
Involv'd with me?   If I were wrong to fly,
I did so thinking how yourself would act
In a like case.
    Gil   'T is true, I cannot blame you.
Ah! he said truer may be than he meant,
Who liken'd a true friend to a true mirror,
That shows one all oneself indeed, but all
Revers'd; that when I look into your breast
To see my honour, I but see disgrace
Reflected there.   I must begone at once
To Salvatierra; for, to leave my name
In danger is to let it run to shame.

                    Enter ALONSO

Oh, Don Alonso, you are come in time.
If aught that I have ever done for you
Deserve return, requite me, I beseech you,
By giving Manuel here the Ensigncy
I must throw up.

Alon. But why?

Gil I must at once
To Salvatierra, where my honour lies
In the utmost peril.

Alon. But —

Gil I am resolv'd.

Alon. I fain might try dissuade you, but I know
Your honour will not call in vain. Enough:
Be 't as you will — on one condition.

Gil Well?

Alon. That I may go with you, and share your risk,
Who more than shar'd, and conquer'd mine.

Man. Nay, sir,
If any one do that it must be I,
His older friend, who bringing this ill news
Must see him safely through it.

Alon. But 't was I
Who drew him from his home, where, till I came,
He liv'd in peace and quiet, but where now
This outrage has grown up in his forc'd absence.
And surely, the world over, 't is ill manners
For one who, having drawn a friend from home,
Lets him return alone.

Man. Well, be you courteous,
I'll not be cowardly.

Gil Oh, this rivalry
Proves the nobility of both! But, friends,
Neither must go with me; you both are here
Fled in like peril of your lives from home,
And how could I avail me of your love
At such a price? Nay, I may want you both
In greater risks hereafter; and whom look to,
If you be lost?

Alon. True, but if one of us
Went with you now, the other —

Man. And that one
Must be myself.

Alon. You see, sir, one *will* go.
Do you choose which.

Man. Content.

Gil   How shall I choose,
When to choose one must needs the other hurt!
But if it needs must be —
I say that Don Alonso, so engag'd
In high and even holy business here,
Must not forego 't for mine.   If one will come,
Let it be Manuel.
    Alon.   I live to hear
This insult from your lips!   But I'll have vengeance;
Neither shall go unless you take with you
Thus much at least to compensate
For what you leave.   These jewels may assist you
Where my sword cannot.   (*Giving jewels.*)
    Gil   I accept them, sir,
As freely as they're given.   Come, embrace me.
And now to punish an unworthy sister,
And that ill traitor, from whose heart I swear
My bleeding honour with this sword to tear.

SCENE II.   *Outside* GIL PEREZ's *House at Salvatierra; as in*
    ACT I., SCENE I. — *Enter* ISABEL *and* CASILDA.

Isab.   What!   Donna Leonor d'Alvarado, come to Salvatierra?
    Cas.   Yes.
    Isab.   And for what purpose?
    Cas.   They say, to avenge her brother's death.   I myself
have seen her conferring with Juan Baptista.
    Isab.   And what do you infer from that?
    Cas.   He is, they say, chief witness against Don Alonso and
your brother, for this murder.
    Isab.   Against my brother too!   O Casilda, is it not shame-
ful that Juan Baptista should revenge with slanders behind my
brother's back whom he dares not meet face to face!   Nay,
that a traitor be revenged at all on him he has betrayed! thriv-
ing here at home while my brother is banisht!
    Cas.   But there's something else. He charges your brother's
friend Manuel with murdering his men.
    Isab.   In proving which, my honour must be publicly can-
vassed and compromised!

Enter PEDRO

Ped.   Oh, what a long way it has seemed; as it will when
fear fetters one's legs.   Oh, permit me, madam, since fate has
sent me back to your feet, to kiss but the little toe, the pink,
the pearl, the petty Benjamin of those ten toes.   But above
all, tell me, for Heaven's sake, is my master here?

Isab.   No, Pedro, you at least are safe.   He, alas, is far
away.

Ped.   So one might think; but yet on the other hand I'd
swear he must be here.

Isab.   Pedro!

Ped.   Oh yes, his sole vocation now is to dodge my steps
like some avenging ghost of *Capa and Espada.*

Enter JUAN BAPTISTA

Bapt. (*speaking to himself*).   If they condemn him
To death, as on my evidence alone
They must, he'll not return to plague me more
At Salvatierra.   But, fair Isabel,
How blest am I on whom the star of beauty,
Bright rival of the sun,
Beams out such rays of love!

Isab.   Stand off!   Away!
Not rays of love, whatever heretofore
I and my beauty may have beam'd, Baptista,
But now, if rays at all, lightnings of rage
And indignation from my heart and eyes.
Approach them at your peril!   What, false traitor,
You come to court me with my brother's blood
Upon you, shed too in no manly duel,
Face to face, hand to hand, in the open field,
But like a murderer,
Behind his back stabbing him dead with slander —
Never!   [*Exit.*

Bapt.   But, Isabel.

Cas.   Your day is over.   [*Exit.*

Bapt.   And that I should lose her by the very means I
hoped to win her with!

Ped.   Let not this prevent your memory acknowledging

one who has suffered banishment, and lives in terror of his life, on your account.

Bapt.   Pedro!

Ped.   And at your service.

Bapt.   Ah, would you were!

Ped.   Try me.

Bapt.   But are you still Isabel's servant?

Ped.   I trust so.

Bapt.   Oh, good Pedro, I would fain explain to her, and wipe out (as I easily can) the offence she has taken against me; and if you will but be my friend, and leave the door ajar to-night, that I may tell her the whole story, I'll pay you well for it.

Ped.   Well, I think there can be no danger in that. Why, if you should happen to call loudly outside the door to-night, and I let you in, forgetting to ask who it is — surely I shall not be to blame?

Bapt.   'T is well; the sun is already setting; go you to your post, and I shall be at mine immediately.

[*Exeunt severally.*

SCENE III.   *A Room in* GIL PEREZ'S *House.* — *Enter* ISABEL *and* CASILDA.

Isab.   Casilda, now the flaming sun has set,
See to the doors; and you and Ines there
Sing to me — 't will beguile my melancholy.
No merry song, however; something sad
As my own fancies.   (*They sing within.*)
                    Hark! what noise is that?
One calling at the door at such an hour! —
Again! — Bid Pedro see —
Why, what is it that makes me tremble so?
From head to foot —

Enter PEDRO *hurriedly*

Ped.   O madam!
Isab.   Well?
Ped.   O madam —
Opening the door — only to ask — a man
All muffled up ran by me — (*Aside.*)   'T is all right.

Enter GIL PEREZ, *cloakt*

Isab.   Who's this?

Gil (discovering himself).   I, Isabel.

Isab.   Oh heavens!

Gil   Well, sister,

What troubles you?

Ped.   Oh Lord, oh Lord, oh Lord!   *(Hides.)*

Isab.   O Gil, how have you dared to venture here,

Your very life at stake!

Gil   Small risk to one

Whom your ill doings have half kill'd already.

Isab.   I do not understand you —

Gil   You need not:

I come not to explain, but to avenge;

And, mark my words, what I have come to do,

I'll do.

Isab.   Alas! is it my fault then, brother,

That traitors of their gold can make them wings

To fly into my house?

Gil   Be not afraid;

I shall not judge of you or any one

Unheard, as others seem to judge of me.

What is the matter?

Isab.   Nay, I only know

You are accus'd of aiding, how I know not,

In Don Diego's death — on evidence,

As 't is believ'd, the Judge (who now is here,

Inflam'd by Donna Leonor) declares

Sufficient to convict you of your life

And property — Alas, alas, my brother!

Gil   You shall away with me; for 't is not well

To leave you here alone and unprotected.

But I must see first what this mighty Judge

Has got against me.

Isab.   But how get at it?

Gil   Why from the fountain-head.   But, by the Lord,

If I must fly or die for 't,

It shall not be for nothing; I'll begin

My vengeance on this rascal.   *(Pulling out* PEDRO.)

Ped.   Oh begin
On some one else and sum up all on me!
   Gil   How come you here?
   Ped.   Oh, I will tell the truth
And nothing but the truth.
   Gil   Well?
   Ped.   Being assur'd
That you were coming hither —
   Gil   Well?
   Ped.   I came
Before.
   Gil   And why, when —
   Ped.   That by doing so
You should not see my face, (which you declar'd,
Seeing again, you'd kill me,) but my back,
Which as you never swore at —
   Gil (striking him).   Villain, die!
   Ped. (falling as dead).   Oh! I am slain!
   Gil   Come, Isabel, 't is I
Must bear you on my shoulders through the flames
That rise all round.   [*Exeunt* GIL *and* ISABEL.
   Ped. (rising).   Oh, angel of sham death,
How much I owe your out-spread wings to-day,
Under whose shadow — Yo escaparè.   [*Exit.*

SCENE IV. *An open Gallery in the Judge's House at Sal-*
   vatierra. — Enter Judge, and attendants, with lights, &c.

   Judge   Here in this gallery where the air is cool
Set out my desk and papers.
I must examine all these depositions.
   1st Attendant   'T is done, my lord.
   2nd Attendant   My lord, a stranger asks
Admittance — upon something, as he says,
Important to the matter now in hand.
   Judge   Admit him, then.
   Gil (without).   Manuel, keep the door;
And, till my lord and I have had our talk,
Let no one enter.
   Man. (without).   Trust me.

Enter GIL

Gil	First permit me

To kiss your lordship's hand.   And secondly,
Having important matter to disclose
About this business, I would tell it you
Alone —

Judge (to attendants).   Retire!   [*Exeunt attendants.*
Gil   And with your lordship's leave
Will take a chair.
Judge   Sit, sir.
Gil   May I presume
To ask your lordship how Gallicia
Agrees with you?
Judge   I thank you, very well.
Gil   I'm very glad of that.   Humph — as I take it,
Your lordship is come down into these parts
On a great trial?
Judge   Yes, the case is this;
A certain Don Alonso de Tordoya,
And one Gil Perez of this place, are charg'd
With slaying Don Diego d'Alvarado.
Gil   Slaying?
Judge   In duel, sir.
Gil   I marvel much
They should have dragg'd your lordship from the city
And from the court that you so much adorn,
Into this beggarly place, to try a cause
That happens almost every day in Spain.
Judge   True, sir, but this is not by any means
The whole, or kernel, of the case.   These men,
Beside, and after, the said homicide,
Resisted the king's officers; this Perez
Especially — a notable ruffian
Who lives among these hills a lawless life
Of violence and murder — struck the Sheriff,
And — but I'm scarce entitled to say more
To one whose very name I know not.
Gil   Oh!
My name is quickly told, if that be all.

Judge   What is it then?
Gil   Gil Perez.
Judge   Ho! without!
Man. (appearing at the door).   My lord!
Judge   And who are you?
Gil   A friend of mine.
Man.   Who will take care that no one else comes in,
Till you have done.   [*Exit.*
    Gil   Your lordship sees how 't is —
Be not alarm'd — pray take your chair again —
I've much to say to you.
    Judge (aside).   Better submit.
This desperate man may have a score beside —
Well, sir, your business with me?
    Gil   Why, my lord,
I for these many days have been, so please you,
Away from home; suddenly coming back,
My friends here tell me of a mortal suit
Your lordship has against me; when I ask
For the particulars, some say one thing,
And some another.   I, who naturally
Am somewhat interested in the truth,
Think it the wisest course to come at once
Straight to head-quarters.
    Judge   This is strange proceeding.
    Gil   Oh, if your lordship scruple telling me,
These papers will not.   I'd not for the world
Annoy your lordship.   *(Takes the depositions.)*
    Judge   What are you about, sir!
    Gil   Conning my brief.
    Judge   But, sir —
    Gil   Now pray, my lord,
Resume your seat; let me not ask you this
So very often.   *(Reading.)*   Ah — the bare indictment
I know in a rough way, no need read that;
But for the evidence.   Ah, here it is.
Humph; the first witness called, Andrew Ximenes:
"Andrew Ximenes, being duly sworn,
"Deposeth thus: that he was cutting wood,
"When the two gentlemen came out to fight;

"And stood to watch them; that, after some passes,
"Don Diego fell; and the officers of justice
"Then coming up, the other leap'd on horse,
"And fled: but being brought to ground by a shot
"That kill'd his horse, then ran, until he reach'd
"Gil Perez's house," — here enter I, — "who first
"Courteously ask'd the Sheriff to desist
"Hunting the gentleman; but when the Sheriff
"Persisted, drew on him and on his people,
"And fought them back; but how and when exactly
"The wound was given, deponent cannot say.
"And all this he deposeth upon oath,
"Andrew Ximenes —"   And he says the truth;
Andrew is a good, honourable fellow.
Now for the second, Gil Parrado; humph.
"Parrado, duly sworn, deposeth thus;
"That, hearing a commotion, he ran out
"And got in time to see" — here enter I —
"Gil Perez fighting with the officers,
"Then on a sudden running to the river
"Plunge in.   And that is all he knows of it."
How short and sweet!
"Next and third witness, Juan Baptista," — ay,
Now for this exemplary Christian —
"Juan Baptista sworn, deposeth thus:
"That, as luck fell, he was behind a tree
"When the two gentlemen came out to fight;
"That they fought fairly hand to hand, until" —
Here enter I — "Gil Perez suddenly
"Rush'd from a thicket by, and join'd himself
"With Don Alonso, and the two together
"Maliciously and treacherously slew
"Don Diego."   Pray, my lord, what is the worth
Of such a witness, who himself admits
He stood behind a tree watching two men
Set on a third, and slay him, and yet never
Ran to his help?   Well — humph — "And after this,
"Saw Don Alonso jump upon a horse
"And fly, while Perez drew his sword upon
"The officers of justice, and slew one,

"And maim'd another."   Give me leave, my lord,
To take this leaf.   (*Tears it out.*)
                            I'll bring it back to you
When I have made this rascal Jew confess
(If ever Jews confess) what he *did* see,
If any thing; but fair that if a judge
Decide on evidence, that evidence
At least be true; that he should hear moreover
Both sides, accus'd as well as his accuser.
As to that Sheriff's wounds — the only count
To which I own — I never sought the fray;
The fray sought me, as I stood innocently
At my own door; and pray what man of honour —
What would your lordship's sober self have done
In such a case?
 Judge Within! within there! ho!
Perez himself is here! the culprit!   Seize him!
 Man. (appearing).   Ay, do, if you can catch him.
 Gil   Manuel,
Let them come up; I have no more to say.
And you and I, who walk'd in by the door,
Can jump out of the window.
 Voices (within).   Seize him!   Seize him!
 Judge   One word, Gil Perez; if you yield at once,
I'll be your friend.
 Gil   I make no friends of lawyers,
And never trust their promises.
 Judge   If not,
As sure as Heav'n, I'll bring you to the scaffold.
 Gil   If you can catch me.
 Judge   Cannot I?
 Gil   Well, try.
 Judge   Ho there! upon him; and if he resist,
Cut him down!
 Man. Now then, Gil!
 Gil   Now, Manuel!
Out with the lights! or wanting them, we two
Will strike them, knaves, in plenty out of you.
                            (*Confusion and Melée, in which* GIL
                                and MANUEL *escape.*)

ACT III

Gil THIS mountain then, upon whose wrinkled edge
The weary moon reclines, must be our fort;
Where, in some green and shady spot of it,
(Hung round with savage, inaccessible rocks,)
While Isabel and your Juana rest,
You and I, Manuel, will steal into
The little village nestled there below,
And of such travellers as come this way,
Demand (our own all gone) a scanty living,
By fair entreaty, not by violence;
Until, pursuit giv'n up, we may retreat
Elsewhere, to live upon what little means
Injustice leaves us.
    Man.   Gil, 't is nothing new
For criminals to hide
Ev'n where they did the crime, where vengeance least
Expects to find them, and hunts round in vain.
And even should they light upon the place,
Surely we two, back'd by these friendly rocks,
Can keep at bay the rabble that we foil'd
On level ground.
    Isab.   I have listen'd to you both,
And take it ill you reckon on yourselves
Alone; when I, who, though a woman, having yet
Your blood, Gil Perez, running in my veins,
And something of your spirit in my heart,
Am at your side.

Jua.   And I, who, like a coward,
Chime in the last; yet, if with little power,
With right good will indeed.
     Gil   Well spoken both!
But I maintain it as a golden law,
Women be women ever; keep you quiet,
And comforting yourselves as best you may,
While Manuel and I, as becomes men,
Provide for you in all.
     Isab.   Well, we at least,
If fit for nothing else, can pray for you.

                         [*Exeunt* ISABEL *and* JUANA.

     Gil   Now they are gone, I want to talk with you
On a grave matter, Manuel. 'T is this.
Among those depositions at the Judge's,
One rascal, and a rascal too whose gold
Makes weigh his witness against honesty,
Declar'd on oath he saw me, me, Gil Perez,
Abetting Don Alonso treacherously
To slay Don Diego.
     Man.   Who was this?
     Gil   Why one
Who has not this alone to answer for,
As you will know when I name — Juan Baptista.
     Man.   A coward, who, as all such villains do,
Flies to the tongue for vengeance, not the sword;
Behind one's back too —
Why, let us go at once, and in broad day
Before all eyes, before the very Judge's
He lied to, drag the rascal from his house,
And make him eat his words in the very place
He spit them forth in.
     Gil   All this we will do,
But at some better opportunity,
And fitter place.   I've heard my grandsire say,
          "If you begin the fray, why then
               You must abide the how and when;
               But who's drawn into it, I trow,
               May suit himself with when and how."
But footsteps!   Hark! —

Now to commence our calling, as new members
Of the most courteous cut-purse company.

Enter LEONARDO, *travelling*

Leon. (speaking as he enters).   Lead on the horses, Mendo,
    't is so pleasant
Under the shade of these wooded rocks,
I'll walk some way alone.
    Gil   Your servant, sir.
    Leon.   Sir, God be with you.
    Gil   Travelling all alone?
And whither, may I ask?
    Leon.   To Lisbon, sir.
    Gil   And whence?
    Leon.   I started at the break of day
From Salvatierra.
    Gil   Ay?   Then you can tell
What news is stirring there.
    Leon.   Oh, nothing, sir.
Unless perhaps the exploits of a fellow
The terror of that country; one Gil Perez,
I think; who, when justice was at his heels
After some crime or other I forget,
Wounded the Sheriff, kill'd his officer,
And then was impudent enough to walk
Into the very Judge's house, and there,
Before his very eyes, snatch up and read
The depositions drawn up against him.
    Gil   A very curious story, that!
    Leon.   And then,
Though half the place was up in arms on him,
He, and another who is, as I hear,
Much such another rascal as himself,
Broke through them all and got away scot free!
But they are after him.
    Gil   This is the news?
    Leon.   All that I know of.
    Gil   Well — before you go,
I'll ask you, sir, who by your speech and bearing

Seem a good fellow.   If a friend of yours
Came flying for his life, the Philistines
Close on his heels, and fell before your feet,
At your own door, exhausted, and beseeching
Help and protection of you — let me ask
What would you do?

    Leon.   What do? why, give it him.

    Gil   You would? and would you, in so doing,
Deserve the name of rascal for your pains?

    Leon.   No, certainly.

    Gil   And when a writ was out
Against you for so doing, charging you
With murder, threatening death and confiscation,
Would you be more a rascal for demanding
Such needful information of the Judge
As he alone could give of evidence
Which you suspected, and found false?

    Leon.   No, truly.

    Gil   One question more.   If, damn'd by such false witness,
You were found guilty, all your property
Confiscated, yourself condemn'd to die,
Might not you fly the misdirected sword
Of justice, and of those who well could spare
Beg a poor tithe of what she robb'd you wholly,
And be no rascal still?

    Leon.   Oh clearly, clearly.

    Gil   This granted then, look to the inference.
I am Gil Perez; I who struck the Sheriff,
And kill'd his man, and read the Judge's papers,
And flying hither, shorn of house and home,
Ask you for that of which the law robs me;
Which, having plenty, if you will not give,
By your own free admission I may take,
And be no rascal still.

    Leon.   You need not use
My argument against me; I respect
And pity you, Gil Perez; take this chain;
If it be not enough, I pledge my word
I'll bring you more hereafter.

    Gil   All you say

Tells of a generous heart.   But ere I take
Your present, tell me — do you give it me
For fear, alone, and in my power, may be,
Or of good will?
 Leon.   Good will!   I swear to you,
Gil Perez, I would even do the same
Had I a squadron at my side.
 Gil   As such
I take it, then.   For when my life must pay,
As soon or late it must, the penalty
Of hungry vengeance, I shall lay it down
Contented in my conscience, and report
That I but took from those who had to give,
And freely gave; the only retribution
My evil star allow'd me.
 Leon.   True enough.
Is there aught else that I can do for you?
 Gil Nothing.
 Leon.   Farewell — and may a better fate
Await you.
 Gil Farewell — shall I see you safe
Over the mountain?
 Leon.   Not a step — adieu.   [*Exit.*
 Man. Sure never robbery was known to wear
So fair a face.
 Gil Tut, tut, you're not to call it
Robbery, but preferment, Manuel.
But who are these?

Enter two Farmers

 1st Farm. I tell you I have bought the stock of vines
Upon his farm.
 2nd Farm. What, Gil's?
 1st Farm.   Yes; sold, you know,
To pay the costs of prosecution,
Judges and Alguazils and such; and I
Am carrying them the money.
 Man.   Fair game this.
 Gil I know him, a near neighbour.   Well, friend Antony,
How goes it with you?

1st Farm.   What! Gil Perez! you!
When the whole country's after you?
   Gil   And if they catch me nobody's the worse
Except myself.   But till they catch and kill me,
(When I shall want, you know, no more to live on,)
I've not a stiver; clipt of the estate
Whose price you carry in your pocket there.
Now, I'd not starve; but, on the other hand,
Would not wrong any one to keep me from 't:
How shall we settle that?
   1st Farm.   Oh easily —
Take this — and this *(offers money)* — I had better give it up
At once, for fear.   *(Aside.)*
   Gil   But do you give me this
Of free good will?
   1st Farm.   Why as to that, Gil Perez,
My will is good to serve you; but, you see,
I am not very rich.
   Gil   You mean by that
You would not give this money could you help it?
   1st Farm.   Why certainly.
   Gil   Then keep it and begone
In peace.
   1st Farm.   Gil Perez!
   Gil   I'll not have it said
I robb'd — not shamed to beg in my distress.
   2nd Farm.   And I pray, Gil, and he who likes may hear
      me,
God keep you from your enemies.   I have here
Six pieces that my wife knows nothing of;
You're welcome.
   Gil   Not a penny; go your ways,
Or night will reach you ere you reach your homes.
                           [*Exeunt Farmers.*
   Man.   Gil, while you talk'd with them, I've heard a sound
As of pursuit — listen! — and many too.
   Gil   Let us up higher then!
   Man.   Beware, the trees
Will whisper of our whereabout.
   Gil   Then here

Behind the rocks that tell no tales.
Man.   Quick, quick!

> *(They hide.)*

Enter DONNA LEONOR, JUAN BAPTISTA, *Judge, Alguazils, &c.*

Bapt.   Here, madam, till the scorching sun be sunk,
Tarry awhile.
Leonor   My cousin's grievous sickness
Calls me with all speed homeward.
Judge   And as yet
No vestige of these ruffians, whom to find
And bring to justice, madam, in your cause,
I'll peril my own life.
Gil   Hist, Manuel!
Man.   Ay, but speak lower.
Gil   When better than now
Can I avenge Alonso and myself,
When judge, accus'd, accuser, and false witness,
Are all together?
Man.   Wait awhile.
Gil   But —
Man.   See,
Fresh comers.
Gil   I shall lose the golden moment.

> *Enter some, dragging along* PEDRO

Judge   A prisoner?
1st Man   One of Gil Perez's knaves, my lord, whom we
have just now caught creeping over to Portugal.   The very
day Perez swam over there this fellow was missed from Sal-
vatierra, and returned on the very evening of his return.
Judge   Very suspicious indeed.
Pedro   Very, my lord, grant it.   Yes, wherever I go, to
Portugal, Flanders, Germany, China, Japan, 't is all the same.
I am sure to find him there.
Judge   You know then where he is now?
Ped.   Oh, doubtless close at hand; he must be, I being
here; he is such a constant master, that if you put me in
prison he'll soon surrender only to follow me there.
Judge   Point out the place, then.

Ped.   Would to Heav'n I could, for were he clapt up safe
I'd not follow *him*, I promise you.   Indeed, my lord,
I live in terror of my life from him.
Flying from him it was I fled from home
To Portugal; where the first man I saw
Was he I thought I'd left at Salvatierra:
Flying to Andalusia, the first face
I saw was his I left in Portugal:
Till, rushing homeward in despair, the man
I thought I'd left behind in Andalusia,
Met me at once, and having knockt me down,
Left me for dead.   Well, I got up at last,
And fled again: but, scarcely got a mile,
Your people seize me on suspicion
Of knowing where he hides, and so far justly,
That carrying me by way of a decoy,
I'll lay my life he soon were in the trap.

Judge   Your folly, or your cunning, sir, shall not mislead
us; tell me where your master is at once, or the wooden horse —

Ped.   Alas, I'm a bad rider.

Judge   Take him to the village and keep him close. By his
looks I doubt not, spite of this affected simplicity, he's a desperate ruffian.

Ped.   I seem such a desperate fellow to him!   Dear me, of
the four men here let one depart, and leave three, and one of
the three leave two, and one of the two one; and that one
leave half himself; and that half his half; and that quarter his
half, till it comes to *nil:* it would still be nilly willy with me.

[*Exit, guarded by Alguazils.*

Gil   Manuel,
The Alguazils are gone.

Man.   Now for it then.

Gil (appearing).   God save this noble company.

All   Gil Perez!

Gil   Be not alarm'd; I have but a few words
To say to one of you, this Juan Baptista.

Judge   Holloa! my guards!

Man.   Judge, never strain your throat,
Unless you would be answer'd by such guards
As waited on you yesterday.

Judge   Is this the way that I, and, in my person,
That justice is insulted?
Gil   Nay, my lord,
You least of all should tax a criminal
Who so punctiliously respects yourself,
And the realm's Justice in your belly lodg'd,
That not to waste you in a vain pursuit,
He waits on you himself.
   Judge   Impudent man!
And this before that most illustrious lady
Your treachery has render'd brotherless;
And who with daily prayers —
   Gil   And 't is for this —
That she may hear my vindication
Ev'n from the very lips that made the charge,
And cease an unjust persecution,
Unworthy of her noble name and blood,
That I am here.   For, madam, if I prove
That Don Alonso in fair duel slew
Your brother, and without my treacherous help,
Or any man's, would you pursue us still?
   Leonor   No, sir; for though the laws of duel are
For men alone, I know enough of them
To pardon all that was in honour done,
Ev'n to my cost.   Prove what you say you will,
And Don Alonso may take sanctuary
In my own house against myself and all.
   Gil   'T is nobly said.   On this I take my stand:
And since 't is general and accepted law
That what a witness first shall swear, and then
Forswear, stand for no evidence at all,
Stand forth, Juan Baptista;
Here is your deposition; I will read it
Before the very Judge you swore it to,
And before this great lady, and do you
Substantiate or deny it point by point.
   Judge   Audacity!
   Gil (reading).   In the first place you swear,
That, "As luck fell, you were behind a tree
"When the two gentlemen came out to fight."

Say, is this true?

Bapt.   It is.

Gil   "And that they fought
"Hand to hand fairly, until suddenly
"Gil Perez, rushing from a thicket, sided
"With Don Alonso."   Now, bethink you well;
Is this the truth, Baptista?

Bapt.   Yes.   I swear it.

Gil   Infamous liar!   *(Shoots him with a pistol.)*

Bapt. (falling).   Heav'n have mercy on me!

Gil   My lord, you must another murder add
To my black catalogue.   Come, Manuel,
We must away while we have time.   Farewell.

                              [*Exeunt* GIL *and* MANUEL.

Judge   By the most sacred person of my king,
I swear to punish this audacity,
If it should cost my life.

Bapt.   Oh, listen, lady;
While I have breath to speak.   I'm justly slain.
I tried to swear Gil Perez's life away
To gain his sister; he has told you true:
In fair and open duel, hand to hand,
Was Don Diego slain.   Oh let my death
Atone for this, and my last dying words
Attest it.   *(Dies.)*

Enter the Alguazils with PEDRO

Alg.   We heard a pistol, and returned, my lord, to see.

Judge   It was Gil Perez; that is his work.   *(Pointing to* BAPTISTA.*)*

Ped.   There, said I not the truth?

Judge   He must not escape; after him!   As to this fellow here, who is plainly in his secrets, let two Alguazils keep guard upon him here, lest he do further mischief; the rest come with me.

Ped.   What crime have I committed?   Did I not tell you, my lord, he would come, and did he not come?

Judge   Peace, traitor!   Come, madam.   [*Exeunt.*

SCENE II. *Another Pass in the same Mountain — firing and shouting heard; after which, enter* ISABEL *and* JUANA *on a platform of rock above the stage.*

Isab.   That arquebuss! of which only the thunder
Has reach'd us of perhaps some deadly bolt
On one of those we love!
Why tarry they so long?   What think you, Juana?
   Jua.   Oh what, but share your fears!
   Isab.   Let us descend,
And learn the truth at once; better at once
To die, than by this torture.

   (As they are about to descend, enter to them suddenly
        GIL PEREZ *and* MANUEL.*)*

Gil   Wait!
Isab.   My brother!
Jua.   Manuel!
Gil   They are coming; hide we here;
There is no time —

        Enter Judge, LEONOR, *Alguazils, &c.*

Judge   After them! after them!
By Heav'n, this mountain-top shall be the scaffold
On which the wretch shall expiate his crimes.
Two thousand scudi for the man who brings,
Dead or alive, Gil Perez!
   Gil (appearing above).   By the Lord,
You rate me cheap, my lord; I'll set you higher —
I say four thousand scudi for the Judge,
Alive or stuff'd!
   Judge   There he is!   Fire!   *(Alguazil fires and wounds*
        GIL.*)*
   Gil (falling).   God help me!
   Judge   Yield.
   Gil (struggling).   I've an arm left yet.
   Alg.   He'll fight when dead.
   Judge   Away with him!   *(Judge and Alguazils carry off*
        GIL.*)*
   Man. (struggling with JUANA*).*   Leave hold of me, I say.

Jua.   Oh! Manuel!

Isab.   Oh! my brother!

Man.   Let me go,

Or I will dash you headlong with myself.   (*He rushes down,*
ISABEL *and* JUANA *after him.*)

SCENE III.   *Same as* SCENE I. — PEDRO *discovered
guarded by two Alguazils.*

Ped.   Shots and shouting!   They must be at work.   Perhaps you gentlemen will wait, while I go and see.

Alg.   Be quiet, or two bullets —

Ped.   Oh, one would be enough, thank you.   Well, if I
mustn't go, will you two gentlemen? and leave me to wait for
you?   I'm quite indifferent.

Alg.   We leave you not an instant or an inch.

Ped.   Were ever guards half so polite!   Sure, I must be a
holiday to be so strictly kept.

Alg.   Hark!   They are coming.

Enter Judge and Alguazils with GIL, *a cloak thrown over him*

Judge   Where is the other prisoner?

Alg.   Here, my lord.

Judge   March on with us.

Alg. II   My lord, this man will faint with loss of blood and
weariness.

Judge   Halt then, and let him breathe awhile.

                    (*They uncover* GIL, *and* PEDRO *sees him.*)

Ped.   I might have guessed it!   Let me be in the bilboes,
on the very scaffold, he must be with me: he will die on purpose to lie in the same grave with me, I think!

Gil   Whose voice is that?

Ped.   Nobody's.

Gil   Pedro?   Courage, my poor boy.   My day is over.   Oh,
vanity of mortal strength!

Judge   But who are these?

Enter DONNA LEONOR, *with* ISABEL, JUANA, *and Servants*

Leonor   I, Donna Leonor, who, falling in

With these sad ladies, do repent me much,
That, mis-directed by a lying tongue,
I have pursued this gentleman — I doubt
To death — if not, I charge you from this moment
Leave him at liberty.
  Isab.   Or else —

Enter suddenly MANUEL *and* DON ALONSO, *and Followers*

  Alon.   Or else,
Look to it.
  Gil Don Alonso! whom I thought
Far off upon the seas?
  Alon.   And should have been,
But when my foot was on the very plank
That rock'd upon the foam along the beach,
I, who could never get you from my heart,
And knew that you had come to peril hither,
Could but return once more to him who sav'd
My life, though he had wav'd me from his side.
Enough; I am in time. I tell you, sir,
Give up this man at once. *(To the* JUDGE.)
  Judge   Not for you all!
  Alon. Then at him and his people!

(ALONSO, MANUEL, *and their people rush on the Judge,
  Alguazils, &c., disarm them, and beat them out.*)

  Alon. (embracing GIL). My friend is free.
  Gil And what first use shall make
Of freedom?
  Ped. Why, turn Friar; you can then
Be free and easy too, and leave me so.
Oh, sir, have I not had enough of terror,
Exile, and hunger, to deserve your pardon?
Plead for me, Don Alonso.
  Alon.   Gil —
  Gil   Nay, nay,
What could you seem about to ask of me
But granted ere 't was said? Go. I forgive you.

With which magnanimous forbearance now
Gil Perez, the Gallician, makes his bow.

"Thus ends," says Calderon, "the first part of the *hazañas no-tables* of Luis Perez," whose name I have, for sundry reasons, (and without offence to the hero, I hope,) changed to *Gil*. He was "a notorious robber," says Mr. Ticknor, a kind of Spanish Rob Roy perhaps; at all events, one whose historical reality is intimated by greater distinctness of character than is usual in these plays. Of such gentry examples are never wanting in Spain, where so little alters to this day; witness the career of the famous José Maria, quite lately ended; and who, I read in a book of Travels, was, like Gil, a farmer, for his first calling; a most merciful robber when he took to his second; and who performed Gil's feat of confronting, if not a Judge, a Prime Minister in his own den.

Gil perhaps had better have "played his pranks" (as Fuller says of Robin Hood) in prose; but he was a lawless fellow, and blank verse lay in his way. Those who think his style altogether too heroic for a country robber, will at least find my version more than excused by the original.

THREE JUDGMENTS AT A BLOW

DRAMATIS PERSONÆ

PEDRO IV., *King of Aragon*
DON MENDO TORELLAS, *his Minister*
DONNA VIOLANTE, *Mendo's Daughter*
ELVIRA, *her Maid*
DON LOPE DE URREA
DONNA BLANCA, *his Wife*
DON LOPE, *their Son*
BEATRICE, *their Servant*
DON GUILLEN, *a Friend of Don Lope's*
VICENTE, *Young Lope's Servant*

ROBBERS, OFFICERS, ROYAL SUITE, &C.

ACT I

SCENE I. *A Mountain Pass near Saragossa. Shot within. Then enter* DON MENDO *and* VIOLANTE *pursued by robbers, among whom is* VICENTE.

Men.   VILLAINS, let steel or bullet do their worst,
I'll die ere yield.
Viol.   Heav'n help us!
Robber I   Fool, to strive
Against such odds — upon their own ground too,
Red with the blood of hundreds like yourselves.
Vic.   Come, sir, no more ado;
But quietly give my young madam up,
Nice picking for our captain.
Men.   Not while a drop of blood is in my body.
Robbers   Here's at you then!
Viol.   My father!

(*As the Robbers attack* MENDO, *enter* DON LOPE.)

Lope   How now? whom have you here?
Vic.   Oh, noble captain,
We found this lady resting from the sun
Under the trees, with a small retinue,
Who of course fled.
All but th.. ancient gentleman, who still
Holds out against us.
Lope (to MENDO). What can you expect
Against such numbers?
Men.   Not my life, but death.
You come in time —
Upon my knees I do beseech of you (*kneels*)

No other mercy save of instant death
To *both* of us.
  Lope   Arise! you are the first
Has mov'd me to the mercy you decline.
This lady is — your wife?
  Men.   My only daughter!
  Viol. In spirit as in blood. If by his death
You think to make you masters of my life,
Default of other weapon, with these hands
I'll cease the breath of life, or down these rocks
Dash myself headlong.
  Lope   Lady, calm yourself;
Your beauty has subdued an angry devil
One like yourself first rais'd within my soul.
Your road lies whither, sir?
  Men.   To Saragossa.
Where if I could requite —
  Lope   Your name?
  Men.   Don Mendo
Torellas, after a long embassage
To Paris, Rome, and Naples, summon'd back
By Pedro, king of Aragon — with whom
If 't be (as oft) some youthful petulance,
Calling for justice or revenge at home,
Drives you abroad to these unlawful courses,
I pledge my word —
  Lope   Alas, sir, I might hail
Your offer could I hope that your deserts,
However great, might cancel my account
Of ill-deserving. But indeed my crimes
Have gather'd so in number, and in weight,
And condemnation — committed, some of them,
To stave away the very punishment
They must increase at last; others, again,
In the sheer desperation of forgiveness
That all had heap'd upon me —
  Men.   Nay, nay, nay;
Despair not; trust to my good offices;
In pledge of which here, now, before we part,
I swear to make your pardon the first boon

I'll ask for or accept at the king's hand.
Your name?

Lope   However desperate, and asham'd
To tell it, you shall hear it — and my story.
Retire!   *(To the Robbers, who exeunt.)*
          Don Mendo, I am Lope, son
Of Lope de Urrea, of some desert,
At least in virtue of my blood.

Men.   Indeed!
Urrea and myself were, I assure you,
Intimate friends of old, — another tie,
If wanting one, to bind me to your service.

Lope   I scarce can hope it, sir; if I, his son,
Have so disgrac'd him with my evil ways,
And so impoverisht him with my expenses,
Were you his friend, you scarcely can be mine.
And yet, were I to tell you all, perhaps
I were not all to blame.

Men.   Come, tell me all;
'T is fit that I should hear it.

Viol.   I begin
To breathe again.

Lope   Then listen, sir.   My father in his youth,
As you perhaps may know, but *why* I know not,
Held off from marriage; till, bethinking him,
Or warn'd by others, what a shame it were
So proud a name should die for want of wearer,
In his late years he took to wife a lady
Of blameless reputation, and descent
As noble as his own, but so unequal
In years, that she had scarcely told fifteen
When age his head had whiten'd with such snows
As froze his better judgment.

Men.   Ay, I know
Too well — too well!   *(Aside.)*

Lope   Long she repell'd his suit,
Feeling how ill ill-sorted years agree;
But, at the last, before her father's will
She sacrific'd her own.   Oh sacrifice
That little lacks of slaughter!   So, my father

Averse from wedlock's self, and she from him,
Think what a wedlock this must be, and what
The issue that was like to come of it!
While other sons cement their parents' love,
My birth made but a wider breach in mine.
Just in proportion as my mother lov'd
Her boy, my father hated him — yes, hated,
Even when I was lisping at his knees
That little language charms all fathers' hearts.
Neglecting me himself, as I grew up
He neither taught, nor got me taught, to curb
A violent nature, which by love or lash
May even be corrected in a wolf:
Till, as I grew, and found myself at large,
Spoilt both by mother's love and father's hate,
I took to evil company, gave rein
To every passion as it rose within,
Wine, dice, and women — what a precipice
To build the fabric of a life upon!
Which, when my father
Saw tottering to its fall, he strove to train
The tree that he had suffered to take root
In vice, and grow up crooked — all too late!
Though not revolting to be ruled by him,
I could not rule myself.   And so we liv'd
Both in one house, but wholly apart in soul,
Only alike in being equally
My mother's misery.   Alas, my mother!
My heart is with her still!   Why, think, Don Mendo,
That, would she see me, I must creep at night
Muffled, a tip-toe, like a thief, to her,
Lest he should know of it! why, what a thing
That such a holy face as filial love
Must wear the mask of theft!   But to sum up
The story of my sorrows and my sins
That have made me a criminal, and him
Almost a beggar; —
In the full hey-day of my wilfulness
There liv'd a lady near, in whom methought
Those ancient enemies, wit, modesty,

And beauty, all were reconcil'd; to her,
Casting my coarser pleasures in the rear,
I did devote myself — first with mute signs,
Which by and by began to breathe in sighs,
And by and by in passionate words that love
Toss'd up all shapeless, but all glowing hot,
Up from my burning bosom, and which first
Upon her willing ears fell unreprov'd,
Then on her heart, which by degrees they wore
More than I us'd to say her senseless threshold
Wore by the nightly pressure of my feet.
She heard my story, pitied me
With her sweet eyes; and my unruly passion,
Flusht with the promise of first victory,
Push'd headlong to the last; not knowing, fool!
How in love's world the shadow of disappointment
Exactly dogs the substance of success.
In fine, one night I stole into her house,
Into her chamber; and with every vow
Of marriage on my tongue; as easy then
To utter, as thereafter to forswear,
When in the very jewel I coveted
Very compliance seem'd to make a flaw
That made me careless of it when possess'd.
From day to day I put our marriage off
With false pretence, which she at last suspecting,
Falsely continued seeming to believe,
Till she had got a brother to her side,
(A desperate man then out-law'd, like myself,
For homicide,) who, to avenge her shame,
With other two waylaid me on a night
When as before I unsuspectingly
Crept to her house; and set upon me so,
All three at once, I just had time to parry
Their thrusts, and draw a pistol, which till then
They had not seen, when —
    Voices (within).   Fly!   Away!   Away!

Enter VICENTE

    Lope   What is the matter now?

Vic.   Captain!
Lope   Well, speak.
Vic.   We must be off; the lady's retinue
Who fled have rous'd the soldiery, and with them
Are close upon our heels.   We've not a moment.
     Lope   Then up the mountain!
     Men.   Whither I will see
They shall not follow you; and take my word
I'll not forget my promise.
     Lope   I accept it.
     Men.   Only, before we part, give me some token,
The messenger I send may travel with
Safe through your people's hands.
     Lope (giving a dagger).   This then.
     Men.   A dagger?
An evil-omen'd pass-word.
     Lope   Ah, Don Mendo,
What has a wretched robber got to give
Unless some implement of death!   And see,
The wicked weapon cannot reach your hand,
But it must bite its master's.   *(His hand bleeding.)*
Ill-omen'd as you say!
     Voices (within).   Away!   Away!
     Vic.   They're close upon us!
     Viol.   O quick! begone!   My life hangs on a thread
While yours is in this peril.
     Lope   That alone
Should make me fly to save it.   Farewell, lady.
Farewell, Don Mendo.
     Men. and Viol.   Farewell!
     Lope   What strange things
One sun between his rise and settings brings.   [*Exit.*
     Men.   Let us anticipate, and so detain
The soldiers.   That one turn of Fortune's wheel
Years of half-buried memory should reveal!
     Viol.   Could I believe that crime should ever be
So amiable!   How fancy with us plays,
And with one touch colours our future days!
                                        [*Exeunt severally.*

SCENE II.   *An Audience Hall in the Palace of* PEDRO, *King of Aragon. — Enter* DON LOPE DE URREA *and* DON GUILLEN.

Guil.   Such bosom friends, sir, as from infancy
Your son and I have been, I were asham'd,
You being in such trouble, not to offer
My help and consolation.   Tell me aught
That I can serve you in.
 Urr.   Believe me, sir,
My heart most deeply thanks your courtesy.
When came you to the city?
 Guil.   Yesterday,
From Naples.
 Urr. Naples?
 Guil.   To advance a suit
I have in Aragon.
 Urr.   I too am here
For some such purpose; to beseech the king
A boon I doubt that he will never grant.
 Guil.   Ev'n now his Highness comes.

Enter King PEDRO *and Train*

Urr.   So please your Majesty, listen to one,
Of whom already you have largely heard —
Don Lope de Urrea.
 King   Oh!   Don Lope!
 Urr.   I come not hither to repeat in words
The purport of so many past petitions,
My sorrows now put on a better face
Before your Highness' presence.   I beseech you
To hear me patiently.
 King   Speak, Urrea, speak!
 Urr.   Speak if I can, whose sorrow rising still
Clouds its own utterance.   My liege, my son,
Don Lope, lov'd a lady here; seduc'd her
By no feign'd vows of marriage, but compell'd
By me, who would not listen to a suit
Without my leave contracted, put it off
From day to day, until the lady, tired

Of a delay that argued treachery,
Engag'd her brother in the quarrel; who
With two companions set upon my son
One night to murder him.   The lad, whose mettle
Would never brook affront, nor car'd for odds,
Drew on all three; slew one — a homicide
That nature's common law of self-defence
Permits.   The others fled, and set on him
The officers of justice, one of whom
In his escape he struck —
A self-defence against your laws I own
Not so to be excus'd — then fled himself
Up to the mountains.   I must needs confess
He better had deserv'd an after-pardon
By lawful service in your camp abroad
Than aggravating old offence at home,
By lawless plunder; but your Highness knows
It is an ancient law of honour here
In Aragon, that none of noble blood
In mortal quarrel quit his native ground.
But to return.   The woman, twice aggriev'd,
Her honour and her brother lost at once,
(For him it was my son slew of the three,)
Now seeks to bring her sorrows into port:
And pitying my grey hairs and misery,
Consents to acquit my son on either count,
Providing I supply her wherewithal
To hide her shame within some holy house;
Which, straiten'd as I am, (that, by my troth,
I scarce, my liege, can find my daily bread,)
I have engag'd to do; not only this,
But, in addition to the sum in hand,
A yearly income — which to do, I now
Am crept into my house's poorest rooms,
And, (to such straits may come nobility!)
Have let for hire what should become my rank
And dignity to an old friend, Don Mendo
Torellas, who I hear returns to-day
To Saragossa.   It remains, my liege,
That, being by the plaintiff's self absolv'd,

My son your royal pardon only needs;
Which if not he nor I merit ourselves,
Yet let the merits of a long ancestry,
Who swell your glorious annals with their names
Writ in their blood, plead for us not in vain;
Pity the snows of age that misery
Now thaws in torrents from my eyes; yet more,
Pity a noble lady — my wife — his mother —
Who sits bow'd down with sorrow and disgrace
In her starv'd house.
    King   This is a case, Don Lope,
For my Chief Justice, not for me.
    Urr.   Alas!
How little hope has he who, looking up
To dove-ey'd mercy, sees but in her place
Severely-sworded justice!
    King   Is 't not fit
That the tribunal which arraign'd the crime
Pronounce the pardon also?
    Urr.   Were it so,
I know not where to look for that tribunal,
Or only find it speechless, since the death
Of Don Alfonso.
    King   His successor's name
This day will be announc'd to Aragon.
    Urr.   Yet let a father's tears —
    King   They might indeed
The marble heart of justice make to bleed.
                     [*Exeunt* KING, DON GUILLEN, *and Train.*
    Urr.   And thus to satisfy the exigence
Of public estimation, one is forc'd
To sacrifice entreaty and estate
For an ill son.
Yet had but this petition been inflam'd
With love, that love of his had lit in me,
My prayer had surely prosper'd.   But 't is done,
Fruitless or not: *well* done, for Blanca's sake;
Poor Blanca, though indeed she knows it not,
And scarcely would believe it —
But who comes here? — the friend of better days,

Don Mendo!   I would hide me from his eye,
But, oh indignity, his ancient friend,
Equal in birth and honour to himself,
Must now, reduc'd to 't by a shameless son,
Become his tavern-keeper!   For the present
I may hold back — the King too! come to meet
And do him honour.

Enter, meeting, KING, *with Train, and* DON MENDO

Men.   My royal master, let me at your feet
Now and for ever —
　　King   Rise, Don Mendo, rise,
Chief Justice of all Aragon.
　　Men.   My liege,
How shall I rise with such a weight of honour
And solemnest responsibility,
As you have laid upon my neck!
　　King   'T is long
Since we have met.   How fare you?
　　Men.   How but well,
On whom your royal favour shines so fair!
　　King   Enough.   You must be weary.   For to-day
Go rest yourself, Chief Justice.   And to-morrow
We'll talk together.   I have much to tell,
And much to ask of you.
　　Men.   Your Highness knows
How all my powers are at your sole command,
And only well employ'd in doing it.   [*Exit* KING *with Train.*
　　Urr.   If it be true that true nobility
Slowly forgets what once it has esteem'd,
I think Don Mendo will not turn away
From Lope de Urrea.
　　Men.   My old friend!
I must forget myself, as well as honour,
When I forget the debt I owe your love.
　　Urr.   For old acquaintance then I kiss your hand;
And on two other counts.   First, as your host,
You know, on your arrival; be assur'd
That I shall do my best to entertain you:

And, secondly, congratulating you
On your new dignity, which you hardly don
Before I am your suitor.

    Men.   Oh, Don Lope,
How gladly shall I serve you!

    Urr.   This memorial
I had presented to the king, and he
Referr'd to his Chief Justice.

    Men.   Oh trust to me,
And to my loyal friendship in the cause.

    Urr.   A son of mine, Don Mendo —

    Men.   Nay, no more —
I am appriz'd of all.

    Urr.   I know that men
Think my heart harden'd toward my only son.
It might have been so; not, though, till my son's
Was flint to me.   O Mendo, by his means
My peace of mind, estate, and good repute
Are gone for ever!

    Men.   Nay, be comforted:
I fill a post where friendship well can grant
What friendship fairly asks.   Think from this hour
That all is ended.   Not for your sake only,
But for your son's; to whom (you soon shall hear
The whole strange history) I owe my life,
And sure shall not be slack to save his own.
All will be well.   Come, let us to your house,
Whither, on coming to salute the king,
I sent my daughter forward.

    Urr.   I rejoice
To think how my poor Blanca will rejoice
To do her honour.   You remember Blanca?

    Men.   Remember her indeed, and shall delight
To see her once again.   *(Aside.)*   O lying tongue,
To say so, when the heart beneath would fain
We had not met, or might not meet again!

SCENE III.   *A Room in* URREA's *House. — Enter* BLANCA *and*
VIOLANTE *in travelling dress, meeting.*

    Blan.   How happy am I that so fair a guest

Honours my house by making it her own,
And me her servant!
To welcome and to wait on Violante
I have thus far intruded.

   Viol.   Nay, Donna Blanca,
Mine is the honour and the happiness,
Who, coming thus to Aragon a stranger,
Find such a home and hostess.   Pardon me
That I detain you in this ante-room,
My own not ready yet.

   Blan.   You come indeed
Before your people look'd for you.

   Viol.   But not
Before my wishes, lady, I assure you:
Not minding on the mountains to encounter
Another such a risk.

   Blan.   There was a first then?

   Viol.   So great that I assure you (and too truly) *(aside)*
My heart yet beats with it.

   Blan.   How was 't?

   Viol.   Why, thus:
In wishing to escape the noon-day sun,
That seem'd to make both air and land breathe fire,
I lighted from my litter in a spot
That one might almost think the flowers had chosen
To tourney in, so green and smooth the sward
On which they did oppose their varied crests,
So fortified above with closing leaves,
And all encompass'd by a babbling stream.
There we sat down to rest; when suddenly
A company of robbers broke upon us,
And would have done their worst, had not as suddenly
A young and gallant gentleman, their captain,
Arrested them, and kindly — but how now?
Why weep you, Donna Blanca?

   Blan.   Weeping, yes,
My sorrows with your own — But to your tale.

   Viol.   Nay, why should I pursue it if my trouble
Awake the memory of yours?

   Blan.   Your father,

Saw he this youth, this robber cavalier
Who grac'd disgrace so handsomely?
   Viol.   Indeed
And owes his life and honour to him.
   Blan.   Oh!
He had aton'd for many a foregone crime
By adding that one more!   But I talk wild;
Pardon me, Violante.
I have an anguish ever in my breast
At times will rise, and sting me into madness;
Perhaps you will not wonder when you hear
This robber was my son, my only son,
Whose wicked ways have driv'n him where he is,
From home, and law, and love!
   Viol.   Forgive me, lady,
I mind me now — he told us —
But I was too confus'd and terrified
To heed to names.   Else credit me —

Enter URREA *and* MENDO

   Urr.   Largess! a largess, wife! for bringing you
Joy and good fortune to our house, from which
They have so long been banisht.
   Blan.   Long indeed!
   Urr.   So long, methinks, that coming all at once
They make me lose my manners. (*To* VIOLANTE.)   This
     fair hand
Must, as I think it will, my pardon sign;
Inheriting such faculty.   Oh, Blanca,
I must not let one ignorant moment slip —
You know not half our joy.
Don Mendo, my old friend, and our now guest,
Grac'd at the very threshold by the King
With the Chief-Justiceship of Aragon,
Points his stern office with an act of mercy,
By pardoning your Lope — whom we now
Shall have once more with us, I trust, for ever.
Oh join with me in thanking him!
   Blan.   I am glad,

Don Mendo, that we meet under a roof
Where I can do you honour.   For my son,
I must suppose from what your daughter says,
You would, without our further prayer or thanks,
Have done as you have done.
  Men.   Too true — I know —
And you still better, lady — that, all done,
I am your debtor still.

Enter ELVIRA

  Elv. Madam, your room is ready.
  Viol.   May I then
Retire?
  Blan. If I may wait upon you thither.
  Urr. Nay, nay, 't is I that as a grey-hair'd page
Must do that office.
  Men.   Granted, on condition
That I may do as much for Donna Blanca.
  Viol. As master of the house, I must submit
Without condition.   [*Exeunt* VIOLANTE *and* URREA.
  Blan.   You were going, sir? —
  Men. To wait upon you, Blanca.
  Blan.   Nay, Don Mendo,
Least need of that.
  Men.   Oh, Blanca, Heaven knows
How much I have desir'd to talk with you!
  Blan. And to what purpose, sir? —
No longer in your power — perhaps, nor will —
To do as well as talk.
  Men.   If but to say
How to my heart it goes seeing you still
As sad as when I left you years ago.
  Blan. "As sad? — as when you left me years ago" —
I understand you not — am not aware
I ever saw you till to-day.
  Men.   Ah, Blanca,
Have pity!
  Blan. Nay, Don Mendo, let us cease
A conversation, uselessly begun,

To end in nothing.   If your memory,
Out of some dreamt-of fragments of the past,
Attach to me, the past is dead in time;
Let it be buried in oblivion.
    Men.   Oh, with what courage, Blanca, do you wield
Your ready woman's wit!
    Blan.   I know not why
You should say that.
    Men.   But *I* know.
    Blan.   If 't be so,
Agree with me to say no more of it.
    Men.   But how?
    Blan.   By simple silence.
    Men.   How be silent
Under such pain?
    Blan.   By simple suffering.
    Men.   Oh, Blanca, how learn that?
    Blan.   Of me — and thus.
Beatrice!

Enter BEATRICE

    Beat.   Madam?
    Blan.   Light Don Mendo to
His chamber.   Thus be further trouble sped.
    Men.   Nay, rather coals of fire heap'd on my head!
                                  [*Exeunt severally.*

ACT II

SCENE I. *A Room in* URREA's *House. — Enter* URREA *and* BLANCA *on one side, and* LOPE *and* VICENTE *on the other.*

Lope   THRICE blessed be the day that brings me back
In all humility and love, my father,
To kiss your feet once more.
    Urr.   Rise up, my son,
As welcome to your parents as long lookt for.
Rise and embrace me.
    Lope   Till I have your hand
I scarcely dare.
    Urr.   Then take it, Lope — there —
And may God make thee virtuous as thy father
Can pray for thee.   Thy mother too —
    Lope   O madam,
I scarcely dare with anguish and repentance
Lift up my eyes to those I have made weep
So many bitter tears —
    Blan.   You see, my son,
You keep them weeping still — not bitter tears,
But tears of joy — Oh, welcome home again!
    Vic.   Where is there any room for a poor devil
Who has done penance upon rock and water
This many a day, and much repents him of
His former sins?
    Urr.   What you alive too?
    Vic.   Yes, sir,
This saddle's pad, *(showing* LOPE,) or, if you like, the beast
That bears the saddle — or, by another rule,—

That where the cat jumps also goes her tail.

   Lope (to his father).   You see, sir, in such godly company
I must repent.

   Vic.   Why, devil take 't —

   Urr.   What, swearing?

   Vic.   But some poor relic of our former life
That yet will stick.   Madam, permit me,
If not to kiss your hand, nor ev'n your feet,
At least the happy ground on which they walk.

   Blan.   Rise, rise.   How can I less than welcome one
Who has so loyally stood by my son,
Through evil and through good?

   Vic.   A monument
As one might say, madam, *ad perpetuam
Fidelis Amicitiæ Memoriam.*

Enter BEATRICE

   Beat.   What! is my master home?   Then, by the saints,
Saving your presence, and before your faces,
I must embrace him.

   Lope   Thanks, good Beatrice.

   Urr.   You see how all rejoice to see you, Lope,
But none so more than I; believe 't.   But now
'T is time you wait on Mendo, and acknowledge
The kindness he has done us.   See, Beatrice,
If he be in his room, or busy there.   [*Exit* BEATRICE.
Meanwhile, my son, I crave one patient hearing
To what I have to say.

   Vic.   Now for a lecture.

   Lope   Silence, sir!   Coming here, we must expect
And bear such things.   Pray speak, sir.

   Urr.   You see, Lope,
(And doubtless must have heard of it before,)
In what ill plight we are: my property,
What yet remains of it, embroil'd and hamper'd,
And all so little, that this last expense,
Of getting (as I have) your Estifania,
Who has already cost us all so much,
Into a convent; to do this, I say,

I have been forc'd to let my house for hire
To my old friend; yea, almost, I assure you,
To beg from door to door.   Enough of that.
'T is done; and you are now at last restor'd
To home, and station — wealth I cannot say —
But all is well that ends well.   All I ask,
(And 't is with tears and with a broken voice
I ask it: I would ask it on my knees
If these white hairs forbade not such descent,)
That from this day, in pity to us all —
Perhaps in gratitude — you would repent
Your past excess; yea, surfeited with that,
Would henceforth tame your headlong passions down
Into a quiet current.   Help me, son,
Rebuild the shaken credit of our house,
And show — let us *both* show — that misery
Has taught us not in vain.   Let us be friends
Henceforth; no rivalry of love or hate
Between us; each doing what in him lies
To make what may remain of life to each
Happy and honourable.   On my part
I stake a father's love and tenderness;
And will not you as freely on your side
Wager your filial obedience?
Your father asks, implores you.   Oh, consider
You may not always have a friend in need
To rescue you as now: nay, disappoint
His mercy and again provoke the laws
He now remits, that friend may turn to foe
And sacrifice the life he vainly spar'd.

 Vic.   There only wants, "in sæcula sæculorum,"
To finish off with.

 Lope   Sir, I promise you
Amendment, that shall make the past a foil
To set the future off.

     Enter MENDO

 Men.   I come in time
To vouch fulfilment of so fair a vow.

Lope   Oh, sir —

Men.   I knew you on your road to me;
Your errand too; and thus much have forestall'd
Of needless courtesy.

Lope   Pray God reward you
With such advancement in your prince's love
As envy, the court Hydra, shall not hiss,
But general love and acclamation
Write in gold letters in our history,
For ages and for ages.   Sir, your hand!

Men.   My heart, my heart, you shame me by your thanks,
For service that the veriest churl had paid
For what you did me, Lope.
Why, I'm your debtor still.   But now, enough!
I cannot steal more time from business;
The king expects me.

Urr.   I too must abroad.

Lope   Would I could wait on both — but, as it is,
I think my father's self would waive his right,
In favour of our common benefactor.

Urr.   Indeed, indeed, I do rejoice you should.

                                    [*Exit with* BLANCA.

Men.   And I, not knowing if your choice be right,
Know that I would not lose you for a moment,
So glad your presence makes me.   [*Exit with* LOPE.

Vic.[1]   Beatrice!   Beatrice!

Beat.   Well?

Vic.   Think you not, now that our principals are fairly out
of the way, you owe me a kiss on my arrival?

Beat.   Ay, hot from the oven.

Vic.   Ah Beatrice! if you only knew what heartaches you've
cost me.

Beat.   You indeed, robbing and murdering, and I don't
know what beside, up in the mountains! and then my new
madam that's come with you, Donna Violante; with her fine
Elvira, — I know, sir, when your master was courting his
mistress, you —

Vic.   Now, my own Beatrice, if you could only know what

---

[1] Vicente's flirtation with the two Criadas, and its upshot, is
familiar to English play-goers in the comedy of "The Wonder."

you are talking of as well as I, how little jealousy could such a creature as that give you!

Beat. Well — but why?

Vic. Not a woman at all, neither maid nor mermaid — Why, didn't I catch her with all those fine locks of hers clean off her head?

Beat. Clean off her head!

Vic. The woman's bald.

Beat. Bald?

Vic. As my hand! besides, all that fine white *chevaux-de-frise* that ornaments her gums.

Beat. Well?

Vic. All sham.

Beat. What, my fine madam there false teeth?

Vic. Oh, and half a dozen villainous things I could tell you, did it become a gentleman to tell tales of ladies. But see, here is master coming back.

Beat. Good bye then, for the present, Vicente. False teeth and a wig!   [*Exit.*

Enter DON LOPE

Lope Vicente, have you by any chance seen Violante?

Vic. Not that I know of, sir; she may however have passed without my knowing her.

Lope Vicente still! As if it were possible one who had once seen such beauty could ever forget it.

Vic. Why, sir, if her maid Elvira happened to be by her side —

Lope Fool!

Vic. Pray it is impossible in the system of things that the maid should be handsomer than the mistress?

Lope Oh could I but see her!

Vic. Take care, take care, sir. Beware of raising the old devil — and now we are but just out of the frying-pan —

Lope Beware *you*, sir! I tell you I ill liked my father's lecture; do not you read me another. It were best that no one crossed me, or by heaven! — But who comes here?

Vic. Don Guillen de Azagra.

Enter DON GUILLEN

Lope   What?
Ask what reward you will of me, Vicente.
Don Guillen de Azagra back again!

Guil.   And could not wait a moment, hearing you
Were also back, Don Lope, till I found you,
As well to give you welcome as receive it.

Lope   Our old affection asks for nothing less
On both sides.   Oh, you are welcome!

Guil.   Well can he come, who comes half dead between
Dead hope and quickening passion!

Lope   How is that?

Guil.   Why, you remember how three years ago
I went to Naples — to the wars there?

Lope   Yes,
We parted, I remember, sadly enough
On both sides, in the Plaza del Aseo;
Unconsciously divining the sad days
That were about to dawn on one of us.

Guil.   Nay, upon both.   I am no stranger, Lope,
To your misfortunes; and Heav'n knows I felt them!
But they are over, Heav'n be thankt! mine yet
Are sadly acting.   You can help me now,
If not to conquer, to relieve them.

Lope   Ay,
And will strain every nerve for you.   But first
Must hear your story.

Guil.   Well — I went to Naples,
Where, as you know, our King by force of arms
Was eager to revenge the shameful death
Of Norandino, whom the king of Naples
Had on the scaffold treacherously murder'd.
Of which, and Naples too, I say no more
Than this; that, entering the city,
I saw a lady in whom the universe
Of beauty seem'd to centre; as it might be
The sun's whole light into a single beam,
The heavenly dawn into one drop of dew,
Or the whole breathing spring into one rose.

You will believe I lov'd not without cause,
When you have heard the lady that I speak of
Is —
Vic.   Donna Violante!
Lope   Knave and fool!
Vic.   Why so, sir! only for telling you I saw the lady coming this way; but, I suppose, seeing people here, she has turned back.
Lope   Will you retire awhile, Don Guillen? this lady is my father's guest.
Guil. (aside).   Beside, she might be angry finding me here.
                                                    [*Exit.*
Lope   'Fore Heaven, my mind misgave me it was she he spoke of!
Vic.   Well, you have got the weather-gage.   Tackle her now.

Enter VIOLANTE *and* ELVIRA

Lope   Nay, lady, turn not back.   What you, the sun
I see by, to abridge my little day
By enviously returning to the west
As soon as ris'n, and prematurely drawing
The veil of night over the blush of dawn!
Oh, let me not believe I fright you now,
As yesterday I did, fair Violante,
Arm'd among savage rocks with savage men,
From whose rude company your eyes alone
Have charm'd me, and subdued for the first time
A fierce, unbridled will.
Viol.   It were not strange,
Don Lope, if my bosom trembled still
With that first apparition.   But in truth
I had not hesitated,
Had I not seen, or fancied, at your side
Another stranger.
Lope   Oh, a friend; and one
Who spoke with me of *you;* nay, who retired
Only for fear of drawing new disdain
Upon old love; and left me here indeed,
To speak in his behalf.

Viol.   Alas, Elvira,
Was 't not Don Guillen?
   Elv.   Yes.
   Viol.   Don Lope plead
Another's, and Don Guillen's love!

                                (*She is going.*)

   Lope   At least
Let me attend you to my mother's door.
   Viol. Nay, stay, sir.
   Lope   Stay! and lose my life in losing
This happy opportunity!
   Viol.   Are life
And opportunity the same?
   Lope   So far,
That neither lost ever returns again.
   Viol. If you have aught to tell me, tell it here
Before I go.
   Lope   Only to ask if you
Confess yourself no debtor to a heart
That long has sigh'd for you?
   Viol.   You, sir, are then
Pleading another's cause?
   Lope   I might be shy
To plead in my own person — a reserve
That love oft feels — and pardons.
   Viol.   'T is in vain.
I will not own to an account of sighs
Drawn up against me without my consent;
So tell your friend; and tell him he mistakes
The way to payment making you, of all,
His agent in the cause.
   Lope   Nay, nay, but wait.
   Viol. No more — Adieu!   [*Exit.*
   Lope   She thought I only us'd
Another's suit as cover to my own,
And cunningly my seeming cunning turns
Against myself.   But I will after her;
If Don Guillen come back, tell him, Vicente,
I'll wait upon him straight.   [*Exit.*
   Vic. Madam Elvira!

Elv.   Well, Monsieur Cut-throat?

Vic.   Well, you are not scared at my face now?

Elv.   I don't know that — your face remains as it was.

Vic.   Come, come, my queen, do me a little favour.

Elv.   Well, what is that?

Vic.   Just only die for love of me; I always make a point of never asking impossibilities of any woman.

Elv.   Love is out of the question!   I perhaps might *like* you, did I not know the lengths you go with that monkey Beatrice.

Vic.   With whom?

Elv.   I say with Beatrice.   Bystanders see as much, sir, as players.

Vic.   I with Beatrice!   Lord! lord! if you only knew half what I know, Elvira, you'd not be jealous of her.

Elv.   Why, what do you know of her?

Vic.   A woman who, could she breed at all, would breed foxes and stoats — a tolerable outside, but only, only go near her — Foh! such a breath! beside other peculiarities I don't mention out of respect to the sex.   But this I tell you, one of those sparkling eyes of hers is glass, and her right leg a wooden one.

Elv.   Nonsense!

Vic.   Only you look, and see if she don't limp on one side, and squint on the other.

Don Guillen (entering at one side).   I can wait no longer.

Don Lope (entering at the other).   It is no use; she is shut up with my mother.   Now for Don Guillen.

Elv.   They are back.

Vic.   We'll settle our little matter by and by.

Elv.   Glass eyes and wooden legs!   [*Exit.*

Lope (To DON GUILLEN*).*   Forgive my leaving you so long;
          I have been
Waiting on one who is my father's guest,
The lady Violante.

Guil.   So sweet duty
Needs no excuse.

Lope   Now to pursue your story —

Guil.   Ah — where did I leave off?

Lope   About the truce

Making at Naples, when you saw a lady —

Guil.   Ay, but I must remember one thing, Lope,
Most memorable of all.   The ambassador
Empower'd to treat on our good king's behalf
Was Mendo de Torellas, whose great wisdom
And justice, both grown grey in state affairs,
Well fitted him for such authority;
Which telling you, and telling you beside,
That when the treaty made, and he left Naples,
I left it too, still following in his wake
The track of a fair star who went with him
To Saragossa, to this very house —
Telling you this, I tell you all — tell who
My lady is — his daughter — Violante,
Before whose shrine my life and soul together
Are but poor offerings to consecrate.

Vic. (aside).   A pretty market we have brought our pigs to!
Who'll bet upon the winner?

Lope (aside).   Oh confusion!
But let us drain the cup at once.   Don Guillen,
Your admiration and devotedness
Needed the addition of no name to point
Their object out.   But tell me,
Ere I advise with you, how far your prayer
Is answer'd by your deity?

Guil.   Alas!
Two words will tell —

Lope   And those?

Guil.   Love unreturn'd!
Or worse, return'd with hate.

Vic. (aside).   Come, that looks better.

Guil.   My love for her has now no hope, Don Lope,
But in your love for me.   She is your guest,
And I as such, beside my joy in you,
May catch a ray of her — may win you even
To plead for me in such another strain
As has not yet wearied her ears in vain;
Or might you not ev'n now, as she returns,
Give her a letter from me; lest if first
She see, or hear from others of my coming,

She may condemn my zeal for persecution,
And make it matter of renew'd disdain.
I'll write the letter now, and bring it to you
Ere she be back.   [*Exit.*

   Vic. (*To* LOPE.) Good bye, sir.
   Lope   Whither now,
Vicente?
   Vic. To the mountains — I am sure
You'll soon be after me.
   Lope   I understand —
But stay awhile.
True, I love Violante, and resent
Don Guillen's rivalry: but he's my friend —
Confides to me a passion myself own,
And cannot blame.
Wait we awhile, Vicente, and perhaps
A way will open through the labyrinth
Without our breaking through.
   Vic.   How glad I am
To see you take 't so patiently! Now, sir,
Would you be rul'd —
   Lope   What then?
   Vic.   Why simply, sir,
Forget the lady — but a few days' flame,
And then —
   Lope   Impossible!
   Vic.   What's to be done then?
   Lope I know not — But she comes.

Enter VIOLANTE

   Viol.   Still here, Don Lope!
   Lope Ah, what in nature will its centre leave,
Or, forc'd away, recoils not faster still!
So rivers yearn along their murmuring beds
Until they reach the sea; the pebble thrown
Ever so high, still faster falls to earth;
Wind follows wind, and not a flame struck out
Of heavy wood or flint, but it aspires
Upward at once and to its proper sphere.

Viol.   All good philosophy, I make no doubt
But how apply it here?

Lope   How easily!
Your beauty being that to which my soul
Ever flies fastest, and most slowly leaves.

Viol.   Surely this sudden rapture ill agrees
With what I heard before.

Lope   How, Violante?

Viol.   Have you not haply chang'd parts in the farce,
And ris'n from second character to first?

Lope   My second did not please you — come what will,
Casting feign'd speech and character aside,
I'll e'en speak for myself in my own person.
Listen to me — Don Guillen —

Guil. (listening at the side).   Just a moment
To hear him plead my cause.

Lope   Following your beauty, as a flower the sun,
Has come from Italy to Aragon,
And, as my friend, by me entreats of you
To let him plead his suit.

Guil.   Would I could stay
To hear the noble Lope plead my cause,
But summon'd hence —   [*Exit.*

Viol.   Ill does your second part
Excuse your ill performance of the first;
One failure might be pardon'd, but two such
Are scarce to be excus'd.

Lope   Oh, tell me then
Which chiefly needs apology!

Viol.   I will.
First for your friend Don Guillen; bid him cease
All compliment and courtship, knowing well
How all has been rejected hitherto,
And will hereafter, to the ruthless winds.

Lope   And on the second count — my own?

Viol.   How easily
Out of his answer you may draw your own!

Lope   Alas!

Viol.   For when the judge has to pronounce
Sentence on two defendants, like yourselves,

Whose charge is both alike, and bids the one
Report his condemnation to the other;
'T is plain —

    Lope   That both must suffer?

    Viol.   Nay, if so
The judge had made one sentence serve for both.

    Lope   Great Heavens!

    Guil. (listening at the side).   The man dismissed, I'll hear
       the rest.

    Viol.   Oh, let it be enough to tell you now
The heart that once indeed was adamant,
Resisting all impression — but at last
Ev'n adamant you know —

    Guil.   Oh, she relents!

    Lope   Oh, let me kiss those white hands for those words!

    Guil.   Excellent friend! he could not plead more warmly
Were 't for himself.

    Lope   Oh for some little token
To vouch, when you have vanisht from my eyes,
That all was not a dream!

    Viol. (giving him a rose).   This rose, whose hue
Is of the same that should my cheek imbue!   [*Exit.*

Enter GUILLEN

    Guil.   Oh how twice welcome is my lady's favour,
Sent to me by the hand of such a friend!
How but in such an attitude as this
Dare I receive it? *(Kneels.)*

    Lope   Rise, Don Guillen, rise:
Flowers are but fading favours that a breath
Can change and wither.

    Guil.   What mean you by this?

    Lope   Only that though the flower in my hands
Is fresh from Violante's, I must tell you
It must not pass to yours.

    Guil.   Did I not hear you
Pleading my cause?

    Lope   You might —

    Guil.   And afterwards,

When I came back again, herself confess
That, marble as she had been to my vows,
She now relented tow'rd me!

Lope   If you did,
'T would much disprove the listener's adage.

   Guil.   How?

   Lope   You set your ears to such a lucky tune,
As took in all the words that made for you,
But not the rest that did complete the measure.

   Guil.   But did not Violante, when you urg'd her
In my behalf, say she relented?

Lope   Yes.

   Guil.   To whom then?

Lope   To myself.

Vic.   The cat's unbagg'd!

   Guil.   To you!

Lope   To me.

   Guil.   Don Lope, you must see
That ev'n my friendship for you scarce can stomach
Such words — or credit them.

Lope   Let him beware
Who doubts my words, stomach them as he can.

   Guil.   But 't is a jest:
Bearing my happy fortune in your hands,
You only, as old love has leave to do,
Tantalise ere you give it me.   Enough,
Give me the rose.

Lope   I cannot, being just
Given to me, and for me.

   Guil.   His it is
Whose right it is, and that is mine; and I
Will have it.

Lope   If you can.

   Guil.   Then follow me,
Where (not in your own house) I may chastise
The friendship that must needs have play'd me false
One way or other   [*Exit.*

Lope   Lead the way then, sir.

Enter hurriedly DONNA BLANCA *and* VIOLANTE *from
opposite sides*

Viol. Don Lope, what is this?
Lope   Nothing, Violante.
Viol. I heard your angry voices in my room,
And could not help —
Blan.   And I too.   O my son,
Scarce home with us, and all undone already!
Where are you going?
Lope   No where; nothing; leave me.
Viol. Tell me the quarrel — Oh!   I dread to hear.
Lope What quarrel, lady? let me go — your fears
Deceive you.
Blan.   Lope, not an hour of peace
When you are here!
Lope   Nay, madam, why accuse me,
Before you know the cause?

Enter URREA

Urr.   How now? — disputing?
Blanca and Violante too?   What is it?
Blan. Oh, nothing! (I must keep it from his father.)
Nothing — he quarrell'd with Vicente here,
And would have beat him — and we interposed;
Indeed, no more.
Vic.   The blame is sure to fall
Upon my shoulders.
Urr.   Is 't not very strange,
Your disposition, Lope? never at peace
With others or yourself.
Lope   'T is nothing, sir.
Vic. He quarrell'd with me, sir, about some money
He thought he ought to have, and couldn't find it
In his breeches' pocket.
Urr.   Go, go — get you gone, knave.
Vic. Always fair words from you at any rate. *(Aside.)*
Urr. And for such trifles, Lope, you disturb
My house, affright your mother and her guest
With your mad passion.
Lope   I can only, sir,
Answer such charge by silence, and retire.

Now for Don Guillen.   [*Exit.*

    Blan.   Oh let him not go!

    Urr. Why not? 't is a good riddance. Violante,
You must excuse this most unseemly riot
Close to your chamber. My unruly son,
When his mad passion's rous'd, neither respects
Person or place.

    Viol.   Nay, sir, I pardon him.
And should, for I'm the cause!   (*Aside.*)

    Blan.   Ah, wretched I,
Who, by the very means I would prevent
His going forth, have op'd the door to him.

> (*Noise within of swords, and the voices of* LOPE *and*
> GUILLEN *fighting.*)

    Urr. What noise is that again?

> *Enter* ELVIRA

    Elv.   'T is in the street.

> *Enter* BEATRICE

    Beat. Oh, my young master fighting — run, sir, run!

    Urr. And 't is for this I've sacrific'd myself!

> *Enter, fighting,* LOPE *and* GUILLEN; *Gentlemen and*
> *others trying to part them*

    Urr. (*going between them*). Hold, Lope! Hold, Don
    Guillen!

    Voices   Part them! part them!

    Guil. Traitor!

    Lope   Traitor! — I say that he's the traitor
Whoever —

    Urr.   Madman, will you not forbear
When your grey-headed father holds your sword!

    Lope And in so doing robs me of the honour
I never got from him.

    Urr.   Oh! ruffian!

But if this graceless son respect me not,
His father, my white hairs appeal to you,
Don Guillen.

    Guil.   And shall not appeal in vain —
Out of respect, sir, for your age and name,
And for these gentlemen who interpose,
I shall refer the issue of this quarrel
To other time and place.

    Lope   A good excuse
For fear to hide in.

    Guil.   Fear!

    Urr.   Madman! again!
That the respect his rival shows to me
Should make my son despise him.   By these heav'ns
This staff shall teach you better.

    Lope   Strike me not!
Beware — beware!

    Urr.   Why, art thou not asham'd —

    Lope Yes, of respect for you that's fear of me.

    Guil. Whoever says or thinks what I have done
Is out of fear of you, I say —

    Urr.   He lies!
I'll top your sentence for you.

    Lope   Then take thou
The answer! *(Strikes* URREA, *who falls; confusion.)*

    A voice What have you done?

    Another   Help, help!

    Voices After him, after him! — the parricide!

             (LOPE *rushes out and the people after him.)*

    Guil. I know not how to leave the poor old man —
Come, let me help you, sir.

    Urr.   Parricide!
May outrag'd Heaven that has seen thy crime,
Witness my curse, and crush thee! Every sword
That every pious hand against thee draws,
Caught up by the revenging elements,
Turn thunderbolt, (as every weapon shall
Drawn in God's cause,) and reach thee to the centre!
That sacrilegious hand which thou hast rais'd
Against this snow-white head — how shall it face

Heaven's judgment bar; yea, how can Heav'n now
Behold this deed, nor quench its visual sun,
Veil its pure infinite blue with awful cloud,
And with a terrified eclipse of things
Confound the air you breathe, the light you see,
The ground you walk on!

    Guil.   Pray, sir, compose yourself —
Your cloak — your staff —

    Urr.   My staff! what use is that?
When it is steel that must avenge my wrong?
Yet give it me — fit instrument
Wherewith to chastise a rebellious child —
Ay, and he did not use his sword on me,
Mark that, nor I on him — give me my staff.
Alas, alas! and I with no strength left
To wield it, only as I halt along,
Feeling about with it to find a grave,
And knocking at deaf earth to let me in.[1]

    Guil.   Nay, calm yourself,
The population of the place is up
After the criminal.

    Urr.   And to what purpose?
They cannot wipe away my shame by that.
Call them back rather
To gaze upon a man disgraced
Disgrac'd by him to whom he gave a being.
I say, behold me all — the wretched man

        [1] *Como me podrè vengar*
          Si aquel, que me ha de ayudar
          A sustentarme, me advierte
          Que armado en la tierra dura
          Solo ha de irme aprovechando
          De aldaba, con que ir llamando
          A mi misma sepultura?

      Ne deth, alas! ne will not han my lif.
      Thus walke I like a resteles caitif,
      And on the ground, which is my modres gate,
      I knocke with my staf erlich and late,
      And say to hire, "Leve mother, let me yn."
              CHAUCER's *Pardoner's Tale*

By his own flesh and blood insulted, and
On his own flesh and blood crying Revenge!
Revenge! revenge! revenge!
Not to the heavens only, nor to Him
Who sits in judgment there, do I appeal,
But to the powers of earth.　Give me my hat,
I'll to the king forthwith.
  Vic.   Consider, sir;
You would not enter in the palace gates
So suddenly, and in this plight?
  Urr.   Why not,
Whose voice should leap the glittering walls of Heaven,
And unannounced and uninvited
The palace-doors of God —
King Pedro! king of Aragon!　Christian king!
Whom fools the Cruel call, and Just the wise,
I call on you, King Pedro[1] —
  King (entering with MENDO *and Train.)*　Who calls the
   king?
  Urr.　A wretch who, falling at your feet, implores
Your royal justice.
  King   I remember you;
Don Lope de Urrea, whose son I pardon'd.
What would you of me?
  Urr.   That you would, my king,
Unpardon him you pardon'd; draw on him
The disappointed sword of justice down.
That son — *my* son — if he indeed be mine —
(Oh, Blanca, pure as the first blush of day,
Blush'd not to be so pure,
Pardon me such a word!) has, after all
My pain and sacrifice in his behalf;
Has, in defiance of the laws of man

[1] The Biographie Universelle says it was Don Pedro of *Castile* about whose cognomen there was some difference of opinion; a defence of him being written in 1648 by Count de Roca, ambassador from Spain to Venice, entitled, "El Rey Don Pedro, llamado el Cruel, el Justiciero, y el Necessitado, defendido." It is he, I suppose, figures in the "Medico de su Honra." He flourished at the same time, however, with his namesake of Aragon.

And God, and of that great commandment, which,
Though fifth * on the two tables, yet comes first
After God's jealous honour is secur'd,
Has struck me — struck his father — in a fray
Wherein that father tried to save his life.
I have no vindication; *will* have none,
But at your hands and by your laws; unless,
If you deny me that, I do appeal
Unto the King of kings to do me justice;
Which I will have, that heav'n and earth may know
How a bad son begets a ruthless sire!

King   Mendo!

Men.   My liege.

King   I must again refer
This cause to you.   (*To* URREA.)   Where is your son?

Urr.   Fled! fled!

King (to MENDO).   After him then, use all the powers I own
To bring the wretch to justice.   See me not
Till that be done.

Men.   I'll do my best, my liege.

King   I have it most at heart.   In all the rolls
Of history, I know of no like quarrel:
And the first judgment on it shall be done
By the Fourth Pedro, king of Aragon.   [*Exeunt severally.*

[* *Although the table of Errata says* "for *fifth* read *fourth*," *it
seems obvious that the fifth commandment is the one referred to.*
                                                            Ed.]

ACT III

1st Officer   HERE, my lord, where the Ebro, swollen with her mountain streams, runs swiftest, he will try to escape.
    Men.   Hunt for him then, leaving neither rock nor thicket unexplored.   *(They disperse.)*
Oh, what a fate is mine,
Seeking for that which most I dread to find,
Once thought the curse of jealousy alone!
The iron king will see my face no more
Unless I bring Don Lope to his feet:
Whom, on the other hand, my gratitude
And love would save from justice,
Oh, how —

Enter some, fighting with DON LOPE

    Lope   I know I cannot save my life,
But I will sell it dear.
    Men.   Hold off! the king
Will have him taken, but not slain.   *(Aside.)*   And I,
Can I but save him now, shall find a mean
Hereafter —
Don Lope!
    Lope   I should know that voice; the face
I cannot, blind with fury, dust, and blood.
Or was 't the echo of some inner voice,
Some far off thunder of the memory,

That moves me more than all these fellows' swords!
Is it Don Mendo?

    Men.   Who demands of you
Your sword, and that you yield in the king's name.

    Lope   I yield?

    Men.   Ay, sir, what can you do beside?

    Lope   Slaying be slain.   And yet my heart relents
Before your voice; and now I see your face
My eyes dissolve in tears.   Why, how is this?
What charm is on my sword?

    Men.   'T is but the effect
And countenance of justice that inspires
Involuntary awe in the offender.

    Lope   Not that.   Delinquent as I am, I could,
With no more awe of justice than a mad dog,
Bite right and left among her officers;
But 't is yourself alone: to you alone
Do I submit myself; yield up my sword
Already running with your people's blood,
And at your feet —

    Men.   Rise, Lope.   Heaven knows
How gladly would your judge change place with you
The criminal; far happier to endure
Your peril than my own anxiety.
But do not you despair, however stern
Tow'rds you I carry me before the world.
The king is so enrag'd —

    Lope   What, he has heard!

    Men.   Your father cried for vengeance at his feet.

    Lope   Where is my sword?

    Men.   In vain.   'T is in my hand.

    Lope   Where somehow it affrights me — as before
When giving you my dagger, it turn'd on me
With my own blood.

    Men.   Ho there!
Cover Don Lope's face, and carry him
To prison after me.   *(Aside.)*   Hark, in your ear,
Conduct him swiftly, and with all secrecy,
To my own house — in by the private door,
Without his knowing whither,

And bid my people watch and wait on him.
I'll to the king — Alas, what agony,
I know not what, grows on me more and more!   [*Exeunt.*

SCENE II.   *A Room in the Palace.* — *Enter* KING.

King   Don Mendo comes not back, and must not come,
Till he have done his errand.   I myself
Can have no rest till justice have her due.
A son to strike his father in my realm
Unaw'd, and then unpunisht!
But by great Heav'n the laws shall be aveng'd
So long as I shall reign in Aragon.
Don Mendo!

Enter MENDO

Men.   Let me kiss your Highness' hand.
King   Welcome, thou other Atlas of my realm,
Who shar'st the weight with me.   For I doubt not,
Coming thus readily into my presence,
You bring Don Lope with you.
Men.   Yes, my liege;
Fast prisoner in my house, that none may see
Or talk with him.
King   Among your services
You have not done a better.
The crime is strange, 't is fit the sentence on it
Be memorably just.
Men.   Most true, my liege,
Who I am sure will not be warp'd away
By the side current of a first report,
But on the whole broad stream of evidence
Move to conclusion.   I do *know* this charge
Is not so grave as was at first reported.
King   But is not thus much clear — that a son smote
His father?
Men.   Yes, my liege.
King   And can a charge
Be weightier?
Men.   I confess the naked fact,

But 't is the special cause and circumstance
That give the special colour to the crime.
    King   I shall be glad to have my kingdom freed
From the dishonour of so foul a deed
By any extenuation.
    Men.   Then I think
Your Majesty shall find it here.   'T is thus:
Don Lope, on what ground I do not know,
Fights with Don Guillen — in the midst o' the fray,
Comes old Urrea, at the very point
When Guillen was about to give the lie
To his opponent — which the old man, enrag'd
At such unseemly riot in his house,
Gives for him; calls his son a fouler name
Than gentleman can bear, and in the scuffle
Receives a blow that in his son's blind rage
Was aim'd abroad — in the first heat of passion
Throws himself at your feet, and calls for vengeance,
Which, as I hear, he now repents him of.
He's old and testy — age's common fault —
And, were not this enough to lame swift justice,
There's an old law in Aragon, my liege,
That in our courts father and son shall not
Be heard in evidence against each other;
In which provision I would fain persuade you
Bury this quarrel.
    King   And this seems just to you?
    Men.   It does, my liege.
    King   Then not to me, Don Mendo,
Who will examine, sentence, and record,
Whether in such a scandal to the realm
The son be guilty of impiety,
Or the sire idle to accuse him of 't.
Therefore I charge you have Urrea too
From home to-night, and guarded close alone;
It much imports the business.
    Men.   I will, my liege.
                           [*Exeunt severally.*

Scene III. *A Corridor in* urrea's *House, with three doors in front. — Enter from a side door* violante *and* elvira.

Viol. Ask me no more, Elvira; I cannot answer when my thoughts are all locked up where Lope lies.

Elv. And know you where that is? Nearer than you think; there, in my lord your father's room.

Viol. There! Oh, could I but save him!

Elv. You can at least comfort him.

Viol. Something must be done. Either I will save his life, Elvira, or die with him. Have you the key?

Elv. I have one; my lord has the master-key.

Viol. Yours will do, give it me. I am desperate, Elvira, and in his danger drown my maiden shame; see him I will at least. Do you rest here and give me a warning if a footstep come. *(She enters centre door.)*

Scene IV. *An inner Chamber in* urrea's *House. —* lope *discovered.*

Lope Whither then have they brought me? Ah, Violante, Your beauty costs me dear! And even now
I count the little I have yet to live
Minute by minute, like one last sweet draught,
But for your sake. Nay, 't is not life I care for,
But only Violante.

Viol. (entering unseen). Oh, his face
Is bathed in his own blood; he has been wounded.
Don Lope!

Lope Who is it calls on a name
I thought all tongues had buried in its shame?

Viol. One who yet — pities you.

Lope (turning and seeing her). Am I then dead,
And thou some living spirit come to meet me
Upon the threshold of another world;
Or some dead image that my living brain
Draws from remembrance on the viewless air,
And gives the voice I love to? Oh, being here,

Whatever thou may'st be, torment me not
By vanishing at once.
    Viol.   No spirit, Lope,
And no delusive image of the brain;
But one who, wretched in your wretchedness,
And partner of the crime you suffer for,
All risk of shame and danger cast away,
Has come — but hark! — I may have but a moment —
The door I came by will be left unlockt
To-night, and you must fly.
    Lope   Oh, I have heard
Of a fair flower of such strange quality,
It makes a wound where there was none before,
And heals what wound there was.   Oh, Violante,
You who first made an unscath'd heart to bleed,
Now save a desperate life!
    Viol.   And I have heard
Of two yet stranger flowers that, severally,
Each in its heart a deadly poison holds,
Which, if they join, turns to a sovereign balm.
And so with us, who in our bosoms bear
A passion which destroys us when apart,
But when together —
    Elv. (calling within).   Madam! madam! your father!
    Viol.   Farewell!
    Lope   But you return?
    Viol.   To set you free.
    Lope   That as it may; only return to me.
                      [*Exit* VIOLANTE, *leaving* LOPE.

SCENE V.   *Same as* SCENE III.   ELVIRA *waiting.* — *Enter*
              VIOLANTE *from centre door.*

    Viol.   Quick! lock the door, Elvira, and away with me on
wings.   My father must not find me here.
    Elv.   Nay, you need not be frightened, he has gone to my
lady Blanca's room by the way.
    Viol.   No matter, he must not find me; I would learn too
what is stirring in the business.

Oh would I ever drag my purpose through,
I must be desperate and cautious too.   [*Exit.*

Elv. (*locking the door*).   Well, that's all safe, and now myself to hear what news is stirring.

Vicente (*talking as he enters*).   In the devil's name was
there ever such a clutter made about a blow?   People all up
in arms, and running here and there, and up and down, and
every where, as if the great Tom of Velilla was a ringing.

Elv.   Vicente! what's the matter?

Vic.   Oh, a very great matter, Elvira.   I am very much
put out indeed.

Elv.   What about, and with whom?

Vic.   With all the world, and my two masters, the young
and old one, especially.

Elv.   But about what?

Vic.   With the young one for being so ready with his fists,
and the old one bawling out upon it to heaven and earth, and
then Madam Blanca, she must join in the chorus too; and then
your grand Don Mendo there, with whom seizing's so much in
season, he has seized my master, and my master's father, and
Don Guillen, and clapt them all up in prison.   Then I've a
quarrel with the king!

Elv.   With the king!   You must be drunk, Vicente.

Vic.   I only wish I was.

Elv.   But what has the king done?

Vic.   Why, let me be beaten at least fifty thousand times,
without caring a jot: and now forsooth because an old fellow
gets a little push, his eyes flash axe and gibbet.   Then, Elvira,
I'm very angry with you.

Elv.   And why with me?

Vic.   Because, desperately in love with me as you are, you
never serenade me, nor write me a billet-doux, nor ask me for
a kiss of my fair hand.

Elv.   Have I not told you, sir, I leave that all to Beatrice?

Vic.   And have I not told you, Beatrice may go hang for
me?

Elv.   Oh, Vicente, could I believe you!

Vic.   Come, give me a kiss on credit of it; in case I lie, I'll
pay you back.

Elv.   Well, for this once.

Enter BEATRICE

Beat.   The saints be praised, I've found you at last!

Vic.   Beatrice!

Elv.   Well, what's the matter?

Vic.   You'll soon see.

Beat.   Oh, pray proceed, proceed, good folks. Never mind me: you've business — don't interrupt it — I've seen quite enough, besides being quite indifferent who wears my cast-off shoes.

Elv.   I beg to say, madam, I wear no shoes except my own, and if I *were* reduc'd to other people's, certainly should not choose those that are made for a wooden leg.

Beat.   A wooden leg?   Pray, madam, what has a wooden leg to do with me?

Elv.   Oh, madam, I must refer you to your own feelings.

Beat.   I tell you, madam, these hands should tear your hair up by the roots, if it had roots to tear.

Vic.   Now for her turn.

Elv.   Why, does she mean to insinuate my hair is as false as that left eye of hers?

Beat.   Do you mean to insinuate my left eye is false?

Elv.   Ay; and say it to your teeth.

Beat.   More, madam, than I ever could say to yours, unless, indeed, you've *paid*, madam, for the set you wear.

Elv.   Have you the face to say my teeth are false?

Beat.   Have *you* the face to say my eye's of glass?

Elv.   I'll teach you to say I wear a wig.

Beat.   Would that my leg *were* wood just for the occasion.

Vic.   Ladies, ladies, first consider where we are.

Beat.   Oh ho!   I think I begin to understand.   ⎫

Elv.   Oh, and so methinks do I.   ⎪

Beat.   It is this wretch —   ⎪

Elv.   This knave —   ⎬ *Spoken together.*

Beat.   This rascal —   ⎪

Elv.   This vagabond —   ⎪

Beat.   Has told all these lies.   ⎪

Elv.   Has done all this mischief.   ⎭

(They set upon and pinch him, &c.)

Vic.   Ladies, ladies — Mercy! oh! ladies! just listen!

Elv. Listen indeed! If it were not that I hear people
coming —

Vic. Heaven be praised for it!

Beat. We will defer the execution then — And in the mean
while shall we two sign a treaty of peace?

Elv. My hand to it — Agreed!

Beat.   Adieu!

Elv. Adieu!   [*Exeunt* BEATRICE *and* ELVIRA.

Vic. The devil that seiz'd the swine sure has seiz'd you,
And all your pinches make me tenfold writhe
Because you never gave the king his tithe.   [*Exit.*

SCENE VI. DONNA BLANCA's *Apartment: it is dark. — Enter
the* KING *disguised, and* BLANCA *following him.*

Blan. Who is this man,
That in the gathering dusk enters our house,
Unaskt and muffled thus? what is 't you want?
To croak new evil in my ears? for none
But ravens now come near us — Such a silence
Is not the less ill-omen'd. Beatrice!
A light! my blood runs cold — Answer me, man,
What want you with me?

King   Let us be alone,
And I will tell you.

Blan.   Leave us, Beatrice —
I'll dare the worst — And now reveal yourself.

King   Not till the door be lockt.

Blan.   Help, help!

King   Be still.

Blan.   What would you? and who are you then?

King (discovering himself).   The king.

Blan.   The king!

King   Do you not know me?

Blan.   Yea, my liege,
Now the black cloud has fallen from the sun.
But cannot guess why, at an hour like this,
And thus disguis'd — Oh, let me know at once
Whether in mercy or new wrath you come
To this most wretched house!

King   In neither, Blanca;

But in the execution of the trust
That Heav'n has given to kings.
  Blan.   And how, my liege,
Fall I beneath your royal vigilance?
  King   You soon shall hear: but, Blanca, first take breath,
And still your heart to its accustom'd tune,
For I must have you all yourself to answer
What I must ask of you.   Listen to me.
Your son, in the full eye of God and man,
Has struck his father — who as publicly
Has cried to me for vengeance — such a feud
Coming at length to such unnatural close,
Men 'gin to turn suspicious eyes on you, —
You, Blanca, so mixt up in such a cause
As in the annals of all human crime
Is not recorded.   Men begin to ask
Can these indeed be truly son and sire?
This is the question; and to sift it home,
I am myself come hither to sift you
By my own mouth.   Open your heart to me,
Relying on the honour of a king
That nothing you reveal to me to-night
Shall ever turn against your good repute.
We are alone, none to way-lay the words
That travel from your lips; speak out at once;
Or, by the heavens, Blanca, —
  Blan.   Oh, my liege,
Not in one breath
Turn royal mercy into needless threat;
Though it be true my bosom has so long
This secret kept close prisoner, and hop'd
To have it buried with me in my grave,
Yet if I peril my own name and theirs
By such a silence, I'll not leave to rumour
Another hour's suspicion; but reveal
To you, my liege, yea, and to heav'n and earth,
My most disastrous story.
  King   I attend.
  Blan.   My father, though of lineage high and clear
As the sun's self, was poor; and knowing well
How ill in this world honour fares alone,

Betroth'd the beauty of my earliest years
(The only dowry that I brought with me)
To Lope de Urrea, whose estate
Was to supply the much he miss'd of youth.
We married — like December wed to May,
Or flower of earliest summer set in snow;
Yet heaven witness that I honour'd, ay,
And lov'd him; though with little cause of love,
And ever cold returns; but I went on
Doing my duty toward him, hoping still
To have a son to fill the gaping void
That lay between us — yea, I pray'd for one
So earnestly, that God, who has ordain'd
That we should ask at once for all and nothing
Of Him who best knows what is best for us,
Denied me what I wrongly coveted.
Well, let me turn the leaf on which are written
The troubles of those ill-assorted years,
And to my tale.   I had a younger sister,
Whom to console me in my wretched home,
I took to live with me — of whose fair youth
A gentleman enamour'd — Oh, my liege,
Ask not his name — yet why should I conceal it,
Whose honour may not leave a single chink
For doubt to nestle in?   Sir, 't was Don Mendo,
Your minister; who, when his idle suit
Prosper'd not in my sister's ear, found means,
Feeing one of the household to his purpose,
To get admittance to her room by night;
Where, swearing marriage soon should sanction love,
He went away the victor of an honour
That like a villain he had come to steal;
Then, but a few weeks after, (so men quit
All obligation save of their desire,)
Married another, and growing great at court,
Went on your father's bidding into France
Ambassador, and from that hour to this
Knows not the tragic issue of his crime.
I, who perceiv'd my sister's alter'd looks,
And how in mind and body she far'd ill,
With menace and persuasion wrung from her

The secret I have told you, and of which
She bore within her bosom such a witness
As doubly prey'd upon her life.   Enough;
She was my sister; why reproach her then,
And to no purpose now the deed was done?
Only I wonder'd at mysterious Heav'n,
Which her misfortune made to double mine,
Who had been pining for the very boon
That was her shame and sorrow; till at last,
Out of the tangle of this double grief
I drew a thread to extricate us both,
By giving forth myself about to bear
The child whose birth my sister should conceal.
'T was done — the day came on — I feign'd the pain
She felt, and on my bosom as my own
Cherish'd the crying infant she had borne,
And died in bearing — for even so it was;
I and another matron (who alone
Was partner in the plot)
Assigning other illness for her death.
This is my story, sir — this is the crime,
Of which the guilt being wholly mine, be mine
The punishment; I pleading on my knees
My love both to my husband and my sister
As some excuse.   Pedro of Aragon,
Whom people call the Just, be just to me:
I do not ask for mercy, but for justice,
And that, whatever be my punishment,
It may be told of me, and put on record,
That, howsoever and with what design
I might deceive my husband and the world,
At least I have not sham'd my birth and honour.
    King (apart).   Thus much at least is well; this free con-
        fession
Of this unnatural feud the blackest part
Washes away, although it swell the list
Of knotted doubts that Justice must resolve;
As thus: — Don Lope has revil'd and struck
One whom himself and all the world believe
His father — a belief that I am pledg'd

Not to disprove.   Don Mendo has traduc'd
A noble lady to her death; and Blanca
Contriv'd an ill imposture on her lord:
Two secret and one public misdemeanour,
To which I must adjudge due punishment —
Blanca, enough at present, you have done
Your duty; Fare you well.

Blan.   Heav'n keep your Highness!
Don Mendo (knocking within).   Open the door.
King   Who calls?
Blan.   I know not, sir.
King   Open it, then, but on your life reveal not
That I am here.

                              (KING *hides,* BLANCA *opens the door.*)

Blan.   Who is 't?

                    Enter MENDO

Men.   I, Blanca.
Blan.   Your errand?
Men.   Only, Blanca, to beseech you
Fear not, whatever you may hear or see
Against your son.   His cause is in my hands,
His person in my keeping; being so,
Who shall arraign my dealings with him?
King (coming forth).   I.
Men.   My liege, if you —
King   Enough; give me the key
Of Lope's prison.
Men.   This it is, my liege,
Only —
King   I know enough.   Blanca, retire.
Mendo, abide you here.   To-night shall show
If I be worthy of my name or no.   [*Exit.*
Men.   What is the matter, Blanca?
Blan.   Your misdeeds
And mine, Don Mendo, which just Heaven now
Revenges with one blow on both of us.
After the King! nor leave him till he swear
To spare my Lope, who, I swear to you,

Is not my son, but yours, and my poor Laura's!

Men.   Merciful Heav'ns!   But I will save his life
Come what come may to me.

Blan.   Away, away, then!

                              [*Exeunt severally.*

SCENE VII.   *Same as* SCENE III. — *Enter* VIOLANTE *and*
                 ELVIRA *at a side door.*

Elv.   Consider, madam.

Viol.   No!

Elv.   But think —

Viol.   I tell you it must be done.

Elv.   They will accuse your father.

Viol.   Let them; I tell you it must be done, and *now:* I
ask'd you not for advice, but to obey me.   Unlock the door.

Elv.   Oh how I tremble!   Hark!

Viol.   A moment!   They must not find him passing out —
the attempt and not the deed confounding us.[1]   Listen!

Elv. (listening at a side door).   I can hear nothing distinct,
only a confused murmur of voices.

Viol.   Let me — hush! — Hark! they are approaching!

                    Enter MENDO

Men.   Anguish, oh! anguish!

Viol.   My father!

Men.   Ay, indeed,
And a most wretched one.

Viol.   What is it, sir?
Tell me at once.

Men.   I know not.   Oh, 't is false!
I know too well, and you must know it too.
My daughter, the poor prisoner who lies there
Is my own son, not Blanca's, not Urrea's,
But my own son, your brother, Violante!

Viol.   My brother!

                 [1] *Y se queda su intencion*
                 Sin su efecto discubierta.

Men.   Ay, your brother, my own son,
Whom we must save!
  Viol.   Alas, sir, I was here
On the same errand, ere I knew — but hark!
All's quiet now.   *(A groan within.)*
  Men.   Listen!   What groan was that?
  Viol.   My hand shakes so, I cannot —
  Lope (within).   Mercy, O God!
  Men.   The key, the key! — but hark! they call again
At either door; we must unlock.
(They unlock the side doors. — Enter through one BLANCA *and*
  BEATRICE, *through the other* URREA *and* VICENTE.)
  Urr.   Don Mendo,
The king desires me from your mouth to learn
His sentence on my son.
  Blan.   Oh, Violante!
  Men.   From me! from me! to whom the king as yet
Has not deliver'd it. —
But what is this?   Oh, God!
(The centre door opens and DON LOPE *is discovered, garrotted,*
  with a paper in his hand, and lights at each side.)
  Urr.   A sight to turn
Rancour into remorse.
  Men.   In his cold hand
He holds a scroll, the sentence, it may be,
The king referr'd you to.   Read it, Urrea;
I cannot.   Oh, my son, the chastisement
I only merited has fall'n on both
And doubled the remorse that I alone
Must feel — and stifle.
  Urr. (reading).   "He that reviles and strikes whom he be-
          lieves
His father, let him die for 't; and let those
Who have disgrac'd a noble name, or join'd
An ill imposture, see his doom; and show
Three judgments summ'd up in a single blow."

THE MAYOR OF ZALAMEA

DRAMATIS PERSONÆ

KING PHILIP II
DON LOPE DE FIGUEROA
DON ALVARO DE ATAIDE
PEDRO CRESPO, *a Farmer of Zalamea*
JUAN, *his Son*
ISABEL, *his Daughter*
INES, *his Niece*
DON MENDO, *a poor Hidalgo*
NUÑO, *his Servant*
REBOLLEDO, *a Soldier*
CHISPA, *his Mistress*

A SERGEANT, A NOTARY, SOLDIERS, LABOURERS,
CONSTABLES, ROYAL SUITE, &C.

ACT I

SCENE I. *Country near Zalamea. — Enter* REBOLLEDO, CHISPA, *and Soldiers.*

Reb. CONFOUND, say I, these forced marches from place to place, without halt or bait; what say you, friends?

All Amen!

Reb. To be trailed over the country like a pack of gypsies, after a little scrap of flag upon a pole, eh?

1st Soldier Rebolledo's off!

Reb. And that infernal drum which has at last been good enough to stop a moment stunning us.

2nd Sold. Come, come, Rebolledo, don't storm: we shall soon be at Zalamea.

Reb. And where will be the good of that if I'm dead before I get there? And if not, 't will only be from bad to worse: for if we all reach the place alive, as sure as death up comes Mr. Mayor to persuade the Commissary we had better march on to the next town. At first Mr. Commissary replies very virtuously, "Impossible! the men are fagged to death." But after a little pocket persuasion, then it's all "Gentlemen, I'm very sorry; but orders have come for us to march forward, and immediately" — and away we have to trot, foot weary, dust bedraggled, and starved as we are. Well, I swear if I do get alive to Zalamea to-day, I'll not leave it on this side o' sun-rise for love, lash, or money. It won't be the first time in my life I've given 'em the slip.

1st Sold. Nor the first time a poor fellow has had the slip given him for doing so. And more likely than ever now that Don Lope de Figueroa has taken the command, a fine brave fellow they say, but a devil of a Tartar, who'll have every inch of duty done, or take the change out of his own son, without waiting for trial either.[1]

Reb.   Listen to this now, gentlemen!   By Heaven, I'll be beforehand with him.

2nd Sold.   Come, come, a soldier shouldn't talk so.

Reb.   I tell you it isn't for myself I care so much, as for this poor little thing that follows me.

Chis.   Signor Rebolledo, don't you fret about me; you know I was born with a beard on my heart, if not on my chin, if ever girl was; and your fearing for me is as bad as if I was afeard myself.   Why, when I came along with you I made up my mind to hardship and danger for honour's sake; else if I'd wanted to live in clover, I never should have left the Alderman who kept such a table as all Aldermen don't, I promise you.   Well, what's the odds?   I chose to leave him and follow the drum, and here I am, and if I don't flinch, why should you?

Reb.   'Fore Heaven, you're the crown of womankind!

Soldiers   So she is, so she is, Viva la Chispa!

Reb.   And so she is, and one cheer more for her, hurrah! especially if she'll give us a song to lighten the way.

Chis.   The castanet shall answer for me.

Reb.   I'll join in — and do you, comrades, bear a hand in the chorus.

Soldiers   Fire away!

Chispa sings.

I.

> *Titiri tiri, marching is weary,*
> > *Weary, weary, and long is the way:*
> *Titiri tiri, hither, my deary,*
> > *What meat have you got for the soldier to-day?*
> *"Meat have I none, my merry men,"*
> *Titiri tiri, then kill the old hen.*
> *"Alas and a day! the old hen is dead!"*

[1] Don Lope de Figueroa, who figures also in the *Amar despues de la Muerte,* was (says Mr. Ticknor) "the commander under whom Cervantes served in Italy, and probably in Portugal, when he was in the *Tercio de Flandes,*—the Flanders Regiment,—one of the best bodies of troops in the armies of Philip II.," and the very one now advancing, with perhaps Cervantes in it, to Zalamea.

Then give us a cake from the oven instead.
   Titiri titiri titiri tiri,
Give us a cake from the oven instead.

                          II.

Admiral, admiral, where have you been-a?
   "I've been fighting where the waves roar."
Ensign, ensign, what have you seen-a?
   "Glory and honour and gunshot galore;
Fighting the Moors in column and line,
Poor fellows, they never hurt me or mine —
   Titiri titiri titiri tina" —

1st Sold.   Look, look, comrades — what between singing and grumbling we never noticed yonder church among the trees.

Reb.   Is that Zalamea?

Chis.   Yes, that it is, I know the steeple.   Hurrah! we'll finish the song when we get into quarters, or have another as good; for you know I have 'em of all sorts and sizes.

Reb.   Halt a moment, here's the sergeant.

2nd Sold.   And the captain too.

              Enter Captain and Sergeant

Capt.   Good news, gentlemen, no more marching for to-day at least; we halt at Zalamea till Don Lope joins with the rest of the regiment from Llerena.   So who knows but you may have a several days' rest here?

Reb. and Solds.   Huzzah for our captain!

Capt.   Your quarters are ready, and the Commissary will give every one his billet on marching in.

Chis. (singing).   Now then for

           Titiri tiri, hither, my deary,
           Heat the oven and kill the old hen.

                                    [*Exit with Soldiers.*

Capt.   Well, Mr. Sergeant, have you my billet?

Serg.   Yes, sir.

Capt.   And where am I to put up?

Serg.   With the richest man in Zalamea, a farmer, as proud as Lucifer's heir-apparent.

Capt.   Ah, the old story of an upstart.

Serg.   However, sir, you have the best quarters in the place, including his daughter, who is, they say, the prettiest woman in Zalamea.

Capt.   Pooh! a pretty peasant! splay hands and feet.

Serg.   Shame! shame!

Capt.   Isn't it true, puppy?

Serg.   What would a man on march have better than a pretty country lass to toy with?

Capt.   Well, I never saw one I cared for, even on march. I can't call a woman a woman unless she's clean about the hands and fetlocks, and otherwise well appointed — a lady in short.

Serg.   Well, any one for me who'll let me kiss her.   Come, sir, let us be going, for if you won't be at her, I will.

Capt.   Look, look, yonder!

Serg.   Why, it must be Don Quixote himself with his very Rosinante too, that Miguel Cervantes writes of.

Capt.   And his Sancho at his side.   Well, carry you my kit on before to quarters, and then come and tell me when all's ready.   [*Exeunt.*

Scene II.   *Zalamea, before* crespo's *House.* — *Enter*
don mendo *and* nuño.

Men.   How's the gray horse?

Nuñ.   You may as well call him the *Dun;* so screw'd he can't move a leg.

Men.   Did you have him walk'd gently about?

Nuñ.   Walk'd about! when it's corn he wants, poor devil!

Men.   And the dogs?

Nuñ.   Ah, now, they might do if you'd give them the horse to eat.

Men.   Enough, enough — it has struck three.   My gloves and tooth-pick!

Nuñ.   That sinecure tooth-pick!

Men.   I tell you I would brain any body who insinuated to me I had not dined — and on game too.   But tell me,

Nuño, haven't the soldiers come into Zalamea this afternoon?

Nuñ. Yes, sir.

Men. What a nuisance for the commonalty who have to quarter them!

Nuñ. But worse for those who haven't.

Men. What do you mean, sir?

Nuñ. I mean the squires. Ah, sir; if the soldiers aren't billeted on them, do you know why?

Men. Well, why?

Nuñ. For fear of being starved — which would be a bad job for the king's service.

Men. God rest my father's soul, say I, who left me a pedigree and patent all blazon'd in gold and azure, that exempts me from such impositions.

Nuñ. I wish he'd left you the gold in a more available shape, however.

Men. Though indeed when I come to think of it, I don't know if I owe him any thanks; considering that unless he had consented to beget me an Hidalgo at once, I wouldn't have been born at all, for him or any one.

Nuñ. Humph! Could you have help'd it?

Men. Easily.

Nuñ. How, sir?

Men. You must know that every one that is born is the essence of the food his parents eat —

Nuñ. Oh! Your parents did eat then, sir? You have not inherited *that* of them, at all events.

Men. Which forthwith converts itself into proper flesh and blood — ergo, if my father had been an eater of onions, for instance, he would have begotten me with a strong breath; on which I should have said to him, "Hold, I must come of no such nastiness as that, I promise you."

Nuñ. And now I see the old saying is true.

Men. What is that?

Nuñ. That hunger sharpens wit.

Men. Knave, do you insinuate —

Nuñ. I only know it is now three o'clock, and we have neither of us yet had any thing but our own spittle to chew.

Men. Perhaps so, but there are distinctions of rank. An Hidalgo, sir, has no belly.

Nuñ. Oh Lord! that I were an Hidalgo!

Men. Possibly; servants must learn moderation in all things. But let me hear no more of the matter; we are under Isabel's window.

Nuñ. There again — if you are so devoted an admirer, why on earth, sir, don't you ask her in marriage of her father? by doing which you would kill two birds with one stone: get yourself something to eat, and his grandchildren squires.

Men. Hold your tongue, sir, it is impious. Am I, an Hidalgo with such a pedigree, to demean myself with a plebeian connexion just for money's sake?

Nuñ. Well, I've always heard say a mean father-in-law is best; better stumble on a pebble than run your head against a post. But, however, if you don't mean marriage, sir, what do you mean?

Men. And pray, sir, can't I dispose of her in a convent in case I get tired of her? But go directly, and tell me if you can get a sight of her?

Nuñ. I'm afraid lest her father should get a sight of me.

Men. And what if he do, being my man? Go and do as I bid you.

Nuñ. (after going to look). Come, sir, you owe one meal at least now — she's at the window with her cousin.

Men. Go again, and tell her something about her window being another East, and she a second Sun dawning from it in the afternoon. (ISABEL *and* INES *come to the window.*)

Ines For heaven's sake, cousin, let's stand here and see the soldiers march in.

Isab. Not I, while that man is in the way, Ines; you know how I hate the sight of him.

Ines With all his devotion to you!

Isab. I wish he would spare himself and me the trouble.

Ines I think you are wrong to take it as an affront.

Isab. How would you have me take it?

Ines Why, as a compliment.

Isab. What, when I hate the man?

Men. Ah! 'pon the honour of an Hidalgo, (which is a sacred oath,) I could have sworn that till this moment the sun had not risen. But why should I wonder? when indeed a second Aurora —

Isab. Signor Don Mendo, how often have I told you not to waste your time playing these fool's antics before my window day after day.

Men. If a pretty woman only knew, la! how anger improved its beauty! her complexion needs no other paint than indignation. Go on, go on, lovely one, grow angrier, and lovelier still.

Isab. You shan't have even that consolation; come, Ines.

[*Exit.*

Ines Beware of the portcullis, sir knight.

(*Shuts down the blind in his face.*)

Men. Ines, beauty must be ever victorious, whether advancing or in retreat.

Enter CRESPO

Cres. That I can never go in or out of my house without that squireen haunting it!

Nuñ. Pedro Crespo, sir!

Men. Oh — ah — let us turn another way; 't is an ill-conditioned fellow.

As he turns, enter JUAN

Juan That I never can come home but this ghost of an Hidalgo is there to spoil my appetite.

Nuñ. His son, sir!

Men. He's worse. (*Turning back.*) Oh, Pedro Crespo, good day, Crespo, good man, good day.   [*Exit with* NUÑO.

Cres. Good day indeed; I'll make it bad day one of these days with you, if you don't take care.   But how now, Juanito, my boy?

Juan I was looking for you, sir, but could not find you; where have you been?

Cres.   To the barn, where high and dry,
       The jolly sheaves of corn do lie,
       Which the sun, arch-chemist old,
       Turn'd from black earth into gold,
       And the swinging flail one day
       On the barn-floor shall assay,
       Separating the pure ore

From the drossy chaff away.
This I've been about — And now,
Juanito, what hast thou?

Juan Alas, sir, I can't answer in so good rhyme or reason.
I have been playing at fives, and lost every bout.

Cres. What signifies if you paid?

Juan But I could not, and have come to you for the
money.

Cres. Before I give it you, listen to me.
There are things two
Thou never must do;
Swear to more than thou knowest,
Play for more than thou owest;
And never mind cost,
So credit's not lost.

Juan Good advice, sir, no doubt, that I shall lay by for
its own sake as well as for yours. Meanwhile, I have also
heard say,
Preach not to a beggar till
The beggar's empty hide you fill.

Cres. 'Fore Heaven, thou pay'st me in my own coin.
But —

Enter Sergeant

Serg. Pray, does one Pedro Crespo live hereabout?

Cres. Have you any commands for him, if he does?

Serg. Yes, to tell him of the arrival of Don Alvaro de
Ataide, captain of the troop that has just marcht into Zalamea,
and quartered upon him.

Cres. Say no more; my house and all I have is ever at the
service of the king, and of all who have authority under him.
If you will leave his things here, I will see his room is got
ready directly; and do you tell his Honour that, come when
he will, he shall find me and mine at his service.

Serg. Good — he will be here directly. [*Exit.*

Juan I wonder, father, that, rich as you are, you still submit yourself to these nuisances.

Cres. Why, boy, how could I help them?

Juan You know; by buying a patent of Gentility.

Cres. A patent of Gentility! upon thy life now dost think
there's a soul who doesn't know that I'm no gentleman at all,
but just a plain farmer? What's the use of my buying a patent of Gentility, if I can't buy the gentle blood along with it!
will any one think me a bit more of a gentleman for buying
fifty patents? Not a whit; I should only prove I was worth
so many thousand royals, not that I had gentle blood in my
veins, which can't be bought at any price. If a fellow's been
bald ever so long, and buys him a fine wig, and claps it on,
will his neighbours think it is his own hair a bit the more? No,
they will say, "So-and-so has a fine wig; and, what's more, he
must have paid handsomely for it too." But they know his
bald pate is safe under it all the while. That's all he gets
by it.

Juan Nay, sir, he gets to look younger and handsomer,
and keeps off sun and cold.

Cres. Tut! I'll have none of your wig honour at any
price. My grandfather was a farmer, so was my father, so is
yours, and so shall you be after him. Go, call your sister.

Enter ISABEL *and* INES

Oh here she is. Daughter, our gracious king (whose life
God save these thousand years!) is on his way to be crowned
at Lisbon; thither the troops are marching from all quarters,
and among others that fine veteran Flanders regiment, com-
manded by the famous Don Lope de Figueroa, will march into
Zalamea, and be quartered here to-day; some of the soldiers
in my house. Is it not as well you should be out of the way?

Isab. Sir, 't was upon this very errand I came to you,
knowing what nonsense I shall have to hear if I stay below.
My cousin and I can go up to the garret, and there keep so
close, the very sun shall not know of our whereabout.

Cres. That's my good girl. Juanito, you wait here to receive them in case they come while I am out looking after
their entertainment.

Isab. Come, Ines.

Ines Very well —
Though I've heard in a song what folly 't would be
To try keep in a loft what won't keep on the tree.   [*Exeunt.*

Enter Captain and Sergeant

Serg. This is the house, sir.

Capt. Is my kit come?

Serg. Yes, sir, and (*aside*) I'll be the first to take an inventory of the pretty daughter. [*Exit.*

Juan Welcome, sir, to our house; we count it a great honour to have such a cavalier as yourself for a guest, I assure you. (*Aside.*) What a fine fellow! what an air! I long to try the uniform, somehow.

Capt. Thank you, my lad.

Juan You must forgive our poor house, which we devoutly wish was a palace for your sake. My father is gone after your supper, sir; may I go and see that your chamber is got ready for you?

Capt. Thank you, thank you.

Juan Your servant, sir. [*Exit.*

Enter Sergeant

Capt. Well, sergeant, where's the Dulcinea you told me of?

Serg. Deuce take me, sir, if I haven't been looking every where in parlour, bed-room, kitchen, and scullery, up-stairs and down-stairs, and can't find her out.

Capt. Oh, no doubt the old fellow has hid her away for fear of us.

Serg. Yes, I ask'd a serving wench, and she confess'd her master had lock'd the girl up in the attic, with strict orders not even to look out so long as we were in the place.

Capt. Ah! these clodpoles are all so jealous of the service. And what is the upshot? Why, I, who didn't care|a pin to see her before, shall never rest till I get at her now.

Serg. But how, without a blow-up?

Capt. Let me see; how shall we manage it?

Serg. The more difficult the enterprise, the more glory in success, you know, in love as in war.

Capt. I have it!

Serg. Well, sir?

Capt. You shall pretend — but no, here comes one will serve my turn better.

Enter REBOLLEDO *and* CHISPA

Reb. (to CHISPA). There he is; now if I can get him into a good humour —

Chis. Speak up then, like a man.

Reb. I wish I'd some of your courage; but don't you leave me while I tackle him. Please your Honour —

Capt. (to Sergeant). I tell you I've my eye on Rebolledo to do him a good turn; I like his spirit.

Serg. Ah, he's one of a thousand.

Reb. (aside). Here's luck! Please your Honour —

Capt. Oh, Rebolledo — Well, Rebolledo, what is it?

Reb. You may know I am a gentleman who has, by ill luck, lost all his estate; all that ever I had, have, shall have, may have, or can have, through all the conjugations of the verb *"to have."* And I want your Honour —

Capt. Well?

Reb. To desire the ensign to appoint me roulette-master to the regiment, so I may pay my liabilities like a man of honour.

Capt. Quite right, quite right; I will see it done.

Chis. Oh, brave captain! Oh, if I only live to hear them all call me Madam Roulette!

Reb. Shall I go at once and tell him?

Capt. Wait. I want you first to help me in a little plan I have.

Reb. Out with it, noble captain. Slow said slow sped, you know.

Capt. You are a good fellow; listen. I want to get into that attic there, for a particular purpose.

Reb. And why doesn't your Honour go up at once?

Capt. I don't like to do it in a strange house without an excuse. Now look here; you and I will pretend to quarrel; I can get angry and draw my sword, and you run away up stairs, and I after you, to the attic, that's all; I'll manage the rest.

Chis. Ah, we get on famously.

Reb. I understand. When are we to begin?

Capt. Now directly.

Reb. Very good. *(In a loud voice.)* This is the reward of my services — a rascal, a pitiful scoundrel, is preferred, when a man of honour — a man who has seen service —

Chis.   Halloa!   Rebolledo up!   All is not so well.

Reb.   Who has led you to victory —

Capt.   This language to me, sir?

Reb.   Yes, to you, who have so grossly insulted and defrauded —

Capt.   Silence! and think yourself lucky if I take no further notice of your insolence.

Reb.   If I restrain myself, it is only because you are my captain, and as such — but, 'fore God, if my cane were in my hand —

Chis. (advancing).   Hold!   Hold!

Capt.   I'll show you, sir, how to talk to me in this way.

(Draws his sword.)

Reb.   It is before your commission, not you, I retreat.

Capt.   That shan't save you, rascal!

(Pursues REBOLLEDO out.)

Chis.   Oh, I shan't be Madam Roulette after all. Murder! murder!   [*Exit calling.*

SCENE III.   ISABEL's *Garret.* — ISABEL *and* INES.

Isab.   What noise is that on the stairs?

Enter REBOLLEDO

Reb.   Sanctuary!   Sanctuary!

Isab.   Who are you, sir?

Enter Captain

Capt.   Where is the rascal?

Isab.   A moment, sir!   This poor man has flown to our feet for protection; I appeal to you for it; and no man, and least of all an officer, will refuse that to any woman.

Capt.   I swear no other arm than that of beauty, and beauty such as yours, could have withheld me.   (*To* REBOLLEDO.)   You may thank the deity that has saved you, rascal.

Isab.   And I thank you, sir.

Capt.   And yet ungratefully slay me with your eyes in return for sparing him with my sword.

Isab. Oh, sir, do not mar the grace of a good deed by poor compliment, and so make me less mindful of the real thanks I owe you.

Capt. Wit and modesty kiss each other, as well they may, in that lovely face. *(Kneels.)*

Isab. Heavens! my father!

Enter CRESPO *and* JUAN *with swords*

Cres. How is this, sir? I am alarmed by cries of murder in my house — am told you have pursued a poor man up to my daughter's room; and, when I get here expecting to find you killing a man, I find you courting a woman.

Capt. We are all born subjects to some dominion — soldiers especially to beauty. My sword, though justly rais'd against this man, as justly fell at this lady's bidding.

Cres. No lady, sir, if you please; but a plain peasant girl — my daughter.

Juan (aside). All a trick to get at her. My blood boils. *(Aloud to Captain.)* I think, sir, you might have seen enough of my father's desire to serve you to prevent your requiting him by such an affront as this.

Cres. And, pray, who bid thee meddle, boy? Affront! what affront? The soldier affronted his captain; and if the captain has spared him for thy sister's sake, pray what hast thou to say against it?

Capt. I think, young man, you had best consider before you impute ill intention to an officer.

Juan I know what I know.

Cres. What! you will go on, will you?

Capt. It is out of regard for you I do not chastise him.

Cres. Wait a bit; if that were wanting, 't would be from his father, not from you.

Juan And, what's more, I wouldn't endure it from any one but my father.

Capt. You would not?

Juan No! death rather than such dishonour!

Capt. What, pray, is a clodpole's idea of honour?

Juan The same as a captain's — no clodpole no captain, I can tell you.

Capt. 'Fore Heaven, I must punish this insolence.

(About to strike him.)

Cres. You must do it through me, then.

Reb. Eyes right! — Don Lope!

Capt. Don Lope!

Enter DON LOPE

Lope How now? A riot the very first thing I find on joining the regiment? What is it all about?

Capt. (aside). Awkward enough!

Cres. (aside). By the lord, the boy would have held his own with the best of 'em.

Lope Well! No one answer me? 'Fore God, I'll pitch the whole house, men, women, and children, out of windows, if you don't tell me at once. Here have I had to trail up your accursed stairs, and then no one will tell me what for.

Cres. Nothing, nothing at all, sir.

Lope Nothing? that would be the worst excuse of all, but swords aren't drawn for nothing; come, the truth?

Capt. Well, the simple fact is this, Don Lope: I am quartered upon this house; and one of my soldiers —

Lope Well, sir, go on.

Capt. Insulted me so grossly I was obliged to draw my sword on him. He ran up here where it seems these two girls live; and I, not knowing there was any harm, after him; at which these men, their father or brother, or some such thing, take affront. This is the whole business.

Lope I am just come in time then to settle it. First, who is the soldier that began it with an act of insubordination?

Reb. What, am I to pay the piper?

Isab. (pointing to REB.) This, sir, was the man who ran up first.

Lope This? handcuff him!

Reb. Me! my lord?

Capt. (aside to REB.) Don't blab, I'll bear you harmless.

Reb. Oh, I dare say, after being marcht off with my hands behind me like a coward. Noble commander, 't was the captain's own doing; he made me pretend a quarrel, that he might get up here to see the women.

Capt. I *had* some cause for quarrel, you see.

Lope Not enough to peril the peace of the town for. Halloa there! beat all to quarters on pain of death. And, to prevent further ill blood here, do you *(to the Captain)* quarter yourself elsewhere till we march. I'll stop here.

Capt. I shall of course obey you, sir.

Cres. (to ISABEL). Get you in. *(Exeunt* ISAB. *and* INES.) I really ought to thank you heartily for coming just as you did, sir; else, I'd done for myself.

Lope How so?

Cres. I should have killed this popinjay.

Lope What, sir, a captain in his Majesty's service?

Cres. Ay, a general, if he insulted me.

Lope I tell you, whoever lays his little finger on the humblest private in the regiment, I'll hang him.

Cres. And I tell you, whoever points his little finger at my honour, I'll cut him down before hanging.

Lope Know you not, you are bound by your allegiance to submit?

Cres. To all cost of property, yes; but of honour, no, no, no! My goods and chattels, ay, and my life — are the king's; but my honour is my own soul's, and that is — God Almighty's!

Lope 'Fore God, there's some truth in what you say.

Cres. 'Fore God, there ought to be, for I've been some years saying it.

Lope Well, well. I've come a long way, and this leg of mine (which I wish the devil who gave it would carry away with him!) cries for rest.

Cres. And who prevents its taking some? the same devil I suppose who gave you your leg, gave me a bed (which I don't want him to take away again, however) on which your leg may lie if it like.

Lope But did the devil, when he was about it, make your bed as well as give it?

Cres. To be sure he did.

Lope Then I'll unmake it — Heaven knows I'm weary enough.

Cres. Heaven rest you then.

Lope (aside). Devil or saint alike he echoes me.

Cres. (aside). I and Don Lope never shall agree.

ACT II

Scene I. *In Zalamea. — Enter* DON MENDO *and* NUÑO.

Men. WHO told you all this?

Nuñ. Ginesa, her wench.

Men. That, whether that riot in the house were by accident or design, the captain has ended by being really in love with Isabel?

Nuñ. So as he has as little of comfort in his quarters as we of eatable in ours — ever under her window, sending her messages and tokens by a nasty little soldier of his.

Men. Enough, enough of your poisoned news.

Nuñ. Especially on an empty stomach.

Men. Be serious, Nuño. And how does Isabel answer him?

Nuñ. As she does you. Bless you, she's meat for your masters.

Men. Rascal! This to me! *(Strikes him.)*

Nuñ. There! two of my teeth you've knockt out, I believe: to be sure they weren't of much use in your service.

Men. By Heaven, I'll do so to that captain, if —

Nuñ. Take care, he's coming, sir.

Men. *(aside to* NUÑO*).* This duel shall be *now* — though night be advancing on — before discretion come to counsel milder means. Come, and help me arm.

Nuñ. Lord bless me, sir, what arms have you got except the coat over the door?

Men. In my armoury I doubt not are some pieces of my ancestors that will fit their descendant. [*Exeunt.*

Enter Captain, Sergeant, and REBOLLEDO

Capt. I tell you my love is not a fancy; but a passion, a tempest, a volcano.

Serg. What a pity it is you ever set eyes on the girl!

Capt. What answer did the servant give you?

Serg. Nay, sir, I have told you.

Capt. That a country wench should stand upon her virtue as if she were a lady!

Serg. This sort of girls, captain, don't understand gentlemen's ways. If a strapping lout in their own line of life courted them in their own way, they'd hear and answer quick enough. Besides, you really expect too much, that a decent woman should listen after one day's courtship to a lover who is perhaps to leave her to-morrow.

Capt. And to-day's sun-setting!

Serg. Your own love too, but from one glance —

Capt. Is not one spark enough for gunpowder?

Serg. You too, who would have it no country girl could be worth a day's courtship!

Capt. Alas, 't was that was my ruin — running unawares upon a rock. I thought only to see a splay-footed gawky, and found a goddess. Ah, Rebolledo, could you but get me one more sight of her?

Reb. Well, captain, you have done me one good turn, and though you had like to run me into danger, I don't mind venturing again for you.

Capt. But how? how?

Reb. Well, now, look here. We've a man in the regiment with a fair voice, and my little Chispa — no one like her for a flash song. Let's serenade at the girl's window; she must, in courtesy or curiosity, look out; and then —

Capt. But Don Lope is there, and we mustn't wake him.

Reb. Don Lope? When does he ever get asleep with that leg of his, poor fellow? Besides, you can mix along with us in disguise, so as at least *you* won't come into question.

Capt. Well, there is but this chance, if it be but a faint one; for if we should march to-morrow! — come, let us set about it; it being, as you say, between ourselves that I have anything to do with it. [*Exeunt Captain and Sergeant.*

Enter CHISPA

Chis. He's got it, at any rate.

Reb. What's the matter now, Chispa?

Chis. Oh, I mark'd his face for him.

Reb. What, a row?

Chis. A fellow there who began to ask questions as to my fair play at roulette — when I was all as fair as day too — I answered him with this. *(Showing a knife.)* Well, he's gone to the barber's to get it dressed.

Reb. You still stand kicking when I want to get to the fair. I wanted you with your castanets, not your knife.

Chis. Pooh! one's as handy as the other.   What's up now?

Reb. Come with me to quarters; I'll tell you as we go along.   [*Exeunt.*

SCENE II. *A trellis of vines in* CRESPO's *garden. — Enter* CRESPO *and* DON LOPE.

Cres. Lay the table here. *(To* LOPE.) You'll relish your supper here in the cool, sir.   These hot August days at least bring their cool nights by way of excuse.

Lope A mighty pleasant parlour this!

Cres. Oh, a little strip my daughter amuses herself with; sit down, sir.   In place of the fine voices and instruments you are us'd to, you must put up with only the breeze playing on the vine leaves in concert with the little fountain yonder. Even the birds (our only musicians) are gone to bed, and wouldn't sing any the more if I were to wake them.   Come, sit down, sir, and try to ease that poor leg of yours.

Lope I wish to heaven I could.

Cres. Amen!

Lope Well, I can at least bear it.   Sit down, Crespo.

Cres. Thank you, sir. *(Hesitating.)*

Lope Sit down, sit down, pray.

Cres. Since you bid me then, you must excuse my ill manners. *(Sits.)*

Lope Humph — Do you know, I am thinking, Crespo, that yesterday's riot rather overset your good ones?

Cres. Ay?

Lope Why how else is it that you, whom I can scarce get

to sit down at all to-day, yesterday plump'd yourself down at once, and in the big chair too?

Cres.   Simply because yesterday you *didn't* ask me. To-day you are courteous, and I am shy.

Lope   Yesterday you were all thistle and hedgehog; to-day as soft as silk.

Cres.   It is only because you yourself were so.   I always answer in the key I'm spoken to; yesterday you were all out of tune, and so was I.   It is my principle to swear with the swearer, and pray with the saint; all things to all men.   So much so as I declare to you your bad leg kept me awake all night.   And, by the by, I wish, now we are about it, you would tell me which of your legs it is that ails you: for, not knowing, I was obliged to make sure by swearing at both of mine: and one at a time is quite enough.

Lope   Well, Pedro, you will perhaps think I have some reason for my tetchiness, when I tell you that for thirty years during which I have served in the Flemish wars through summer's sun, and winter's frost, and enemy's bullets, I have never known what it is to be an hour without pain.

Cres.   God give you patience to bear it!

Lope   Pish! can't I give it myself?

Cres.   Well, let him leave you alone then!

Lope   Devil take patience!

Cres.   Ah, let him! he wants it; only it's too good a job for him.

Enter JUAN *with table, &c.*

Juan   Supper, sir.

Lope   But what are my people about, not to see to all this?

Cres.   Pardon my having been so bold to tell them I and my family would wait upon you, so, I hope, you shall want for nothing.

Lope   On one condition then, that as you have no fear of your company now, your daughter may join us at supper.

Cres.   Juan, bid your sister come directly.   [*Exit* JUAN.

Lope   My poor health may quiet all suspicion on that score, I think.

Cres.   Sir, if you were as lusty as I wish you, I should have no fear.   I bid my daughter keep above while the regiment was here because of the nonsense soldiers usually talk to girls. If all were gentlemen like you, I should be the first to make her wait on them.

Lope (aside).   The cautious old fellow!

Enter JUAN, ISABEL, *and* INES

Isab. (to CRESPO*).*   Your pleasure, sir.

Cres.   It is Don Lope's, who honours you by bidding you to sup with him.

Lope (aside).   What a fair creature!   Nay, 't is I that honour myself by the invitation.

Isab.   Let me wait upon you.

Lope   Indeed no, unless waiting upon me mean supping with me.

Cres.   Sit down, sit down, girl, as Don Lope desires you.

[*They sit at table.   Guitar heard within.*

Lope   Music too!

Cres.   None of ours.   It must be some of your soldiers, Don Lope.

Lope   Ah, Crespo, the troubles and dangers of war must have a little to sweeten them betimes.   The uniform sits very tight, and must be let out every now and then.

Juan   Yet 't is a fine life, sir.

Lope   Do you think you would like to follow it?

Juan   If I might at your Excellency's side.

SONG *(within).*

Ah for the red spring rose,
Down in the garden growing,
Fading as fast as it blows,
Who shall arrest its going?
Peep from thy window and tell,
Fairest of flowers, Isabel.

Lope (aside).   Pebbles thrown up at the window too!   But I'll say nothing, for all sakes.   *(Aloud.)*   What foolery!

Cres.   Boys!   Boys!   *(Aside.)*   To call her very name too! If it weren't for Don Lope —

Juan (going).   I'll teach them —

Cres.   Halloa, lad, whither away?
Juan   To see for a dish —
Cres.   They'll see after that.   Sit still where thou art.

SONG *(within).*

Wither it would, but the bee
Over the blossom hovers,
And the sweet life ere it flee
With as sweet art recovers,
Sweetest at night in his cell,
Fairest of flowers, Isabel.

Isab. (aside).   How have I deserved this?
Lope (knocking over his chair).   This is not to be borne!
Cres. (upsetting the table).   No more it is!
Lope   I meant my leg.
Cres.   And I mine.
Lope   I can eat no more, and will to bed.
Cres.   Very good; so will I.
Lope   Good night, good night, to you all.
All   Good night, sir.
Lope (aside).   I'll see to them.   [*Exit.*
Cres. (aside).   I'll shut the girls up, and then look after 'em.   *(Aloud.)* Come, to bed. *(To* JUAN.) Halloa, lad, again!   This is the way to thy room, is it not?

                                        [*Exeunt severally.*

SCENE III.   *Outside* CRESPO'S *House. — The Captain, Sergeant,* REBOLLEDO, CHISPA, &c., *with guitars. — At one corner,* MENDO *in old armour, with* NUÑO, *observing them. — It is dark.*

Men. (aside to NUÑO).   You see this?
Nuñ.   And hear it.
Men.   I am bloodily minded to charge into them at once, and disperse them into chaos; but I will see if she is guilty of answering them by a sign.
Capt.   No glance from the window yet!
Reb.   Who'd stir for a sentimental love song?   Come, Chispa, you can give us one that would make her look out of the grave.

Chis.   Here am I on my pedestal.   Now for it.

(She sings.)

> *There once was a certain Sampayo*
>   *Of Andalusia the fair;*
> *A Major he was in the service,*
>   *And a very fine coat did he wear.*
> *And one night, as to-night it might happen,*
>   *That as he was going his round,*
> *With the Garlo half drunk in a tavern —*

Reb.   Asonante to "happen," you know.
Chis.   Don't put me out, Rebolledo — *(Sings.)*

> *With the Garlo half drunk in a tavern*
> *His lovely Chillona he found.*

CHORUS

> *With the Garlo half drunk in a tavern*
> *His lovely Chillona he found.*

SECOND STANZA

> *Now this Garlo, as chronicles tell us,*
>   *Although rather giv'n to strong drinks,*
> *Was one of those terrible fellows*
>   *Is down on a man ere he winks.*
> *And so while the Major all weeping*
>   *Upbraided his lady unkind,*
> *The Garlo behind him came creeping*
>   *And laid on the Major behind.*

CHORUS

> *The Garlo, &c.*

(During Chorus, DON LOPE *and* CRESPO *have entered at different sides with swords, and begin to lay about them.)*

Cres.   What something in this way, perhaps! ⎫
Lope   After this fashion, may be!   ⎬ *Together.*
                                      ⎭

(The Soldiers are driven off.)

Lope   Well, we're quit of them, except one.   But I'll soon settle him.

Cres.   One still hanging about.   Off with you!

Lope   Off with *you*, rascal!   *(They fight).*   By Heaven, he fights well!

Cres.   By Heaven, a handy chap at his tool!

Enter JUAN with sword and torch

Juan   Where is Don Lope?

Lope   Crespo!

Cres.   Don Lope!

Lope   To be sure, didn't you say you were going to bed?

Cres.   And didn't you?

Lope   This was my quarrel, not yours.

Cres.   Very well, and I come out to help you in it.

Re-enter Captain and Soldiers with swords

1st Sold.   We'll soon settle them.

Capt.   Don Lope!

Lope   Yes, Don Lope.   What is all this, sir?

Capt.   The soldiers were singing and playing in the street, sir, doing no offence to any one, but were set upon by some of the town's people, and I came to stop the riot.

Lope   You have done well, Don Alvaro, I know your prudence; however, as there is a grudge on both sides, I shall not visit the town's people this time with further severity; but, for the sake of all parties, order the regiment to march from Zalamea to-morrow — nay, to-day, for it is now dawn.   See to it, sir: and let me hear of no such disgraceful riots hereafter.

Capt.   I shall obey your orders, sir.

[Exit with Soldiers, &c.

Cres. (aside).   Don Lope is a fine fellow; we shall cog together after all.

Lope (to CRESPO *and* JUAN).   You two keep with me, and don't be found alone.   [*Exeunt.*

Re-enter MENDO, and NUÑO wounded

Men.   'T is only a scratch.

Nuñ. A scratch? Well, I could well have spared that.

Men. Ah, what is it compared to the wound in my heart!

Nuñ. I would gladly exchange for all that.

Men. Well, he did lay upon your head handsomely, didn't he?

Nuñ. Ah, and on my tail too; while you, under that great shield of yours, — *(Drum.)*

Men. Hark! what's that?

Nuñ. The soldiers' reveillee. I heard say they were to leave Zalamea to-day.

Men. I am glad of it, since they'll carry that detestable captain off with them at all events.   [*Exeunt.*

SCENE IV.   *Outside Zalamea. — Enter Captain, Sergeant,*
REBOLLEDO, *and* CHISPA.

Capt. March you on, Sergeant, with the troop. I shall lie here till sun-down, and then steal back to Zalamea for one last chance.

Serg. If you are resolved on this, sir, you had better do it well attended, for these bumpkins are dangerous, once affronted.

Reb. Where, however, (and you ought to tip me for my news,) you have one worst enemy the less.

Capt. Who's that?

Reb. Isabel's brother. Don Lope and the lad took a fancy to each other and have persuaded the old father to let him go for a soldier; and I have only just met him as proud as a peacock, with all the sinew of the swain and the spirit of the soldier already about him.

Capt. All works well; there is now only the old father at home, who can easily be disposed of. It only needs that he who brought me this good news help me to use it.

Reb. Me do you mean, sir? So I will, to the best of my power.

Capt. Good; you shall go with me.

Serge. But if Don Lope should happen on you?

Capt. He is himself obliged to set off to Guadalupe this evening, as the king is already on the road. This I heard from himself when I went to take his orders. Come with me,

Sergeant, and settle about the troops marching, and then for
my own campaign.   [*Exeunt Captain and Sergeant.*

Chis.   And what am I to do, Rebolledo, meanwhile? I
shan't be safe alone with that fellow whose face I sent to be
stitcht by the barber.

Reb.   Ah, how to manage about that?   You wouldn't dare
go with us?

Chis.   Not in petticoats; but in the clothes of that runaway
stable boy?   I can step into them free of expense.

Reb.   That's a brave girl.

Chis. (singing).

> And now who shall say
> The love of a soldier's wife lasts but a day?

                                                        [*Exeunt.*

SCENE V.   CRESPO's *Garden Porch.* — DON LOPE,
                        CRESPO, JUAN.

Lope   I have much to thank you for, Crespo, but for nothing so much as for giving me your son for a soldier. I do thank
you for that with all my heart.

Cres.   I am proud he should be your servant.

Lope   The king's! the king's! — *my* friend.   I took a fancy
to him from the first for his spirit and affection to the service.

Juan   And I will follow you to the world's end, sir.

Cres.   Though you must make allowance for his awkward-
ness at first, sir, remembering he has only had ploughmen for
teachers, and plough and pitch-forks for books.

Lope   He needs no apology.   And now the sun's heat
abates towards his setting, I will be off.

Juan   I will see for the litter.   [*Exit.*

Enter ISABEL *and* INES

Isab.   You must not go, sir, without our adieu.

Lope   I would not have done so; nor without asking
pardon for much that is past, and even for what I am now
about to do.   But remember, fair Isabel, 't is not the price
of the gift, but the good will of the giver, makes its value.
This brooch, though of diamond, becomes poor in your hands,

and yet I would fain have you wear it in memory of Don Lope.

Isab. I take it ill you should wish to repay us for an entertainment —

Lope No, no, no repayment; that were impossible if I wished it. A free keepsake of regard.

Isab. As such I receive it then, sir. Ah, may I make bold to commit my brother to your kindness?

Lope Indeed, indeed, you may rely on me.

Enter JUAN

Juan The litter is ready.

Lope Adieu, then, all.

All Adieu, adieu, sir.

Lope Ha, Peter! who, judging from our first meeting, could have prophesied we should part such good friends?

Cres. I could, sir, had I but known —

Lope (*going*). Well?

Cres. That you were at once as good as crazy. (*Exit* LOPE.) And now, Juan, before going, let me give thee a word of advice in presence of thy sister and cousin; thou and thy horse will easily overtake Don Lope, advice and all. By God's grace, boy, thou com'st of honourable if of humble stock; bear both in mind, so as neither to be daunted from trying to rise, nor puffed up so as to be sure to fall. How many have done away the memory of a defect by carrying themselves modestly; while others again have gotten a blemish only by being too proud of being born without one. There is a just humility that will maintain thine own dignity, and yet make thee insensible to many a rub that galls the proud spirit. Be courteous in thy manner, and liberal of thy purse; for 't is the hand to the bonnet and in the pocket that makes friends in this world; of which to gain one good, all the gold the sun breeds in India, or the universal sea sucks down, were a cheap purchase. Speak no evil of women; I tell thee the meanest of them deserves our respect; for of women do we not all come? Quarrel with no one but with good cause; by the Lord, over and over again, when I see masters and schools of arms among us, I say to myself, "This is not the thing we want at all, *How to fight,* but, *Why to fight?* that is the lesson we want to learn." And I verily believe if but one master of the *Why to fight* advertised among us he would carry off all the scholars. Well — enough — You have not (as you once said to me) my advice this time on an empty stomach — a fair outfit of clothes and money — a good horse — and a good sword — these, together with Don Lope's countenance, and my blessing — I trust in God to live to see thee home again with honour and advancement on thy back. My son, God bless thee! There — And now go — for I am beginning to play the woman.

Juan   Your words will live in my heart, sir, so long as it lives. *(He kisses his father's hand.)* Sister! *(He embraces her.)*

Isab.   Would I could hold you back in my arms!

Juan   Adieu, cousin!

Ines   I can't speak.

Cres.   Be off, else I shall never let thee go — and my word is given!

Juan   God bless you all!   [*Exit.*

Isab.   Oh, you never should have let him go, sir.

Cres. (aside).   I shall do better now. *(Aloud.)* Pooh, why, what the deuce could I have done with him at home here all his life — a lout — a scape-grace perhaps. Let him go serve his king.

Isab.   Leaving us by night too!

Cres.   Better than by day, child, at this season — Pooh! — *(Aside.)* I must hold up before them.

Isab.   Come, sir, let us in.

Ines   No, no, cousin, e'en let us have a little fresh air now the soldiers are gone.

Cres.   True — and here I may watch my Juan along the white, white road. Let us sit. *(They sit.)*

Isab.   Is not this the day, sir, when the Town Council elects its officers?

Cres.   Ay, indeed, in August — so it is. And indeed this very day.

(As they talk together, the Captain, Sergeant, REBOLLEDO *and* CHISPA *steal in.)*

Capt. (whispering).   'T is she! you know our plan; I seize her, and you look to the others.

Isab. What noise is that?

Ines Who are these?

(The Captain seizes and carries off ISABEL — *the Sergeant and* REBOLLEDO *seize* CRESPO.)

Isab. (within). My father! My father!

Cres. Villains! A sword! A sword!

Reb. Kill him at once.

Serg. No, no.

Reb. We must carry him off with us then, or his cries will rouse the town. [*Exeunt, carrying* CRESPO.

ACT III

SCENE I. *A Wood near Zalamea. — It is dark. — Enter* ISABEL.

Isab. OH never, never might the light of day arise and show me to myself in my shame! Oh, fleeting morning star, mightest thou never yield to the dawn that even now presses on thy azure skirts! And thou, great Orb of all, do thou stay down in the cold ocean foam; let night for once advance her trembling empire into thine! For once assert thy voluntary power to hear and pity human misery and prayer, nor hasten up to proclaim the vilest deed that Heaven, in revenge on man, has written on his guilty annals! Alas! even as I speak, thou liftest thy bright, inexorable face above the hills! Oh! horror! What shall I do? whither turn my tottering feet? Back to my own home? and to my aged father, whose only joy it was to see his own spotless honour spotlessly reflected in mine, which now — And yet if I return not, I leave calumny to make my innocence accomplice in my own shame! Oh that I had stayed to be slain by Juan over my slaughter'd honour! But I dared not meet his eyes even to die by his hand. Alas! — Hark! What is that noise?

Cres. (within). Oh in pity slay me at once!

Isab. One calling for death like myself?

Cres. Whoever thou art —

Isab. That voice!   [*Exit.*

SCENE II. *Another place in the Wood. —* CRESPO *tied to a tree. — Enter to him* ISABEL.

Isab. My father!

Cres. Isabel! Unbind these cords, my child.

Isab. I dare not — I dare not yet, lest you kill before you hear my story — and you must hear that.

Cres. No more, no more! Misery needs no remembrancer.

Isab. It must be.

Cres. Alas! Alas!

Isab. Listen for the last time. You know how, sitting last night under the shelter of those white hairs in which my maiden youth had grown, those wretches, whose only law is force, stole upon us. He who had feign'd that quarrel in our house, seizing and tearing me from your bosom as a lamb from the fold, carried me off; my own cries stifled, yours dying away behind me, and yet ringing in my ears like the sound of a trumpet that has ceas'd! — till here, where out of reach of pursuit, — all dark — the very moon lost from heaven — the wretch began with passionate lies to excuse his violence by his love — his love! — I implored, wept, threatened, all in vain — the villain — But my tongue will not utter what I must weep in silence and ashes for ever! Yet let these quivering hands and heaving bosom, yea, the very tongue that cannot speak, speak loudliest! Amid my shrieks, entreaties, imprecations, the night began to wear away and dawn to creep into the forest. I heard a rustling in the leaves; it was my brother — who in the twilight understood all without a word — drew the sword you had but just given him — they fought — and I, blind with terror, shame, and anguish, fled till — till at last I fell before your feet, my father, to tell you my story before I die! And now I undo the cords that keep your hands from my wretched life. So — it is done! and I kneel before you — your daughter — your disgrace and my own. Avenge us both; and revive your dead honour in the blood of her you gave life to!

Cres. Rise, Isabel; rise, my child. God has chosen thus to temper the cup that prosperity might else have made too sweet. It is thus he writes instruction in our hearts: let us bow down in all humility to receive it. Come, we will home, my Isabel, lean on me. *(Aside.)* 'Fore Heaven, an' I catch that captain! *(Aloud.)* Come, my girl! Courage, so.

Voice (within). Crespo! Peter Crespo!

Cres. Hark!

Voice Peter! Peter Crespo!

Cres. Who calls?

Enter Notary

Not. Peter Crespo! Oh, here you are at last!

Cres. Well?

Not. Oh, I've had a rare chase. Come — a largess for my news. The corporation have elected you Mayor!

Cres. Me!

Not. Indeed. And already you are wanted in your office. The king is expected almost directly through the town; and, beside that, the captain who disturbed us all so yesterday has been brought back wounded — mortally, it is thought — but no one knows by whom.

Cres. (to himself). And so when I was meditating revenge, God himself puts the rod of justice into my hands! How shall I dare myself outrage the law when I am made its keeper? *(Aloud.)* Well, sir, I am very grateful to my fellow-townsmen for their confidence.

Not. They are even now assembled at the town hall, to commit the wand to your hands; and indeed, as I said, want you instantly.

Cres. Come then.

Isab. Oh, my father!

Cres. Ay, who can now see that justice is done you. Courage! Come.   [*Exeunt.*

SCENE III.   *A Room in Zalamea. — Enter the Captain, wounded, and Sergeant.*

Capt. It was but a scratch after all. Why on earth bring me back to this confounded place?

Serg. Who could have known it was but a scratch till 't was cured? Would you have liked to be left to bleed to death in the wood?

Capt. Well, it is cured, however; and now to get clear away before the affair gets wind. Are the others here?

Serg. Yes, sir.

Capt. Let us be off then before these fellows know; else we shall have to fight for it.

Enter REBOLLEDO

Reb. Oh, sir, the magistrates are coming!

Capt. Well, what's that to me?

Reb. I only say they are at the door.

Capt. All the better. It will be their duty to prevent any riot the people might make if they knew of our being here.

Reb. They know, and are humming about it through the town.

Capt. I thought so. The magistrates must interfere, and then refer the cause to a court martial, where, though the affair is awkward, I shall manage to come off.

Cres. (within). Shut the doors; any soldier trying to pass, cut him down!

Enter CRESPO, *with the wand of office in his hand,*
Constables, Notary, &c.

Capt. Who is it dares give such an order?

Cres. And why not?

Capt. Crespo! Well, sir. The stick you are so proud of has no jurisdiction over a soldier.

Cres. For the love of Heaven don't discompose yourself, captain; I am only come to have a few words with you, and, if you please, alone.

Capt. Well then, *(to soldiers, &c.)* retire awhile.

Cres. (to his people). And you — but hark ye; remember my orders.   [*Exeunt Notary, Constables, &c.*

Cres. And now, sir, that I have used my authority to make you listen, I will lay it by, and talk to you as man to man. *(He lays down the wand.)* We are alone, Don Alvaro, and can each of us vent what is swelling in his bosom; in mine at least, till it is like to burst!

Capt. Well, sir?

Cres. Till last night (let me say it without offence) I knew not, except perhaps my humble birth, a single thing fortune had left me to desire. Of such estate as no other farmer in the district; honoured and esteemed (as now appears) by my fellow-townsmen, who neither envied me my wealth, nor taunted me as an upstart; and this even in a little community, whose usual, if not worst, fault it is to canvass each other's weaknesses. I had a daughter too — virtuously and modestly brought up, thanks to her whom heaven now holds! Whether fair, let what has passed — But I will leave what I may to silence — would to God I could leave all, and I should not now be coming on this errand to you! But it may not be: — you must help time to redress a wound so great, as, in spite of myself, makes cry a heart not used to overflow. I must have redress. And how? The injury is done — by you: I might easily revenge myself for so public and shameful an outrage, but I would have retribution, not revenge. And so, looking about, and considering the matter on all sides, I see but one way which perhaps will not be amiss for either of us. It is this. You shall forthwith take all my substance, without reserve of a single farthing for myself or my son, only what you choose to allow us; you shall even brand us on back or forehead, and sell us like slaves or mules by way of adding to the fortune I offer you — all this, and what you will besides, if only you will with it take my daughter to wife, and restore the honour you have robbed. You will not surely eclipse your own in so doing; your children will still be your children if my grandchildren; and 't is an old saying in Castile, you know, that, " 'T is the horse redeems the saddle." This is what I have to propose. Behold, *(he kneels,)* upon my knees I ask it — upon my knees, and weeping such tears as only a father's anguish melts from his frozen locks! And what is my demand? But that you should restore what you have robbed: so fatal for us to lose, so easy for you to restore; which I could myself now wrest from you by the hand of the law, but which I rather implore of you as a mercy on my knees!

Capt. You have done at last? Tiresome old man! You may think yourself lucky I do not add your death, and that of your son, to what you call your dishonour. 'T is your daughter saves you both; let that be enough for all. As to the wrong you talk of, if you would avenge it by force, I have little to fear. As to your magistrate's stick there, it does not reach my profession at all.

Cres. Once more I implore you —

Capt. Have done — have done!

Cres. Will not these tears —

Capt. Who cares for the tears of a woman, a child, or an old man?

Cres. No pity?

Capt. I tell you I spare your life, and your son's: pity enough.

Cres. Upon my knees, asking back my own at your hands that robbed me?

Capt. Nonsense!

Cres. Who could extort it if I chose?

Capt. I tell you you could not.

Cres. There is no remedy then?

Capt. Except silence, which I recommend you as the best.

Cres. You are resolved?

Capt. I am.

Cres. (*rising, and resuming his wand*). Then, by God, you shall pay for it! Ho there!

Enter Constables, &c.

Capt. What are these fellows about?

Cres. Take this captain to prison.

Capt. To prison! you can't do it.

Cres. We'll see.

Capt. Am I a bonâ fide officer or not?

Cres. And am I a straw magistrate or not? Away with him!

Capt. The king shall hear of this.

Cres. He shall — doubt it not — perhaps to-day; and shall judge between us. By the by, you had best deliver up your sword before you go.

Capt. My sword!

Cres. Under arrest, you know.

Capt. Well — take it with due respect then.

Cres. Oh yes, and you too. Hark ye, (*to Constables, &c.,*) carry the captain with due respect to Bridewell; and there with due respect clap on him a chain and hand-cuffs; and not only him, but all that were with him, (all with due respect,) respectfully taking care they communicate not together. For I mean with all due respect to examine them on the business, and if I get sufficient evidence, with the most infinite respect of all, I'll wring you by the neck till you're dead, by God!

Capt. Set a beggar on horseback!

[*They carry him off.*

Enter Notary and others with REBOLLEDO, *and*
CHISPA *in boy's dress*

Not. This fellow and the page are all we could get hold
of. The other got off.

Cres. Ah, this is the rascal who sung. I'll make him sing
on t' other side of his mouth.

Reb. Why, is singing a crime, sir?

Cres. So little that I've an instrument shall make you do
it as you never did before. Will you confess?

Reb. What am I to confess?

Cres. What pass'd last night?

Reb. Your daughter can tell you that better than I.

Cres. Villain, you shall die for it!   [*Exit.*

Chis. Deny all, Rebolledo, and you shall be the hero of a
ballad I'll sing.

Not. And you too were of the singing party?

Chis. Ah, ah, and if I was, you can't put me to the question.

Not. And why not, pray?

Chis. The law forbids you.

Not. Oh, indeed, the law? How so, pray?

Chis. Because I'm in the way ladies like to be who love
Rebolledo.   [*Exeunt, carried off, &c.*

SCENE IV.   *A Room in* CRESPO's *House.* — *Enter* JUAN
pursuing ISABEL *with a dagger.*

Isab. Help, help, help!   [*Exit.*

Juan You must not live!

Enter CRESPO, *who arrests him*

Cres. Hold! What is this?

Juan My father! To avenge our shame —

Cres. Which is to be avenged by other means, and not by
you. How come you here?

Juan Sent back by Don Lope last night, to see after some

missing soldiers, on approaching the town I heard some cries —

Cres. And drew your sword on your officer, whom you wounded, and are now under arrest from me for doing it.

Juan Father!

Cres. And Mayor of Zalamea. Within there!

Enter Constables

Take him to prison.

Juan Your own son, sir?

Cres. Ay, sir, my own father, if he transgressed the law I am made guardian of. Off with him! *(They carry off* JUAN.) So I shall keep him out of harm's way at least. And now for a little rest. *(He lays by his wand.)*

Lope (calling within). Stop! Stop!

Cres. Who's that calling without? Don Lope!

Enter LOPE

Lope Ay, Peter, and on a very confounded business too. But at least I would not put up any where but at your friendly house.

Cres. You are too good. But, indeed, what makes you back, sir, so suddenly?

Lope A most disgraceful affair; the greatest insult to the service! One of my soldiers overtook me on the road, flying at full speed, and told me — Oh, the rascal!

Cres. Well, sir?

Lope That some little pettifogging Mayor of the place had got hold of a captain in my regiment, and put him in prison! In prison! 'Fore Heaven, I never really felt this confounded leg of mine till to-day, that it prevented me jumping on horseback at once to punish this trumpery Jack-in-office as he deserves. But here I am, and, by the Lord, I'll thrash him within an inch of his life.

Cres. You will?

Lope Will I!

Cres. But will he stand your thrashing?

Lope Stand it or not, he shall have it.

Cres. Besides, might your captain happen to deserve what he met with?

Lope And, if he did, *I* am his judge, not a trumpery mayor.

Cres. This mayor is an odd sort of customer to deal with, I assure you.

Lope Some obstinate clodpole, I suppose.

Cres. So obstinate, that if he's made up his mind to hang your captain, he'll do it.

Lope Will he? I'll see to that. And if you wish to see too, only tell me where I can find him.

Cres. Oh, close here.

Lope You know him?

Cres. Very well, I believe.

Lope And who is it?

Cres. Peter Crespo. *(Takes his wand.)*

Lope By God, I suspected it!

Cres. By God, you were right.

Lope Well, Crespo, what's said is said.

Cres. And, Don Lope, what's done is done.

Lope I tell you, I want my captain.

Cres. And I tell you, I've got him.

Lope Do you know he is the king's officer?

Cres. Do you know he ravished my daughter?

Lope That you are outstripping your authority in meddling with him?

Cres. Not more than he is in meddling with me.

Lope Do you know my authority supersedes yours?

Cres. Do you know I tried first to get him to do me justice with no authority at all, but the offer of all my estate?

Lope I tell you, *I'll* settle the business for you.

Cres. And I tell you I never leave to another what I can do for myself.

Lope I tell you once more and for all, I must have my man.

Cres. And I tell you once more and for all, you shall — when you have cleared him of the depositions.

Lope The depositions! What are they?

Cres. Oh, only a few sheets of parchment tagged together with the evidence of his own soldiers against him.

Lope Pooh! I'll go myself, and take him from the prison.

Cres. Do, if you like an arquebuss ball through your body.

Lope I am accustomed to that. But I'll make sure. Within there!

Enter Orderly

Have the regiment to the market-place directly under arms. I'll see if I'm to have my prisoner or not.   [*Exit.*

Cres. And I — Hark ye!

[*Exit, whispering to a Constable.*

SCENE V. *Before the Prison in Zalamea. — A Street in the centre. — Enter on one side* DON LOPE *with Troops; at the other, before the Prison, Labourers, Constables, &c. armed; and afterward,* CRESPO.

Lope Soldiers, there is the prison where your captain lies. If he be not given up instantly at my last asking, set fire to the prison; and, if further resistance be made, to the whole town.

Cres. Friends and fellow-townsmen, there is the prison where lies a rascal capitally convicted —

Lope They grow stronger and stronger. Forward, men, forward! (*As the Soldiers are about to advance, trumpets and shouts of "God save the King," within.*)

Lope The king!

All The king!

Enter KING PHILIP II. *through centre Street, with Train, &c. Shouting, Trumpets, &c.*

King What is all this?

Lope 'T is well your Majesty came so suddenly, or you would have had one of your whole towns by way of bonfire on your progress.

King What has happened?

Lope The mayor of this place has had the impudence to seize a captain in your Majesty's service, clap him in prison, and refuses to surrender him to me, his commander.

King Where is this mayor?

Cres. Here, so please your Majesty.

King Well, Mr. Mayor, what have you to offer in defence?

Cres. These papers, my Liege: in which this same captain

is clearly proved guilty, on the evidence of his own soldiers, of carrying off and violating a maiden in a desolate place, and refusing her the satisfaction of marriage though peaceably entreated to it by her father with the endowment of all his substance.

Lope This same mayor, my Liege, is the girl's father.

Cres. What has that to do with it? If another man had come to me under like circumstances, should I not have done him like justice? To be sure. And therefore, why not do for my own daughter what I should do for another's? Besides, I have just done justice against my own son for striking his captain; why should I be suspected of straining it in my daughter's favour? But here is the process; let his Majesty see for himself if the case be made out. The witnesses are at hand too; and if they or any one can prove I have suborned any evidence, or any way acted with partiality to myself, or malice to the captain, let them come forward, and let my life pay for it instead of his.

King (after reading the papers). I see not but the charge is sustantiated: and 't is indeed a heavy one. Is there any one here to deny these depositions? *(Silence.)* But, be the crime proved, *you* have no authority to judge or punish it. You must let the prisoner go.

Cres. You must send for him then, please your Majesty. In little towns like this, where public officers are few, the deliberative is forced sometimes to be the executive also.

King What do you mean?

Cres. Your Majesty will see. *(The prison gates open, and the Captain is seen within, garrotted in a chair.)*

King And you have dared, sir! —

Cres. Your Majesty said the sentence was just; and what is well said cannot be ill done.

King Could you not have left it for my imperial Court to execute?

Cres. All your Majesty's justice is only one great body with many hands; if a thing be to be done, what matter by which? Or what matter erring in the inch, if one be right in the ell?

King At least you might have beheaded him, as an officer and a gentleman.

Cres.   Please your Majesty, we have so few Hidalgos here-about, that our executioner is out of practice at beheading. And this, after all, depends on the dead gentleman's taste; if he don't complain, I don't think any one else need for him.

King   Don Lope, the thing is done; and, if unusually, not unjustly — Come, order all your soldiers away with me toward Portugal; where I must be with all despatch.   For you — (*to* CRESPO,) what is your name?

Cres.   Peter Crespo, please your Majesty.

King   Peter Crespo, then, I appoint you perpetual Mayor of Zalamea.   And so farewell.   [*Exit with Train.*

Cres. (kneeling).   God save your Highness!

Lope   Friend Peter, his Highness came just in time.

Cres.   For your captain, do you mean?

Lope   Come now — confess, wouldn't it have been better to have given up the prisoner, who, at my instance, would have married your daughter, saved her reputation, and made her wife of an Hidalgo?

Cres.   Thank you, Don Lope, she has chosen to enter a convent and be the bride of one who is no respecter of Hidalgos.

Lope   Well, well, you will at least give me up the other prisoners, I suppose?

Cres.   Bring them out.   (JUAN, REBOLLEDO, CHISPA, *brought out.*)

Lope   Your son too!

Cres.   Yes, 't was he wounded his captain, and I must punish him.

Lope   Come, come, you have done enough — at least give *him* up to his commander.

Cres.   Eh? well, perhaps so; I'll leave his punishment to you.

      With which now this true story ends —
      Pardon its many errors, friends.

Mr. Ticknor thinks Calderon took the hint of this play from Lope de Vega's "Wise Man at Home"; and he quotes (though without noticing this coincidence) a reply of Lope's hero to some one advising him to assume upon his wealth, that is much of a piece with Crespo's answer to Juan on a like score in the first act of this piece. Only that in Lope the answer *is* an answer: which, as Juan says, in Calderon it is not; so likely to happen with a borrowed answer.

This is Mr. Ticknor's version from the older play:

> *He that was born to live in humble state*
> *Makes but an awkward knight, do what you will.*
> *My father means to die as he has liv'd,*
> *The same plain collier that he always was;*
> *And I too must an honest ploughman die.*
> *'T is but a single step or up or down;*
> *For men there must be that will plough or dig,*
> *And when the vase has once been fill'd, be sure*
> *'T will always savour of what first it held.*

I must observe of the beginning of Act III., that in this translation Isabel's speech is intentionally reduced to prose, not only in measure of words, but in some degree of idea also. It would have been far easier to make at least verse of almost the most elevated and purely beautiful piece of Calderon's poetry I know; a speech (the beginning of it) worthy of the Greek Antigone, which, after two Acts of homely talk, Calderon has put into his *Labradora's* mouth. This, admitting for all culmination of passion, and Spanish passion, must excuse my tempering it to the key in which (measure only kept) Calderon himself sets out.

BEWARE OF SMOOTH WATER

DRAMATIS PERSONÆ

Don Alonso
Donna Clara }
Donna Eugenia } *his Daughters*
Don Torribio, *his Nephew*
Mari Nuño }
Brigida } *his Servants*
Otañez }
Don Felix }
Don Juan } *Gallants*
Don Pedro }
Hernando, *Don Felix's Servant*

ACT I

Scene I. *A Room in* don alonso's *House at Madrid. —*
Enter alonso *and* otañez, *meeting.*

Otañ.   My own dear master!
Alon.   Welcome, good Otañez,
My old and trusty servant!
Otañ.   Have I liv'd
To see what I so long have long'd to see,
My dear old master home again!
Alon.   You could not
Long for 't, Otañez, more than I myself.
What wonder, when my daughters, who, you know,
Are the two halves that make up my whole heart,
Silently call'd me home, and silently
(For maiden duty still gagg'd filial love)
Out of the country shade where both have grown,
Urg'd me to draw the blossom of their youth
Where it might ripen in its proper day.
Otañ.   Indeed, indeed, sir.   Oh that my dear lady
Were but alive to see this happy hour!
Alon.   Nay, good Otañez, mar it not recalling
What, ever sleeping in the memory,
Needs but a word to waken into tears.
God have her in his keeping!   He best knows
How I have suffered since the king, my master,
Despatching me with charge to Mexico,
I parted from her ne'er to see her more;
And now come back to find her gone for ever!
You know 't was not the long and roaring seas

Frighted her for herself, but these two girls —
For them she stay'd — and full of years and honour
Died, when God will'd! and I have hasten'd home
Well as I may, to take into my hands
The charge death slipp'd from hers.

  Otañ.   Your own good self!
Though were there ever father, who could well
Have left that charge to others, it was you,
Your daughters so religiously brought up
In convent with their aunt at Alcalá.
Well, you are come, and God be prais'd for it!
And, at your bidding, here are they, and I,
And good old Mari Nuño — all come up
To meet you at Madrid. I could not wait
The coach's slower pace, but must spur on
To kiss my old master's hand.

  Alon.   Myself had gone
To meet them; but despatches of the king's
Prevented me. They're well?

  Voices (within).   Make way there — way!

  Otañ. And lovely as the dawn. And hark! are here
To answer for themselves.

  Enter CLARA, EUGENIA, MARI NUÑO, *as from travel*

  Clara (kneeling). Sir, and my father — by my daily prayers
Heav'n, won at last in suffering me to kiss
These honour'd hands, leaves me no more to ask,
Than at these honour'd feet to die,
With its eternal blessing afterward.

  Eug. And I, my father, grateful as I am
To Heav'n, for coming to your feet once more,
Have yet this more to ask — to live with you
For many, many happy years to come!

  Alon. Oh, not in vain did nature fix the heart
In the mid bosom, like a sun to move
Each circling arm with equal love around!
Come to them — one to each — and take from me
Your lives anew. God bless you!
Come, we are here together in Madrid,

And in the sphere where you were born to move.
This is the house that is to be your own
Until some happy lover calls you his;
Till which I must be father, lover, husband,
In one.   Brigida!

Enter BRIGIDA

Brig.   Sir?
Alon.   My daughters' rooms
Are ready?
Brig.   Ay, sir, as the sky itself
For the sun's coming.
Alon.   Go and see them then,
And tell me how you like what I have bought,
And fitted up for your reception.
Clara   I thank you, sir, and bless this happy day,
Though leaving my lov'd convent far away.
Eug. (aside).   And I twice bless it, that no longer hid
In a dull cell, I come to see Madrid.
                          [*Exeunt* CLARA *and* EUGENIA.
Mari Nuño   Now the young ladies, sir, have had their turn,
Shall not I kiss your hand?
Alon.   Oh, welcome too,
Good Mari Nuño; who have been so long
A mother to them both.   And, by the by,
Good Mari Nuño, now we are alone,
I'd hear from you, who know them both so well,
Their several characters and dispositions,
And not, as 't were, come blindfold to the charge
That Heav'n has laid upon me.
Mari   You say well, sir.
Well, I might say at once, and truly too,
That nothing need be said in further praise
But that they are your daughters.   But to pass,
Lest you should think I flatter,
From general to individual,
And to begin with the eldest, Donna Clara;
Eldest in years and in discretion too,
Indeed the very pearl of prudence, sir,

And maidenly reserve; her eyes still fixt
On earth in modesty, or heav'n in prayer;
As gentle as a lamb, almost as silent;
And never known to say an angry word:
And, such her love of holy quietude,
Unless at your desire, would never leave
Her cloister and her missal.   She's, in short,
An angel upon earth, whom to be near
And wait on, one would sell oneself a slave.
So much for her.   Donna Eugenia,
Though unexceptionable in heart and head,
As, God forgive me, any child of yours
Must be, is different, — not for me to say
Better or worse, — but very different:
Of a quick spirit, loving no control;
Indeed, as forward as the other shy;
Quick to retort, and sharply; so to speak,
Might sometimes try the patience of a saint;
Longing to leave a convent for the world,
To see and to be seen; makes verses too;
Would not object, I think, to have them made
(Or love, may be) to her — you understand;
Not that I mean to say —
   Alon.   Enough, enough.
Thanks for your caution as your commendation:
How could I fortify against weak points
Unless I knew of them?   And, to this end,
Although Eugenia be the younger sister,
I'll see her married first; husband and children
The best specific for superfluous youth:
And, to say truth, good Mari, the very day
Of my arrival hither, I despatch'd
A letter to my elder brother's son,
Who still maintains our dwindled patrimony
Up in the mountains, which I would reclaim,
Or keep it rather in its lawful line,
By an alliance with a child of mine.
All falls out luckily.   Eugenia
Wedded to him shall make herself secure,
And the two stems of Cuadradillos so
Unite and once more flourish, at a blow.   [*Exeunt.*

SCENE II.　*A Room in* DON FELIX's *House;* DON FELIX,
and HERNANDO *dressing him.*

Hern.　Such fine ladies, sir, come to be our neighbours.

Fel.　So they ought to be, such a noise as they made in coming.

Hern.　One of them already betroth'd, however.

Fel.　So let her, and married too, if she would only let me sleep quiet.　But what kind of folks are they?

Hern.　Oh, tip-top.　Daughters of the rich old Indian who has bought the house and gardens opposite, and who will give them all his wealth when they marry, which they say he has brought them to Madrid expressly to do.

Fel.　But are they handsome?

Hern.　I thought so, sir, as I saw them alighting.

Fel.　Rich and handsome then?

Hern.　Yes, sir.

Fel.　Two good points in a woman, at all events, of which I might profit, such opportunities as I have.

Hern.　Have a care, sir, for the old servant who told me this, told me also that the papa is a stout fiery old fellow, who'd stick the Great Turk himself if he caught him trifling with his daughters.

Fel.　That again is not so well; for, though I'm not the Great Turk, I've no mind to share that part of his fortune. But of the two girls, what said your old servant? who, as such, I suppose told you all that was amiss in them at least.

Hern.　Well, you shall judge.　One, the oldest, is very discreet.

Fel.　Ah, I told you so.

Hern.　The other lively.

Fel.　Come, that sounds better.　One can tackle her hand to hand, but the grave one one can only take a long shot at with the eyes.

Hern.　Whichever it be, I should like to see you yourself hit one of these days, sir.

Fel.　Me?　The woman is not yet cast who will do that. If I meddle with these it is only because they lie so handy.

Hern.　And handsome as well as handy!

Fel. Pooh! I wouldn't climb a wall to pluck the finest fruit in the world. But hark! some one's at the door. See who 't is.

Enter DON JUAN *in travelling dress*

Juan I, Felix, who seeing your door open, could not but walk in without further ceremony.

Fel. You know that it and my heart are ever open to you. Welcome, welcome, Don Juan! all the more welcome for being unexpected: for though I had heard we might one day have you back, I did not think so soon.

Juan Why, the truth is, I got my pardon sooner than I expected.

Fel. Though not than I prayed for. But tell me all about it.

Juan You know I was obliged to fly to Italy after that unlucky duel. Well, there the great duke of Terranova, who (as good luck would have it) was then going ambassador to Hungary, took a fancy to me, and carried me with him; and, pleased with what service I did him, interested himself in my fortunes, and one good day, when I was least expecting it, with his own hand put my pardon into mine.

Fel. A pardon that never should have needed asking, all of an unlucky quarrel at cards.

Juan So you and the world suppose, Felix: but in truth there was something more behind.

Fel. Ah?

Juan Why, the truth is, I was courting a fair lady, and with fair hope of success, though she would not confess it, urging that her father being away at the time, her mother would not consent in his absence. Suddenly I found I had a rival, and took occasion of a casual dispute at cards to wipe out the score of jealousy; which I did with a vengeance to both of us, he being killed on the spot, and I, forc'd to fly the country, must, I doubt, ere this, have died out of my lady's memory, where only I cared to live.

Fel. Ay, you know well enough that in Madrid Oblivion lies in the very lap of Remembrance, whether of love or loathing.   I thank my stars I never pinn'd my faith on woman yet.

Juan   Still the same sceptic?

Fel.   Ay, they are fine things, but my own heart's ease is finer still; and if one party must be deceived, I hold it right in self-defence it should not be I.   But come; that you may not infect me with your faith, nor I you with my heresy, tell me about your journey.

Juan   How could it be otherwise than a pleasant one, such pageants as I had to entertain me by the way?

Fel.   Oh, you mean our royal master's nuptials?

Juan   Ay!

Fel.   I must hear all about them, Juan; even now, upon the spot.

Juan   Well, then, you know at least, without my telling you, how great a debt Germany has owed us —

Enter DON PEDRO *hastily*

Ped.   My dear Don Felix!

Fel.   Don Pedro!   By my faith, my door must be the door of heaven, I think; for all the good keep coming in by 't.   But how comes your University term so soon over?

Ped.   Alas, it's *not* over, but —

Fel.   Well?

Ped.   I'll tell you.

Juan   If I be in your way —

Ped.   No, no, sir, if you are Felix's friend you have the key of my confidence.   My story is easily told.   A lady I am courting in Alcalá is suddenly come up to Madrid, and I am come after her.   And to escape my father's wrath at playing truant, I must beg sanctuary in your house awhile.

Fel.   And this once will owe me thanks for your entertainment, since I have Don Juan's company to offer you.

Juan   Nay, 't is I have to thank you for Don Pedro's.

Fel.   Only remember, both of you, that however you may amuse one another, you are not to entertain me with your several hearts and darts.   Hernando, get us something to eat; and till it comes you shall set off rationally at least, Juan, with the account of the royal nuptials you were beginning just as Don Pedro came in.

Juan   On condition you afterwards recount to me your re-
joicings in Madrid meanwhile.

Fel.   Agreed.

Ped.   I come in happy time to hear you both.

Juan   You know, as I was saying, what a debt
Germany has ow'd us since our fair Maria
Her title of the Royal Child of Spain
Set in the crown of Hungary — a debt
They only could repay us as they do,
Returning us one of the self-same stock,
So like herself in beauty and desert,
We seem but taking what we gave away.
If into Austria's royal hand we gave
Our royal rose, she now returns us one
Sprung of the self-same stem, as fair, as sweet
In maiden graces; and if double-dyed
In the imperial purple, yet so fresh,
She scarce has drunk the dawns of fourteen Aprils.
The marriage contract sign'd, the marriage self
Delay'd, too long for loyal Spain's desire,
That like the bridegroom for her coming burn'd,
(But happiness were hardly happiness
Limp'd it not late,) till her defective years
Reach'd their due blossom — Ah, happy defect,
That every uncondition'd hour amends!
At last arose the day — the day of days —
When from her royal eyrie in the North
The imperial eaglet flew.   Young Ferdinand,
King of Bohemia and Hungary
Elect, who not in vain Rome's holy hand
Awaits to bind the laurel round his brow,
As proxy for our king espous'd her first,
And then, all lover-like, as far as Trent
Escorted her, with such an equipage
As when the lords and princes of three realms
Out-do each other in magnificence
Of gold and jewel, ransackt from the depths
Of earth and sea, to glitter in the eye
Of Him who sees and lights up all from heav'n.
So, like a splendid star that trails her light

Far after her, she cross'd fair Italy,
When Doria, Genoa's great Admiral,
Always so well-affected to our crown,
Took charge of her sea-conduct; which awhile,
Till winds and seas were fair, she waited for
In Milan; till, resolv'd to wait no more,
The sea, that could not daunt her with his rage,
Soon as her foot was on his yellow shore,
Call'd up his Tritons and his Nereids
Who love and make a calm, to smooth his face
And still his heaving breast; on whose blue flood
The golden galley in defiance burn'd,
Her crew in wedding pearl and silver drest;
Her silken sail and cordage, fluttering
With myriad flags and streamers of all dye,
Sway'd like a hanging garden over-head,
Amid whose blossoms stood the royal bride,
A fairer Venus than did ever float
Over the seas to her dominions
Quivering the arrows of diviner love.
Then to the sound of trump and clarion
The royal galley, and with her forty more
That followed in her wake as on their queen,
Weigh'd, shook out sail, and dipp'd all oars at once,
Making the flood clap hands in acclamation;
And so with all their streamers, as 't were spring
Floating away to other hemispheres,
Put out to sea; and touching not the isles
That gem the midway deep — not from distrust
Of friendly France in whose crown they are set,
And who (as mighty states contend in peace
With courtesies as with hard blows in war)
Swell'd the triumphal tide with pageantries
I may not stop to tell — but borne upon,
And (as I think) bearing, fair wind and wave,
The moving city on its moving base
With sail and oar enter'd the Spanish Main,
Which, flashing emerald and diamond,
Leap'd round the golden prow that clove between
And kiss'd the happy shore that first declin'd

To meet its mistress.   Happy Denia,
That in her golden sand holds pearly-like
The first impression of that royal foot!
I will not tell — let Felix, who was here,
And has new breath — how, landed happily,
Our loyal Spain — yea, with what double welcome —
Receiv'd the niece and consort of our king,
Whom, one and both, and both in one, may Heav'n
Bless with fair issue, and all happiness,
For years and years to come!

Enter HERNANDO

Hern.   Sir, sir!

Fel.   Well?

Hern.   Your two new neighbours — just come to the window.

Fel.   Gentlemen, we must waive my story then, for, as the proverb goes, "*My lady first.*" (*He looks out.*) By Heaven, they are divine!

Juan   Let me see. (*Aside.*) By Heaven, 't is she!

Ped.   Come, it is my turn now. (*Aside.*) Eugenia! I must keep it to myself.

Fel.   I scarce know which is handsomest.

Juan   Humph! both pretty girls enough.

Ped.   Yes, very well.

Fel.   Listen, gentlemen; whether handsome, or pretty, or very well, or all three, you must not stare at them from my window so vehemently; being the daughters of a friend of mine, and only just come to Madrid.

Juan (aside).   That the first thing I should see on returning to Madrid, is she for whose love I left it!

Ped. (aside).   That the first thing I see here is what I came for the very purpose of seeing!

Hern. (entering).   Table is serv'd, sir.

Fel.   To table, then. I know not how it is with you, gentlemen, but for myself, my appetite is stronger than my love.

Juan (aside to FELIX*).*   You jest as usual; but I assure you it is one of those very ladies on whom my fortune turns!

[*Exit.*

Fel.   Adieu to one then.

Ped.   All this is fun to you, Felix; but believe me, one of
those ladies is she I have followed from Alcalá.   [*Exit.*

Fel.   Adieu to both then — unless indeed you are both of
you in love with the same.   But, thank God,

> I that am in love with neither,
> Need not plague myself for either.
> The least expense of rhyme or care
> That man can upon woman spare.

But they are very handsome nevertheless.   [*Exit.*

SCENE III.   *An Apartment in* DON ALONSO'S *House.* —
Enter CLARA *and* EUGENIA.

Clara   Is 't not a pretty house, Eugenia,
And all about it?
    Eug.   I dare say you think so.
    Clara   But do not you then?
    Eug.   No — to me it seems
A sort of out-court and repository,
Fit but for old Hidalgos and Duennas,
Too stale and wither'd for the blooming world,
To wear away in.
    Clara   I like its quietude;
This pretty garden too.
    Eug.   A pretty thing
To come for to Madrid — a pretty garden!
I tell you were it fuller of all flowers
Than is a Dutchman's in his tulip-time,
I want the lively street whose flowers are shops,
Carriages, soldiers, ladies, cavaliers,
Plenty of dust in summer, dirt in winter,
And where a woman sitting at her blind
Sees all that passes.   Then this furniture!
    Clara   Well — surely velvet curtains, sofas, chairs,
Rich Indian carpets, beds of Damascene,
Chandeliers, gilded mirrors, pictures too —
What would you have, Eugenia?
    Eug.   All very well,
But, after all, no marvellous result
Of ten years spent in golden India.

Why, one has heard how fine a thing it is
To be my Lord Mayor's daughter; what must be,
Methought, to own a dowry from Peru!
And when you talk about the furniture,
Pictures, chairs, carpets, mirrors, and all that —
The best of all is wanting.
    Clara   What is that?
    Eug.   Why, a coach, woman!   Heav'n and earth, a coach!
What use is all the money-bonds and gold
He has been boasting of in all his letters,
Unless, now come at last, he plays the part
We've heard so long rehearsing?
    Clara   Not to spare
Your father even, Eugenia!   For shame!
'T is time to tie your roving tongue indeed.
Consider, too, we are not in the country,
Where tongue and eyes, Eugenia, may run wild
Without offence to uncensorious woods;
But in a city, with its myriad eyes
Inquisitively turn'd to watch, and tongues
As free and more malicious than yours
To tell — where honour's monument is wax,
And shame's of brass.   I know, Eugenia,
High spirits are not in themselves a crime;
But if to men they *seem* so? — that's the question.
For it is almost better to do ill
With a good outward grace than well without;
Especially a woman; most of all
One not yet married; whose reputation
One breath of scandal, like a flake of snow,
May melt away; one of those tenderest flowers
Whose leaves ev'n the warm breath of flattery
Withers as fast as envy's bitterest wind,
That surely follows short-liv'd summer praise.
Ev'n those who praise your beauty, grace, or wit,
Will be the first, if you presume on them,
To pull the idol down themselves set up,
Beginning with malicious whispers first,
Until they join the storm themselves have rais'd.
And most if one be giv'n oneself to laugh

And to make laugh: the world will doubly yearn
To turn one's idle giggle into tears.
I say this all by way of warning, sister,
Now we are launcht upon this dangerous sea.
Consider of it.

    Eug.   "Which that all may do
May Heav'n —"   Come, Clara, if the sermon's done,
Pray finish it officially at once,
And let us out of church.   These homilies
In favour of defunct proprieties,
Remind one of old ruff and armour worn
By Don Punctilio and Lady Etiquette
A hundred years ago, and past with them
And all their tedious ancestors for ever.
I am alive, young, handsome, witty, rich,
And come to town, and mean to have my fling,
Not caring what malicious people say,
If nothing true to say against my honour.
And so with all sail set, and streamers flying,
(A coach shall be my ship, and I will have it!)
I mean to glide along the glittering streets
And down the Prado, as I go along
Capturing what eyes and hearts I find by the way,
Heedless of every little breath of scandal
That such as you turn back affrighted by.
I'll know the saints' days better than the saints
Themselves; the holidays and festivals
Better than over-done apprentices.
If a true lover comes whom I can like
As he loves me, I shall not turn away:
As for the rest who flutter round in love,
Not with myself, but with my father's wealth,
Or with themselves, or any thing but me,
You shall see, Clara, how I'll play with them,
Till, having kept them on my string awhile
For my own sport, I'll e'en turn them adrift
And let them go, the laugh all on my side.
And therefore when you see —

    Clara   How shall I dare
To see what even now I quake to hear!

Enter ALONSO

Alon. Clara! Eugenia!

Both Sir?

Alon. Good news, good news, my girls! What think you? My nephew, Don Torribio Cuadradillos, my elder brother's elder son, head of our family and inheritor of the estate, is coming to visit me; will be here indeed almost directly. What think you now!

Eug. (aside). One might have thought, from such a flourish of trumpets, the king was coming at least.

Alon. Mari Nuño!

Mari (entering). Sir?

Alon. Let a chamber be got ready for my nephew, Don Torribio, directly. Brigida!

Brig. (entering). Sir?

Alon. See that linen be taken up into Don Torribio's room. Otañez, have dinner ready for my nephew, Don Torribio, directly he arrives. And you two, *(to his daughters,)* I expect you will pay him all attention; as head of the family, consider. Ay, and if he *should* take a fancy to one of you — I know not he will — but if he *should*, I say, whichever it be, she will take precedence of her sister for ever. *(Aside.)* This I throw out as a bait for Eugenia.

Eug. It must be Clara, then, sir, for she is oldest, you know.

Clara Not in discretion and all wife-like qualities, Eugenia.

Eug. Clara!

Alon. Hark! in the court!

Don Torribio (speaking loud within). Hoy! good man there! Can you tell me if my uncle lives hereabout?

Alon. 'T is my nephew, surely!

Torr. (within). Why, fellow, I mean of course Don Alonso — who has two daughters, by the token I'm to marry one of 'em.

Alon. 'T is he! I will go and receive him.   [*Exit.*

Torr. (within). Very well, then. Hold my stirrup, Lorenzo.

Eug. What a figure!

Enter ALONSO *and* TORRIBIO

Alon. My nephew, Don Torribio, giving thanks to Heaven

for your safe arrival at my house, I hasten to welcome you as its head.

Torr. Ay, uncle, and a head taller, I promise you, than almost any body in the parish.

Alon. Let me introduce your cousins to you, who are so anxious for your acquaintance.

Torr. Ah, that's proper of 'em, isn't it?

Both Welcome, sir.

Alon. And how are you, nephew?

Torr. Very tired, I promise you: for the way is long and my horse a rough goer, so as I've lost leather.

Alon. Sit down, and rest till they bring dinner.

Torr. Sitting an't the way to mend it. But, however — (*Sits.*) Nay, though I be head of the house, I an't proud — you can all of you sit down too.

Clara (aside). Amiable humility!

Eug. (aside). No wonder the house is crazy if this be its head!

Torr. Well, now I come to look at you, cousins, I may say you are both of you handsome girls, indeed; which'll put me to some trouble.

Clara How so, cousin?

Torr. Why, didn't you ever hear that if you put an ass between two bundles of hay, he'll die without knowing which to begin on, eh?

Alon. His father's pleasant humour!

Clara A courteous comparison!

Eug. (aside). Which holds as far as the ass at least.

Torr. Well, there's a remedy. I say, uncle, mustn't cousins get a dispensation before they marry?

Alon. Yes, nephew.

Torr. Well, then, when you're about it, you can get two dispensations, and I can marry both my cousins. Aha! Well, but, uncle, how are you? I had forgot to ask you that.

Alon. Quite well, in seeing you in my house at last, and to reap, I trust, the fruits of all my travel.

Torr. Ah, you may say that. Oh, cousins, if you could only see my pedigree and patent, in a crimson velvet case; and all my forefathers painted in a row — I have it in my saddle-bags, and if you'll wait a minute —

Enter MARI NUÑO

Mari   Dinner's ready.

Torr. (looking at MARI*).*   Lord a' mercy, uncle, what's this? something you brought from India, belike; does it speak?

Alon.   Nay, nephew, 't is our Duenna.

Torr.   A what?

Alon.   A Duenna.

Torr.   A tame one?

Alon.   Come, come, she tells us dinner's ready.

Torr.   Yes, if you believe her; but I've heard say, Duennas always lie.   However, I'll go and see for myself.   [*Exit.*

Clara   What a cousin!

Eug.   What a lover!

Mari   Foh!   I wonder how the watch came to let the plague into the city!   [*Exit.*

Alon.   You are silent, both of you?

Both   Not I, sir.

Alon.   I understand you; Don Torribio
Pleases you not — well, he's a little rough;
But wait a little; see what a town life
Will do for him; all come up so at first,
The finest diamonds, you know, the roughest —
Oh, I rejoice my ancestor's estate
Shall to my grandchildren revert again!
For this I tell you — one, I care not which,
But one of you, shall marry Don Torribio:
And let not her your cousin does not choose,
For one more courtly think herself reserv'd;
By Heaven she shall marry, if e'er marry,
One to the full as rough and country-like.
What, I to see my wealth, so hardly won,
Squander'd away by some fine town gallant,
In silks and satins! see my son-in-law
Spend an estate upon a hat and feather!
I'll tell you I'll not have it.   One of you
Must marry Don Torribio.   [*Exit.*

Clara   I'll die first.

Eug.   And I'll live an old maid — which much is worst.

ACT II

SCENE I. *A Room in* DON FELIX's *House.* — FELIX *and* HERNANDO; *to whom enter* JUAN.

Fel.   WELL, Juan, and how slept you?
Juan   As one must
In your house, Felix; had not such a thought
No house can quiet, woke me long ere dawn.
  Fel.   Indeed!   How so?
Juan   Felix, the strangest thing —
But now we are alone I'll tell you all.
Last night — the very moment that I saw
That angel at the window, as at Heaven's gate —
The fire that I myself had thought half dead
Under the ashes of so long an absence,
Sprung up anew into full blaze.   Alas!
But one brief moment did she dawn on us,
Then set, to rise no more all the evening,
Watch as I would.   But day is come again,
And as I think, Felix, the holyday
When our new Queen shall make her solemn entry
Into Madrid; and she, my other Queen,
Will needs be up — be up and out betimes;
So I forestall the sun in looking for her,
And now will to the door beneath her window
Better to watch her rising.
But, as you love me, not a word of this
Breathe to Don Pedro.   [*Exit.*
    Fel.   'T was wisely said
Because his memory of her is quick,

Hers is of him? Aha!

Hern.   Nay, if he like it,
"Oh, let him be deceiv'd!"

Fel.   'T was wisely said
By him who self-deception us'd to call
The cheapest and the dearest thing of all.
Ha! here's the other.
I begin to think
My house is turn'd into a Lazar-house
Of crazy lovers. *(Enter* PEDRO.*)*
Good day, Don Pedro.

Ped.   As it needs must be
To one who hails it in your house, and opposite
My lady's! Oh, you cannot think, my Felix,
With what a blessed consciousness of this
I woke this morning! I can scarce believe 't.
Why, in your house, I shall have chance on chance,
Nay, certainty of seeing her — *to-day*
Most certainly. But I'll go post myself
Before the door; she will be out betimes
To mass.

Fel. Well, you will find Don Juan there.

Ped. Eh? Well, so much the better, I can do 't
With less suspicion; nay, with none at all
If you will go with us. Only, Don Felix,
Breathe not a word to him about my love.

As he is going, re-enter JUAN

Fel. Juan again?

Juan   I only came to ask
What church we go to? *(Aside to* FELIX.*)* Let us keep at
      home.

Fel. Don Pedro, what say you?

Ped.   Oh, where you please.
(Aside.) Stir not!

Fel. (aside). How easy to oblige two friends
Who ask the same, albeit with divers ends!
(Aloud.) What, are your worships both in love, perhaps,
As Spanish cavaliers are bound to be,

And think I've nothing else to do, forsooth,
Than follow each upon his wildgoose chase?
Forgetting I may take 't into my head
To fall in love myself — perhaps with one,
Or both, of those fair ladies chance has brought
Before my windows.   Now I think upon 't,
I am, or mean to be, in love with one;
And, to decide with which, I'll e'en wait here
Till they both sally forth to church themselves.
So, gentlemen, would you my company,
I must not go with you, you stay with me.

    Ped.   Willingly.

    Juan   Oh, most willingly!   (*Aside to* FELIX.)   How well
You manag'd it.

    Ped. (aside to FELIX).   'T is just as I could wish.

    Fel. (aside).   And just as I, if thereby I shall learn
Whether they love the same; and, if the same,
Whether the one — But come, come! 't is too late
For wary me to wear love's cap and bells.

    Juan   Since we must do your bidding on this score,
We'll e'en make you do ours upon another,
And make you tell us, as you promis'd both,
And *owe* to me — what, when our Queen was landed,
You fine folks of Madrid did in her honour.

    Ped.   Ay, if you needs will fetter our free time,
Help us at least to pass it by the story
You had begun.

    Fel.   Well then, to pick it up
Where Juan left it for us, on the shore.
There, when our Queen was landed, as I hear,
The Countess Medellin, her Chamberlain,
Of the Cardona family, receiv'd her,
And the Lord Admiral on the King's part,
With pomp that needed no excuse of haste,
And such a retinue (for who claims not
To be the kinsman, friend, or follower,
Of such a name?) as I believe Castile
Was almost drain'd to follow in his wake.
Oh, noble house! in whom the chivalry
Of courage, blameless worth, and loyalty,

Is nature's patent of inheritance
From generation to generation!
And so through ringing Spain, town after town,
And every town a triumph, on they pass'd.
Madrid meanwhile —

    Juan   Stop, stop!   They're coming out!

    Ped.   Where!   Let me see.

    Juan   The servant only.

    Fel.   Nay,
They'll follow soon.

    Juan   Till when, on with your story.

    Fel.   Madrid then, sharing in the general joy
Of her king's marriage, and with one whose mother
Herself had nurst — though, as you said, half sick
Of hope deferr'd, had, at the loyal call,
That never fails in Spain, drawn to her heart
The life-blood of the realm's nobility
To do her honour; not only when she came,
But, in anticipation of her coming,
With such prelusive pomps, as if you turn
Far up time's stream as history can go,
In hymeneals less august than these,
You shall find practis'd — torchéd troop and masque,
With solemn and preliminary dance,
Epithalamium and sacrifice,
Invoking Hymen's blessing.   So Madrid,
Breathing new Christian life in Pagan pomp,
With such epithalamium as all Spain
Rais'd up to Heav'n, into sweet thunder tun'd
Beyond all science by a people's love,
Began her pageant.   First, the nightly masque,
So fair as I have never seen the like,
Nor shall again; nor which, unless you draw
On your imagination for the type
Of what I tell, can I depict to you;
When, to the sound of trumpet and recorder,
The chiming poles of Spain and Germany
Beginning, drew the purple mountain down,
Glittering with veins of ore and silver trees,
All flower'd with plumes, and taper-starr'd above,

With monster and volcano breathing fire,
While to and fro torch-bearing maskers ran
Like meteors; all so illuminating night,
That the succeeding sun hid pale in cloud,
And wept with envy, till he dawn'd at length
Upon the famous Amphitheatre,
Which, in its masonry out-doing all
That Rome of a like kind in ruin shows,
This day out-did itself,
In number, rank, and glory of spectators,
Magnificence of retinue, multitude,
Size, beauty, and courage, of the noble beasts
Who came to dye its yellow dust with blood;
As each horn'd hero of the cloven hoof,
Broad-chested, and thick-neckt, and wrinkle-brow'd,
Rush'd roaring in, and tore the ground with 's foot,
As saying, "Lo! this grave is yours or mine!"
While that yet nobler beast, noblest of all,
Who knights the very knighthood that he carries,
Proud in submission to a nobler will,
Spurn'd all his threats, and, touch'd by the light spur,
His rider glittering like a god aloft,
Turn'd onset into death.   Fight follow'd fight,
Till darkness came at last, sending Madrid
Already surfeited with joy, to dream
Of greater, not unanxious that the crown
And centre of the centre of the world
Should not fall short of less renowned cities
In splendour of so great a celebration;
While too the hundreds of a hundred nations,
In wonder or in envy cramm'd her streets;
Until her darling come at last, whose spouse
Shall lay his own two empires at her feet,
And crown her thrice; as Niece, and Spouse, and Queen.

   Juan   A charming story, finisht just in time,
For look!   *(They look out.)*

    Fel.   That is the father, Don Alonso.

    Juan   Indeed!

    Ped. (aside).   That's he then!   But that strange man with
       him,

Who's he?

Hern.   Oh, I can tell you that;
His nephew, an Asturian gentleman,
Betroth'd to one of the daughters.

Juan (aside).   Not to mine!

Ped. (aside).   Not my Eugenia, or by Heav'n —
But we shall scarcely see them, Felix, here,
Wrapt in their mantles too.

Fel.   And I would pay
My compliment to Don Alonso.

Juan   Come,
Let us go down with you into the street.
(Aside.)   Oh love, that in her memory survive
One thought of me, not dead if scarce alive!

Ped. (aside).   Oh, may her bosom whisper her 't is still
Her eyes that draw me after where they will!   [*Exeunt.*

SCENE II.   *Street between the Houses of* ALONSO *and* FELIX:
ALONSO *and* TORRIBIO *waiting.*

Alon.   If you really affect Eugenia, nephew, — *(aside)* as
I wished — I will communicate with her after church, and if
all be well (as I cannot doubt) get a dispensation forthwith.
But they are coming.

Enter from ALONSO'S *door* CLARA, EUGENIA, *in mantles, the
latter with a handkerchief in her hand;* MARI NUÑO, BRIGIDA,
and OTAÑEZ *behind; and at the same time* FELIX, JUAN, *and*
PEDRO *opposite.*

Clara   Cover your face, Eugenia.   People in the street.

Eug.   Well, I'm not ashamed of it.   *(Aside.)*   Don Pedro!
and Don Juan!

Fel. (whispers).   Which is it, Don Juan?

Juan   She with the handkerchief in her hand.   I'll go wait
for her at the church.   [*Exit.*

Ped. (to FELIX).   That is she with the white kerchief·in her
hand.   I'll follow them.

Fel. (aside).   The same, then!

Clara   Eugenia, lend me your handkerchief, it is hot.
(Takes the handkerchief and uncovers her face towards FELIX.)
And let us go, and do not you look behind you.

Fel.   And she I most admired.

                [*Exeunt* CLARA, EUGENIA, &c., PEDRO *after them.*

Torr.   Uncle, what are these fellows hanging about our doors for?

Alon.   Nay, 't is the public street, you know.

Torr.   What, my cousins' street?

Alon.   To be sure.

Torr.   I'll not suffer any one I don't like to hang about it, however, and least of all these perfumery puppies.

Alon.   But if they happen to live here, nephew?

Torr.   Don't let 'em live here, then.

Alon.   But if they own houses here?

Torr.   They mustn't own houses, then.

Fel.   Don Alonso, permit me to kiss your hand on your arrival among us.   I ought indeed first to have waited upon you in your own house; but this happy chance makes me anticipate etiquette.

Torr.   Coxcomb!

Alon.   Thank you, sir; had I known you intended me such a favour, I should have anticipated your anticipation by waiting upon you.   Give me leave to present to you my nephew, Don Torribio de Cuadradillos, who will also be proud of your acquaintance.

Torr.   No such thing, I shan't at all.

Alon.   Nephew, nephew!

Fel.   I trust you are well, sir?

Torr.   Oh, so, so, thank ye, for the matter of that, neither well nor ill, but mixt-like.   (ALONSO *salutes* FELIX *and exit with* TORRIBIO.)

Fel.   Now then, I know both face, and dress, and name.
And that my rival friends both love the same;
The same too that myself of the fair pair
Thought yester-eve the fairest of the fair.
Was 't not enough for my two friends that they
Turn enemies — must I too join the fray?
Oh, how at once to reconcile all three,
Those two with one another, and with me!

Re-enter JUAN *hastily*

Juan   On seeing me, my friend, her colour chang'd:

She loves me still, Don Felix!   I am sure
She loves me!   Is not the face — we know it is,
The tell-tale index of the heart within?
Oh happiness! at once within your house,
And next my lady's!   What is now to do
But catch the ball good fortune throws at us!
You know her father, you will visit him
Of course, and then — and then — what easier?
Draw me in with you, or after you — or perhaps
A letter first — ay, and then afterward —
But why so dumb?
  Fel.   I scarce know how to answer.
Juan, you know I am too much your friend
To do you any spite?
  Juan   How could I dream it?

     Enter PEDRO *hastily*

  Ped. Oh, Felix, if my love —
  Fel. (aside).   The other now!
He must be stopt.   A moment, gentlemen,
Before you speak, and let me tell you first
A case of conscience you must solve for me.
You both have mighty matters, I doubt not,
To tell me, such as warm young gentlemen
Are never at a loss for in Madrid;
But I may have my difficulties too.
(Aside.)   The same will serve for both.
  Ped. Well, let us hear.
  Fel. Suppose some friend of yours, dear as you will,
Loving your neighbour's daughter — (such a case
Will do as well as any) — ask'd of you
To smuggle him, his letters, or himself,
Into that neighbor's house, there secretly
To ply a stolen love; what would you do?
  Ped. Do it of course!
  Juan   Why not?
  Fel.   Well, I would not.
  Ped. But why?
  Fel.   Because, however it turn'd out,

I must do ill; if one friend's love succeeded
I had play'd traitor to the other still;
If unsuccessful, not that cost alone,
But also, without counter-profiting
Him whom I sacrific'd so much to serve.

 Ped. If that be your determination,
I have no more to say.   [*Exit.*

 Juan   Nor I: farewell;
I must find other means.   [*Exit.*

 Fel.   Of all the plagues,
For one with no love profit of his own
Thus to be pester'd with two lovers' pains!
And yet, what, after all, between the two —
Between the *three*, perhaps, am I to do?
'Fore Heav'n, I think, 't will be the only way
To get her to untie who drew the knot;
No woman ever at a loss
To mend or mar a matter as she wills.
Yet 't is an awkward thing to ask a lady,
"Pray, madam, which of these two sighing swains
"Like you the best? or both? or neither, madam?"
Were not a letter best? But then who take it?
Since to commit her letter, would so far
Commit her honour to another's hands?
By Heav'n, I think I've nothing left to do,
But ev'n to write it, and to take it too;
A ticklish business — but may fair intent
And prudent conduct lead to good event! [*Exit.*

   Scene III. *An Apartment in* don alonso's *House.* —
    Enter clara, eugenia, mari nuño, &c.

 Clara Here, take my mantle, Mari. Oh, I wish we had a
chaplain of our own in the house, not to go abroad through
the crowded streets!

 Eug. And I, that church were a league of crowded street
off, and we obliged to go to it daily.

 Mari I agree with Señora Clara.

 Brigida And I with Señora Eugenia.

 Mari And why, pray?

Brig. Oh, madam, I know who it is deals most in sheep's eyes.

Enter DON ALONSO

Alon. (talking to himself as he enters). How lucky he should have pitcht on the very one I wanted! *(Aloud.)* Oh, Eugenia, I would speak with you. Nay, retire not, Clara, for I want you to pardon me for the very thing Eugenia is to thank me for.

Clara A riddle, sir. I pardon you?

Alon. Listen, both of you. Your cousin Don Torribio has declared his love for Eugenia: and though I could have wish'd to marry you, Clara, first, and to the head of our house too, yet my regret at your missing it is almost cancell'd by the joy of your sister's acceptance.

Clara And so with me, believe me, sir. I am well content to be slighted so long as she is happy: which may be with my cousin these thousand years to come. *(Aside.)* Oh, providential rejection! [*Exit.*

Torribio (peeping in). Ah! what a wry face she makes!

Alon. And you, Eugenia, what say you?

Eug. (aside). Alas! surprise on surprise! *(Aloud.)* Nay, sir, you know, I hope, that I am ever ready to obey you.

Alon. I look'd for nothing else of you.

Torr. Nor I.

Alon. Your cousin is waiting your answer in his chamber. I will tell him the good news, and bring him to you. [*Exit.*

Eug. Only let him come! Alas!

Torr. (entering). How lightly steps a favour'd lover forth! Give you joy, cousin.

Eug. The wretch!

Torr. Being selected by the head of your house.

Eug. Sir, one word; I wouldn't marry you if it should cost me my life.

Torr. Ah, you are witty, cousin, I know.

Eug. Not to you, sir. And now especially, I mean to tell you sober truth, and abide by it, so you had better listen. I tell you once again, and once for all, I wouldn't marry you to save my life!

Torr. Cousin! After what I heard you tell your father?

Eug. What I said then was out of duty to him; and what I now say is out of detestation of you.

Torr. I'll go and tell him this, I declare I will.

Eug. Do, and I'll deny it. But I mean it all the same, and swear it.

Torr. Woman, am I not your cousin?

Eug. Yes.

Torr. And head of the family?

Eug. I dare say.

Torr. An Hidalgo?

Eug. Yes.

Torr. Young?

Eug. Yes.

Torr. Gallant?

Eug. Very.

Torr. And dispos'd to you?

Eug. Very possibly.

Torr. What do you mean then?

Eug. Whatever you choose, so long as you believe I mean what I say. I'll never marry you. You might be all you say, and fifty other things beside, but I'll never marry any man without a capacity.   [*Exit.*

Torr. Capacity! without a Capacity! I who have the family estate, and my ancestors painted in a row on the patent in my saddle-bags! I who —

Enter ALONSO

Alon. Well, nephew, here you are at last; I've been hunting every where to tell you the good news.

Torr. And what may that be, pray?

Alon. That your cousin Eugenia cordially accepts your offer, and —

Torr. Oh, indeed, does she so? I tell you she's a very odd way of doing it then. Oh uncle, she has said that to me I wouldn't say to my gelding.

Alon. To you?

Torr. Ay, to me — here — on this very spot — just now.

Alon. But what?

Torr. What? why, that I had no Capacity! But I'll soon

settle that; I either have a Capacity or not — if I have, she lies; if not, I desire you to buy me one directly, whatever it may cost.

Alon.   What infatuation!

Torr.   What, it costs so much, does it?   I don't care, I'll not have it thrown in my teeth by her or any other woman; and if you won't, I'll go and buy a Capacity, and bring it back with me, let it cost — ay, and weigh — what it will.   [*Exit.*

Alon.   Nephew, nephew!   Stop him there!

Enter CLARA *and* EUGENIA

Clara   What is the matter, sir?

Alon.   Oh, graceless girl, what have you been saying to your cousin?

Eug.   I, sir?   Nothing.

Alon.   Oh! if you deceive me!   But I must first stop his running after a Capacity!

Eug.   What can I have done?

Clara   Nay, attempt not dissimulation with me, who know how you would risk even your advancement for a sarcasm.

Eug.   It was all for your sake, if I did, Clara.

Clara   For my sake! oh, indeed, you think I can have no lovers but what you reject?   Poor little fool! I could have enough if I chose to lay out for them as some do; but many will pluck at an apple who will retire from a fortress.

Eug.   Hark! they are coming back; I dare not face them both as yet.   [*Exit.*

Enter DON FELIX

Fel.   Permit me, madam —

Clara   Who is this?

Fel.   One, madam,
Who dares to ask one word with you.

Clara   With me?

Fel.   Indeed with you.

Clara   You cannot, sir, mean me.

Fel.   Once more, and once for all, with you indeed;
Let me presume to say so, knowing well
I say so in respect, not in presumption.

Eug. (peeping).   Why, whom has my staid sister got with
    her?

Clara   With me!   My very silence and surprise
Bid you retire at once.

Fel.   Which I will do
When you will let this silence speak to you
With less offence perhaps than could my tongue.

                                 (Offering her a letter.)

Eug.   Oh, if he would but try if fort or apple!

Clara   A letter too! — for me!

Fel.   And, madam, one
It most imports your honour you should read.
For, that being once in question, I make light
That my friends' lives, Don Juan and Don Pedro,
Are in the balance too.

Eug.   Don Juan!   Don Pedro!

Clara   What, sir, is this to me, who neither know
Don Juan, nor Don Pedro, nor yourself?

Fel.   Having then done my duty to my friends,
And (once again I say 't) to yourself, madam,
Albeit in vain — I'll not offend you more
By my vain presence.

Clara   Nay, a moment — wait.
I must clear up this mystery.   Indeed,
I would not be discourteous or ungrateful:
But ere I thank you for your courtesy,
Know you to whom you do it?

Fel.   To Donna Eugenia.

Clara   Well, sir?

Eug.   Oh, the hypocrite!

Fel.   You are the lady?

Clara   Enough — give me the letter, and adieu.

Eug.   I can forbear no longer. *(Coming out.)* Sister, stop!
Oh! what to do! — the letter —

Clara   Well?

Eug.   I tell you
My father and my cousin are coming up,
And if they see —

Clara   Well, if they see! what then?
I wish them both to see and hear it all.

(Calling.) Sir! Father! Cousin! Otañez!

Alon. (within).   Clara's voice?

Fel. What to do now?

Eug.   Alas, to tell the truth,
When I but wish'd to lie!

Clara (calling).   This way, sir, here!

Eug. Will you expose us both?   In here! in here!

> [*She hides* FELIX *behind arras.*

Enter ALONSO, TORRIBIO, MARI NUÑO, OTAÑEZ, &c.

Alon. What is the matter?

Clara There is some one in the house, sir.   A man — I saw
him stealing along the corridor, towards the garret!

Brig. It must be a robber!

Alon. A robber?

Mari What more likely in a rich Indian's house?

Alon. I'll search the house.

Torr. I'll lead the forlorn hope, though that garret were
Maestricht itself.   Now, cousin, you shall see if I've a Capacity or not.   [*Exeunt* ALONSO *and the men.*

Clara Do you two watch in the passage. [*Exeunt* MARI
NUÑO *and* BRIGIDA.]   And now, sir, the door is open, give me
the letter and begone.

Fel. Adieu, madam, neglect not its advice.

Eug. Alas, alas, she has it!

Fel. She's all too fair! come, honour, come, and shame
False love from poaching upon friendship's game!   [*Exit.*

Re-enter ALONSO, &c.

Alon. We can see nothing of him, daughter.

Clara Nay, sir, he probably made off when the alarm was
given.   Take no more trouble.

Alon. Nay, we'll search the whole house.

Torr. What do you say to my Capacity now, cousin?

> [*Exeunt* ALONSO, TORRIBIO, &c.

Clara You see, Eugenia, in what your enterprises end. At
the first crack, you faint and surrender.   I have done all this
to show you the difference between talking and doing.   And
now go; I have got the letter, and want to read it.

Eug. And so do I! but —

Clara Go! I am mistress now. *(Exit* EUGENIA.*)* May
they not have written to me under cover of her name?
let me see. *(Reads.)* "Let not him offend honour by the
very means he takes to secure it; at least let his good intention excuse his ill seeming. Don Juan, more than ever enamoured of you, hangs about your doors; Don Pedro follows
every step you take; they are both in my house; it is impossible
but the secret must soon escape both, who must then refer
their rivalry to the sword, and all to the scandal of your name.
You can, by simply disowning both, secure their lives, your
own reputation, and my peace of mind as their friend and
host.   Adieu!"
Oh what perplexing thoughts this little letter
Buzzes about my brain, both what it says,
And leaves unsaid! — oh, can it be for me?
And is the quiet nun really belov'd
Under the cover of an idle flirt?
Or is it but for her — the vain, pert thing,
Who thinks her eye slays all it looks upon?
If it be so, and she, not I, is lov'd,
I yet may be reveng'd —
       Eug. (entering).   On whom?
       Clara   Eugenia!
This letter that has fallen to my hands,
But meant for you —
       Eug.   Oh, I know all about it.
       Clara   Know all about it! know then that two men
Are even now following your steps like dogs
To tear your reputation between them,
And then each other for that worthless sake,
And yet —
       Eug.   A moment, you shall see at once
How easily I shall secure myself,
And them, and supersede your kind intentions.
Signor Don Pedro!   *(Calls at the window.)*
       Clara   What are you about!
       Eug.   Listen, and you will hear.
       Clara   You dare not do it!
       Eug.   My father's safely lockt up in his room,

(Thanks to the gout your false alarm has brought,)
My cousin gone to buy capacities,
And now's my time.   *(Calling at the window.)*
                              Don Pedro! Signor Don Pedro!
    Ped. (coming below to the window).
He well may wait to have his name thrice call'd
When such a goddess —
    Eug.   Listen, sir, to me.
It is because, I say, *because* this room,
Away from father's and duenna's ears,
Allows some harmless speech, it also bars
All nearer access than the ears and eyes
Of father or duenna both could do.
But, seeing harm of harmless trifling come,
I now entreat, implore, command you, sir,
To leave this window and my threshold clear,
Now and for ever!
    Ped.   Hear me —
    Eug.   Pardon me,
I cannot.
    Ped.   But this once —
    Eug.   If you persist
I must be rude.
    Ped.   Oh, how do worse than —
    Eug. (shutting the blinds down).   Thus!
    Clara   And to your other gallant?
    Eug.   Why not think,
If he were here, I'd do the same to him?
Oh, Clara, be assur'd my levities
Are but the dust on youth's butterfly wing,
Though prudes and sinners too take fright at them;
Like that benighted traveller, you know,
Who, frighted by a shallow brook that jump'd
And bubbled at his right, swerv'd to the left
And tumbled into one that lay quite still,
But deep enough to drown him for his pains.   [*Exit.*
    Clara   What, did she hear what to myself I said?
Or saw my colour change from white to red?
Or only guess'd me waiting for the prey
Her idle chatter ought to fright away?

If chance have done more than all prudence could,
Prudence at least may make occasion good.
And if these lovers by mistake should woo,
Why (by mistake) should I not listen too?
And teach the teacher, to her proper cost,
Those waters are least deep that prattle most.

ACT III

SCENE I. *Room in* ALONSO's *House.* — CLARA *and*
MARI NUÑO.

Clara IT is so, indeed.

Mari You know you can always rely on my old love to you.
But indeed I cannot but wonder at your sister's forwardness.

Clara Yes; to think of two cavaliers after her at once! I
look upon it as my duty to set all to right; to do this I
must once more speak to him who warned me of it; and I want
you to give him this letter — in *her* name, remember — this
will bring him here to-night, and I shall undeceive him for
ever. But hark! some one —

TORRIBIO *is about to enter*

Mari 'T is that wretch.   Stay, sir, no man comes in here.

Torr. Away, troublesome duenna.

Mari It's not decent, I tell you.

Torr. An't my cousin decent; and an't I?

Clara What is the matter?

Torr. This old woman won't let me come in.

Clara She is right, unless my father be with you.

Torr. Oh, I understand —
          Those that are out
          Still will pout.

Clara Well, since she who is in, and may grin, is not here,
you have no business neither.   For me, what grudge I have
against you, be assur'd I can and will repay.   Mari, remember.
                                                    [*Exit.*

Mari Hark! some one at the door.   [*Exit.*

Torr.   By heav'n and earth, I do begin suspect!
I say again I do begin suspect —
And valour rises with suspicion —
I shall ere long be very terrible.
Ancestors!   Saddle-bags!   Capacities!
For passing through the house — let me not say it!
Till I have told my tongue it lies to say it —
In passing though the passage, what saw I
Within Eugenia's room, behind her bed!
I saw —   (*Re-enter* MARI NUÑO *with a letter.*)
   Mari   A letter, madam, — Where is she?
   Torr.   Woman, she was, but is not.   A letter too?
Give it me.
   Mari   You too!
   Torr.   Give it me, or dread
My dreadful vengeance on your wither'd head.
   Mari   Leave hold of it. —
   Torr.   I'll not!   The more you pull,
The more —
   Mari   Then take that on your empty skull!
                              (*Deals him a blow, and calls.*)
Help!   Help!
   Torr.   You crying, when two teeth are out —
   Mari   "As swelling prologues of" — Help! murder! murder!

                Enter EUGENIA, CLARA, ALONSO, BRIGIDA, &c.

   Alon.   What is the matter now?
   Mari   Don Torribio, sir, because I wouldn't let him have
my young lady's letter, has laid violent hands on me.
   Torr.   I?
   All   Don Torribio!
   Torr.   I tell you —
   Alon.   Indeed, nephew, your choleric jealousy carries you
too far.   A respectable female in my house!
   Torr.   I tell you that it is *me* who —
   Alon.   I know — enough — make not the matter worse by
worse excuses.   Give me the letter has been the cause of such
unseemly conduct.
   Eug. (*aside*).   If it should be from one of them!

Clara (aside to EUGENIA). Nothing I hope from your gallants.

Alon. (reads). "My dear nieces, this being the day of the Queen's public entry, I have engag'd a balcony, and will send my coach for you directly to come and see it with me." This, you see, nephew, is all your suspicions amount to! My cousin, Donna Violante, inviting my daughters to witness this august ceremony! If you still suspect; here, take it, and read it for yourself.

Torr. (after looking at the letter). I tell you what, uncle, if they wait till I've read it, they'll not see the sight at all.

Alon. Why so?

Torr. Because I can't read.

Alon. That this should be!

Torr. But that's no matter neither. They can teach me before they go.

Alon. What, when it's to-day? almost directly?

Torr. Can't it be put off?

Alon. 'T is useless saying more. Daughters, such a cere-mony happens, perhaps, but once in a life; you must see it. On with your mantles, whether Don Torribio approve or not. I am lame, you see, and must keep at home; to hear about it all from you on your return.

Clara At your pleasure, sir.

Eug. Shall I stay with you, sir, while Clara —

Alon. No, no. Both of you go.

Clara (aside to MARI, *while putting on her mantle).* Re-member the letter!

Mari Trust to me.

Eug. (aside). I wonder if they will be there!

[*Exeunt all but* TORRIBIO.

Torr. Whether the Queen enter to-day,
To-morrow, or keep quite away,
Let those go see who have a mind;
I am resolved to stay behind:
And now all gone, and coast quite clear,
Clear up the secret I suspect and fear. [*Exit.*

SCENE II. *A Room in* FELIX's *House.* — FELIX *and*
HERNANDO.

Hern. Not going to see the Entry, sir?

Fel.   What use going to a festival if one has no spirits for it?

Hern.   Humph, what makes you out of spirits?

Fel.   Why should you ask?

Hern.   Nay, then, you have already answered me.   You are in love.

Fel.   I scarce know whether you are right or wrong, Hernando.   I have indeed seen a lady whose very beauty forbids all hope of my attaining it.

Hern.   How so, sir?

Fel.   She who has enslav'd Don Juan and Don Pedro has fetter'd me, at last!   I should care little for their rivalry, had not each made me keeper of his love, so that — Hark!

Mari Nuño (within).   Don Felix!

Fel.   Who is that?

Hern.   Some one calling you.

Mari (within).   Señor Don Felix!

Fel.   Well?

Mari (within).   From Donna Eugenia!

[*A letter is thrown in at the window.*

Fel.   From Eugenia!   *(Reads.)*   "Grateful to you for your advice, I have already begun to follow it; but, in order to that, I must see you once again this evening!   Adieu!"   Here is a dilemma!   For if —

Hern.   Don Juan!

Enter JUAN

Juan (aside).   What was that?

Fel.   Don Juan back,
When such a festival —

Juan   And you?   Oh, Felix,
I know not how to speak or hold my tongue!

Fel.   A riddle!   How is that?

Juan   Why, if I speak
I needs must anger you; if not, myself.

Fel.   I do not understand it yet.

Juan   Nor I;
Yet if you give me leave (as leave they give
To children and to fools to say their mind)
I'll say mine.

Fel.　　　Surely say it.

Juan　　　　　　Tell me then —
That letter I saw flying in at the window
As I came up, what was it?

Fel.　　　　　　That of all
That you could ask, Juan, I cannot answer —
Must not — relying on our old regard
For fair construction.

Juan　　　　I believe it, Felix:
Yet seeing that you first excus'd yourself
From helping on my suit, upon the score
Of other obligation; and that now,
Ev'n now, but a few wretched minutes back,
Eugenia herself, in the public street,
Forbad me from her carriage angrily
From following her more — What can I think
But that she loves another? when besides,
Coming back suddenly, I hear her name
Whisper'd — oh, what so loud as an ill whisper! —
By you, and see a letter too thrown in,
Which on my coming up confus'd you hide,
And will not say from whom — I say, Don Felix,
What can I think?

Fel. (aside).　　And I, what can I do?
Who, even if I may excuse myself,
Must needs embroil Don Pedro!

Juan　　　　　　　Answer me.

Fel.　Have I not answered you sufficiently,
In saying that my old and well-tried love
Should well excuse my silence?

Juan　　　　　I confess
Your love, old and well tried as you profess;
And on that very score ask of you, Felix,
What you would do if one as true and tried
In a like case seal'd up his lips to you?

Fel.　Leave them unlockt in fullest confidence.

Juan　Alas! how much, much easier to give
Than follow ev'n the counsel one implores!
Felix, in pity I entreat of you,

Show me that letter!

Fel.   Gladly should you see it
If no one but myself were implicate.

Juan   There *is* then some one else?

Fel.   There is.

Juan   Who else?

Fel.   That's what I cannot tell you.

Juan   Dare not trust
A friend as true to you as you to him?

Fel.   In anything but this.

Juan   What can this do
But aggravate my worst suspicions?

Fel.   I cannot help it.

Juan   I must tell you then
My friendship for you, Felix, may defer,
But not forego, the reading of that letter.

Fel.   I am sorry, sir, your friendship must abide
In ignorance till doomsday.

Juan   You'll not show it?

Fel.   No, never.

Juan   Follow me, sir.

Fel.   Where you please.

As they are going out, enter PEDRO

Ped.   How now?   Don Juan and Felix quarrelling?

Fel.   Nay, only walking out.

Ped.   What, walking out,
With hands upon your swords and inflam'd faces?
You shall not go.

Hern.   That's right, sir, keep them back,
They were about —

Fel.   Peace, rascal!

Ped.   Friends may quarrel,
But surely not to such extremity
But that a third may piece the quarrel up
Without the sword.   The cause of your dispute?

Fel.   I must be silent.

Juan   And so must not I;

Who will not have it thought
That I forgot my manners as a guest
For any idle reason.   You, Don Pedro,
Though lately known to me, are a gentleman,
And you shall hear my story.
    Fel.   Not a word,
Or else —
    Ped.   Nay, Felix —
    Juan   I will speak it out!
Don Pedro, I confided to Don Felix,
My friend and host, the love I long have borne
For one with whom he could advance my suit,
And promis'd so to do it; but instead,
Yea, under the very mask of doing it,
Has urg'd his own; has even now receiv'd
A letter through that ready window thrown,
He dares not show me; and to make all sure,
I heard him whispering as I came upstairs,
The very name of my Eugenia —
    Ped.   Hold!
This is my quarrel.
He who pretends to love Eugenia
Must answer it to me.
    Juan   Two rivals, then!
    Fel.   Two enemies grown out of two old friends
By the very means I us'd to keep them so!
    Juan   Keep them, indeed!
    Ped.   When with base treachery —
    Juan   Hypocrisy —
    Ped.   Under the name of friend —
    Juan   A pretty friend —
    Ped.   You robb'd me —
    Juan (turning to PEDRO).   You!   Dare *you*
Pretend —
    Ped. (to JUAN).   Dare *I!*   Dare *you*, sir?
    Fel.   Peace, I say.
And hear me speak!
    Juan (to FELIX).   The time is past for that.
Follow me, sir.

Ped.   No, *me.*

Fel.   One, or the other, or together both,
I'll either lead or follow, nothing loath!

[*Exeunt wrangling.*

SCENE III.   ALONSO *sitting.* — Enter TORRIBIO.

Torr.   Oh, uncle!

Alon.   Well, what now?

Torr.   Oh, such a thing!   I suspected it!

Alon.   Well, tell me.

Torr.   Such a thing!

Alon.   Speak, man.

Torr.   When we were searching the house for the man cousin Clara told us of —

Alon.   Well?

Torr.   Passing by cousin Eugenia's room, I saw — I have not breath to say it!

Alon.   Speak, sir.

Torr.   Those men in the house — those dandies about the door — I know how they get in now — when I found in my cousin's room — behind her very bed —

Alon.   Don Torribio!

Torr.   The very ladder they climb up by!

Alon.   A ladder?

Torr.   Ah, and a very strong one too, all of iron and cord.

Alon.   If this were true —

Torr.   Wait till I show it you, then.   [*Exit.*

Alon.   Not in vain did Mari Nuño warn me of her dangerous disposition!   If he have such a proof of her incontinence how will he marry her?

Re-enter TORRIBIO *with a fardingale*

Torr.   There, uncle, there it is, hoops, and steps, and all!

Alon.   This a ladder?

Torr.   Ah, that, if it were all let out, would scale the tower of Babel, I believe.

Alon.   I can scarce control my rage.   Fool! this is a fardingale, not a ladder.

Torr. A what-ingale?

Alon. A fardingale, fool![1]

Torr. Why, that's worse than the ladder!

Alon. You will fairly drive me out of my senses! Go, sir, directly, and put it back where you took it from, and for Heaven's sake, no more of such folly.   [*Exit.*

Torr. Well — to think of this! and my cousin that look'd so nice too!

Voices (within). Coach there! coach!

Enter MARI NUÑO

Mari They are come back. I must get lights. Who's this?

Torr. Nobody.

Mari What are you doing with that fardingale; and where did you get it?

Torr. Nothing, and nowhere.

Mari Come, give it me at once, lest I give you the fellow of the cuff I gave you before.

Torr. For fear of which, take that upon your wrinkled chaps. (*Strikes her, and calls out.*) Help! help! Murder! murder! Help!

Enter ALONSO, CLARA, EUGENIA, *&c., in mantles*

Alon. What now?

Torr. Mari Nuño there, only because I wish'd her good night, laid violent hands on me.

---

[1] "A hoop of whalebone, used to spread out the petticoat to a wide circumference"; — Johnson; who one almost wonders did not spread out into a wider circumference of definition about the "*poore verdingales,*" that (according to Heywood)

> —— "*must lie in the streete,*
> *To have them no doore in the citye made meete.*"

The Spanish name is "guarda infanta," which puzzles Don Torribio, as to what his cousin had to do with infants. Our word was first (as Heywood writes) *verdingale*: which, as Johnson tells us, "much exercised the etymology of Skinner, who at last seems to determine that it is derived from *vertu garde.*" This, however, Johnson thinks, does not at all get to the bottom of the etymology, which may, he says, be found in Dutch. Perhaps the old French *petenlair* was of the same kindred.

Mari   Oh the wretch! he wanted to make love to me — and worse — declaring he would none of any who used such a thing as this.   *(Showing fardingale.)*

Alon.   Let us hear no more of such folly.   There is something else to-day to tell of.   Well, *(to his daughters,)* you have seen this procession?

Eug.   Ay, sir; the greatest sight, I believe, that Spain has seen since she was greatest of nations.

Alon.   I, who could not go myself, am to see it, you know, in your recital.

Eug.   As best we can, sir.

Clara (aside to MARI NUÑO*).*   Have you seen Don Felix?

Mari (aside).   Enough, he will be here.   But when?

Clara   When the story is done, and all weary are gone to bed.

Mari   Good.   [*Exit; the rest sit down.*

Clara   Begin you then, Eugenia, I will chime in.

Eug.   This being the long-expected day
When our fair Spain and fairest Mariana
Should quicken longing hope to perfect joy,
Madrid awoke, and dress'd her squares and streets
In all their glory; through all which we pass'd
Up to the Prado, where the city's self,
In white and pearl array'd, by ancient usage,
Waited in person to receive the bride
By a triumphal arch that rose heaven-high,
The first of four all nam'd and hung about
With emblems of the four parts of the world,
(Each with a separate element distinct,)
Of which our sovereign lord was now to lay
The four crowns at his sovereign lady's feet.

Clara   And this first arch was Europe; typified
By the wide Air, which temperatest she breathes,
And which again, for double cognizance,
Wore the imperial eagle for its crest;
With many another airy symbol more,
And living statutes supplementary
Of Leon and Castile, each with its crown,
Austria, the cradle of the royal bride,
And Rome, the mistress of the faith of all.

Eug.   Here then, when done the customary rite
Of kissing hands and due obeisance,
Drum, trumpet, and artillery thundering,
With that yet lordliest salute of all,
A people's universal acclamation;
(And never in the world were subjects yet
So proud, and bow'd, and with so good a cause;)
Under a golden canopy she mov'd
Tow'rd San Geronimo, whose second arch,
Of no less altitude and magnificence,
Deckt with the sixty crowns of Asia,
Receiv'd her next, wearing for cognizance
Earth, of which Asia is the largest piece;
Which Earth again carried a lion's mane,
As proclamation of her noblest growth.
     Clara   Thence passing on, came to where Africa,
Her waste of arid desert embleming
By Fire, whose incarnation, the Sun,
Burn'd on this arch as in his house in heaven,
Bore record of the trophies two great Queens
Upon the torrid continent had won,
Who, one with holy policy at home,
The other in Granada by the sword,
Extirpated deadly Mahometism.
     Eug.   Last, to the Holy Virgin dedicate,
From whose cathedral by the holy choir
Chaunted Te Deum, rose in splendid arch
America, wearing for her device
The silver image of the Ocean,
That roll'd the holy cross to the New World.
And so all pass'd to the Escurial,
In front of which, in two triumphal cars,
Two living statues were — one Mercury,
Who, as divine ambassador, thus far
Had brought the royal bride propitiously;
The other, Hymen, who took up the charge
Mercury left, and with unquenching torch,
While cannon, trumpet, choir, and people's voice
Thunder'd her praises, took the palfrey's rein,
Who gloried in the beauty that he bore,
And brought and left her at her palace door.

Alon. Well done, well done, both of you, in whose lively antiphony I have seen it all as well as if I had been there.

Torr. Well, for my part I neither wanted to see it nor hear of it.

Alon. No? why so, nephew?

Torr. Lord, I've seen twice as good as that down in my country many a time, all the boys and girls dancing, and the mayor, and the priest, and —

Alon. Peace, peace. Come, Brigida, light me to my room, I am sleepy.

Eug. And I; with sight-seeing, and sight-telling, I suppose. (*Aside.*) And with a heavy heart, alas!

[*Exeunt* ALONSO, EUGENIA, *and* BRIGIDA.

Clara Will not you to bed too, sir?

Torr. Not till I've had my supper, I promise you. Oh, I don't care for all your sour looks, not I, nor your threats of revenge neither.

Clara You don't?

Torr. No, I defy you.

Clara Not if I were to prove to you that she you slighted me for loves another?

Torr. Oh, cousin Clara!

Clara Shall I prove it to you?

Torr. Oh, if my ancestors could hear this, what would they say?

Clara I don't know. But you may hear if you like what she says to your rival.

Torr. Ha!

Clara Go into this balcony, and you will hear her talking to him in the street.

Torr. I knew! I guess'd! the ladder!

(*He goes into the balcony and she shuts him in.*)

Clara There cool yourself in the night till I let you out. And now to have *you* safe too. (*Locks* EUGENIA's *door.*) And now, all safe, for the first time in my life Love and I meet in fair field. Mari Nuño! (*Enter* MARI.) Where is the Cavalier?

Mari Waiting in my chamber.

Clara Bring him. You understand it is all for Eugenia's good?

Mari I understand.   [*Exit, and returns with* FELIX.
Fel. I fly, madam, to your feet. *(Kneels.)*
Clara Rise, sir, 't is about your letter I sent to you.
Fel. Alas, madam, all is worse than ever!
Clara What has happened?
Fel. Not only did my two friends fall out with each other, as I expected, but with me for the very good services I was doing them; insulted me till I could withhold my sword no longer; we went out to fight; were seen, pursued, and disperst by the alguazils. I return'd home to await them, but as yet know nothing more of them.
Clara Alas, sir, what do I not owe you for your care on my behalf?
Fel. More perhaps than you imagine.
Clara Tell me all at least, that I may at least know my debt, if unable to repay it.
Fel. Alas, I dare not say what is said in not saying.
Clara Said, and not said? I do not understand!
Fel. I, alas, too well!
Clara Explain to me then, sir.
Fel. No, madam. If what I feel is so much on my friends' account, it is still more for their sakes that I keep it unsaid.
Clara Hark! what noise is that? Mari Nuño, what is the matter?

Enter MARI NUÑO

Mari Oh, madam, some one is getting over the garden wall! Your father has heard the noise; and is got up with his sword.
Clara If he should find you!
Fel. He need not. This balcony —
Clara No, no!
Torribio (within). Thieves! Murder! Help!

(He opens the balcony; TORRIBIO *falls forward on him, push'd in by* JUAN *with his sword drawn.)*

Torr. Murder! Murder!
Juan (to FELIX*).* Thou too here, traitor!   } *All at once.*
Fel. (drawing his sword). Who are these?

(Confusion, in which enter ALONSO *with drawn sword,* OTAÑEZ, BRIGIDA, *&c.)*

Alon. Two! Torribio, to my side.

Fel. Wait! wait! Let me explain.

Alon. Don Felix!

Fel. Listen to me, all of you, I say! I was sent for to prevent, not to do, mischief, by Donna Eugenia herself —

Enter EUGENIA

Eug. By *me*, sir!

Clara Hold, hold, Eugenia.

Eug. I will *not* hold when my name is in question without my — Sent for by me, sir!

Fel. Not by you, madam; by Donna Eugenia, *(pointing to* CLARA,) to prevent —

Alon. and Eug. Clara!

Torr. Ah, 't was she put me to freeze in the balcony, too.

Clara (to FELIX). Sir, you come here to save another from peril. Leave me not in it.

Fel. I leave you, madam, who would lay down my life for you! and all the rather if you are *not* Donna Eugenia.

Alon. None but her father or her husband must do that.

Fel. Then let me claim to do it as the latter. *(Kneels to* CLARA.)

Alon. But, Clara?

Clara Sir, I am ready to obey my father — and my husband.

Eug. And I, sir. And to prove my duty, let me marry my cousin at once, and retire with him to the mountains.

Torr. Marry me! No, indeed! No Capacities, and ladders, and — what-d'ye-call-'ems — for me. I'll e'en go back as I came, with my ancestors safe in my saddle-bags, I will.

Juan (to ALONSO). Permit me, sir. I am Don Juan de Mendoza; a name at least not unknown to you. I have loved your daughter long; and might have had perchance favourable acceptation from her mother long ago, had not you yourself been abroad at the time.

Alon. I now remember to have heard something of the kind. What say you, Eugenia?

Eug. I am ready to obey my father — and my husband.
       With which at last our comedy shall close,
       Asking indulgence both of friends and foes.
Clara And ere we part our text for envoy give, —
Beware of all smooth waters while you live!

This Comedy seems an Occasional Piece, to celebrate the marriage of Philip IV. with Anna Maria of Austria, and the pageants that Calderon himself was summoned to devise and manage. This marriage was in 1649; when Calderon, as old as the century, was in his prime: and I think the airy lightness of the dialogue, the play of character, the easy intrigue, and the happily introduced wedding rhapsodies, make it one of the most agreeable of his comedies.

As I purposely reduced the swell of Isabel's speech in the last play, I must confess that the present version of these wedding pageants, though not unauthorized by the original, had perhaps better have been taken in a lighter tone to chime in with so much common dialogue. But they were done first, to see what could be made of them: and, as little dramatic interest is concerned, are left as they were; at least not the less like so much in Calderon, where love and loyalty are concerned; and to be excused by the reader as speeches *spouted* by boys on holiday occasions.

THE MIGHTY MAGICIAN

AURELIO, *Viceroy of Antioch*
LELIO, *his Son*
FABIO, *a chief Officer in Antioch*
FLORO, *his Son*
LISANDRO, *an aged Christian*
JUSTINA, *his Daughter*
LIVIA, *their servant*
CIPRIANO, *a Professor of Learning*
EUSEBIO ⎫
⎬ *his Scholars*
JULIAN ⎭
LUCIFER, *the Evil Spirit*

CITIZENS, SOLDIERS, &c.

ACT I

SCENE I. *A retired Grove near Antioch. — Enter* CIPRIANO,
EUSEBIO, *and* JULIAN, *with books.*

   Cipr.   THIS is the place, this the sequester'd spot
Where, in the flower about and leaf above,
I find the shade and quiet that I love,
And oft resort to rest a wearied wing;
And here, good lads, leave me alone, but not
Lonely, companion'd with the books you bring:
That while the city from all open doors
Abroad her gaping population pours,
To swell the triumph of the pomp divine
That with procession, sacrifice, and song
Convoys her tutelary Zeus along
For installation in his splendid shrine;
I, flying from the hubbub of the throng
That overflows her thoroughfares and streets,
And here but faintly touches and retreats,
In solitary meditation may
Discount at ease my summer holiday.
You to the city back, and take your fill
Of festival, and all that with the time's,
And your own youth's, triumphant temper chimes;
Leaving me here alone to mine; until
Yon golden idol reaching overhead,
Dragg'd from his height, and bleeding out his fires
Along the threshold of the west, expires,
And drops into the sea's sepulchral lead.
     Eusebio   Nay, sir, think once again, and go with us,

Or, if you will, without us; only, go;
Lest Antioch herself as well as we
Cry out upon a maim'd solemnity.
   Julian   Oh, how I wish I had not brought the books,
Which you have ever at command — indeed,
Without them, all within them carry — here —
Garner'd — aloft —
   Euseb.   In truth, if stay you will,
I scarcely care to go myself.
   Cipr.   Nay, nay,
Good lads, good boys, all thanks, and all the more,
If you but leave it simply as I say.
You have been somewhat overtaxed of late,
And want some holiday.
   Julian   Well, sir, and you?
   Cipr.   Oh, I am of that tougher age and stuff
Whose relaxation is its work.   Besides,
Think you the poor Professor needs no time
For solitary tillage of his brains
Before such shrewd ingatherers as you
Come on him for their harvest unawares?
Away, away! and like good citizens
Help swell the general joy with two such faces
As such as mine would only help to cloud.
   Euseb.   Nay, sir —
   Cipr.   But I say, Yea, sir! and my scholars
By yea and nay as I would have them do.
   Euseb.   Well, then, farewell, sir.
   Cipr.   Farewell, both of you.
                     [*Exeunt* EUSEBIO *and* JULIAN.
Away with them, light heart and wingéd heel,
Soon leaving drowsy Pallas and her dull
Professor out of sight, and out of mind.
And yet not so perhaps; and, were it so,
Why, better with the frolic herd forgetting
All in the youth and sunshine of the day
Than ruminating in the shade apart.
Well, each his way and humour; some to lie
Like Nature's sickly children in her lap,
While all the stronger brethren are at play;

When ev'n the mighty Mother's self would seem
Drest out in all her festival attire
In honour of the universal Sire
Whom Antioch as for her own to-day
Propitiates.   Hark, the music! — Speed, good lads,
Or you will be too late.   Ah, needless caution!
Ev'n now already half way down the hill,
Spurr'd by the very blood within their veins,
They catch up others, who catching from them
The fire they re-inflame, the flying troop
Consuming fast to distance in a cloud
Of dust themselves have kindled, whirls away
Where the shrill music blown above the walls
Tells of the solemn work begun within.
Why, ev'n the shrieking pipe that pierces here,
Shows me enough of all the long procession
Of white-robed priest and chanting chorister,
The milkwhite victim crown'd, and high aloft
The chariot of the nodding deity,
Whose brazen eyes that as their sockets see,
Stare at his loyal votaries.   Ah me! —
Well, here too happier, if not wiser, those
Who, with the heart of unsuspicious youth,
Take up tradition from their fathers' hands
To pass it on to others in their turn;
But leaving me behind them in the race
With less indeed than little appetite
For ceremonies, and to gods, like these,
That, let the rabble shout for as they please,
Another sort begin to shake their heads at,
And heav'n to rumble with uneasily
As flinging out some antiquated gear.
So wide, since subtle Greece the pebble flung
Into the sleeping pool of superstition,
Its undulation spreads to other shores,
And saps at the foundation of our schools.
— Why, this last Roman, Caius Plinius —
Who drawing nature's growth and history
Down to her root and first cause — What says he? —
Ev'n at the very threshold of his book

A definition laying over which
The clumsy mimic idols of our shrines
Stumble and break to pieces — oh, here it is —
"*Quapropter effigiem Dei formamque quærere,*
Imbecillitatis humanæ reor" —
"All visible effigies of God
But types of human imbecility." —
But what has Antioch to say to that,
Who at such cost of marble and of gold
Has built the very temple into which
She drags her tutelary Zeus to-day? —
Zeus veritable God, this effigy
Is none of him at all!   But then, alas!
This same *Quapropter* follows a premiss
That elbows out Zeus with his effigy.
For — as I gather from his foreign word —
Wherever, or Whatever, Deity —
Si modo est alius — if distinct at all
From universal Nature — it must be
One all-informing, individual Whole,
All eye, all ear, all self, all sense, all soul —
Whereas this Zeus of ours, though Chief indeed —
Nay, *because* chief of other gods than he,
Comes from this Roman's hand no God at all! —
This is a knotty question.
    Lucifer (without).   Nor while I
Tangle, for you, good doctor, to untie.
    Cipr.   What!   The poor bird scarce settled on the bough,
Before the fowler after him!   How now?
Who's there?
    Lucifer (entering habited as a Merchant).   A stranger;
       therefore pardon him,
Who somehow parted from his company
And lost in his own thoughts (a company
You know one cannot lose so easily)
Has lost his way to Antioch.
    Cipr.   Antioch!
Whose high white towers and temples ev'n from here
Challenge the sight, and scarce a random line
Traced by a wandering foot along the grass

But thither leads for centre.

Luc.   The old story,
Of losing what one should have found on earth
By staring after something in the clouds —
Is it not so?

Cipr.   To-day too, when so many
Are flocking thither to the festival,
Whose current might have told — and taken — you
The way you wished to go.

Luc.   To say the truth,
My lagging here behind as much I think
From a distaste for that same festival
(Of which they told us as we came along)
As inadvertency — my way of life
Busied enough, if not too much, with men
To care for them in crowd on holidays,
When business stands, and neither they nor I
Gaping about can profit one another;
And therefore, by your leave — but only so —
I fain would linger in this quiet place
Till evening, under whose dusky cloak
I may creep unobserv'd to Antioch.

Cipr. (aside).   Humane address, at least.   And why should I
Grudge him the quiet I myself desire? —
(Aloud.) Nay, this is public ground — for you, as me,
To use it at your pleasure.

Luc.   Still with yours —
Whom by your sober suit and composed looks,
And by this still society of books,
I take to be a scholar —

Cipr.   And if so?

Luc.   Ill brooking idle company.

Cipr.   Perhaps;
But that no wiser traveller need be —
And, if I judge of you as you of me,
Though with no book hung out for sign before,
Perchance a scholar too.

Luc.   If so, more read
In men than books, as travellers are wont.
But, if myself but little of a bookman,

Addicted much to scholars' company,
Of whom I meet with many on my travels,
And who, you know, themselves are living books.
    Cipr.   And you have travell'd much?
    Luc.   Aye, little else,
One may say, since I came into the world
Than going up and down it: visiting
As many men and cities as Ulysses,
From first his leaving Troy without her crown,
Along the charméd coasts he pass'd, with all
The Polyphemes and Circes in the way,
Right to the Pillars where his ship went down.
Nay, and yet farther, where the dark Phœnician
Digs the pale metal which the sun scarce deigns
With a slant glance to ripen in earth's veins:
Or back again so close beneath his own
Proper dominion, that the very mould
Beneath he kindles into proper gold,
And strikes a living Iris into stone.
    Cipr.   One place, however, where Ulysses was,
I think you have not been to — where he saw
Those he left dead upon the field of Troy
Come one by one to lap the bowl of blood
Set for them in the fields of Asphodel.
    Luc.   Humph! — as to that, a voyage which if all
Must take, less need to brag of; or perchance
Ulysses, or his poet, apt to err
About the people and their doings there —
But let the wonders in the world below
Be what they may; enough in that above
For any sober curiosity,
Without one's diving down before one's time:
Not only countries now as long ago
Known, till'd, inhabited, and civilized;
As Egypt, Greece, and Rome, with all their arts,
Trades, customs, polities, and history:
But deep in yet scarce navigated seas,
Countries uncouth, with their peculiar growths
Of vegetation or of life; where men
Are savage as the soil they never till;

Or never were, or were so long ago,
Their very story blotted from the page
Of earth they wrote it on; unless perchance
From riot-running nature's overgrowth
Of swarming vegetation, peeps some scarce
Decypherable monument which yet,
To those who find the key, perchance has told
Stories of men, more mighty men, of old,
Or of the gods themselves who walk'd the world
When with the dews of first creation wet.

   Cipr.   Oh knowledge from the fountain freshly drawn
Without the tedious go-between of books!
But with fresh soul and senses unimpair'd
What from the pale reflection of report
We catch at second hand, and much beside
That in our solitary cells we miss.

   Luc.   Aye, truly we that travel see strange things,
Though said to tell of stranger; some of us,
Deceived ourselves, or seeking to deceive,
With prodigies and monsters which the world,
As wide and full of wonders as it is,
Never yet saw, I think, nor ever will:
Which yet your scholars use for clay and straw
Of which to build your mighty folios —
For instance this same bulky Roman here,
Whose leaf you turn'd, I doubt impatiently,
When my intrusion rustled in the leaves —

   Cipr.   Hah!   But how knew you —
   Luc.   Nay, if some stray words
Of old familiar Latin met my ear
As I stood hesitating.

   Cipr. (holding up the book).   This at least
You read then?

   Luc.   One might say before 't was written.

   Cipr.   But how so?

   Luc.   Oh, this same sufficient Roman,
What is he but another of the many
Who having seen a little and heard more
That others pick'd as loosely up before,
Constructs his little bird's-nest universe

Of shreds and particles of false and true
Cemented with some thin philosophy,
All filch'd from others, as from him to be
By the next pilfering philosopher,
Till blown away before the rising wind
Of true discovery, or dropt to nothing
After succeeding seasons of neglect.
    Cipr. (aside).   A strange man this — sharp wit and biting
       word.
(Aloud.) Yet surely Man, after so many ages
Of patient observation of the world
He lives in, is entitled by the wit
Vouchsafed him by the Maker of the world
To draw into some comprehensive whole
The stray particulars.
    Luc.   Aye, and forsooth,
Not only the material world he lives in;
But, having of this undigested heap
Composed a world, must make its Maker too,
Of abstract attributes, of each of which
Still more unsure than of the palpable,
Forthwith he draws to some consistent One
The accumulated ignorance of each
In so compact a plausibility
As light to carry as it was to build.
    Cipr.   But, since (I know not how) you hit upon
The question I was trying when you came;
And, spite of your disclaiming scholarship,
Seem versed in that which occupies the best —
If Pliny blunder with his single God,
As in our twilight reason well he may,
Confess however that a Deity
Plural and self-discordant, as he says,
Is yet more like frail man's imagination,
Who, for his own necessities and lusts,
Splits up and mangles the Divine idea
To pieces, as he wants a piece of each;
Not only gods for all the elements
Divided into land, and sea, and sky;
But gods of health, wealth, love, and fortune; nay,

Of war and murder, rape and robbery;
Men of their own worse nature making gods
To serve the very vices that suggest them,
Which yet upon their fellow-men they visit
(Else were an end of human polity)
With chain and fine and banishment and death.
So that unless man made such gods as these,
Then are these gods worse than the man they made.
And for the attributes, which though indeed
You gibe at us for canvassing, yourself
Must grant — as whether one or manifold,
Deity in its simplest definition
Must be at least eternal —

  Luc.   Well? —

  Cpr.   Yet those
Who stuff Olympus are so little that,
That Zeus himself, the sovereign of all,
Barely escaped devouring at his birth
By his own father, who anticipated
And found some such hard measure for himself;
And as for Zeus' own progeny — some born
Of so much baser matter than his brain,
As from his eggs, which the almighty swan
Impregnated, and mortal Leda laid;
And whose two chicken-deities once hatch'd
Now live and die on each alternate day.

  Luc. Aye, but if much of this be allegory
In which the wisdom of antiquity
Veils the pure Deity from eyes profane —

  Cipr. — Deity taking arms against itself
Under Troy walls, wounding and wounded — aye
And, trailing heavenly ichor from their wounds,
So help'd by others from the field to one
Who knew the leech's art themselves did not.

  Luc. Softly — if not to swear to allegory,
Still less to all the poets sing of heaven,
High up Parnassus as they think to sit.

  Cipr. But these same poets, therefore sacred call'd,
They are who these same allegories spin
Which time and fond tradition consecrate;

What might have been of the divine within
So overgrown with folly and with sin
As but a spark of God would such impure
Assimilation with himself abjure,
Which yet with all the nostril that he may
Zeus snuffs from Antioch's sacrifice to-day.
Besides, beyond the reach of allegory
The gods themselves in their own oracles
Doubly themselves convict —
As when they urge two nations on to war,
By promising the victory to each;
Whereby on one side their omniscience
Suffers, as their all-goodness on the other.

    Luc.   What if such seeming contradictions aim
Where human understanding cannot reach?
But granting for the sake of argument,
And for that only, what you now premise;
What follows?

    Cipr.   Why, that if, as Pliny writes,
Deity by its very definition
Be one, eternal, absolute, all wise,
All good, omnipotent, all ear, all eyes,
Incapable of disintegration —
If this be Deity indeed —

    Luc.   Then what?

    Cipr.   Simply — that we in Antioch know him not.

    Luc.   Rash leap to necessary non-conclusion
From a premiss that quarrels with itself
More than the deity it would impugn;
For if one God eternal and all wise,
Omnipotent to do as to devise,
Whence this disorder and discordance in —
Not only this material universe,
That seems created only to be rack'd
By the rebellion of its elements,
In earthquake and tempestuous anarchy —
But also in the human microcosm
You say created to reflect it all?
For Deity, all goodness as all wise,
Why create man the thing of lust and lies

You say reflects himself in his false god?—
By modern oracle no more convicted
Of falsehood, than by that first oracle
Which first creation settled in man's heart.
No, if you must define, premise, conclude,
Away with all the coward squeamishness
That dares not face the universe it questions;
Blinking the evil and antagonism
Into its very constitution breathed
By him who, but himself to quarrel with,
Quarrels as might the many with each other.
Or would you be yourself one with yourself,
Catch hold of such as Epicurus' skirt,
Who, desperately confounded this confusion
Of matter, spirit, good and evil, yea,
Godhead itself, into a universe
That is created, roll'd along, and ruled,
By no more wise direction than blind Chance.
Trouble yourself no more with disquisition
That by sad, slow, and unprogressive steps
Of wasted soul and body lead to nothing:
And only sure of life's short breathing-while,
And knowing that the gods who threaten us
With after-vengeance of the very crimes
They revel in themselves, are nothing more
Than the mere coinage of our proper brain
To cheat us of our scanty pleasure here
With terror of a harsh account hereafter; —
Eat, drink, be merry; crown yourselves with flowers
About as lasting as the heads they garland;
And snatching what you can of life's poor feast,
When summon'd to depart, with no ill grace,
Like a too greedy guest, cling to the table
Whither the generations that succeed
Press forward famish'd for their turn to feed.
Nay, or before your time self-surfeited,
Wait not for nature's signal to be gone,
But with the potion of the spotted weed,
That peradventure wild beside your door
For some such friendly purpose cheaply grows,

Anticipate too tardy nature's call:
Ev'n as one last great Roman of them all
Dismiss'd himself betimes into the sum
Of universe; not nothing to become;
For that can never cease that was before;
But not that sad Lucretius any more.

    Cipr.   Oh, were it not that sometimes through the dark
That walls us about, a random ray
Breaks in to tell one of a better day
Beyond —

Enter LELIO *and* FLORO, *as about to fight*

    Lelio   Enough — these branches that exclude the sun
Defy all other inquisition.
No need of further way.
    Floro   Nor further word;
Draw, sir, at once —
    Lelio   Nay, parry that yourself
Which waited not your summons to be drawn.
    Cipr.   Lelio, and Floro?
    Floro   What, will the leaves blab?
    Lelio   And with their arms arrest a just revenge?
    Cipr.   And well indeed may trees begin to talk,
When men as you go babbling.
    Floro   Whoso speaks
And loves his life, hold back.
    Lelio   I know the voice,
But dazzled with the darkness — Cipriano!
    Cipr.   Aye; Cipriano, sure enough; as you
Lelio and Floro.
    Floro   Well, let that suffice,
And leave us as you find us.
    Cipr.   No, not yet —
    Floro   Not yet!
    Lelio   Good Cipriano —
    Cipr.   Till I know
How it has come to pass that two such friends,
Each of the noblest blood in Antioch,
Are here to shed it by each other's hands.

Lelio Sudden surprise, and old respect for you,
Suspend my sword a moment, Cipriano,
That else —
     Floro Stand back, stand back!   You are a scholar,
And better versed in logic than the laws
Of honour; and perhaps have yet to learn
That when two noblemen have drawn the sword,
One only must return it to the sheath.
     Lelio 'T is so indeed — once more, stand off.
     Cipr.   And once more
Back, both of you, say I; if of your lives
Regardless, not of mine, which thus, unarm'd,
I fling between your swords —
Lelio, I look to you — Floro, as ever
Somewhat hot-headed and thrasonical —
Or do you hold with him the scholar's gown
Has smother'd all the native soldiery
That saucy so-call'd honour to itself
Alone mis-arrogates!   You are deceived:
I am like you by birth a gentleman,
Under like obligation to the laws
Of that true honour, which my books indeed
May help distinguish from its counterfeit,
But, older as I am, have yet not chill'd
From catching fire at any just affront —
And let me tell you this too — those same books,
Ancient and modern, tell of many a hand
That, turning most assiduously the leaf,
When the time came, could wield as well the sword.
I am unarm'd: but you, with all your swords,
I say you shall not turn them on each other
Till you have told me what the quarrel is;
Which after hearing if I own for one
That honour may not settle with good word,
I pledge my own to leave it to the sword.
Now, Lelio? —
     Lelio   One answer does for both:
He loves where I love.
     Floro   No — I thus much more —
He dares to love where I had loved before;

Betrayéd friendship adding to the score
Of upstart love.
    Lelio   You hear him, Cipriano?
And after such a challenge —
    Cipr.   Yet a moment.
As there are kinds of honour, so of love —
And ladies —
    Lelio   Cipriano, Cipriano!
One friend my foe for daring love where I,
Let not another, daring doubt that he
Honours himself in so dishonouring me —
    Floro   Slanting your sharp divisions on a jewel
That if the sun turn'd all his beams upon
He could not find, or make, a flaw —
    Cipr.   Nor I then,
With far less searching scrutiny than Phœbus —
I am to understand then, such a fair
Jewel as either would in wedlock wear.
    Floro   And rather die than let another dare.
    Cipr.   Enough, enough! of Lelio's strange logic,
And Floro's more intelligible rant,
And back to sober metaphor.   Which of you
Has this fair jewel turn'd her light upon?
    Floro (after a pause).   Why, who would boast —
    Lelio   Indeed, how could she be
The very pearl of chastity she is,
Turn'd she her glances either left or right?
    Cipr.   Which therefore each, as he obliquely steals,
Counts on as given him only —
    Floro   To have done
With metaphor and logic, what you will,
So as we fall to work;
Or if you must have reason, this, I say,
Resolves itself to a short syllogism —
Whether she give or we presume upon —
If one of us devote himself to win her,
How dares another cross him?
    Cipr.   But if she
Not only turn to neither, but still worse,
Or better, turn from both?

Lelio   But love by long devotion may be won,
That only one should offer —
  Floro   And that one
Who first —
  Lelio   Who first! —
  Cipr.   And all this while, forsooth,
The lady, of whose purity one test
Is her unblemisht unpublicity,
Is made a target for the common tongue
Of Antioch to shoot reproaches at
For stirring up two noblemen to blood.
From which she only can escape, forsooth,
By choosing one of two she cares not for
At once; or else, to mend the matter, when
He comes to claim her by the other's blood.
  Lelio   At least she will not hate him, live or dead,
Who staked his life upon her love.
    Cipr.   Small good
To him who lost the stake; and he that won —
Will she begin to love whom not before
For laying unloved blood upon her door;
Or, if she ever loved at all, love more?
Is this fair logic, or of one who knows
No more of woman's honour than of man's?
Come, come, no more of beating round the bush,
You know how I have known and loved you both,
As brothers — say as sons — upon the score
Of some few years and some few books read more —
Though two such fiery fine young gentlemen,
Put up your swords and be good boys again,
Deferring to your ancient pedagogue;
If cold by time and studies, as you say,
Then fitter for a go-between in love,
And warm at least in loyalty to you.
These jewels — to take up the metaphor
Until you choose to drop it of yourselves —
These jewels have their caskets, I suppose —
Kindred and circumstance, I mean —
    Lelio   Oh such
As by their honourable poverty

Do more than doubly set the jewel off!

Cipr.   Ev'n so?   And may not one, who, you agree,
Proof-cold against suspicion of the kind,
Be so far trusted, as, if not to see,
To hear, at least, of where, and how, enshrined?

    Floro   I know not what to answer.   How say you?

    Lelio   Relying on your honour and tried love —
Justina, daughter of the old Lisandro.

    Cipr.   I know them; her if scarcely, yet how far
Your praises short of her perfections are;
Him better, by some little service done
That rid him of a greater difficulty,
And would again unlock his door to me —
— And who knows also, if you both agree,
Her now closed lips; if but a sigh between
May tell which way the maiden heart may lean?

    Floro   Again, what say you, Lelio?

    Lelio   I, for one,
Content with that decision.

    Floro   Be it so.

    Cipr.   Why, after all, behold how luckily
You stumbled on this rock in honour's road,
That serves instead for Cupid's stepping-stone.
And when the knightly courage of you both
Was all at fault to hammer out the way,
Who knows but some duenna-doctor may?
And will — if but like reasonable men,
Not angry boys, you promise to keep sheath'd
Your swords, while from her father or herself
I gather, from a single sigh perhaps,
To which, if either, unaware she turns;
Provided, if to one, the other yield;
But if to neither, both shall quit the field.
What say you both to this?

    Lelio   Aye — I for one.

    Floro   And I; provided on the instant done.

    Cipr.   No better time than now, when, as I think,
The city, with her solemn uproar busy,
Shuts her we have to do with close within.
But you must come along with me, for fear

Your hands go feeling for your swords again
If left together: and besides to know
The verdict soon as spoken.

    Lelio   Let us go.   [*Exeunt.*

    Lucifer (re-appearing). Aye, Cipriano, faster than you
        think;

For I will lend you wings to burn yourself
In the same taper they are singed withal. —
By the quick feelers of iniquity
That from hell's mouth reach through this lower world,
And tremble to the lightest touch of mischief,
Warn'd of an active spirit hereabout
Of the true God inquisitive, and restless
Under the false by which I rule the world,
Here am I come to test it for myself.
And lo! two fools have put into my hand
The snare that, wanting most, I might have miss'd;
That shall not him alone en-mesh, but *her*
Whom I have long and vainly from the ranks
Striv'n to seduce of Him, the woman-born,
Who is one day to bruise the serpent's head —
So is it written; but meanwhile my hour
On earth is not accomplisht, and I fain
Of this detested race would hinder all
From joining in the triumph of my fall
Whom I may hinder; and of these, these twain;
Each other by each other snaring; yea,
Either at once the other's snare and prey.
Oh, my good doctor, you must doubt, you must,
And take no more the good old gods on trust;
To Antioch then away; but not so fast
But I shall be before you, starting last.   [*Exit.*

    SCENE II.   *A Room in* LISANDRO's *house.* — *Enter*
            LISANDRO, JUSTINA, *and* LIVIA.

    Justina   At length the day draws in.
    Lisandro   And in with it
The impious acclamation that all day,
Block up our doors and windows as we may,

Insults our faith, and doubly threatens it.
Is all made fast, Justina?

Just. All shall be, sir,
When I have seen you safely to your rest.

Lis. You know how edict after edict aim'd
By Rome against the little band of Christ —
And at a time like this, the people drunk
With idol-ecstasy —

Just. Alas, alas!

Lis. Oh, gladly would I scatter these last drops
That now so scarcely creep along my veins,
And these thin locks that tremble o'er the grave,
In such a martyrdom as swept to heav'n
The holy Paul who planted, and all those
Who water'd here the true and only faith,
Were't not for thee, for fear of thee, Justina,
Drawing you down at once into my doom,
Or leaving you behind, alone, to hide
From insult and suspicion worse than death —
I dare not think of it. Make fast; keep close;
And then, God's will be done! You know we lie
Under a double danger.

Just. How so, sir?

Lis. Aurelio and Fabio, both, you know,
So potent in the city, and but now
Arm'd with a freshly whetted sword of vengeance
Against the faith, but double-edged on us,
Should they but know, as know they must, their sons
Haunting the doors of this suspected house.

Just. Alas, alas!
That I should draw this danger on your head!
Which yet you know —

Lis. I know, I know — God knows,
My darling daughter; but that chaste reserve
Serves but to quicken beauty with a charm
They find not in the wanton Venus here:
Drawn as they are by those withdrawing eyes
Irradiate from a mother's, into whose
The very eyes of the Redeemer look'd,
And whom I dare not haste to join in heav'n

At cost of leaving thee defenceless here.

Just.   Sufficient for the day!   And now the day
Is done.   Come to your chamber — lean on me —
Livia and I will see that all is fast;
And, that all seen to, ere we sleep ourselves,
Come to your bedside for your blessing.   Hark!
Knocking ev'n now!   See to it, Livia.

(She leads out LISANDRO, *and returns.)*

Oh, well I got my father to his chamber!
What is it? —

Livia   One would see your father, madam.

Just.   At such an hour!   He cannot, Livia;
You know the poor old man is gone to rest —
Tell him —

Livia   If not your father, then yourself,
On matter that he says concerns you both.

Just.   Me too! — Oh, surely neither of the twain
We both so dread?

Livia   No, madam; rather one
I think that neither need have cause to fear, —
Cipriano.

Just.   Cipriano!   The great scholar,
Who did my father service, as I think,
And now may mean another; and God knows
How much, or quickly, needed!

Livia   So he says.

Just.   What shall I do!   Will not to-morrow —

Cipriano (entering).   Oh, lady,
You scarce can wonder more than I myself
At such a visit, and at such an hour,
Only let what I come to say excuse
The coming, and so much unmannerly.

Just.   My father is withdrawn, sir, for the night,
Never more wanting rest; I dare not rouse him,
And least of all with any troubled news.
Will not to-morrow —

Cipr.   What I have to say
Best told to-night, at once; and not the less
Since you alone, whom chiefly it concerns,
Are here to listen.

Just.   I! — Well, sir, relying
On your grave reputation as a scholar,
And on your foregone favour to my father,
If I should dare to listen —
    Cipr.   And alone?
    Just. Livia, leave us.   [*Exit* LIVIA.
    Cipr.   Oh, lady — oh, Justina —
(Thus stammers the ambassador of love
In presence of its sovereign) —
You must — cannot but — know how many eyes
Those eyes have wounded —
    Just.   Nay, sir —
    Cipr.   Nay, but hear.
I do not come for idle compliment,
Nor on my own behalf; but in a cause
On which hang life and death as well as love.
Two of the noblest youths in Antioch,
Lelio and Floro — Nay, but hear me out:
Mine, and till now almost from birth each other's
Inseparable friends, now deadly foes
For love of you —
    Just.   Oh, sir!
    Cipr.   I have but now
Parted their swords in mortal quarrel cross'd.
    Just. Oh, that was well.
    Cipr.   I think, for several sakes —
Their own, their fathers', even Antioch's
That would not lose one of so choice a pair;
And, I am sure you think so, lady, yours,
So less than covetous of public talk,
And least of all at such a fearful cost.
    Just. Oh, for all sakes all thanks!
    Cipr.   Yet little due
For what so lightly done, and it may be
So insufficiently; this feud not stopt —
Suspended only, on a single word —
Which now at this unseasonable hour
I stand awaiting from the only lips
That can allay the quarrel they have raised.
    Just. Alas, why force an answer from my lips

So long implied in silent disregard?

Cipr.   Yet, without which, like two fierce dogs, but more
Exasperated by the holding back,
They will look for it in each other's blood.

Just.   And think, poor men, to find their answer there!
Oh, sir, you are the friend, the friend of both,
A famous scholar; with authority
And eloquence to press your friendship home.
Surely in words such as you have at will
You can persuade them for all sakes — and yet
No matter mine perhaps — but, as you say,
Their fathers', Antioch's, their own —

Cipr.   Alas!
I doubt you know not in your maiden calm
How fast all love and logic such as that
Burns stubble up before a flame like this!

Just. (aside).   And none in heav'n to help them!

Cipr.   All I can
But one condition hardly wringing out
Of peace, till my impartial embassy
Have ask'd on their behalf, which of the twain —
How shall I least offend? — you least disdain?

Just.   Disdain is not the word, sir; oh, no, no!
I know and honour both as noblemen
Of blood and station far above my own;
And of so suitable accomplishments.
Oh, there are many twice as fair as I,
And of their own conditions, who, with half
My wooing, long ere this had worn the wreath
Tied with a father's blessing, and all Antioch
To follow them with Hymeneal home.

Cipr.   But if these fiery men, do what one will,
Will look no way but this? —

Just.   Oh, but they will;
Divert their eyes awhile, a little while,
Their hearts will follow; such a sudden passion
Can but have struck a shallow root — perhaps
Ere this had perish'd, had not rival pride
Between them blown it to this foolish height.

Cipr.   Disdain is not the word then.   Well, to seek,

What still as wide as ever from assent —
Could you but find it in your heart to feel
If but a hair's-breadth less — say dis-esteem
For one than for the other —
    Just.   No, no, no!
Even to save their lives I could not say
What is not — cannot — nay, and if it could
And I could say that was that is not — *can* not —
How should that hair's-breadth less of hope to one
Weigh with the other to desist his suit,
Both furious as you tell me?
    Cipr.   And both are:
But ev'n that single hair thrown in by you
Will turn the scale that else the sword must do.
    Just.   But surely must it not suffice for both
That they who drew the sword in groundless hope
Sheathe it in sure despair? Despair! Good God!
For a poor creature like myself, despair!
That men with souls to which a word like that
Lengthens to infinite significance,
Should pin it on a wretched woman's sleeve!
But as men talk — I mean, as far as I
Can make them, as they say, despair of that
Of which, even for this world's happiness,
Despair is better hope of better things —
Will not my saying — and as solemnly
As what one best may vouch for; that so far
As any hope of my poor liking goes,
Despair indeed they must — why should not this
Allay their wrath, and let relapsing love
In his own channel all the clearer run
For this slight interjection in the current?
Why should it not be so?
    Cipr.   Alas, I know not:
For though as much they promised, yet I doubt
When each, however you reject him now,
Believes you might be won hereafter still,
Were not another to divide the field;
Each upon each charging the exigence
He will not see lies in himself alone,

Might draw the scarcely sheathéd sword at once;
Or stifled hate under a hollow truce
Blaze out anew at some straw's provocation,
And I perhaps not by to put it out.
    Just.   What can, what can be done then!
    Cipr.   Oh, Justina,
Pardon this iteration.   Think once more,
Before your answer with its consequence
Travels upon my lip to destiny.
I know you more than maiden-wise reserved
To other importunities of love
Than those which ev'n the pure for pure confess;
Yet no cold statue, which, however fair,
Could not inflame so fierce a passion; but
A breathing woman with a beating heart,
Already touch'd with pity, you confess,
For these devoted men you cannot love.
Well, then — I will not hint at such a bower
As honourable wedlock would entwine
About your father's age and your own youth,
Which ev'n for him — and much less for yourself —
You would not purchase with an empty hand.
But yet, with no more of your heart within
Than what you now confess to — pity — pity,
For generous youth wearing itself away
In thankless adoration at your door,
Neglecting noble opportunities;
Turning all love but yours to deadly hate —
Sedate, and wise, and modestly resolved,
Can you be, lady, of yourself so sure —
(And surely they will argue your disdain
As apt to yield as their devotion) —
That, all beside so honourably faced,
You, who now look with pity, and perhaps
With gratitude, upon their blundering zeal,
May not be won to turn an eye less loath
On one of them, and blessing one, save both?
    Just.   Alas! I know it is impossible —
Not if they wasted all their youth in sighs,
And even slavish importunities,

I could but pity — pity all the more
That all the less what only they implore
To yield; so great a gulf between us lies.
    Cipr.   What — is the throne pre-occupied?
    Just.   If so,
By one that Antioch dreams little of.
But it grows late: and if we spoke till dawn,
I have no more to say.
    Cipr.   Nor more will hear?
    Just.   Alas, sir, to what purpose?   When, all said,
Said too as you have said it —
And I have but the same hard answer still;
Unless to thank you once and once again,
And charge you with my thankless errand back,
But in such better terms,
As, if it cannot stop ill blood, at least
Shall stop blood-shedding 'tween these hapless men.
    Cipr.   And shall the poor ambassador who fail'd
In the behalf of those who sent him here,
Hereafter dare to tell you how he sped
In making peace between them?
    Just.   Oh, do but that,
And what poor human prayer can win from Heav'n,
You shall not be the poorer.   So, good-night!   [*Exit.*
    Cipr.   Good-night, good-night!   Oh Lelio and Floro!
If ever friends well turn'd to deadly foes,
Wiser to fight than I to interpose.
    Lucifer (passing from behind).   The shaft has hit the mark;
        and by the care
Of hellish surgery shall fester there.   [*Exit.*

ACT II

SCENE I. *The sea-shore; a storm raging.*

Cipriano (cavalierly drest).   OH, mad, mad, mad, ambition! to the skies
Lifting to drop me deep as Hades down! —
What!   Cipriano — what the once so wise
Cipriano — quit his wonted exercise
Among the sober walks of old renown,
To fly at love — to swell the wind with sighs
Vainer than learning — doff the scholar's gown
For cap and feather, and such airy guise
In which triumphant love is wont to go,
But wins less acceptation in her eyes —
The only eyes in which I cared to show —
My heart beneath the borrow'd feather bleeding —
Than in the sable suit of long ago,
When heart-whole for another's passion pleading.
She loves not Floro — loves not Lelio,
Whose quarrel sets the city's throat agape,
And turns her reputation to reproof
With altercation of some dusky shape
Haunting the twilight underneath her roof —
Which each believes the other: — and, for me,
The guilty one of the distracted three,
She closest veils herself, or waves aloof
In scorn; or in such self-abasement sweet
As sinks me deep and deeper at her feet,
Bids me return — return for very shame,
Back to my proper studies and good name,

Nor waste a life on one who, let me pine
To death, will never but in death be mine.
Oh, she says well — oh, heart of stone and ice
Unworthy of the single sacrifice
Of one true heart's devotion.   Oh divine
Creature, whom all the glory and the worth
That ever ravaged or redeem'd the earth
Were scanty worship offered at your shrine!
Oh Cipriano, master-fool of all
The fools that unto thee for wisdom call;
Of supercilious Pallas first the mock,
And now blind Cupid's scorn, and laughing-stock;
Who in fantastic arrogance at odds
With the Pantheon of your people's gods
Ransack'd the heavens for one more pure and whole
To fill the empty temple of the soul,
Now caught by retribution in the mesh
Of one poor piece of perishable flesh —
What baser demon of the pit would buy
With all your ruin'd aspirations!
   Lucifer (within).   I! —
   Cipr.   What!   The very winds and waters
        Hear, and answer to the cry
        She is deaf to! — Better thrown
        On distracted nature's bosom
        With some passion like my own
        Torn and tortured: where the sun
        In the elemental riot
        Ere his daily reign half done,
        Leaves half-quencht the tempest-drencht
        Welkin scowling on the howling
        Wilderness of waves that under
        Slash of whirlwind, spur of lightning,
        Roar of thunder, black'ning, whit'ning,
        Fling them foaming on the shore —
        Let confusion reign and roar! —
        Lightnings, for your target take me!
        Waves, upon the sharp rock break me;
        Or into your monstrous hollow
        Back regurgitating hurl;

Let the mad tornado whirl me
To the furthest airy circle
Dissipated of the sky,
Or the gaping earth down-swallow
To the centre! —

Lucifer (entering).   By-and-bye.

Cipr.   Hark again! and in her monstrous
Labour, with a human cry
Nature yearning — what portentous
Glomeration of the storm
Darkly cast in human form,
Has she bolted! —

Luc.   As among
Flashes of the lightning flung
Beside you, in its thunder now
Aptly listen'd —

Cipr.   What art thou?

Luc.   One of a realm, though dimly in your charts
Discern'd, so vast that as from out of it
As from a fountain all the nations flow,
Back they shall ebb again; and sway'd by One
Who, without Oriental over-boast,
Because from him all kings their crowns derive,
Is rightfully saluted King of kings,
Whose reign is as his kingdom infinite,
Whose throne is heaven, and earth his footstool, and
Sun, moon, and stars his diadem and crown.
Who at the first disposal of his kingdom
And distribution into sea and land —
Me, who for splendour of my birth and grand
Capacities above my fellows shone,
Star of the Morning, Lucifer, alone —
Me he made captain of the host who stand
Clad as the morning star about his throne.
Enough for all ambition but my own;
Who discontented with the all but all
Of chiefest subject of Omnipotence
Rebell'd against my Maker; insolence
Avenged as soon as done on me and all
Who bolster'd up rebellion, by a fall

Far as from heav'n to Hades. Madness, I know;
But worse than madness whining to repent
Under a rod that never will relent.
Therefore about the land and sea I go
Arm'd with the very instrument of hate
That blasted me: lightnings anticipate
My coming, and the thunder rolls behind;
Thus charter'd to enlarge among mankind,
And to recruit from human discontent
My ranks in spirit, not in number, spent.
Of whom, in spite of this brave gaberdine,
I recognize thee one: thee, by the line
Scarr'd on thy brow, though not so deep as mine;
Thee by the hollow circles of those eyes
Where the volcano smoulders but not dies:
Whose fiery torrent running down has scarr'd
The cheek that time had not so deeply marr'd.
Do not I read thee rightly?
    Cipr.   But too well;
However come to read me —
    Luc.   By the light
Of my own darkness reading yours — how deep!
But not, as mine is, irretrievable:
Who from the fulness of my own perdition
Would, as I may, revenge myself on him
By turning to fruition your despair —
What if I make you master at a blow,
Not only of the easy woman's heart
You now despair of as impregnable,
And waiting but my word to let you in,
But lord of nature's secret, and the lore
That shall not only with the knowledge, but
Possess you with the very power of him
You sought so far and vainly for before:
So far All-eyes, All-wise, Omnipotent —
If not to fashion, able yet to shake
That which the other took such pains to make —
As in the hubbub round us; I who blurr'd
The spotless page of nature at a word
With darkness and confusion, will anon

Clear it, to write another marvel on. —
　　　　By the word of power that binds
　　　　And loosens; by the word that finds
　　　　Nature's heart through all her rinds,
　　　　Hearken, waters, fires, and winds;
　　　　Having had your roar, once more
　　　　Down with you, or get you gone.
　　Cipr.　With the clatter and confusion
　　　　Of the universe about me
　　　　Reeling — all within, without me, —
　　　　Dizzy, dazzled — if delusion,
　　　　Waking, dreaming, seeing, seeming —
　　　　Which I know not — only, lo!
　　　　Like some mighty madden'd beast
　　　　Bellowing in full career
　　　　Of fury, by a sudden blow
　　　　Stunn'd, and in a moment stopp'd
　　　　All the roar, or into slow
　　　　Death-ward-drawing murmur, leaving
　　　　Scarce the fallen carcase heaving,
　　　　With the fallen carcase dropp'd. —
Behold! the word scarce fallen from his lips,
Swift almost as a human smile may chase
A frown from some conciliated face,
The world to concord from confusion slips:
The winds that blew the battle up dead slain,
Or with their tatter'd standards swept amain
From heav'n; the billows of the erected deep
Roll'd with their crests into the foaming plain;
While the scared earth begins abroad to peep
And smooth her ruffled locks as from a rent
In the black centre of the firmament,
Revenging his unnatural eclipse,
The Lord of heav'n from its ulterior blue
That widens round him as he pierces through
The folded darkness, from his sovereign height
Slays with a smile the dragon-gloom of night.
　　Luc.　All you have heard and witness'd hitherto
But a foretaste to quicken appetite
For that substantial after-feast of power

That I shall set you down to take your fill of:
When not the fleeting elements alone
Of wind, and fire, and water, floating wrack,
But this same solid frame of earth and stone,
Yea, with the mountain loaded on her back,
Reluctantly, shall answer to your spell
From a more adamantine heart stone-cold
Than hers you curse for inaccessible.
What, you would prove it?   Let the mountain there
Step out for witness.   Listen, and behold.

      Monster upshot of upheaving[1]
      Earth, by fire and flood conceiving;
      Shapeless ark of refuge, whither,
      When came deluge creeping round,
      Man retreated — to be drown'd —
      Now your granite anchor, fast
      In creation's centre, cast,
      Come with all your tackle cleaving
      Down before the magic blast —
Cipr.   And the unwieldly vessel, lo!
      Rib and deck of rock, and shroud
      Of pine, top-gallanted with cloud,
      All her forest-canvas squaring,
      Down the undulating woodland
      As she flounders to and fro.
      All before her tearing, bearing
      Down upon us —
Luc.   Anchor, ho! —
Behold the ship in port!   And what if freighted
With but one jewel, worthy welcome more
Than ever full-fraught Argosy awaited,
At last descried by desperate eyes ashore;
From the first moment of her topsail showing
Like a thin cobweb spun 'twixt sea and sky;
Then momently before a full wind blowing
Into her full proportions, till athwart
The seas that bound beneath her, by and bye

---

[1] The Phenomena that follow, and are here supposed to be the magic illusions created in Cipriano's eyes, are in the original represented by theatrical machinery.

She sweeps full sail into the cheering port —
> Strangest bark that ever plied
> In despite of wind and tide,
> At the captain's magic summons
> Down your granite ribs divide,
> And show the jewel hid inside.

Cipr.   Justina! —

Luc.   Soft!   The leap that looks so easy
Yet needs a longer stride than you can master.

Cipr.   Oh divine apparition, that I fain
Would all my life as in Elysium lose
Only by gazing after; and thus soon
As rolling cloud across the long'd-for moon,
The impitiable rocks enclose again! —
But was it she indeed?

Luc.   She that shall be,
And yours, by means that, bringing her to you,
Possess you of all nature, which in vain
You sigh'd for ere for nature's masterpiece.
And thus much, as I told you, only sent
As foretaste of that great accomplishment,
Which if you will but try for, you can reach
By means which, if I practise, I can teach.

Cipr.   And at what cost?

Luc.   You that have flung so many years away
In learning and in love that came to nothing,
Think not to win the harvest in a day!
The God you search for works, you know, by means
(That your philosophers call second cause),
And we by means must underwork him —

Cipr.   Well? —

Luc.   To comprehend, and, after, to constrain
Whose mysteries you will not count as vain
A year in this same mountain lock'd with me? —

Cipr.   Where she is? —

Luc.   As I told you, where shall be.
At least this mountain after a short labour
Has brought forth something better than a mouse;
And what then after a whole year's gestation
Accomplish under our joint midwifery,

Under a bond by which you bind you mine
In fewer and no redder drops than needs
The leech of land or water when he bleeds?
Let us about — but first upon his base
The mountain we must study in replace,
That else might puzzle your geography.
Come, take your stand upon the deck with me,
Till with her precious cargo safe inside,
And all her forest-colours flying wide,
The mighty vessel put again to sea —
What, are you ready? — Wondrous smack,
      As without a turn or tack
      Hither come, so thither back,
      And let subside the ruffled deep
      Of earth to her primæval sleep. —
How steadily her course the good ship trims,
While Antioch far into the distance swims,
With all her follies bubbling in the wake;
Her scholars that more hum than honey make:
Muses so chaste as never of their kind
Would breed, and Cupid deaf as well as blind:
For Cipriano, wearied with the toil
Of so long working on a thankless soil,
At last embarking upon magic seas
In a more wondrous Argo than of old,
Sets sail with me for such Hesperides
As glow with more than dragon-guarded gold.   [*Exeunt.*

ACT III

SCENE I. *Before the mountain.* CIPRIANO.

Cipriano   Now that at last in his eternal round
Hyperion, after skirting either pole,
Of his own race has set the flaming goal
In heav'n of my probation under-ground:
Up from the mighty Titan with his feet
Touching the centre, and his forest-hair
Entangling with the stars; whose middle womb
Of two self-buried lives has been the tomb;
At last, my year's apprenticeship complete,
I rise to try my cunning, and as one
Arm'd in the dark who challenges the sun.
You heav'ns, for me your azure brows with cloud
Contract, or to your inmost depth unshroud:
Thou sapphire-floating counterpart below,
Obsequious of my moon-like magic flow:
For me you mountains fall, you valleys rise,
With all your brooks and fountains far withdrawn;
You forests shudder underneath my sighs;
And whatsoever breathes in earth and skies;
You birds that on the bough salute the dawn;
And you wild creatures that through wood and glen
Do fly the hunter, or the hunter flies;
Yea, man himself, most terrible to men;
Troop to my word, about my footstep fawn;
Yes, ev'n you spirits that by viewless springs
Move and perplex the tangled web of things,
Wherever in the darkest crypt you lurk

Of nature, nature to my purpose work;
That not the dead material element,
But complicated with the life beyond
Up to pure spirit, shall my charm resent,
And take the motion of my magic wand;
And, once more shaken on her ancient throne,
In me old nature a new master own.

   Lucifer   But how is this, Cipriano, that misled
By hasty passion you affront the day
Ere master of the art of darkness?

   Cipr.   Nay,
By that same blazing witness overhead
Standing in heav'n to mark the time foretold,
Since first imprison'd in this mountain-hold
My magic so preluded with the dread
Preliminary kingdom of the dead,
That not alone the womb of general earth
Which Death has crowded thick with second birth
But monuments with marble lips composed
To dream till doomsday, suddenly disclosed,
And woke their sleepers centuries too soon
To stare upon the old remember'd moon.
Wearied of darkness, I will see the day:
Sick of the dead, the living will assay:
And if the ghastly year I have gone through
Bear half its promised harvest, will requite
With a too warm good-morrow the long night
That one cold living heart consigned me to.

   Luc.   Justina!

   Cipr.   Aye, Justina: now no more
Obsequiously sighing at the door
That never open'd, nor the heart of stone
On which so long I vainly broke my own;
But of her soul and body, when and how
I will, I claim the forfeit here and now.

   Luc. Enough: the hour is come; do thou design
The earth with circle, pentagram, and trine;
The wandering airs with incantation twine;
While through her sleep-enchanted sense I shake
The virgin constancy I cannot break.

(Clouds, roll before the mountain, hiding CIPRIANO.*)*

Thou nether realm of darkness and despair,
Whose fire-enthronéd emperor am I;
Where many-knotted till the word they lie,
Your subtlest spirits at the word untie,
And breathe them softly to this upper air;
With subtle soft insinuation fair
Of foul result encompass and attaint
The chastity of the rebellious saint
Who dares the Spirit of this world defy.
Spirits that do shapeless float
In darkness as in light the mote,
At my summons straightway take
Likeness of the fairest make,
And, her sleeping sense about
Seal'd from all the world without,
Through the bolted eyelids creep;
Entheatre the walls of sleep
With an Eden where the sheen
Of the leaf and flower between
All is freshest, yet with Eve's
Apple peeping through the leaves;
Through whose magic mazes may
Melancholy fancy stray
Till she lose herself, or into
Softer passion melt away:
While the scent-seducing rose
Gazing at her as she goes
With her turning as she turns,
Into her his passion burns;
While the wind among the boughs
Whispers half-remember'd vows;
Nightingale interpreters
Into their passion translate hers;
And the murmurs of a stream
Down one current draw the dream.
While for hidden chorus, I
At her dreaming ear supply
Such a comment as her own
Heart to nature's shall atone:

Till the secret influence
Of the genial season even
Holy blood that sets to heaven
Draws into the lower sense;
Till array'd in angel guise
Earthly memories surprise
Ev'n the virgin soul and win
Holy pity's self to sin.

(The clouds roll away, and discover JUSTINA *asleep in her chamber.)*

Lucifer (at her ear).   Come forth, come forth, Justina, come; for scared
Winter is vanisht, and victorious Spring
Has hung her garland on the boughs he bared:
Come forth; there is a time for every thing.

Justina (in her sleep).   That was my father's voice — come, Livia —
My mantle — oh, not want it? — well then, come.

Luc.   Aye, come abroad, Justina; it is Spring;
The world is not with sunshine and with leaf
Renew'd to be the tomb of ceaseless grief;
Come forth: there is a time for every thing.

Just.   How strange it is —
I think the garden never look'd so gay
As since my father died.

Luc.   Ev'n so: for now
Returning with the summer wind, the hours
Dipt in the sun re-dress the grave with flowers,
And make new wreaths for the survivor's brow;
Whose spirit not to share were to refuse
The power that all creating, all renews
With self-diffusive warmth, that, with the sun's,
At this due season through creation runs,
Nor in the first creation more exprest
Than by the singing builder of the nest
That waves on this year's leaf, or by the rose
That underneath them in his glory glows;
Life's fountain, flower, and crown; without whose giving
Life itself were not, nor, without, worth living.

Chorus of Voices　Life's fountain, flower, and crown; without whose giving
Life itself were not, nor, without, worth living.

Song

Who that in his hour of glory
Walks the kingdom of the rose,
And misapprehends the story
Which through all the garden blows;
Which the southern air who brings
It touches, and the leafy strings
Lightly to the touch respond;
And nightingale to nightingale
Answering a bough beyond —
CHORUS　*Nightingale to nightingale*
Answering a bough beyond.

Just.　These serenaders — singing their old songs
Under one's window —
Luc.　Aye, and if nature must decay or cease
Without it; what of nature's masterpiece?
Not in her outward lustre only, but
Ev'n in the soul within the jewel shut;
What but a fruitless blossom; or a lute
Without the hand to touch it music-mute:
Incense that will not rise to heav'n unfired;
By that same vernal spirit uninspired
That sends the blood up from the heart, and speaks
In the rekindled lustre of the cheeks?
Chorus　Life's fountain, flower, and crown; without whose
giving
Life itself were not, nor, without, worth living.

Song

Lo, the golden Girasolé,
That to him by whom she burns,
Over heaven slowly, slowly,
As he travels ever turns;
And beneath the wat'ry main
When he sinks, would follow fain,
Follow fain from west to east,
And then from east to west again.

CHORUS *Follow would from west to east,*
        And then from east to west again.

Just. He beckon'd us, and then again was gone;
Oh look! under the tree there, Livia —
Where he sits — reading — scholar-like indeed! —
With the dark hair that was so white upon
His shoulder — but how deadly pale his face! —
And, statue-still-like, the quaint evergreen
Up and about him creeps, as one has seen
Round some old marble in a lonely place.
    Luc. Aye, look on that — for, as the story runs,
Ages ago, when all the world was young,
That ivy was a nymph of Latium,
Whose name was Hedera: so passing fair
That all who saw fell doting on her; but
Herself so icy-cruel, that her heart
Froze dead all those her eyes had set on fire.
Whom the just God who walk'd that early world,
By right-revenging metamorphosis
Changed to a thing so abject-amorous,
She grovels on the ground to catch at any
Wither'd old trunk or sapling, in her way:
So little loved as loath'd, for strangling those
Whom once her deadly-deathless arms enclose.

Song
So for her who having lighted
    In another heart the fire,
Then shall leave it unrequited
    In its ashes to expire:
After her that sacrifice
Through the garden burns and cries;
In the sultry breathing air:
In the flowers that turn and stare —
"What has she to do among us,
Falsely wise and frozen fair?"

    Luc. Listen, Justina, listen and beware.
    Just. Again! That voice too? — But you know my father
Is ill — is in his chamber —
How sultry 't is — the street is full and close —

Let us get home — why do they stare at us?
And murmur something — "Cipriano? — Where
"Is Cipriano? — lost to us — some say,
"And to himself, — self-slain — mad — Where is he?
Alas, alas, I know not —
  Luc.   Come and see —
  Justina (waking). Mercy upon me! Who is this?
  Luc.   Justina, your good angel,
Who, moved by your relenting to the sighs
Of one who lost himself for your disdain,
Will lead you to the cavern where he lies
Subsisting on the memory of your eyes —
  Just. 'T was all a dream! —
  Luc.   That dreaming you fulfil.
  Just. Oh, no, with all my waking soul renounce.
  Luc. But, dreaming or awake, the soul is one,
And the deed purposed in Heaven's eyes is done.
  Just. Oh Christ! I cannot argue — I can pray,
Christ Jesus, oh, my Saviour, Jesu Christ!
Let not hell snatch away from Thee the soul
Thou gav'st Thy life to save! — Livia! — Livia!

Enter LIVIA

Where is my father? where am I? Oh, I know —
In my own chamber — and my father — oh! —
But, Livia, who was it that but now
Was here — here in my very chamber —
  Livia   Madam?
  Just. You let none in? oh, no! I know it — but
Some one there was — here — now — as I cried out —
A dark, strange figure —
  Livia   My child, compose yourself;
No one has come, or gone, since you were laid
In your noon-slumber. This was but a dream.
The air is heavy; and the melancholy
You live alone with since your father's death —
  Just. A dream, a dream indeed — oh Livia,
That leaves his pressure yet upon my arm —
And that without the immediate help of God

I had not overcome — Oh, but the soul,
The soul must be unsteady in the faith,
So to be shaken even by a dream.
Oh, were my father here!   But he's at rest —
I know he is — upon his Saviour's breast;
And — who knows! — may have carried up my cries
Ev'n to His ear upon whose breast he lies!
Give me my mantle, Livia; I'll to the church;
Where if but two or three are met in prayer
Together, He has promised to be there —
And I shall find Him.
 Livia   Oh, take care, take care!
You know the danger — in broad daylight too —
Or take me with you.
 Just.   And endanger two?
Best serve us both by keeping close at home,
Praying for me as I will pray for you.   [*Exeunt.*

SCENE II. *Entrance to the mountain cavern.* CIPRIANO *in a
   magician's dress, with wand, &c.*

What! do the powers of earth, and air, and hell,
Against their upstart emperor rebel?
Lo, in obedience to the rubric dark
The dusky cheek of earth with mystic mark
Of pentagram and circle I have lined,
And hung my fetters on the viewless wind,
And yet the star of stars, for whose ascent
I ransack all the lower firmament,
In unapparent darkness lags behind.
Whom once again with adjuration new
Of all the spirits whom these signs subdue,
Whether by land or water, night or day,
Whether awake or sleeping, yea or nay,
I summon now before me. —

   Enter slowly a veiled Figure of JUSTINA.

 The Figure   What dark spell
From the sequester'd sadness of my cell,
Through the still garden, through the giddy street,

And up the solitary mountain-side,
Leads me with sleep-involuntary feet? —
   Cipr.   'T is she, as yet though clouded! — oh divine
Justina! —
   The Figure   Cipriano! —
   Cipr.   At last here,
In such a chamber where ev'n Phœbus fails
To pierce, and baffled breezes tell no tales,
At last, to crown the labour of a year
Of solitary toil and darkness — here! —
And at a price beside — but none too dear —
Oh year-long night well borne for such a day!
Oh soul, for one such sense well sold away!
Oh Now that makes for all the past amends,
Oh moment that eternal life transcends
To such a point of ecstasy, that just
About to reap the wishes that requite
All woes —
   The Figure (unveiling a skull and vanishing as it speaks).
         Behold the World and its delight
Is dust and ashes, dust and ashes, dust —
   Cipr. (flinging down his Wand).   Lucifer! Lucifer! Luci-
     fer! —
   Luc.   My son!
   Cipr.   Quick! with a word —
                How now? —
                      With a word — at once —
With all your might —
   Luc.   Well, what with it? —
   Cipr.   The charm —
Shatter it! shatter it, I say! — Is 't done?
Is 't vanisht —
   Luc.   What has thus unsensed you?
   Cipr.   Oh! —
You know it — saw it — did it —
   Luc.   Come — be a man:
What, scared with a mere death's-head?
   Cipr.   Death's, indeed! —
   Luc.   What was it more? —
   Cipr.   Justina's seeming self —

After what solitary labour wrought,
And after what re-iterated charms,
Step by step here in all her beauty brought
Within the very circle of these arms,
Then to death's grisly lineaments resign'd
Slipt through them, and went wailing down the wind
"Ashes and dust and ashes" —
Nay, nay, pretend not that the fault was mine —
The written incantation line by line
I mutter'd, and the mystic figure drew;
You only are to blame — you only, you,
Cajoling me, or by your own cajoled,
Bringing me fleshless death for the warm life
For which my own eternal life is sold.

    Luc.   You were too rash, — I warn'd you, and if not,
Who thinks at a first trial to succeed?
Another time —

    Cipr.   No, no!   No more of it!
What, have I so long dabbled with the dead,
That all I touch turns to corruption?
Were it indeed herself — her living self —
Till underneath my deadly contact slain;
Or having died during the terrible year
I have been living worse than dead with you,
What I beheld not she, but what she was,
Out of the tomb that only owns my spell
Drawn into momentary lifeliness
To mock me with the phantom of a beauty
Whose lineaments the mere impalpable air
Let in upon disfeatures — was it she?

    Luc.   She lives, and shall be yours.

    Cipr.   Not if herself,
In more than all her living beauty breathing,
Came to efface that deadly counterfeit! —
Oh, what have I been doing all this while,
From which I wake as from a guilty dream,
But with my guilt's accomplice at my side
To prove its terrible reality?
Where were my ears, my eyes, my senses? where
The mother-wit which serves the common boor,

Not to resent that black academy,
Mess-mating with dead men and living fiends,
And not to know no good could come of it? —
My better self — the good that in me grew
By nature, and by good instruction till'd,
Under your shadow turn'd to poisonous weed;
And ev'n the darker art you bribed me with,
To master, if by questionable ways,
The power I sigh'd for in my better days,
So little reaching to the promised height,
As sinking me beneath the lowest fiend,
Who, for the inestimable self I sold,
Pays the false self you made me with false gold!

   Luc.   When will blind fury, falling foul of all,
Light where it should?   Suppose a fault so far,
As knowledge working through unpractised hands
Might fail at first encounter; all men know
How a mere sand will check a vast machine;
And in these complicated processes
An agency so insignificant
As to be wholly overlookt it was
At the last moment foil'd us.

   Cipr.   But she lives!
Lives — from your clutches saved, and saved from mine —
Ev'n from that only shadow of my guilt
That could have touch'd her, saved — unguilty shame,
That now is left with all the guilt to me.
Oh that I knew a God in all the heav'ns
To thank, or ev'n of Tartarus — ev'n thee,
Thee would I bless, whatever power it be
That with that shadow saved her, and mock'd me
Back to my better senses.   If not she,
What was it?

   Luc.   What you saw.

   Cipr.   A phantom?

   Luc.   Well,
A phantom.

   Cipr.   But how raised?

   Luc.   What if by her?
She is a sorcerer as her father was.

Cipr.   A sorcerer!   She a sorcerer! oh, black lie
To whiten your defeat! and, were it true,
Oh mighty doctor to be foil'd at last
By a mere woman! — If a sorcerer,
Then of a sort you deal not with, nor hell —
And ev'n Olympus likes the sport too well —
Raising a phantom not to draw me down
To deeper sin, but with its ghastly face
And hollow voice both telling of the tomb
They came from, warning me of what complexion
Were all the guilty wishes of this world.
But let the phantom go where gone it is —
Not of what mock'd me, but what saved herself,
By whatsoever means — aye, what was it,
That pitiful agency you told me of
So insignificant, as overlookt
At the last moment thwarted us?
   Luc.   What matter?
When now provided for, and which when told
You know not —
   Cipr.   Which I will be told to know —
For as one ris'n from darkness tow'rd the light,
A veil seems clearing from before my sight —
She is a sorcerer, and of the kind
That old Lisandro died suspected of? —
Oh cunning doctor, to outwit yourself,
Outwitted as you have been, and shall be
By him who if your devilish magic fail'd
To teach its purposed mischief,
Thus on his teacher turns it back in full
To force him to confess the counter-power
That foil'd us both.   *(He catches up his wand.)*
   Luc.   Poor creature that you are!
Did not the master from his scholars hold
One sleight of hand that masters all the rest,
What magic needed to compel the devil
To convict those who find him out too late?
Yet to increase your wrath by leaving it
Blind in the pit your guilt consigns you to,
I shall not answer —

Cipr.   Then if your own hell
Cannot enforce you; by that Unknown Power
That saved Justina from your fangs, although
Yourself you cannot master, if you know,
I charge you name him to me! —

    Luc. (after a great flash of lightning, and thunder).
                         Jesus Christ!

    Cipr. (after a pause). Ev'n so! — Christ Jesus — Jesus
        Christ — the same
That poor Lisandro died suspected of,
And I had heard and read of with the rest
But to despise, in spite of all the blood
By which the chosen few their faith confess'd —
The prophet-carpenter of Nazareth,
Poor, persecuted, buffeted, reviled,
Spit upon, crown'd with thorns, and crucified
With thieves — the Son of God — the Son of man,
Whose shape He took to teach them how to live,
And doff'd upon the cross to do away
The sin and death you and your devil-deities
Had heap'd on him from the beginning?

    Luc.   Yea! —

    Cipr. Of the one sun of Deity one ray
That was before the world was, and that made
The world and all that is within it?

    Luc.   Yea!

    Cipr. Eternal and Almighty then: and yet
Infinite Centre as he is of all
The all but infinite universe he made,
With eyes to see me plotting, and with ear
To hear one solitary creature pray,
From one dark corner of his kingdom?

    Luc.   Yea!

    Cipr. All one, all when, all where, all good, all mighty,
All eye, all ear, all self-integrity —
Methinks this must be He of whom I read
In Greek and Roman sages dimly guess'd,
But never until now fully confest
In this poor carpenter of Nazareth,
With poor Justina for his confessor —

And now by thee — by thee — once and again
Spite of thyself — for answer me you must,
Convicted at the bar of your own thunder —
Is this the God for whom I sought so long
In mine own soul and those of other men,
Who from the world's beginning till to-day
Groped or were lost in utter darkness?

  Luc.   Yea!

  Cipr. Enough: and your confession shall be mine —

  Luc. And to like purpose; to believe, confess,
And tremble, in the everlasting fire
Prepared for all who Him against their will
Confess, and in their deeds deny him —

  Cipr.   Oh,
Like a flogg'd felon after full confession
Releast at last!

  Luc.   To bind you mine for ever.

  Cipr. Thine! What art thou?

  Luc.   The god whom you must worship.

  Cipr. There is no God but one, whom you and I
Alike acknowledge, as in Jesus Christ
Reveal'd to man. What other god art thou?

  Luc. Antichrist! He that all confessing Christ
Confess; Satan, the Serpent, the first Tempter,
Who tempted the first Father of mankind
With the same offer to a like result
That I have tempted thee with; yea, had power
Even Him in his humanity to tempt,
Though Him in vain; the god of this world; if
False god, true devil; true angel as I was,
Sun of the morning, Lucifer, who fell
(As first I told thee, hadst thou ears to hear)
For my rebellion down from heaven to hell
More terrible than any Tartarus,
Where over those who fell with me I reign.
Whom, though with them bound in the self-same chain
Of everlasting torment, God allows
To reach my hands out of my prison-house
On all who like me from their God rebel,
As thou hast done.

Cipr.   Not when for God I knew him.

Luc.   Aye, but who but for pride and lust like mine
Had known Him sooner —

Cipr.   And had sooner known
But for thy lying gods that shut Him out.

Luc.   Which others much less wise saw through before.

Cipr.   All happy they then!   But all guilty I,
Yet thus far guiltless of denying Him
Whom even thou confessest.

Luc.   But too late —
Already mine, if not so sworn before,
Yet by this bond —

Cipr.   For service unperform'd!
But unperform'd, or done, and payment due,
I fling myself and all my debt on Him
Who died to undertake them —

Luc.   He is the Saviour of the innocent,
Not of the guilty.

Cipr.   Who alone need saving!

Luc.   Damnation is the sinner's just award,
And He is just.

Cipr.   And being just, will not
For wilful blindness tax the want of light:
And All-good as Almighty, and therefore
As merciful as just, will not renounce
Ev'n the worst sinner who confesses Him,
And testifies confession with his blood.
Which, not to waste a moment's argument,
Too like the old logic that I lost my life in,
And hangs for ever dead upon the cross;
I will forthwith shout my confession,
Into the general ear of Antioch,
And from the evidence of thine own mouth,
Not thee alone, but all thy lying gods,
Convict; and you convicting before God,
Myself by man's tribunal judged and damn'd,
Trust by my own blood mixing with the tide
That flow'd for me from the Redeemer's side,
From those few damning drops to wash me free
That bound me thine for ever —

Luc. (seizing him).   Take my answer —
Cipr. (escaping).   Oh, Saviour of Justina, save Thou me!

                                                            [*Exeunt.*

SCENE III.   *The Hall of Justice in Antioch;* AURELIO, FABIO,
          SENATORS, &c., *just risen from Council.*

Aurelio   You have done well indeed; the very Church
These Christians flock'd to for safe blasphemy
Become the very net to catch them in.
How many, think you?
    Fabio   Not many, sir,
As some that are of the most dangerous.
    Aur.   Among the rest this girl, Lisandro's daughter,
As you and I know, Fabio, to our cost:
But now convicted and condemn'd is safe
From troubling us or Antioch any more.
Come, such good service asks substantial thanks;
What shall it be?
    Fabio   No other, if you please,
Than my son Floro's liberation,
Whom not without good reason for so long
You keep under the city's lock and key.
    Aur.   As my own Lelio, and for a like cause;
Who both distracted by her witchery
Turn'd from fast friends to deadly enemies,
And, in each other's lives, so aimed at ours.
But no more chance of further quarrel now
For one whom Death anticipates for bride
Ere they again gird weapon at their side,
Set them both free forthwith. —   [*Exit* FABIO.
This cursèd woman whose fair face and foul
Behaviour was the city's talk and trouble,
Now proved a sorceress, is well condemn'd;
Not only for my sake and Fabio's,
But for all Antioch, whose better youth
She might, like ours, have carried after her
Through lust and duel into blasphemy.

Re-enter FABIO *with* LELIO *and* FLORO

Lelio   Once more, sir, at your feet —
Aur.   Up, both of you.
Floro and Lelio, you understand
What I have done was of no testy humour,
But for three several sakes —
Your own, your fathers', and the city's peace.
Henceforward, by this seasonable use
Of public law for private purpose check'd,
Your fiery blood to better service turn.
Take hands, be friends; the cause of quarrel gone —
   Lelio   The cause of quarrel gone! —
   Aur.   Be satisfied;
You will know better by and bye; meanwhile
Taking upon my word that so it is;
Which were it not indeed, you were not here
To doubt.
   Floro (aside).   Oh flimsy respite of revenge! —
   Aur.   And now the business of the day well crown'd
With this so happy reconciliation,
You and I, Fabio, to our homes again,
Our homes once more, replenish'd with the peace
We both have miss'd so long. — What noise is that?
   (Cries without.)   Stop him!   A madman!   Stop him! —
   Aur.   What is it, Fabio?
   Fabio   One like mad indeed,
In a strange garb, with flaring eyes, and hair
That streams behind him as he flies along,
Dragging a cloud of rabble after him.
   Aur.   This is no place for either — shut the doors,
And post the soldiers to keep peace without —
   (Cries without.)   Stop him!
   Floro and Lelio   'T is Cipriano! —
   Aur.   Cipriano! —

Enter CIPRIANO

   Cipriano   Aye, Cipriano, Cipriano's self,
Heretofore mad as you that call him so,
Now first himself. — Noble Aurelio,
Who sway'st the sword of Rome in Antioch;

And you, companions of my youthful love
And letters; you grave senate ranged above;
And you whose murmuring multitude below
Do make the marble hall of justice rock
From base to capital — hearken unto me:
Yes, I am Cipriano: I am he
So long and strangely lost, now strangely found —
The famous doctor of your schools, renown'd
Not Antioch only but the world about
For learning's prophet-paragon forsooth;
Who long pretending to provide the truth
For other men in fields where never true
Wheat, but a crop of mimic darnel grew,
Reap'd nothing for himself but doubt, doubt, doubt.
Then 't was that looking with despair and ruth
Over the blasted harvest of my youth,
I saw Justina: saw, and put aside
The barren Pallas for a mortal bride
Divinelier fair than she is feign'd to be:
But in whose deep-entempled chastity
That look'd down holy cold upon my fire,
Lived eyes that but re-double vain desire.
Till this new passion that more fiercely prey'd
Upon the wither'd spirit of dismay'd
Ambition, swiftly by denial blew
To fury that, transcending all control,
I made away the ruin of my soul
To one whom no chance tempest at my feet
In the mid tempest of temptation threw.
Who blinding me with the double deceit
Of loftier aspiration and more low
Than mortal or immortal man should owe
Fulfill'd for me, myself for his I bound;
With him and death and darkness closeted
In yonder mountain, while about its head
The sun his garland of the seasons wound,
In the dark school of magic I so read,
And wrought to such a questionable power
The black forbidden art I travail'd in,
That though the solid mountain from his base

With all his forest I might counterplace,
I could not one sweet solitary flower
Of beauty to my magic passion win.
Because her God was with her in that hour
To guard her virtue more than mountain-fast:
That only God, whom all my learning past
Fail'd to divine, but from the very foe
That would have kept Him from me come to know,
I come to you, to witness and make known:
One God, eternal, absolute, alone;
Of whom Christ Jesus — Jesus Christ, I say —
And, Antioch, open all your ears to-day —
Of that one Godhead one authentic ray,
Visor'd awhile his Godhead in man's make,
Man's sin and death upon Himself to take;
For man made man; by man unmade and slain
Upon the cross that for mankind He bore —
Dead — buried — and in three days ris'n again
To His hereditary glory, bearing
All who with Him on earth His sorrow sharing
With Him shall dwell in glory evermore.
And all the gods I worship'd heretofore,
And all that you now worship and adore,
From thundering Zeus to cloven-footed Pan,
But lies and idols, by the hand of man
Of brass and stone — fit emblems as they be,
With ears that hear not; eyes that cannot see;
And multitude where only One can be —
From man's own lewd imagination built;
By that same devil held to that old guilt
Who tempted me to new.   To whom indeed
If with my sin and blood myself I fee'd
For ever his — that bond of sin and blood
I trust to cancel in the double flood
Of baptism past, and the quick martyrdom
To which with this confession I am come.
Oh delegate of Cæsar to devour
The little flock of Jesus Christ!   Behold
One lost sheep just admitted to the fold
Through the pure stream that rolling down the same

Mountain in which I sinn'd, and as I came
By holy hands administer'd, to-day
Shall wash the mountain of my sins away.
Lo, here I stand for judgment; by the blow
Of sudden execution, or such slow
Death as the devil shall, to maintain his lies,
By keeping life alive in death, devise.
Hack, rack, dismember, burn — or crucify,
Like Him who died to find me; Him that I
Will die to find; for whom, with whom, to die
Is life; and life without, and all his lust
But dust and ashes, dust and ashes, dust —

(He falls senseless to the ground.)

 Aurelio (after a long pause). So public and audacious
  blasphemy
Demands as instant vengeance. Wretched man,
Arise and hear your sentence —
 Lelio   Oh, sir, sir!
You speak to ice and marble — Cipriano!
Oh look'd for long, and best for ever lost!
But he is mad — he knows not what he says —
You would not, surely, on a madman visit
What only sane confession makes a crime?
 Aur. I never know how far such blasphemy,
Which seems to spread like wild-fire in the world,
Be fault or folly: only this I know,
I dare not disobey the stern decree
That Cæsar makes my office answer for.
Especially when one is led away
Of such persuasion and authority,
Still drawing after him the better blood
Of Antioch, to better or to worse.
 Lelio Cipriano! Cipriano! Yet, pray the gods
He be past hearing me!
 Fabio (to AURELIO). Sir, in your ear —
Justina's hour is come; and through the room
Where she was doom'd, she passes to her doom.
 Aur. Let us be gone; they must not look on her,
Nor know she is to die until "to die"
Be past predicament. Here let her wait,

Till he she drew along with her to sin
Revive to share with her its punishment.
Come, Lelio — come, Floro — be assured
I loved and honour'd this man as yourselves
Have honour'd him — but now —

    Lelio   Nay, sir, but —

    Aur.   Nay,

Not I, but Cæsar, Lelio.   Come away.

[*Exeunt. Then* JUSTINA *is brought in by soldiers and left
        alone.*]

    Just.   All gone — all silence — and the sudden stroke,
Whose only mercy I besought, delay'd
To make my pang the fiercer. — What is here? —
Dead? — By the doom perhaps I am to die,
And laid across the threshold of the road
To trip me up with terror — Yet not so,
If but the life, once lighted here, has flown
Up to that living Centre that my own
Now trembles to! — God help him, breathing still? —
— Cipriano! —

    Cipr.   Aye, I am ready — I can rise —
Is my time come? — Oh, God!
Have I repented and confess'd too late,
And this terrible witness of my crime
Stands at the door of death from which it came
To draw me deeper —

    Just.   Cipriano!

    Cipr.   Yet
Not yet disfeatured — nor the voice —
Oh, if not *That* — this time unsummon'd — come
To take me with you where I raised you from —
Once more — once more — assure me! —

    Just. (taking his hand).   Cipriano! —

    Cipr.   And this, too, surely, is a living hand:
Though cold, oh, cold indeed — but yet, but yet,
Not dust and ashes, dust and ashes —

    Just.   No —
But soon to be —

    Cipr.   But soon — but soon to be —
But not as then? —

Just.   I understand you not —
Cipr.   I scarce myself — I must have been asleep —
But now not dreaming?
Just.   No, not dreaming.
Cipr.   No —
This is the judgment-hall of Antioch,
In which — I scarcely mind how long ago —
Is sentence pass'd on me?
Just.   This is indeed
The judgment-hall of Antioch; but why
You here, and what the judgment you await,
I know not —
Cipr.   No. — But stranger yet to me
Why you yourself, Justina. — Oh my God!
What, all your life long giving God his due,
Is treason unto Cæsar? —
Just.   Aye, Cipriano —
Against his edict having crept inside
God's fold with that good Shepherd for my guide,
My Saviour Jesus Christ!
Cipr.   My Saviour too,
And Shepherd — oh, the only good and true
Shepherd and Saviour —
Just.   You confess Him! *You*
Confess Him, Cipriano!
Cipr.   With my blood:
Which being all to that confession pledged,
Now waits but to be paid.
Just.   Oh, we shall die,
And go to heav'n together!
Cipr.   Amen! Amen! —
And yet —
Just.   You do not fear — and yet no shame —
What I have faced so long, that present dread
Is almost lost in long anticipation —
Cipr.   I fear not for this mortal. Would to God
This guilty blood by which in part I trust
To pay the forfeit of my soul with Heav'n
Would from man's hand redeem the innocence
That such atonement needs not.

Just.   Oh, to all
One faith and one atonement —
   Cipr.   But if both,
If both indeed must perish by the doom
That one deserves and cries for — Oh, Justina,
Who upward ever with the certain step
Of faith hast follow'd unrepress'd by sin;
Now that thy foot is almost on the floor
Of heav'n, pray Him who opens thee the door,
Let with thee one repenting sinner in!
   Just. What more am I?   And were I close to Him
As he upon whose breast he lean'd on here,
No intercessor but Himself between
Himself and the worst sinner of us all —
If but repenting we believe in Him.
   Cipr. I do believe — I do repent — my faith
Have sign'd in water, and will seal in blood —
   Just. I have no other hope, but, in that, all.
   Cipr. Oh hope that almost is accomplishment,
Believing all with nothing to repent!
   Just. Oh, none so good as not to need — so bad
As not to find, His mercy.   If you doubt
Because of your long dwelling in the darkness
To which the light was folly — oh 't was shown
To the poor shepherd long before the wise;
And if to me, as simple — oh, not mine,
Not mine, oh God! the glory — not ev'n theirs
From whom I drew it, and — Oh, Cipriano,
Methinks I see them bending from the skies
To take me up to them!
   Cipr.   Whither could I
But into heaven's remotest corner creep,
Where I might only but discern thee, lost
With those you love in glory —
   Just.   Hush! hush! hush!
These are wild words — if I so speak to one
So wise, while I am nothing —
But as you know — Oh, do not think of me,
But Him, into whose kingdom all who come
Are as His angels —

Cipr. Aye, but to come there! —
Where if all intercession, even thine,
Be vain — you say so — yet before we pass
The gate of death together, as we shall —
If then to part — for ever, and for ever —
Unless with your forgiveness!
    Just. I forgive!
Still I, and I, again! Oh, Cipriano,
Pardon and intercession both alike
With Him alone; and had I to forgive —
Did not He pray upon the cross for those
Who slew Him — as I hope to do on mine
For mine — He bids us bless our enemies
And persecutors; which I think, I think,
You were not, Cipriano — why do you shudder? —
Save in pursuit of that — if vain to me,
Now you know all —
    Cipr. I now know all — but you
Not that, which asking your forgiveness for,
I dare not name to you, for fear the hand
I hold as anchor-fast to, break away,
And I drive back to hell upon a blast
That roar'd behind me to these very doors,
But stopt — ev'n in the very presence stopt,
That most condemns me his.
    Just. Alas, alas,
Again all wild to me. The time draws short —
Look not to me, but Him tow'rd whom alone
Sin is, and pardon comes from —
    Cipr. Oh, Justina,
You know not how enormous is my sin —
    Just. I know, not as His mercy infinite.
    Cipr. To Him — to thee — to Him through thee —
    Just. 'T is written,
Not all the sand of ocean, nor the star
Of heav'n so many as His mercies are.
    Cipr. What! ev'n for one who, mad with pouring vows
Into an unrelenting human ear,
Gave himself up to Antichrist — the Fiend —
Though then for such I knew him not — to gain

By darkness all that love had sought in vain!
— Speak to me — if but that hereafter I
Shall never, never, hear your voice again —
Speak to me —

    Just. (after a long pause).   By the Saviour on His cross
A sinner hung who but at that last hour
Cried out to be with Him; and was with Him
In Paradise ere night.

    Cipr.   But was his sin
As mine enormous? —

    Just.   Shall your hope be less,
Offering yourself for Christ's sake on that cross
Which the other only suffer'd for his sin?
Oh, when we come to perish, side by side,
Look but for Him between us crucified,
And call to Him for mercy; and, although
Scarlet, your sin shall be as white as snow!

    Cipr.   Ev'n as you speak, yourself, though yet yourself,
In that full glory that you saw reveal'd
With those you love transfigured, and your voice
As from immeasurable altitude
Descending, tell me that, my shame and sin
Quencht in the death that opens wide to you
The gate, ev'n this great sinner shall pass through,
With Him, with them, with thee! —

    Just.   Glory to God! —
Oh, blest assurance on the very verge
That death is swallow'd up in victory!
And hark! the step of death is at the door —
Courage! — Almighty God through Jesus Christ
Pardon your sins and mine, and as a staff
Guide and support us through the terrible pass
That leads us to His rest! —

    Cipr.   My own beloved!
Whose hand — Oh let it be no sin to say it! —
Is as the staff that God has put in mine —
To lead me through the shadow — yet ev'n now —
Ev'n now — at this last terrible moment —
Which, to secure my being with thee, thee
Forbids to stand between my Judge and me,

And in a few more moments, soul and soul
May each read other as an open scroll —
Yet, wilt thou yet believe me not so vile
To thee, to Him who made thee what thou art,
Till desperation of the only heart
I ever sigh'd for, by I knew not then
How just alienation, drove me down
To that accursèd thing?
    Just.   My Cipriano!
Dost thou remember, in the lighter hour —
That when my heart, although you saw it not,
All the while yearn'd to thee across the gulf
That yet it dared not pass — my telling thee
That only Death, which others disunites,
Should ever make us one?   Behold! and now
The hour is come, and I redeem my vow.

*(Here the play may finish: but for any one who would follow
    Calderon to the end, — Enter* FABIO *with Guard, who lead
    away* CIPRIANO *and* JUSTINA. *Manent* EUSEBIO, JULIAN *and
    Citizens.)*

    Citizen 1   Alas! alas! alas!   So young a pair!
And one so very wise!
    Cit. 2   And one so fair!
    Cit. 3   And both as calmly walking to their death
As others to a marriage festival.
    Julian   Looking as calm, at least, Eusebio,
As when, do you remember, at the last
Great festival of Zeus, we left him sitting
Upon the hill-side with his books?
    Eusebio   I think
Almost the last we saw of him: so soon,
Flinging his studies and his scholars by,
He went away into that solitude
Which ended in this madness, and now death
With her he lost his wits for.
    Cit. 1   And has found
In death whom living he pursued in vain.
    Cit. 2   And after death, as they believe; and so

Thus cheerfully to meet it, if the scaffold
Divorce them to eternal union.

   Cit. 3   Strange that so wise a man
Should fall into so fond a superstition
Which none but ignorance has taken up.

   Cit. 1   Oh, love, you know, like time works wonders.

   Eusebio   Well —
Antioch will never see so great a scholar.

   Julian   Nor we so courteous a Professor —
I would not see my dear old master die
Were all the wits he lost my legacy.

Citizens talking

One says that, as they went out hand in hand,
He saw a halo like about the moon
About their head, and moving as they went.
— *I* saw it. —
   —   Fancy! fancy! —
   —   Any how,
They leave it very dark behind them — Thunder!
— They talk of madness and of blasphemy;
Neither of these, I think, looking much guilty.
— And he, at any rate, I still maintain,
Least like to be deluded by the folly
For which the new religion is condemn'd.
— Before his madness, certainly: but love
First crazed him, as I told you.
   —   Well, if mad,
How guilty?
   —   Hush! hush!   These are dangerous words.
— Be not you bitten by this madness, neighbour.
Rome's arm is long.
   —   Aye, and some say her ears.
— Then, ev'n if bitten, bark not — Thunder again!
— And what unnatural darkness!
   —   Well — a storm —
— They say, you know, he was a sorcerer —
Indeed we saw the mystic dress he wore
All wrought with figures of astrology;
Nay, he confess'd himself as much; and now
May raise a storm to save —

Citizens talking
—   There was a crash!
— A bolt has fallen somewhere — the walls shake —
— And the ground under —
—   Save us, Zeus —
Voices   Away! —
The roof is falling upon us —
(The wall at the back falls in, and discovers a scaffold with
CIPRIANO *and* JUSTINA *dead, and* LUCIFER *above them.)*
Lucifer   Stay! —
And hearken to what I am doom'd to tell.
I am the mighty minister of hell
You mis-call heav'n, and of the hellish crew
Of those false gods you worship for the True;
Who, to revenge *her* treason to the blind
Idolatry that has hoodwinkt mankind,
And *his,* whose halting wisdom, after-knew
What her diviner virtue fore-divined,
By devilish plot and artifices thought
Each of them by the other to have caught;
But, thwarted by superior will, those eyes
That, by my fuel fed, had been a flame
To light them both to darkness down, became
As stars to lead together to the skies,
By such a doom as expiates his sin,
And her pure innocence lets sooner in
To that eternal bliss where, side by side,
They reign at His right hand for whom they died.
While I, convicted in my own despite
Thus to bear witness to the eternal light
Of which I lost, and they have won the crown,
Plunge to my own eternal darkness down.

HÚNDESE

"SUCH STUFF AS DREAMS ARE MADE OF"

DRAMATIS PERSONÆ

BASILIO, *King of Poland*
SEGISMUND, *his Son*
ASTOLFO, *his Nephew*
ESTRELLA, *his Niece*
CLOTALDO, *a General in Basilio's Service*
ROSAURA, *a Muscovite Lady*
FIFE, *her Attendant*

Chamberlain, Lords in Waiting, Officers, Soldiers, &c.,
in Basilio's Service

The Scene of the first and third Acts lies on the Polish
frontier: of the second Act, in Warsaw.

ACT I

SCENE I. *A pass of rocks, over which a storm is rolling away, and the sun setting: in the foreground, half way down, a fortress. Enter first from the topmost rock* ROSAURA, *as from horse-back, in man's attire; and, after her* FIFE.[1]

Rosaura THERE, four-footed Fury, blast-
-engender'd brute, without the wit
Of brute, or mouth to match the bit
Of man — art satisfied at last?
Who, when thunder roll'd aloof,
Tow'rd the spheres of fire your ears
Pricking, and the granite kicking
Into lightning with your hoof,
Among the tempest-shatter'd crags
Shattering your luckless rider
Back into the tempest pass'd?
There then lie to starve and die,
Or find another Phæton
Mad-mettled as yourself; for I,
Wearied, worried, and for-done,
Alone will down the mountain try,

---

[1] As this version of Calderon's drama is not for acting, a higher and wider mountain-scene than practicable may be imagined for Rosaura's descent in the first Act and the soldier's ascent in the last. The bad watch kept by the sentinels who guarded their state-prisoner, together with much else (not all!) that defies sober sense in this wild drama, I must leave Calderon to answer for; whose audience were not critical of detail and probability, so long as a good story, with strong, rapid, and picturesque action and situation, were set before them.

That knits his brows against the sun.

    Fife (as to his mule).   There, thou mis-begotten thing,
Long-ear'd lightning, tail'd tornado,
Griffin-hoof-in hurricano, —
(I might swear till I were almost
Hoarse with roaring Asonante).
Who forsooth because your betters
Would begin to kick and fling —
You forthwith your noble mind
Must prove, and kick me off behind,
Tow'rd the very centre whither
Gravity was most inclined.
There where you have made your bed
In it lie; for, wet or dry,
Let what will for me betide you,
Burning, blowing, freezing, hailing;
Famine waste you: devil ride you:
Tempest baste you black and blue: —
(To Rosaura.)   There!   I think in downright railing
I can hold my own with you.

    Ros.   Ah, my good Fife, whose merry loyal pipe,
Come weal, come woe, is never out of tune —
What, you in the same plight too?

    Fife   Aye;
And madam — sir — hereby desire,
When you your own adventures sing
Another time in lofty rhyme,
You don't forget the trusty squire
Who went with you Don-quixoting.

    Ros.   Well, my good fellow — to leave Pegasus,
Who scarce can serve us than our horses worse —
They say no one should rob another of
The single satisfaction he has left
Of singing his own sorrows; one so great,
So says some great philosopher, that trouble
Were worth encount'ring only for the sake
Of weeping over — what perhaps you know
Some poet calls the "luxury of woe."

    Fife   Had I the poet or philosopher
In place of her that kick'd me off to ride,

I'd test his theory upon his hide.
But no bones broken, madam — sir, I mean? —

Ros.　A scratch here that a handkerchief will heal —
And you? —

Fife　　A scratch in *quiddity*, or kind:
But not in "*quo*" — my wounds are all behind.
But, as you say, to stop this strain,
Which, somehow, once one's in the vein,
Comes clattering after — there again! —
What are we twain — deuce take 't! — we two,
I mean, to do — drencht through and through —
Oh, I shall choke of rhymes, which I believe
Are all that we shall have to live on here.

Ros.　What, is our victual gone too? —

Fife　　　　　　　　　　Aye, that brute
Has carried all we had away with her,
Clothing, and cate, and all.

Ros.　　　　　　And now the sun,
Our only friend and guide, about to sink
Under the stage of earth.

Fife　　　　　And enter Night,
With Capa y Espada — and — pray heav'n —
With but her lanthorn also.

Ros.　　　　　Ah, I doubt
To-night, if any, with a dark one — or
Almost burnt out after a month's consumption.
Well! well or ill, on horseback or afoot,
This is the gate that lets me into Poland;
And, sorry welcome as she gives a guest
Who writes his own arrival on her rocks
In his own blood —
Yet better on her stony threshold die,
Than live on unrevenged in Muscovy.

Fife　Oh what a soul some women have — I mean,
Some men —

Ros.　　Oh, Fife, Fife, as you love me, Fife,
Make yourself perfect in that little part,
Or all will go to ruin!

Fife　　　　　Oh, I will,

Please God we find some one to try it on.
But, truly, would not any one believe
Some fairy had exchanged us as we lay
Two tiny foster-children in one cradle?
   Ros.   Well, be that as it may, Fife, it reminds me
Of what perhaps I should have thought before,
But better late than never — You know I love you,
As you, I know, love me, and loyally
Have follow'd me thus far in my wild venture:
Well! now then — having seen me safe thus far —
Safe if not wholly sound — over the rocks
Into the country where my business lies —
Why should not you return the way we came,
The storm all clear'd away, and, leaving me
(Who now shall want you, though not thank you, less,
Now that our horses gone) this side the ridge,
Find your way back to dear old home again;
While I — Come, come! —
What, weeping, my poor fellow? —
   Fife   Leave you here
Alone — my Lady — Lord! I mean my Lord —
In a strange country — among savages —
Oh, now I know — you would be rid of me
For fear my stumbling speech —
   Ros.   Oh, no, no, no! —
I want you with me for a thousand sakes
To which that is as nothing — I myself
More apt to let the secret out myself
Without your help at all — Come, come, cheer up!
And if you sing again, "Come weal, come woe,"
Let it be that; for we will never part
Until you give the signal.
   Fife   'T is a bargain.
   Ros.   Now to begin, then. "Follow, follow me,
"You fairy elves that be."
   Fife   Aye, and go on —
Something of "following darkness like a dream,"
For that we're after.
   Ros.   No, after the sun;

Trying to catch hold of his glittering skirts
That hang upon the mountain as he goes.

Fife   Ah, he's himself past catching — as you spoke
He heard what you were saying, and — just so —
Like some scared water-bird,
As we say in my country, *dōve* below.

Ros.   Well, we must follow him as best we may.
Poland is no great country, and, as rich
In men and means, will but few acres spare
To lie beneath her barrier mountains bare.
We cannot, I believe, be very far
From mankind or their dwellings.

Fife   Send it so!
And well provided for man, woman, and beast.
No, not for beast.   Ah, but my heart begins
To yearn for her —

Ros.   Keep close, and keep your feet
From serving you as hers did.

Fife   As for beasts,
If in default of other entertainment,
We should provide them with ourselves to eat —
Bears, lions, wolves —

Ros.   Oh, never fear.

Fife   Or else,
Default of other beasts, beastlier men,
Cannibals, Anthropophagi, bare Poles
Who never knew a tailor but by taste.

Ros.   Look, look!   Unless my fancy misconceive
With twilight — down among the rocks there, Fife —
Some human dwelling, surely —
Or think you but a rock torn from the rocks
In some convulsion like to-day's, and perch'd
Quaintly among them in mock-masonry?

Fife   Most likely that, I doubt.

Ros.   No, no — for look!
A square of darkness opening in it —

Fife   Oh,
I don't half like such openings! —

Ros.   Like the loom
Of night from which she spins her outer gloom —

Fife   Lord, madam, pray forbear this tragic vein
In such a time and place —
Ros.   And now again
Within that square of darkness, look! a light
That feels its way with hesitating pulse,
As we do, through the darkness that it drives
To blacken into deeper night beyond.
Fife   In which could we follow that light's example,
As might some English Bardolph with his nose,
We might defy the sunset — Hark, a chain!
Ros.   And now a lamp, a lamp!   And now the hand
That carries it.
Fife   Oh, Lord! that dreadful chain!
Ros.   And now the bearer of the lamp; indeed
As strange as any in Arabian tale,
So giant-like, and terrible, and grand,
Spite of the skin he's wrapt in.
Fife   Why, 't is his own:
Oh, 't is some wild man of the woods; I've heard
They build and carry torches —
Ros.   Never Ape
Bore such a brow before the heav'ns as that —
Chain'd as you say too! —
Fife   Oh, that dreadful chain!
Ros.   And now he sets the lamp down by his side,
And with one hand clench'd in his tangled hair
And with a sigh as if his heart would break —
                    [*During this* SEGISMUND *has entered from the
                              fortress with a torch.*]
Segismund   Once more the storm has roar'd itself away,
Splitting the crags of God as it retires;
But sparing still what it should only blast,
This guilty piece of human handiwork,
And all that are within it.   Oh, how oft,
How oft, within or here abroad, have I
Waited, and in the whisper of my heart
Pray'd for the slanting hand of heav'n to strike
The blow myself I dared not, out of fear
Of that Hereafter, worse, they say, than here,
Plunged headlong in, but, till dismissal waited,

To wipe at last all sorrow from men's eyes,
And make this heavy dispensation clear.
Thus have I borne till now, and still endure,
Crouching in sullen impotence day by day,
Till some such out-burst of the elements
Like this rouses the sleeping fire within;
And standing thus upon the threshold of
Another night about to close the door
Upon one wretched day to open it
On one yet wretcheder because one more; —
Once more, you savage heav'ns, I ask of you —
I, looking up to those relentless eyes
That, now the greater lamp is gone below,
Begin to muster in the listening skies:
In all the shining circuits you have gone
About this theatre of human woe,
What greater sorrow have you gazed upon
Than down this narrow chink you witness still;
And which, did you yourselves not fore-devise,
You register'd for others to fulfil!

  Fife This is some Laureate at a birth-day ode;
No wonder we went rhyming.
  Ros.   Hush! And now
See, starting to his feet, he strides about
Far as his tethered steps —
  Seg.   And if the chain
You help'd to rivet round me did contract
Since guiltless infancy from guilt in act;
Of what in aspiration or in thought
Guilty, but in resentment of the wrong
That wreaks revenge on wrong I never wrought
By excommunication from the free
Inheritance that all created life,
Beside myself, is born to — from the wings
That range your own immeasurable blue,
Down to the poor, mute, scale-imprison'd things,
That yet are free to wander, glide, and pass
About that under-sapphire, whereinto
Yourselves transfusing you yourselves englass!
  Ros. What mystery is this?

Fife   Why, the man's mad:
That's all the mystery.   That's why he's chain'd —
And why —
  Seg.   Nor Nature's guiltless life alone —
But that which lives on blood and rapine; nay,
Charter'd with larger liberty to slay
Their guiltless kind, the tyrants of the air
Soar zenith-upward with their screaming prey,
Making pure heav'n drop blood upon the stage
Of under earth, where lion, wolf, and bear,
And they that on their treacherous velvet wear
Figure and constellation like your own,[1]
With their still living slaughter bound away
Over the barriers of the mountain cage
Against which one, blood-guiltless, and endued
With aspiration and with aptitude
Transcending other creatures, day by day
Beats himself mad with unavailing rage!
  Fife   Why, that must be the meaning of my mule's
Rebellion —
  Ros.   Hush!
  Seg.   But then if murder be
The law by which not only conscience-blind
Creatures, but man too prospers with his kind;
Who leaving all his guilty fellows free,
Under your fatal auspice and divine
Compulsion, leagued in some mysterious ban
Against one innocent and helpless man,
Abuse their liberty to murder mine:
And sworn to silence, like their masters mute
In heav'n, and like them twiring through the mask
Of darkness, answering to all I ask,
Point up to them whose work they execute!
  Ros.   Ev'n as I thought, some poor unhappy wretch,
By man wrong'd, wretched, unrevenged, as I!

---

[1] "Some report that they" — (panthers) — "have one marke on the shoulders resembling the moone, growing and decreasing as she doth, sometimes showing a full compasse, and otherwhiles hollowed and pointed with tips like the hornes." — *Philemon Holland's Pliny*, b. viii, c. 17.

Nay, so much worse than I, as by those chains
Clipt of the means of self-revenge on those
Who lay on him what they deserve.   And I,
Who taunted Heav'n a little while ago
With pouring all its wrath upon my head —
Alas! like him who caught the cast-off husk
Of what another bragg'd of feeding on,
Here's one that from the refuse of my sorrows
Could gather all the banquet he desires!
Poor soul, poor soul!

 Fife   Speak lower — he will hear you.

 Ros. And if he should, what then?   Why, if he would
He could not harm me — Nay, and if he could,
Methinks I'd venture something of a life
I care so little for —

 Seg. Who's that?   Clotaldo?   Who are you, I say,
That, venturing in these forbidden rocks,
Have lighted on my miserable life,
And your own death?

 Ros.   You would not hurt me, surely?

 Seg. Not I; but those that, iron as the chain
In which they slay me with a lingering death,
Will slay you with a sudden — Who are you?

 Ros. A stranger from across the mountain there,
Who, having lost his way in this strange land
And coming night, drew hither to what seem'd
A human dwelling hidden in these rocks,
And where the voice of human sorrow soon
Told him it was so.

 Seg.   Aye?   But nearer — nearer —
That by this smoky supplement of day
But for a moment I may see who speaks
So pitifully sweet.

 Fife   Take care! take care!

 Ros. Alas, poor man, that I myself so helpless,
Could better help you than by barren pity,
And my poor presence —

 Seg.   Oh, might that be all!
But that — a few poor moments — and alas!
The very bliss of having, and the dread

Of losing under such a penalty
As every moment's having runs more near,
Stifles the very utterance and resource
They cry for quickest; till from sheer despair
Of holding thee, methinks myself would tear
To pieces —
   Fife   There, his word's enough for it.
   Seg.   Oh, think, if you who move about at will,
And live in sweet communion with your kind,
After an hour lost in these lonely rocks
Hunger and thirst after some human voice
To drink, and human face to feed upon;
What must one do where all is mute, or harsh,
And ev'n the naked face of cruelty
Were better than the mask it works beneath? —
Across the mountain then!   Across the mountain!
What if the next world which they tell one of
Be only next across the mountain then,
Though I must never see it till I die,
And you one of its angels?
   Ros.   Alas!   Alas!
No angel!   And the face you think so fair,
'T is but the dismal frame-work of these rocks
That makes it seem so; and the world I come from —
Alas, alas, too many faces there
Are but fair visors to black hearts below,
Or only serve to bring the wearer woe!
But to yourself — If haply the redress
That I am here upon may help to yours.
I heard you tax the heav'n's with ordering,
And men for executing, what, alas!
I now behold.   But why, and who they are
Who do, and you who suffer —
   Seg. (pointing upwards).   Ask of them,
Whom, as to-night, I have so often asked,
And ask'd in vain.
   Ros.   But surely, surely —
   Seg.   Hark!
The trumpet of the watch to shut us in.
Oh, should they find you! — Quick!   Behind the rocks!

To-morrow — if to-morrow —
 Ros. (flinging her sword toward him). Take my sword!

ROSAURA and FIFE hide the rocks; Enter CLOTALDO

 Clotaldo These stormy days you like to see the last of
Are but ill opiates, Segismund, I think,
For night to follow; and to-night you seem
More than your wont disorder'd. What! a sword?
Within there!

Enter Soldiers with black visors and torches

 Fife Here's a pleasant masquerade!
 Clo. Whosoever watch this was
Will have to pay head-reckoning. Meanwhile,
This weapon had a wearer. Bring him here,
Alive or dead.
 Seg.   Clotaldo! good Clotaldo! —
 Clo. (to Soldiers who enclose SEGISMUND; *others searching
  the rocks).* You know your duty.
 Soldiers (bringing in ROSAURA *and* FIFE). Here are two of
  them,
Whoever more to follow —
 Clo.   Who are you,
That in defiance of known proclamation
Are found, at night-fall too, about this place?
 Fife Oh, my Lord, she — I mean he —
 Ros.   Silence, Fife,
And let me speak for both. — Two foreign men,
To whom your country and its proclamations
Are equally unknown; and had we known,
Ourselves not masters of our lawless beasts
That, terrified by the storm among your rocks,
Flung us upon them to our cost.
 Fife   My mule —
 Clo. Foreigners? of what country?
 Ros.   Muscovy.
 Clo. And whither bound?
 Ros.   Hither — if this be Poland;
But with no ill design on her, and therefore

Taking it ill that we should thus be stopt
Upon her threshold so uncivilly.

    Clo.   Whither in Poland?

    Ros.   To the capital.

    Clo.   And on what errand?

    Ros.   Set me on the road,
And you shall be the nearer to my answer.

    Clo. (aside).   So resolute and ready to reply,
And yet so young — and — *(aloud)*   Well, —
Your business was not surely with the man
We found you with?

    Ros.   He was the first we saw, —
And strangers and benighted, as we were,
As you too would have done in a like case,
Accosted him at once.

    Clo.   Aye, but this sword?

    Ros.   I flung it toward him.

    Clo.   Well, and why?

    Ros.   And why?
But to revenge himself on those who thus
Injuriously misuse him.

    Clo.   So — so — so!
'T is well such resolution wants a beard —
And, I suppose, is never to attain one.
Well, I must take you both, you and your sword,
Prisoners.

    Fife (offering a cudgel).   Pray take mine, and welcome, sir;
I'm sure I gave it to that mule of mine
To mighty little purpose.

    Ros.   Mine you have;
And may it win us some more kindliness
Than we have met with yet.

    Clo. (examining the sword).   More mystery!
How came you by this weapon?

Ros.   From my father.

    Clo.   And do you know whence he?

    Ros.   Oh, very well:
From one of this same Polish realm of yours,
Who promised a return should come the chance,
Of courtesies that he received himself

In Muscovy, and left this pledge of it —
Not likely yet, it seems, to be redeem'd.
    Clo. (aside).   Oh, wondrous chance — or wondrous
        Providence!
The sword that I myself in Muscovy,
When these white hairs were black, for keepsake left
Of obligation for a like return
To him who saved me wounded as I lay
Fighting against his country; took me home;
Tended me like a brother till recover'd,
Perchance to fight against him once again —
And now my sword put back into my hand
By his — if not his son — still, as so seeming,
By me, as first devoir of gratitude,
To seem believing, till the wearer's self
See fit to drop the ill-dissembling mask.
(Aloud.)   Well, a strange turn of fortune has arrested
The sharp and sudden penalty that else
Had visited your rashness or mischance:
In part, your tender youth too — pardon me,
And touch not where your sword is not to answer —
Commends you to my care; not your life only,
Else by this misadventure forfeited;
But ev'n your errand, which by happy chance,
Chimes with the very business I am on,
And calls me to the very point you aim at.
    Ros.   The capital?
    Clo.   Aye, the capital; and ev'n
That capital of capitals, the Court:
Where you may plead, and I may promise, win
Pardon for this, you say unwilling, trespass,
And prosecute what else you have at heart,
With me to help you forward all I can;
Provided all in loyalty to those
To whom by natural allegiance
I first am bound to.
    Ros.   As you make, I take
Your offer: with like promise on my side
Of loyalty to you and those you serve,
Under like reservation for regards

Nearer and dearer still.

    Clo.   Enough, enough;
Your hand; a bargain on both sides.   Meanwhile,
Here shall you rest to-night.   The break of day
Shall see us both together on the way.

    Ros.   Thus then what I for misadventure blamed,
Directly draws me where my wishes aim'd.   [*Exeunt.*

Scene II. *The Palace at Warsaw. Enter on one side* As-
    tolfo, *Duke of Muscovy, with his train: and, on the other,*
    the princess estrella, *with hers.*

    Astolfo   My royal cousin, if so near in blood,
Till this auspicious meeting scarcely known,
Till all that beauty promised in the bud
Is now to its consummate blossom blown,
Well met at last; and may —

    Estrella   Enough, my Lord,
Of compliment devised for you by some
Court tailor, and, believe me, still too short
To cover the designful heart below.

    Ast.   Nay, but indeed, fair cousin —

    Est.   Aye, let Deed
Measure your words, indeed your flowers of speech
Ill with your iron equipage atone;
Irony indeed, and wordy compliment.

    Ast.   Indeed, indeed, you wrong me, royal cousin,
And fair as royal, misinterpreting
What, even for the end you think I aim at,
If false to you, were fatal to myself.

    Est.   Why, what else means the glittering steel, my Lord,
That bristles in the rear of these fine words?
What can it mean, but, failing to cajole,
To fight or force me from my just pretension?

    Ast.   Nay, might I not ask ev'n the same of you,
The nodding helmets of whose men at arms
Out-crest the plumage of your lady court?

    Est.   But to defend what yours would force from me.

    Ast.   Might not I, lady, say the same of mine?
But not to come to battle, ev'n of words,

With a fair lady, and my kinswoman;
And as averse to stand before your face,
Defenceless, and condemn'd in your disgrace,
Till the good king be here to clear it all —
Will you vouchsafe to hear me?

    Est.   As you will.

    Ast.   You know that, when about to leave this world,
Our royal grandsire, King Alfonso, left
Three children; one a son, Basilio,
Who wears — long may he wear! — the crown of Poland;
And daughters twain: of whom the elder was
Your mother, Clorileña, now some while
Exalted to a more than mortal throne;
And Recisunda, mine, the younger sister,
Who, married to the Prince of Muscovy,
Gave me the light which may she live to see
Herself for many, many years to come.
Meanwhile, good King Basilio, as you know,
Deep in abstruser studies than this world,
And busier with the stars than lady's eyes,
Has never by a second marriage yet
Replaced, as Poland ask'd of him, the heir
An early marriage brought and took away;
His young queen dying with the son she bore him:
And in such alienation grown so old
As leaves no other hope of heir to Poland
Than his two sisters' children; you, fair cousin,
And me; for whom the Commons of the realm
Divide themselves into two several factions;
Whether for you, the elder sister's child;
Or me, born of the younger, but, they say,
My natural prerogative of man
Outweighing your priority of birth.
Which discord growing loud and dangerous,
Our uncle, King Basilio, doubly sage
In prophesying and providing for
The future, as to deal with it when come,
Bids us here meet to-day in solemn council
Our several pretensions to compose.
And, but the martial out-burst that proclaims

His coming, makes all further parley vain,
Unless my bosom, by which only wise
I prophesy, now wrongly prophesies,
By such a happy compact as I dare
But glance at till the Royal Sage declare.

(*Trumpets, &c.* *Enter* KING BASILIO *with his Council.*)

All   The King!   God save the King!
Estrella   ⎫   Oh, Royal sir! —
Astolfo   ⎬ (*kneeling*). God save your Majesty! —
King   Rise, both of you,
Rise to my arms, Astolfo and Estrella;
As my two sisters' children always mine,
Now more than ever, since myself and Poland
Solely to you for our succession look'd.
And now give ear, you and your several factions,
And you, the Peers and Princes of this realm,
While I reveal the purport of this meeting
In words whose necessary length I trust
No unsuccessful issue shall excuse.
You and the world who have surnamed me "Sage"
Know that I owe that title, if my due,
To my long meditation on the book
Which ever lying open overhead —
The book of heav'n, I mean — so few have read;
Whose golden letters on whose sapphire leaf,
Distinguishing the page of day and night,
And all the revolution of the year;
So with the turning volume where they lie
Still changing their prophetic syllables,
They register the destinies of men:
Until with eyes that, dim with years indeed,
Are quicker to pursue the stars that rule them,
I get the start of Time, and from his hand
The wand of tardy revelation draw.
Oh, had the self-same heav'n upon his page
Inscribed my death ere I should read my life,
And, by forecasting of my own mischance,
Play not the victim but the suicide

In my own tragedy! — But you shall hear.
You know how once, as kings must for their people,
And only once, as wise men for themselves,
I woo'd and wedded: know too that my Queen
In childing died; but not, as you believe,
With her, the son she died in giving life to.
For, as the hour of birth was on the stroke,
Her brain conceiving with her womb, she dream'd
A serpent tore her entrail.   And, too surely
(For evil omen seldom speaks in vain)
The man-child breaking from that living tomb
That makes our birth the antitype of death,
Man-grateful, for the life she gave him paid
By killing her: and with such circumstance
As suited such unnatural tragedy;
He coming into light, if light it were
That darken'd at his very horoscope,
When heaven's two champions — sun and moon I mean —
Suffused in blood upon each other fell
In such a raging duel of eclipse
As hath not terrified the universe
Since that that wept in blood the death of Christ:
When the dead walk'd, the waters turn'd to blood,
Earth and her cities totter'd, and the world
Seem'd shaken to its last paralysis.
In such a paroxysm of dissolution
That son of mine was born; by that first act
Heading the monstrous catalogue of crime,
I found fore-written in his horoscope;
As great a monster in man's history
As was in nature his nativity;
So savage, bloody, terrible, and impious,
Who, should he live, would tear his country's entrails,
As by his birth his mother's; with which crime
Beginning, he should clench the dreadful tale
By trampling on his father's silver head.
All which fore-reading, and his act of birth
Fate's warrant that I read his life aright;
To save his country from his mother's fate,
I gave abroad that he had died with her

His being slew: with midnight secrecy
I had him carried to a lonely tower
Hewn from the mountain-barriers of the realm,
And under strict anathema of death
Guarded from men's inquisitive approach,
Save from the trusty few one needs must trust;
Who while his fasten'd body they provide
With salutary garb and nourishment,
Instruct his soul in what no soul may miss
Of holy faith, and in such other lore
As may solace his life-imprisonment,
And tame perhaps the Savage prophesied
Toward such a trial as I aim at now,
And now demand your special hearing to.
What in this fearful business I have done,
Judge whether lightly or maliciously, —
I, with my own and only flesh and blood,
And proper lineal inheritor!
I swear, had his foretold atrocities
Touch'd me alone, I had not saved myself
At such a cost to him; but as a king, —
A Christian king, — I say, advisedly,
Who would devote his people to a tyrant
Worse than Caligula fore-chronicled?
But even this not without grave mis-giving,
Lest by some chance mis-reading of the stars,
Or mis-direction of what rightly read,
I wrong my son of his prerogative,
And Poland of her rightful sovereign.
For, sure and certain prophets as the stars,
Although they err not, he who reads them may;
Or rightly reading — seeing there is One
Who governs them, as, under Him, they us,
We are not sure if the rough diagram
They draw in heav'n and we interpret here,
Be sure of operation, if the Will
Supreme, that sometimes for some special end
The course of providential nature breaks
By miracle, may not of these same stars
Cancel his own first draft, or overrule

What else fore-written all else overrules.
As, for example, should the Will Almighty
Permit the Free-will of particular man
To break the meshes of else strangling fate —
Which Free-will, fearful of foretold abuse,
I have myself from my own son for-closed
From ever possible self-extrication;
A terrible responsibility,
Not to the conscience to be reconciled
Unless opposing almost certain evil
Against so slight contingency of good.
Well — thus perplext, I have resolved at last
To bring the thing to trial: whereunto
Here have I summon'd you, my Peers, and you
Whom I more dearly look to, failing him,
As witnesses to that which I propose;
And thus propose the doing it.   Clotaldo,
Who guards my son with old fidelity,
Shall bring him hither from his tower by night,
Lockt in a sleep so fast as by my art
I rivet to within a link of death,
But yet from death so far, that next day's dawn
Shall wake him up upon the royal bed,
Complete in consciousness and faculty,
When with all princely pomp and retinue
My loyal Peers with due obeisance
Shall hail him Segismund, the Prince of Poland.
Then if with any show of human kindness
He fling discredit, not upon the stars,
But upon me, their misinterpreter;
With all apology mistaken age
Can make to youth it never meant to harm,
To my son's forehead will I shift the crown
I long have wish'd upon a younger brow;
And in religious humiliation,
For what of worn-out age remains to me,
Entreat my pardon both of Heav'n and him
For tempting destinies beyond my reach.
But if, as I misdoubt, at his first step
The hoof of the predicted savage shows;

Before predicted mischief can be done,
The self-same sleep that loosed him from the chain
Shall re-consign him, not to loose again.
Then shall I, having lost that heïr direct,
Look solely to my sisters' children twain;
Each of a claim so equal as divides
The voice of Poland to their several sides,
But, as I trust, to be entwined ere long
Into one single wreath so fair and strong
As shall at once all difference atone,
And cease the realm's division with their own.
Cousins and Princes, Peers and Councillors,
Such is the purport of this invitation,
And such is my design.   Whose furtherance
If not as Sovereign, if not as Seer,
Yet one whom these white locks, if nothing else,
To patient acquiescence consecrate,
I now demand and even supplicate.
  Ast. Such news, and from such lips, may well suspend
The tongue to loyal answer most attuned;
But if to me as spokesman of my faction
Your Highness looks for answer; I reply
For one and all — Let Segismund, whom now
We first hear tell of as your living heir,
Appear, and but in your sufficient eye
Approve himself worthy to be your son,
Then we will hail him Poland's rightful heir.
What says my cousin?
  Est.   Aye, with all my heart.
But if my youth and sex upbraid me not
That I should dare ask of so wise a king —
  King Ask, ask, fair cousin!   Nothing, I am sure,
Not well consider'd; nay, if 't were, yet nothing
But pardonable from such lips as those.
  Est. Then, with your pardon, Sir — If Segismund,
My cousin, whom I shall rejoice to hail
As Prince of Poland too, as you propose,
Be to a trial coming upon which
More, as I think, than life itself depends,
Why, Sir, with sleep disorder'd senses brought

To this uncertain contest with his stars?

King   Well askt indeed!   As wisely be it answer'd! —
Because it is uncertain, see you not?
Far as I think I can discern between
The sudden flaws of a sleep-startled man,
And of the savage thing we have to dread;
If but bewilder'd, dazzled, and uncouth,
As might the sanest and the civilest
In circumstance so strange — nay, more than that,
If moved to any out-break short of blood,
All shall be well with him; and how much more,
If 'mid the magic turmoil of the change,
He shall so calm a resolution show
As scarce to reel beneath so great a blow!
But if with savage passion uncontroll'd
He lay about him like the brute foretold,
And must as suddenly be caged again;
Then what redoubled anguish and despair,
From that brief flash of blissful liberty
Remitted — and for ever — to his chain!
Which so much less, if on the stage of glory
Enter'd and excited through such a door
Of sleep as makes a dream of all between.

  Est.   Oh kindly answer, Sir, to question that
To charitable courtesy less wise
Might call for pardon rather!   I shall now
Gladly, what, uninstructed, loyally
I should have waited.

  Ast.   Your Highness doubts not me,
Nor how my heart follows my cousin's lips,
Whatever way the doubtful balance fall,
Still loyal to your bidding.

  Omnes.   So say all.

  King   I hoped, and did expect, of all no less —
And sure no sovereign never needed more
From all who owe him love or loyalty.
For what a strait of time I stand upon,
When to this issue not alone I bring
My son your Prince, but ev'n myself your King:
And, whichsoever way for him it turn,

Of less than little honour to myself.
For if this coming trial justify
My thus withholding from my son his right,
Is not the judge himself justified in
The father's shame?   And if the judge proved wrong,
My son withholding from his right thus long,
Shame and remorse to judge and father both:
Unless remorse and shame together drown'd
In having what I flung for worthless found.
But come — already weary with your travel,
And ill refresht by this strange history,
Until the hours that draw the sun from heav'n
Unite us at the customary board,
Each to his several chamber: you to rest;
I to contrive with old Clotaldo best
The method of a stranger thing than old
Time has yet among the records told.   [*Exeunt.*

ACT II

SCENE I.　*A Throne room in the Palace.　Music within.*
Enter KING *and* CLOTALDO, *meeting a Lord in waiting.*

King　You for a moment beckon'd from your office,
Tell me thus far how goes it.　In due time
The potion left him?
　　Lord　　　　　　　　At the very hour
To which your Highness temper'd it.　Yet not
So wholly but some lingering mist still hung
About his dawning sense — which to clear,
We fill'd and handed him a morning drink
With sleep's specific antidote suffused;
And while with princely raiment we invested
What nature surely modell'd for a Prince —
All but the sword — as you directed —
　　King　　　　　　　　　　　　Aye —
　　Lord　If not too loudly, yet emphatically
Still with the title of a Prince address'd him.
　　King　How bore he that?
　　Lord　　　　　　　　With all the rest, my liege,
I will not say so like one in a dream
As one himself misdoubting that he dream'd.
　　King　So far so well, Clotaldo, either way,
And best of all if tow'rd the worse I dread,
But yet no violence? —
　　Lord　　　　　　　At most, impatience;
Wearied perhaps with importunities
We yet were bound to offer.

King   Oh, Clotaldo!
Though thus far well, yet would myself had drunk
The potion he revives from!   Such suspense
Crowds all the pulses of life's residue
Into the present moment; and I think,
Whichever way the trembling scale may turn,
Will leave the crown of Poland for some one
To wait no longer than the setting sun!

  Clo.   Courage, my liege!   The curtain is undrawn,
And each must play his part out manfully,
Leaving the rest to heav'n.

  King   Whose written words
If I should misinterpret or transgress!
But as you say —
(*To the Lord, who exit.*)   You, back to him at once;
Clotaldo, you, when he is somewhat used
To the new world of which they call him Prince,
Where place and face, and all is strange to him,
With your known features and familiar garb
Shall then, as chorus to the scene, accost him,
And by such earnest of that old and too
Familiar world, assure him of the new.
Last in the strange procession, I myself
Will by one full and last development
Complete the plot for that catastrophe
That he must put to all; God grant it be
The crown of Poland on his brows! — Hark! hark! —
Was that his voice within? — Now louder — Oh,
Clotaldo, what!   So soon begun to roar! —
Again! above the music — But betide
What may, until the moment, we must hide.
                         [*Exeunt* KING *and* CLOTALDO.

  Segismund (within).   Forbear!   I stifle with your perfume!
      cease
Your crazy salutations! peace, I say —
Begone or let me go, ere I go mad
With all this babble, mummery, and glare,
For I am growing dangerous — Air! room! air! —
                         [*He rushes in.   Music ceases.*

Oh but to save the reeling brain from wreck
With its bewilder'd senses! —

                              [*He covers his eyes for a while.*

                    What!   Ev'n now
That Babel left behind me, but my eyes
Pursued by the same glamour, that — unless
Alike bewitch'd too — the confederate sense
Vouches for palpable: bright-shining floors
That ring hard answer back to the stamp'd heel,
And shoot up airy columns marble-cold,
That, as they climb, break into golden leaf
And capital, till they embrace aloft
In clustering flower and fruitage over walls
Hung with such purple curtain as the West
Fringes with such a gold; or over-laid
With sanguine-glowing semblances of men,
Each in his all but living action busied,
Or from the wall they look from, with fix'd eyes
Pursuing me; and one most strange of all
That, as I pass'd the crystal on the wall,
Look'd from it — left it — and as I return,
Returns, and looks me face to face again —
Unless some false reflection of my brain,
The outward semblance of myself — Myself?
How know that tawdry shadow for myself,
But that it moves as I move; lifts his hand
With mine; each motion echoing so close
The immediate suggestion of the will
In which myself I recognize — Myself! —
What, this fantastic Segismund the same
Who last night, as for all his nights before,
Lay down to sleep in wolf-skin on the ground
In a black turret which the wolf howl'd round,
And woke again upon a golden bed,
Round which as clouds about a rising sun,
In scarce less glittering caparison,
Gather'd gay shapes that, underneath a breeze
Of music, handed him upon their knees
The wine of heaven in a cup of gold,
And still in soft melodious under-song

Hailing me Prince of Poland! — "Segismund,"
They said, "Our Prince!   The Prince of Poland!" and
Again, "Oh, welcome, welcome, to his own,
"Our own Prince Segismund —"
                                        Oh, but a blast —
One blast of the rough mountain air! one look
At the grim features —   *(He goes to the window)*
What they disvisor'd also! shatter'd chaos
Cast into stately shape and masonry,
Between whose channel'd and perspective sides
Compact with rooted towers, and flourishing
To heav'n with gilded pinnacle and spire,
Flows the live current ever to and fro
With open aspect and free step! — Clotaldo!
Clotaldo! — calling as one scarce dares call
For him who suddenly might break the spell
One fears to walk without him — Why, that I,
With unencumber'd step as any there,
Go stumbling through my glory — feeling for
That iron leading-string — aye, for myself —
For that fast-anchored self of yesterday,
Of yesterday, and all my life before,
Ere drifted clean from self-identity
Upon the fluctuation of to-day's
Mad whirling circumstance! — And fool, why not?
If reason, sense, and self-identity
Obliterated from a worn-out brain,
Art thou not maddest striving to be sane,
And catching at that Self of yesterday
That, like a leper's rags, best flung away!
Or if not mad, then dreaming — dreaming? — well —
Dreaming then — Or, if self to self be true,
Not mock'd by that, but as poor souls have been
By those who wrong'd them, to give wrong new relish?
Or have those stars indeed they told me of
As masters of my wretched life of old,
Into some happier constellation roll'd,
And brought my better fortune out on earth
Clear as themselves in heav'n! — Prince Segismund
They call'd me — and at will I shook them off —

Will they return again at my command
Again to call me so? — Within there!   You!
Segismund calls — Prince Segismund —

(He has seated himself on the throne.   Enter CHAMBERLAIN,
with lords in waiting.)

 Chamb.   I rejoice
That unadvised of any but the voice
Of royal instinct in the blood, your Highness
Has ta'en the chair that you were born to fill.
 Seg.   The chair?
 Chamb.   The royal throne of Poland, Sir,
Which may your Royal Highness keep as long
As he that now rules from it shall have ruled
When heav'n has call'd him to itself.
 Seg.   When he? —
 Chamb.   Your royal father, King Basilio, Sir.
 Seg.   My royal father — King Basilio.
You see I answer but as Echo does,
Not knowing what she listens or repeats.
This is my throne — this is my palace — Oh,
But this out of the window? —
 Chamb.   Warsaw, Sir,
Your capital —
 Seg.   And all the moving people?
 Chamb.   Your subjects and your vassals like ourselves.
 Seg.   Aye, aye — my subjects — in my capital —
Warsaw — and I am Prince of it — You see
It needs much iteration to strike sense
Into the human echo.
 Chamb.   Left awhile
In the quick brain, the word will quickly to
Full meaning blow.
 Seg.   You think so?
 Chamb.   And meanwhile
Lest our obsequiousness, which means no worse
Than customary honour to the Prince
We most rejoice to welcome, trouble you,
Should we retire again? or stand apart?

Or would your Highness have the music play
Again, which meditation, as they say,
So often loves to float upon?
  Seg.   The music?
No — yes — perhaps the trumpet — *(Aside.)* Yet if that
Brought back the troop!
  A Lord   The trumpet! There again
How trumpet-like spoke out the blood of Poland!
  Chamb. Before the morning is far up, your Highness
Will have the trumpet marshalling your soldiers
Under the Palace windows.
  Seg.   Ah, my soldiers —
My soldiers — not black-visor'd? —
  Chamb.   Sir?
  Seg.   No matter.
But — one thing — for a moment — in your ear —
Do you know one Clotaldo?
  Chamb.   Oh, my Lord,
He and myself together, I may say,
Although in different vocations,
Have silver'd in your royal father's service;
And, as I trust, with both of us a few
White hairs to fall in yours.
  Seg.   Well said, well said!
Basilio, my father — well — Clotaldo —
Is he my kinsman too?
  Chamb.   Oh, my good Lord,
A General simply in your Highness' service,
Than whom your Highness has no trustier.
  Seg. Aye, so you said before, I think. And you
With that white wand of yours —
Why, now I think on 't, I have read of such
A silver-hair'd magician with a wand,
Who in a moment, with a wave of it,
Turn'd rags to jewels, clowns to emperors,
By some benigner magic than the stars
Spirited poor good people out of hand
From all their woes; in some enchanted sleep
Carried them off on cloud or dragon-back
Over the mountains, over the wide Deep,

And set them down to wake in Fairyland.

Chamb.   Oh, my good Lord, you laugh at me — and I
Right glad to make you laugh at such a price:
You know me no enchanter: if I were,
I and my wand as much your Highness',
As now your chamberlain —

Seg.   My chamberlain? —
And these that follow you? —

Chamb.   On you, my Lord;
Your Highness' lords in waiting.

Seg.   Lords in waiting.
Well, I have now learn'd to repeat, I think,
If only but by rote — This is my palace,
And this my throne — which unadvised — And that
Out of the window there my Capital;
And all the people moving up and down
My subjects and my vassals like yourselves,
My chamberlain — and lords in waiting — and
Clotaldo — and Clotaldo? —
You are an aged, and seem a reverend man —
You do not — though his fellow-officer —
You do not mean to mock me?

Chamb.   Oh, my Lord!

Seg.   Well then — If no magician, as you say,
Yet setting me a riddle, that my brain,
With all its senses whirling, cannot solve,
Yourself or one of these with you must answer —
How I — that only last night fell asleep
Not knowing that the very soil of earth
I lay down — chain'd — to sleep upon was Poland —
Awake to find myself the Lord of it,
With Lords, and Generals, and Chamberlains,
And ev'n my very Gaoler, for my vassals!

Enter suddenly CLOTALDO

Clotaldo   Stand all aside
That I may put into his hand the clue
To lead him out of this amazement.   Sir,
Vouchsafe your Highness from my bended knee
Receive my homage first.

Seg.   Clotaldo!   What,
At last — his old self — undisguised where all
Is masquerade — to end it! — You kneeling too!
What! have the stars you told me long ago
Laid that old work upon you, added this,
That, having chain'd your prisoner so long,
You loose his body now to slay his wits,
Dragging him — how I know not — whither scarce
I understand — dressing him up in all
This frippery, with your dumb familiars
Disvisor'd, and their lips unlockt to lie,
Calling him Prince and King, and madman-like,
Setting a crown of straw upon his head!
     Clo.   Would but your Highness, as indeed I now
Must call you — and upon his bended knee
Never bent Subject more devotedly —
However all about you, and perhaps
You to yourself incomprehensiblest,
But rest in the assurance of your own
Sane waking senses, by these witnesses
Attested, till the story of it all,
Of which I bring a chapter, be reveal'd,
Assured of all you see and hear as neither
Madness nor mockery —
     Seg.   What then?
     Clo.   All it seems:
This palace with its royal garniture;
This capital of which it is the eye,
With all its temples, marts, and arsenals;
This realm of which this city is the head,
With all its cities, villages, and tilth,
Its armies, fleets, and commerce; all your own;
And all the living souls that make them up,
From those who now, and those who shall, salute you,
Down to the poorest peasant of the realm,
Your subjects — Who, though now their mighty voice
Sleeps in the general body unapprized,
Wait but a word from those about you now
To hail you Prince of Poland, Segismund.
     Seg.   All this is so?

Clo.   As sure as anything
Is or can be.
    Seg.   You swear it on the faith
You taught me — elsewhere? —
    Clo. (kissing the hilt of his sword) — Swear it upon this
Symbol, and champion of the holy faith
I wear it to defend.
    Seg. (to himself).   My eyes have not deceived me, nor my
        ears,
With this transfiguration, nor the strain
Of royal welcome that arose and blew,
Breathed from no lying lips, along with it.
For here Clotaldo comes, his own old self,
Who, if not Lie and phantom with the rest —
(Aloud.)   Well then, all this is thus.
For have not these fine people told me so,
And you, Clotaldo, sworn it?   And the Why
And Wherefore are to follow by and bye!
And yet — and yet — why wait for that which you
Who take your oath on it can answer — and
Indeed it presses hard upon my brain —
What I was asking of these gentlemen
When you came in upon us; how it is
That I — the Segismund you know so long —
No longer than the sun that rose to-day
Rose — and from what you know —
Rose to be Prince of Poland?
    Clo.   So to be
Acknowledg'd and entreated, sir.
    Seg.   So be
Acknowledg'd and entreated —
Well — But if now by all, by some at least
So known — if not entreated — heretofore —
Though not by you — For, now I think again,
Of what should be your attestation worth,
You that of all my questionable subjects
Who knówing what, yet left me where, I was,
You least of all, Clotaldo, till the dawn
Of this first day that told it to myself?
    Clo.   Oh, let your Highness draw the line across

Fore-written sorrow, and in this new dawn
Bury that long sad night.
   Seg.   Not ev'n the Dead,
Call'd to the resurrection of the blest,
Shall so directly drop all memory
Of woes and wrongs foregone!
   Clo.   But not resent —
Purged by the trial of that sorrow past
For full fruition of their present bliss.
   Seg.   But leaving with the Judge what, till this earth
Be cancell'd in the burning heav'ns, He leaves
His earthly delegates to execute,
Of retribution in reward to them
And woe to those who wrong'd them — Not as you,
Not you, Clotaldo, knowing not — And yet
Ev'n to the guiltiest wretch in all the realm,
Of any treason guilty short of that,
Stern usage — but assuredly not knowing,
Not knowing 't was your sovereign lord, Clotaldo,
You used so sternly.
   Clo.   Aye, sir; with the same
Devotion and fidelity that now
Does homage to him for my sovereign.
   Seg.   Fidelity that held his Prince in chains!
   Clo.   Fidelity more fast than had it loosed him —
   Seg.   Ev'n from the very dawn of consciousness
Down at the bottom of the barren rocks,
Where scarce a ray of sunshine found him out,
In which the poorest beggar of my realm
At least to human-full proportion grows —
Me!   Me — whose station was the kingdom's top
To flourish in, reaching my head to heav'n,
And with my branches overshadowing
The meaner growth below!
   Clo.   Still with the same
Fidelity —
   Seg.   To me! —
   Clo.   Aye, sir, to you,
Through that divine allegiance upon which
All Order and Authority is based;

Which to revolt against —
   Seg.   Were to revolt
Against the stars, belike!
   Clo.   And him who reads them;
And by that right, and by the sovereignty
He wears as you shall wear it after him;
Aye, one to whom yourself —
Yourself, ev'n more than any subject here,
Are bound by yet another and more strong
Allegiance — King Basilio — your Father! —
   Seg.   Basilio — King — my father! —
   Clo.   Oh, my Lord,
Let me beseech you on my bended knee,
For your own sake — for Poland's — and for his,
Who, looking up for counsel to the skies,
Did what he did under authority
To which the kings of earth themselves are subject,
And whose behest not only he that suffers,
But he that executes, not comprehends,
But only He that orders it —
   Seg.   The King —
My father! — Either I am mad already,
Or that way driving fast — or I should know
That fathers do not use their children so,
Or men were loosed from all allegiance
To fathers, kings, and heav'n that order'd all.
But, mad or not, my hour is come, and I
Will have my reckoning — Either you lie,
Under the skirt of sinless majesty
Shrouding your treason; or if *that* indeed,
Guilty itself, take refuge in the stars
That cannot hear the charge, or disavow —
You, whether doer or deviser, who
Come first to hand, shall pay the penalty
By the same hand you owe it to —
        (*Seizing* CLOTALDO's *sword and about to strike him.*)

       Enter ROSAURA *suddenly*

  Rosaura   Fie, my lord — forbear,
What! a young hand rais'd against silver hair! —

(She retreats through the crowd.)

Seg.   Stay! stay! — What come and vanisht as before —
I scarce remember how — but —
Voices within.   Room for Astolfo, Duke of Muscovy!

Enter ASTOLFO

Astolfo   Welcome, thrice welcome, the auspicious day,
When from the mountain where he darkling lay,
The Polish sun into the firmament
Sprung all the brighter for his late ascent,
And in meridian glory —
    Seg.   Where is he?
Why must I ask this twice? —
    A Lord   The Page, my Lord?
I wonder at his boldness —
    Seg.   But I tell you
He came with Angel written in his face
As now it is, when all was black as hell
About, and none of you who now — he came,
And Angel-like flung me a shining sword
To cut my way through darkness; and again
Angel-like wrests it from me in behalf
Of one — whom I will spare for sparing him:
But he must come and plead with that same voice
That pray'd for me — in vain.
    Chamb.   He is gone for,
And shall attend your pleasure, sir.   Meanwhile,
Will not your Highness, as in courtesy,
Return your royal cousin's greeting?
    Seg.   Whose?
    Chamb.   Astolfo, Duke of Muscovy, my Lord,
Saluted, and with gallant compliment
Welcomed you to your royal title.
    Seg. (to ASTOLFO).   Oh —
You knew of this then?
    Ast.   Knew of what, my Lord?
    Seg.   That I was Prince of Poland all the while,
And you my subject?
    Ast.   Pardon me, my Lord;

But some few hours ago myself I learn'd
Your dignity; but, knowing it, no more
Than when I knew it not, your subject.

  Seg.   What then?

  Ast. Your Highness' chamberlain ev'n now has told you;
Astolfo, Duke of Muscovy,
Your father's sister's son; your cousin, sir:
And who as such, and in his own right Prince,
Expects from you the courtesy he shows.

  Chamb. His Highness is as yet unused to Court,
And to the ceremonious interchange
Of compliment, especially to those
Who draw their blood from the same royal fountain.

  Seg. Where is the lad? I weary of all this —
Prince, cousins, chamberlains, and compliments —
Where are my soldiers? Blow the trumpet, and
With one sharp blast scatter these butterflies,
And bring the men of iron to my side,
With whom a king feels like a king indeed!

  Voices within. Within there! room for the Princess Estrella!

Enter ESTRELLA *with Ladies*

  Estrella Welcome, my Lord, right welcome to the throne
That much too long has waited for your coming:
And, in the general voice of Poland, hear
A kinswoman and cousin's no less sincere.

  Seg. Aye, this is welcome, welcome-worth indeed,
And cousin cousin-worth! Oh, I have thus
Over the threshold of the mountain seen,
Leading a bevy of fair stars, the moon
Enter the court of heav'n — My kinswoman!
My cousin! But my subject? —

  Est.   If you please
To count your cousin for your subject, sir,
You shall not find her a disloyal.

  Seg.   Oh,
But there are twin stars in that heav'nly face,
That now I know for having over-ruled

Those evil ones that darken'd all my past,
And brought me forth from that captivity
To be the slave of her who set me free.

   Est.   Indeed, my Lord, these eyes have no such power
Over the past or present: but perhaps
They brighten at your welcome to supply
The little that a lady's speech commends;
And in the hope that, let whichever be
The other's subject, we may both be friends.

   Seg.   Your hand to that — But why does this warm hand
Shoot a cold shudder through me?

   Est.   In revenge
For likening me to that cold moon, perhaps.

   Seg.   Oh, but the lip whose music tells me so
Breathes of a warmer planet, and that lip
Shall remedy the treason of the hand!

                         (He catches to embrace her.)

   Est.   Release me, sir!

   Chamb.   And pardon me, my Lord,
This lady is a Princess absolute,
As Prince he is who just saluted you,
And claims her by affiance.

   Seg.   Hence, old fool,
For ever thrusting that white stick of yours
Between me and my pleasure!

   Ast.   This cause is mine.
Forbear, sir —

   Seg.   What, sir mouth-piece, you again?

   Ast.   My Lord, I waive your insult to myself
In recognition of the dignity
You yet are new to, and that greater still
You look in time to wear.   But for this lady —
Whom, if my cousin now, I hope to claim
Henceforth by yet a nearer, dearer name —

   Seg.   And what care I?   She is my cousin too:
And if yóu be a Prince — well, am not I?
Lord of the very soil you stand upon?
By that, and by that right beside of blood
That like a fiery fountain hitherto
Pent in the rock leaps toward her at her touch,

Mine, before all the cousins in Muscovy!
You call me Prince of Poland, and yourselves
My subjects — traitors therefore to this hour,
Who let me perish all my youth away
Chain'd there among the mountains; till, forsooth,
Terrified at your treachery foregone,
You spirit me up here, I know not how,
Popinjay-like invest me like yourselves,
Choke me with scent and music that I loathe,
And, worse than all the music and the scent,
With false, long-winded, fulsome compliment,
That "Oh, you are my subjects!" and in word
Reiterating still obedience,
Thwart me in deed at every step I take:
When just about to wreak a just revenge
Upon that old arch-traitor of you all,
Filch from my vengeance him I hate; and him
I loved — the first and only face — till this —
I cared to look on in your ugly court —
And now when palpably I grasp at last
What hitherto but shadow'd in my dreams —
Affiances and interferences,
The first who dares to meddle with me more —
Princes and chamberlains and counsellors,
Touch her who dares! —

> *Ast.*   That dare I —
> *Seg. (seizing him by the throat).*   You dare!
> *Chamb.*   My Lord! —
> *A Lord*   His strength's a lion's —
> *Voices within*   The King!   The King!

Enter KING

> *A Lord*   And on a sudden how he stands at gaze,
> As might a wolf just fasten'd on his prey,
> Glaring at a suddenly encounter'd lion.
> *King*   And I that hither flew with open arms
> To fold them round my son, must now return
> To press them to an empty heart again!
>   *(He sits on the throne.)*

Seg.   That is the King? — My father? —
(After a long pause.)   I have heard
That sometimes some blind instinct has been known
To draw to mutual recognition those
Of the same blood, beyond all memory
Divided, or ev'n never met before.
I know not how this is — perhaps in brutes
That live by kindlier instincts — but I know
That looking now upon that head whose crown
Pronounces him a sovereign king, I feel
No setting of the current in my blood
Tow'rd him as sire.   How is 't with you, old man,
Tow'rd him they call your son? —
    King   Alas!   Alas!
    Seg.   Your sorrow, then?
    King   Beholding what I do.
    Seg.   Aye, but how know this sorrow, that has grown
And moulded to this present shape of man,
As of your own creation?
    King   Ev'n from birth.
    Seg.   But from that hour to this, near, as I think,
Some twenty such renewals of the year
As trace themselves upon the barren rocks,
I never saw you, nor you me — unless,
Unless, indeed, through one of those dark masks
Through which a son might fail to recognize
The best of fathers.
    King   Be that as you will:
But, now we see each other face to face,
Know me as you I know; which did I not,
By whatsoever signs, assuredly
You were not here to prove it at my risk.
    Seg.   You are my father.
And is it true then, as Clotaldo swears,
'T was you that from the dawning birth of one
Yourself brought into being, — you, I say,
Who stole his very birthright; not alone
That secondary and peculiar right
Of sovereignty, but even that prime
Inheritance that all men share alike,

And chain'd him — chain'd him! — like a wild beast's whelp,
Among as savage mountains, to this hour?
Answer if this be thus.

    King   Oh, Segismund,
In all that I have done that seems to you,
And, without further hearing, fairly seems,
Unnatural and cruel — 't was not I,
But One who writes His order in the sky
I dared not misinterpret nor neglect,
Who knows with what reluctance —

    Seg.   Oh, those stars,
Those stars, that too far up from human blame
To clear themselves, or careless of the charge,
Still bear upon their shining shoulders all
The guilt men shift upon them!

    King   Nay, but think:
Not only on the common score of kind,
But that peculiar count of sovereignty —
If not behind the beast in brain as heart,
How should I thus deal with my innocent child,
Doubly desired, and doubly dear when come,
As that sweet second-self that all desire,
And princes more than all, to root themselves
By that succession in their people's hearts?
Unless at that superior Will, to which
Not kings alone, but sovereign nature bows.

    Seg. And what had those same stars to tell of me
That should compel a father and a king
So much against that double instinct?

    King   That,
Which I have brought you hither, at my peril,
Against their written warning, to disprove,
By justice, mercy, human kindliness.

    Seg. And therefore made yourself their instrument
To make your son the savage and the brute
They only prophesied? — Are you not afear'd,
Lest, irrespective as such creatures are
Of such relationship, the brute you made
Revenge the man you marr'd — like sire, like son,
To do by you as you by me have done?

King   You never had a savage heart from me;
I may appeal to Poland.
     Seg.   Then from whom?
If pure in fountain, poison'd by yourself
When scarce begun to flow. — To make a man
Not, as I see, degraded from the mould
I came from, nor compared to those about,
And then to throw your own flesh to the dogs! —
Why not at once, I say, if terrified
At the prophetic omens of my birth,
Have drown'd or stifled me, as they do whelps
Too costly or too dangerous to keep?
     King   That, living, you might learn to live, and rule
Yourself and Poland.
     Seg.   By the means you took
To spoil for either?
     King   Nay, but Segismund!
You know not — cannot know — happily wanting
The sad experience on which knowledge grows,
How the too early consciousness of power
Spoils the best blood; nor whether for your long-
Constrain'd disheritance (which, but for me,
Remember, and for my relenting love
Bursting the bond of fate, had been eternal)
You have not now a full indemnity;
Wearing the blossom of your youth unspent
In the voluptuous sunshine of a court,
That often, by too early blossoming,
Too soon deflowers the rose of royalty.
     Seg.   Aye, but what some precocious warmth may spill,
May not an early frost as surely kill?
     King   But, Segismund, my son, whose quick discourse
Proves I have not extinguish'd and destroy'd
The Man you charge me with extinguishing,
However it condemn me for the fault
Of keeping a good light so long eclipst,
Reflect!   This is the moment upon which
Those stars, whose eyes, although we see them not,
By day as well as night are on us still,
Hang watching up in the meridian heaven

Which way the balance turns; and if to you —
As by your dealing God decide it may,
To my confusion! — let me answer it
Unto yourself alone, who shall at once
Approve yourself to be your father's judge,
And sovereign of Poland in his stead,
By justice, mercy, self-sobriety,
And all the reasonable attributes
Without which, impotent to rule himself,
Others one cannot, and one must not rule;
But which if you but show the blossom of —
All that is past we shall but look upon
As the first out-fling of a generous nature
Rioting in first liberty; and if
This blossom do but promise such a flower
As promises in turn its kindly fruit:
Forthwith upon your brows the royal crown,
That now weighs heavy on my agéd brows,
I will devolve; and while I pass away
Into some cloister, with my Maker there
To make my peace in penitence and prayer,
Happily settle the disorder'd realm
That now cries loudly for a lineal heir.

    Seg.   And so —
When the crown falters on your shaking head,
And slips the sceptre from your palsied hand,
And Poland for her rightful heir cries out;
When not only your stol'n monopoly
Fails you of earthly power, but 'cross the grave
The judgment-trumpet of another world
Calls to count for your abuse of this;
Then, oh then, terrified by the double danger,
You drag me from my den —
Boast not of giving up at last the power
You can no longer hold, and never rightly
Held, but in fee for him you robb'd it from;
And be assured your Savage, once let loose,
Will not be caged again so quickly; not
By threat or adulation to be tamed,
Till he have had his quarrel out with those

Who made him what he is.

 King   Beware! Beware!
Subdue the kindled Tiger in your eye,
Nor dream that it was sheer necessity
Made me thus far relax the bond of fate,
And, with far more of terror than of hope
Threaten myself, my people, and the State.
Know that, if old, I yet have vigour left
To wield the sword as well as wear the crown;
And if my more immediate issue fail,
Not wanting scions of collateral blood,
Whose wholesome growth shall more than compensate
For all the loss of a distorted stem.

 Seg. That will I straightway bring to trial — Oh,
After a revelation such as this,
The Last Day shall have little left to show
Of righted wrong and villany requited!
Nay, Judgment now beginning upon earth,
Myself, methinks, in right of all my wrongs,
Appointed heav'n's avenging minister,
Accuser, judge, and executioner,
Sword in hand, cite the guilty — First, as worst,
The usurper of his son's inheritance;
Him and his old accomplice, time and crime
Inveterate, and unable to repay
The golden years of life they stole away.
What, does he yet maintain his state, and keep
The throne he should be judged from? Down with him,
That I may trample on the false white head
So long has worn my crown! Where are my soldiers?
Of all my subjects and my vassals here
Not one to do my bidding? Hark! A trumpet!
The trumpet —
(He pauses as the trumpet sounds as in ACT I., *and masked
   Soldiers gradually fill in behind the Throne.)*
 King (rising before his throne). Aye, indeed, the trumpet
  blows
A memorable note, to summon those
Who, if forthwith you fall not at the feet
Of him whose head you threaten with the dust,

Forthwith shall draw the curtain of the Past
About you; and this momentary gleam
Of glory, that you think to hold life-fast,
So coming, so shall vanish, as a dream.

   Seg.   He prophesies; the old man prophesies;
And, at his trumpet's summons, from the tower
The leash-bound shadows loosen'd after me
My rising glory reach and over-lour —
But, reach not I my height, he shall not hold,
But with me back to his own darkness!
(He dashes toward the throne and is enclosed by the Soldiers.)
                          Traitors!
Hold off!   Unhand me! — Am I not your king?
And you would strangle him! —
But I am breaking with an inward Fire
Shall scorch you off, and wrap me on the wings
Of conflagration from a kindled pyre
Of lying prophecies and prophet-kings
Above the extinguisht stars — Reach me the sword
He flung me — Fill me such a bowl of wine
As that you woke the day with —

   King   And shall close, —
But of the vintage that Clotaldo knows.

ACT III

Scene I.   *The Tower, &c., as in* Act I., Scene I.
segismund, *as at first, and* clotaldo.

Clotaldo   Princes and princesses, and counsellors,
Fluster'd to right and left — my life made at —
But that was nothing —
Even the white-hair'd venerable King
Seized on — Indeed, you made wild work of it;
And so discover'd in your outward action
Flinging your arms about you in your sleep,
Grinding your teeth — and, as I now remember,
Woke mouthing out judgment and execution,
On those about you.
  Seg.   Aye, I did indeed.
  Clo. Ev'n now your eyes stare wild; your hair stands up —
Your pulses throb and flutter, reeling still
Under the storm of such a dream —
  Seg.   A dream!
That seem'd as swearable reality
As what I wake in now.
  Clo.   Aye — wondrous how
Imagination in a sleeping brain
Out of the uncontingent senses draws
Sensations strong as from the real touch;
That we not only laugh aloud, and drench
With tears our pillow; but in the agony
Of some imaginary conflict, fight
And struggle — ev'n as you did; some, 't is thought,
Under the dreamt-of stroke of death have died.

Seg.   And what so very strange too — In that world
Where place as well as people all was strange,
Ev'n I almost as strange unto myself,
You only, you, Clotaldo — you, as much
And palpably yourself as now you are,
Came in this very garb you ever wore,
By such a token of the past, you said,
To assure me of that seeming present.
  Clo.   Aye?
  Seg.   Aye; and even told me of the very stars
You tell me here of — how in spite of them,
I was enlarged to all that glory.
  Clo.   Aye,
By the false spirits' nice contrivance thus
A little truth oft leavens all the false,
The better to delude us.
  Seg.   For you know
'T is nothing but a dream?
  Clo.   Nay, you yourself
Know best how lately you awoke from that
You know you went to sleep on? —
Why, have you never dreamt the like before?
  Seg.   Never, to such reality.
  Clo.   Such dreams
Are oftentimes the sleeping exhalations
Of that ambition that lies smouldering
Under the ashes of the lowest fortune;
By which when reason slumbers, or has lost
The reins of sensible comparison,
We fly at something higher than we are —
Scarce ever dive to lower — to be kings,
Or conquerors, crown'd with laurel or with gold,
Nay, mounting heav'n itself on eagle wings.
Which, by the way, now that I think of it,
May furnish us the key to this high flight —
That royal Eagle we were watching, and
Talking of as you went to sleep last night.
  Seg.   Last night?   Last night?
  Clo.   Aye, do you remember
Envying his immunity of flight,

As, rising from his throne of rock, he sail'd
Above the mountains far into the West,
That burn'd about him, while with poising wings
He darkled in it as a burning brand
Is seen to smoulder in the fire it feeds?

 Seg. Last night — last night — Oh, what a day was that
Between that last night and this sad To-day!

 Clo. And yet, perhaps,
Only some few dark moments, into which
Imagination, once lit up within
And unconditional of time and space,
Can pour infinities.

 Seg.   And I remember
How the old man they call'd the King, who wore
The crown of gold about his silver hair,
And a mysterious girdle round his waist,
Just when my rage was roaring at its height,
And after which it all was dark again,
Bid me beware lest all should be a dream.

 Clo. Aye — there another specialty of dreams,
That once the dreamer 'gins to dream he dreams,
His foot is on the very verge of waking.

 Seg. Would it had been upon the verge of death
That knows no waking —
Lifting me up to glory, to fall back,
Stunn'd, crippled — wretcheder than ev'n before.

 Clo. Yet not so glorious, Segismund, if you
Your visionary honour wore so ill
As to work murder and revenge on those
Who meant you well.

 Seg.   Who meant me! — me! their Prince
Chain'd like a felon —

 Clo.   Stay, stay — Not so fast,
You dream'd the Prince, remember.

 Seg.   Then in dream
Revenged it only.

 Clo. True. But as they say
Dreams are rough copies of the waking soul
Yet uncorrected of the higher Will,
So that men sometimes in their dreams confess

An unsuspected, or forgotten, self;
One must beware to check — aye, if one may,
Stifle ere born, such passion in ourselves
As makes, we see, such havoc with our sleep,
And ill reacts upon the waking day.
And, by the bye, for one test, Segismund,
Between such swearable realities —
Since Dreaming, Madness, Passion, are akin
In missing each that salutary rein
Of reason, and the guiding will of man:
One test, I think, of waking sanity
Shall be that conscious power of self-control,
To curb all passion, but much most of all
That evil and vindictive, that ill squares
With human, and with holy canon less,
Which bids us pardon ev'n our enemies,
And much more those who, out of no ill will,
Mistakenly have taken up the rod
Which heav'n, they think, has put into their hands.

    Seg.   I think I soon shall have to try again —
Sleep has not yet done with me.

    Clo.   Such a sleep.
Take my advice — 't is early yet — the sun
Scarce up above the mountain; go within,
And if the night deceived you, try anew
With morning; morning dreams they say come true.

    Seg.   Oh, rather pray for me a sleep so fast
As shall obliterate dream and waking too.

                                 [*Exit into the tower.*

    Clo.   So sleep; sleep fast: and sleep away those two
Night-potions, and the waking dream between.
Which dream thou must believe; and, if to see
Again, poor Segismund! that dream must be. —
And yet, and yet, in these our ghostly lives,
Half night, half day, half sleeping, half awake,
How if our waking life, like that of sleep,
Be all a dream in that eternal life
To which we wake not till we sleep in death?
How if, I say, the senses we now trust
For date of sensible comparison, —

Aye, ev'n the Reason's self that dates with them,
Should be in essence or intensity
Hereafter so transcended, and awoke
To a perceptive subtilty so keen
As to confess themselves befool'd before,
In all that now they will avouch for most?
One man — like this — but only so much longer
As life is longer than a summer's day,
Believed himself a king upon his throne,
And play'd at hazard with his fellows' lives,
Who cheaply dreamt away their lives to him.
The sailor dream'd of tossing on the flood:
The soldier of his laurels grown in blood:
The lover of the beauty that he knew
Must yet dissolve to dusty residue:
The merchant and the miser of his bags
Of finger'd gold: the beggar of his rags:
And all this stage of earth on which we seem
Such busy actors, and the parts we play'd,
Substantial as the shadow of a shade,
And Dreaming but a dream within a dream!
    Fife   Was it not said, sir,
By some philosopher as yet unborn,
That any chimney-sweep who for twelve hours
Dreams himself king is happy as the king
Who dreams himself twelve hours a chimney-sweep?
    Clo.   A theme indeed for wiser heads than yours
To moralize upon — How came you here? —
    Fife   Not of my own will, I assure you, sir,
No matter for myself: but I would know
About my mistress — I mean, master —
    Clo.   Oh,
Now I remember — Well, your master-mistress
Is well, and deftly on its errand speeds,
As you shall — if you can but hold your tongue.
Can you?
    Fife   I'd rather be at home again.
    Clo.   Where you shall be the quicker if while here
You can keep silence.
    Fife   I may whistle, then?

Which by the virtue of my name I do,
And also as a reasonable test
Of waking sanity —
  Clo.   Well, whistle then;
And for another reason you forgot,
That while you whistle, you can chatter not.
Only remember — if you quit this pass —
  Fife   (His rhymes are out, or he had call'd it spot) —
  Clo.   A bullet brings you to.
I must forthwith to court to tell the King
The issue of this lamentable day,
That buries all his hope in night.   (*To* FIFE.)   Farewell.
Remember.
  Fife   But a moment — but a word!
What shall I see my mis — mas —
  Clo.   Be content:
All in good time; and then, and not before,
Never to miss your master any more.   [*Exit.*
  Fife   Such talk of dreaming — dreaming — I begin
To doubt if I be dreaming I am Fife,
Who with a lad who call'd herself a boy
Because — I doubt there's some confusion here —
He wore no petticoat, came on a time
Riding from Muscovy on half a horse,
Who must have dreamt she was a horse entire,
To cant me off upon my hinder face
Under this tower, wall-eyed and musket-tongued,
With sentinels, a-pacing up and down,
Crying All's well when all is far from well,
All the day long, and all the night, until
I dream — if what is dreaming be not waking —
Of bells a-tolling and processions rolling
With candles, crosses, banners, San-benitos,
Of which I wear the flamy-finingest,
Through streets and places throng'd with fiery faces
To some black platform —
Oh, I shall take a fire into my hand
With thinking of my own dear Muscovy —
Only just over that Sierra there,
By which we tumbled headlong into — No-land.

Now, if without a bullet after me,
I could but get a peep of my old home —
Perhaps of my own mule to take me there —
All's still — perhaps the gentlemen within
Are dreaming it is night behind their masks —
God send 'em a good nightmare! — Now then — Hark!
Voices — and up the rocks — and armèd men
Climbing like cats — Puss in the corner then.

[He hides.

Enter Soldiers cautiously up the rocks

Captain   This is the frontier pass, at any rate,
Where Poland ends and Muscovy begins.
   Soldier   We must be close upon the tower, I know,
That half way up the mountain lies ensconced.
   Capt.   How know you that?
   Sol.   He told me so — the Page
Who put us on the scent.
   Sol. 2   And, as I think,
Will soon be here to run it down with us.
   Capt.   Meantime, our horses on these ugly rocks
Useless, and worse than useless with their clatter —
Leave them behind, with one or two in charge,
And softly, softly, softly.
                    Soldiers.
   —   There it is!
   — There what? —
   —   The tower — the fortress —
                                That the tower! —
   — That mouse-trap!   We could pitch it down the rocks
With our own hands.
   —   The rocks it hangs among
Dwarf its proportions and conceal its strength;
Larger and stronger than you think.
                                No matter;
No place for Poland's Prince to be shut up in.
At it at once!
   Capt.   No — no — I tell you wait —
Till those within give signal.   For as yet

We know not who side with us, and the fort
Is strong in man and musket.

  Sol.   Shame to wait
For odds with such a cause at stake.

  Capt.   Because
Of such a cause at stake we wait for odds —
For if not won at once, for ever lost:
For any long resistance on their part
Would bring Basilio's force to succour them
Ere we had rescued him we come to rescue.
So softly, softly, softly, still —

  A Soldier (discovering FIFE). Hilloa!

         Soldiers.

  — Hilloa! Here's some one skulking —

 —   Seize and gag him!

 — Stab him at once, say I: the only way
To make all sure.

  —   Hold, every man of you!
And down upon your knees! — Why, 't is the Prince!

 — The Prince! —

  —   Oh, I should know him anywhere,
And anyhow disguised.

       But the Prince is chain'd.

 — And of a loftier presence —

  —   'T is he, I tell you;
Only bewilder'd as he was before.
God save your Royal Highness! On our knees
Beseech you answer us!

  Fife   Just as you please.
Well — 't is this country's custom, I suppose,
To take a poor man every now and then
And set him on the throne; just for the fun
Of tumbling him again into the dirt.
And now my turn is come. 'T is very pretty.

  Sol. His wits have been distemper'd with their drugs.
But do you ask him, Captain.

  Capt.   On my knees,
And in the name of all who kneel with me,
I do beseech your Highness answer to
Your royal title.

Fife   Still, just as you please.
In my own poor opinion of myself —
But that may all be dreaming, which it seems
Is very much the fashion in this country —
No Polish prince at all, but a poor lad
From Muscovy; where only help me back,
I promise never to contest the crown
Of Poland with whatever gentleman
You fancy to set up.
                              Soldiers.
⎡—   From Muscovy?
⎜— A spy then —
⎨—   Of Astolfo's —
⎜—   Spy! a spy! —
⎣— Hang him at once!
     Fife   No, pray don't dream of that!
     Sol.   How dared you then set yourself up for our
Prince Segismund?
     Fife   *I* set up! — I like that —
When 't was yourselves be-siegesmunded me.
     Capt.   No matter — Look! — The signal from the tower.
Prince Segismund!
     Sol. (from the tower).   Prince Segismund!
     Capt.   All's well.
Clotaldo safe secured? —
     Sol. (from the tower).   No — by ill luck,
Instead of coming in, as we had look'd for,
He sprang on horse at once, and off at gallop.
     Capt.   To Court, no doubt — a blunder that — And yet
Perchance a blunder that may work as well
As better forethought.   Having no suspicion,
So will he carry none where his not going
Were of itself suspicious.   But of those
Within, who side with us?
     Sol.   Oh, one and all
To the last man, persuaded or compell'd.
     Capt.   Enough: whatever be to be retrieved,
No moment to be lost.   For though Clotaldo
Have no revolt to tell of in the tower,
The capital will soon awake to ours,

And the King's force come blazing after us.
Where is the Prince?
 Sol.   Within; so fast asleep
We woke him not ev'n striking off the chain
We had so cursedly holp bind him with,
Not knowing what we did; but too ashamed
Not to undo ourselves what we had done.
 Capt.   No matter, nor by whosesoever hands,
Provided done.   Come; we will bring him forth
Out of that stony darkness here abroad,
Where air and sunshine sooner shall disperse
The sleepy fume which they have drugg'd him with.
(They enter the tower, and thence bring out SEGISMUND *asleep*
     on a pallet, and set him in the middle of the stage.)
 Capt.   Still, still so dead asleep, the very noise
And motion that we make in carrying him
Stirs not a leaf in all the living tree.
        Soldiers

If living — But if by some inward blow
For ever and irrevocably fell'd
By what strikes deeper to the root than sleep?
— He's dead!   He's dead!   They've killed him —
—   No — he breathes —
And the heart beats — and now he breathes again
Deeply, as one about to shake away
The load of sleep.
 Capt.   Come, let us all kneel round,
And with a blast of warlike instruments,
And acclamation of all loyal hearts,
Rouse and restore him to his royal right,
From which no royal wrong shall drive him more.
    (They all kneel round his bed: trumpets, drums, &c.)
     Segismund!   Segismund!   Prince Segismund!
Soldiers   King Segismund!   Down with Basilio!
     Down with Astolfo!   Segismund our King! &c.
Soldier 1   He stares upon us wildly.   He cannot speak.
——   2   I said so — driv'n him mad.
——   3   Speak to him, Captain.
 Capt.   Oh, Royal Segismund, our Prince and King,

Look on us — listen to us — answer us,
Your faithful soldiery and subjects, now
About you kneeling, but on fire to rise
And cleave a passage through your enemies,
Until we seat you on your lawful throne.
For though your father, King Basilio,
Now King of Poland, jealous of the stars
That prophesy his setting with your rise,
Here holds you ignominiously eclipst,
And would Astolfo, Duke of Muscovy,
Mount to the throne of Poland after him;
So will not we, your loyal soldiery
And subjects; neither those of us now first
Apprised of your existence and your right:
Nor those that hitherto deluded by
Allegiance false, their visors now fling down,
And craving pardon on their knees with us
For that unconscious disloyalty,
Offer with us the service of their blood;
Not only we and they; but at our heels
The heart, if not the bulk, of Poland follows
To join their voices and their arms with ours,
In vindicating with our lives our own
Prince Segismund to Poland and her throne.

Soldiers {Segismund, Segismund, Prince Segismund!
Our own King Segismund, &c.

(They all rise.)

Seg.   Again?   So soon? — what, not yet done with me?
The sun is little higher up, I think,
Than when I last lay down,
To bury in the depth of your own sea
You that infest its shallows.
    Capt.   Sir!
    Seg.   And now,
Not in a palace, not in the fine clothes
We all were in; but here, in the old place,
And in our old accoutrement —
Only your visors off, and lips unlockt
To mock me with that idle title —

Capt.   Nay,
Indeed no idle title, but your own,
Then, now, and now for ever.   For, behold,
Ev'n as I speak, the mountain passes fill
And bristle with the advancing soldiery
That glitters in your rising glory, sir;
And, at our signal, echo to our cry,
"Segismund, King of Poland!" &c.   *(Shouts, trumpets, &c.)*
     Seg.   Oh, how cheap
The muster of a countless host of shadows,
As impotent to do with as to keep!
All this they said before — to softer music.
     Capt.   Soft music, sir, to what indeed were shadows,
That, following the sunshine of a Court,
Shall back be brought with it — if shadows still,
Yet to substantial reckoning.
     Seg.   They shall?
The white-hair'd and the white-wanded chamberlain,
So busy with his wand too — the old King
That I was somewhat hard on — he had been
Hard upon me — and the fine-feather'd Prince
Who crow'd so loud — my cousin, — and another,
Another cousin, we will not bear hard on —
And — But Clotaldo?
     Capt.   Fled, my Lord, but close
Pursued; and then —
     Seg.   Then, as he fled before,
And after he had sworn it on his knees,
Came back to take me — where I am! — No more,
No more of this!   Away with you!   Begone!
Whether but visions of ambitious night
That morning ought to scatter, or grown out
Of night's proportions you invade the day
To scare me from my little wits yet left,
Begone!   I know I must be near awake,
Knowing I dream; or, if not at my voice,
Then vanish at the clapping of my hands,
Or take this foolish fellow for your sport:
Dressing me up in visionary glories,

Which the first air of waking consciousness
Scatters as fast as from the almander[1] —
That, waking one fine morning in full flower,
One rougher insurrection of the breeze
Of all her sudden honour disadorns
To the last blossom, and she stands again
The winter-naked scare-crow that she was!

  Capt. I know not what to do, nor what to say,
With all this dreaming; I begin to doubt
They have driv'n him mad indeed, and he and we
Are lost together.

  A Soldier (to Captain). Stay, stay; I remember —
Hark in your ear a moment.   *(Whispers.)*

  Capt.   So — so — so? —
Oh, now indeed I do not wonder, sir,
Your senses dazzle under practices
Which treason, shrinking from its own device,
Would now persuade you only was a dream;
But waking was as absolute as this
You wake in now, as some who saw you then,
Prince as you were and are, can testify:
Not only saw, but under false allegiance
Laid hands upon —

  Soldier 1   I, to my shame!
  Soldier 2   And I!

  Capt. Who, to wipe out that shame, have been the first
To stir and lead us — Hark! *(Shouts, trumpets, &c.)*

  A Soldier   Our forces, sir,
Challenging King Basilio's, now in sight,
And bearing down upon us.

  Capt.   Sir, you hear;
A little hesitation and delay,
And all is lost — your own right, and the lives
Of those who now maintain it at that cost;
With you all saved and won; without, all lost.
That former recognition of your right
Grant but a dream, if you will have it so;
Great things forecast themselves by shadows great:

[1] Almander, or almandre, Chaucer's word for *almond-tree*, Rom.
Rose, 1363.

Or will you have it, this like that dream too,
People and place, and time itself, all dream —
Yet, being in 't, and as the shadows come
Quicker and thicker than you can escape,
Adopt your visionary soldiery,
Who, having struck a solid chain away,
Now put an airy sword into your hand,
And harnessing you piece-meal till you stand
Amidst us all complete in glittering,
If unsubstantial, steel —
    Rosaura (without).   The Prince!   The Prince!
    Capt.   Who calls for him?
    Sol.   The Page who spurr'd us hither,
And now, dismounted from a foaming horse —

Enter ROSAURA

    Rosaura   Where is — but where I need no further ask,
Where the majestic presence, all in arms,
Mutely proclaims and vindicates himself.
    Fife   My darling Lady-bird —
    Ros.   My own good Fife,
Keep to my side — and silence! — Oh, my Lord,
For the third time behold me here where first
You saw me, by a happy misadventure
Losing my own way here to find it out
For you to follow with these loyal men,
Adding the moment of my little cause
To yours; which, so much mightier as it is,
By a strange chance runs hand in hand with mine;
The self-same foe who now pretends your right,
Withholding mine — that, of itself alone,
I know the royal blood that runs in you
Would vindicate, regardless of your own:
The right of injured innocence; and, more,
Spite of this epicene attire, a woman's;
And of a noble stock I will not name
Till I, who brought it, have retrieved the shame.
Whom Duke Astolfo, Prince of Muscovy,
With all the solemn vows of wedlock won,

And would have wedded, as I do believe,
Had not the cry of Poland for a Prince
Call'd him from Muscovy to join the prize
Of Poland with the fair Estrella's eyes.
I, following him hither, as you saw,
Was cast upon these rocks; arrested by
Clotaldo: who for an old debt of love
He owes my family, with all his might
Served, and had served me further, till my cause
Clash'd with his duty to his sovereign,
Which, as became a loyal subject, sir,
(And never sovereign had a loyaller,)
Was still his first.   He carried me to Court,
Where, for the second time, I cross'd your path;
Where, as I watch'd my opportunity,
Suddenly broke this public passion out;
Which, drowning private into public wrong,
Yet swiftlier sweeps it to revenge along.
   Seg.   Oh God, if this be dreaming, charge it not
To burst the channel of enclosing sleep
And drown the waking reason!   Not to dream
Only what dreamt shall once or twice again
Return to buzz about the sleeping brain
Till shaken off for ever —
But reassailing one so quick, so thick —
The very figure and the circumstance
Of sense-confest reality foregone
In so-call'd dream so palpably repeated,
The copy so like the original,
We know not which is which; and dream so-call'd
Itself inweaving so inextricably
Into the tissue of acknowledged truth;
The very figures that empeople it
Returning to assert themselves no phantoms
In something so much like meridian day,
And in the very place that not my worst
And veriest disenchanter shall deny
For the too well-remember'd theatre
Of my long tragedy — Strike up the drums!
If this be Truth and all of us awake,

Indeed a famous quarrel is at stake:
If but a Vision I will see it out,
And, drive the Dream, I can but join the rout.

    Capt.   And in good time, sir, for a palpable
Touchstone of truth and rightful vengeance too,
Here is Clotaldo taken.

    Soldiers   In with him!
In with the traitor!   (CLOTALDO *is brought in.*)

    Seg.   Aye, Clotaldo, indeed —
Himself — in his old habit — his old self —
What! back again, Clotaldo, for a while
To swear me this for truth, and afterwards
All for a dreaming lie?

    Clo.   Awake or dreaming,
Down with that sword, and down these traitors theirs,
Drawn in rebellion 'gainst their Sovereign.

    Seg. (about to strike).   Traitor!   Traitor yourself! — But soft
      — soft — soft! —
You told me, not so very long ago,
Awake or dreaming — I forget — my brain
Is not so clear about it — but I know
One test you gave me to discern between,
Which mad and dreaming people cannot master;
Or if the dreamer could, so best secure
A comfortable waking — Was 't not so? —
(To ROSAURA.*)*   Needs not your intercession now, you see,
As in the dream before —
Clotaldo, rough old nurse and tutor too
That only traitor wert, to me if true —
Give him his sword; set him on a fresh horse;
Conduct him safely through my rebel force;
And so God speed him to his sovereign's side!
Give me your hand; and whether all awake
Or all a-dreaming, ride, Clotaldo, ride —
Dream-swift — for fear we dreams should overtake.

        (A Battle may be supposed to take place; after which)

SCENE II. *A wooded pass near the field of battle: drums, trumpets, firing, &c. Cries of "God save Basilio! Segismund," &c. Enter* FIFE *running.*

Fife   God save them both, and save them all! say I! —
Oh — what hot work! — Whichever way one turns
The whistling bullet at one's ears — I've drifted
Far from my mad young — master — whom I saw
Tossing upon the very crest of battle,
Beside the Prince — God save her first of all!
With all my heart I say and pray — and so
Commend her to His keeping — bang! — bang! — bang! —
And for myself — scarce worth His thinking of —
I'll see what I can do to save myself
Behind this rock until the storm blows over.

(*Skirmishes, shouts, firing, &c.   After some time enter*
KING BASILIO, ASTOLFO, *and* CLOTALDO.)

King   The day is lost!
Ast.   Do not despair — the rebels —
King   Alas! the vanquisht only are the rebels.
Clotaldo   Ev'n if this battle lost us, 't is but one
Gain'd on their side, if you not lost in it;
Another moment and too late: at once
Take horse, and to the capital, my liege,
Where in some safe and holy sanctuary
Save Poland in your person.
Ast.   Be persuaded:
You know your son: have tasted of his temper;
At his first onset threatening unprovoked
The crime predicted for his last and worst.
How whetted now with such a taste of blood,
And thus far conquest!
King   Aye, and how he fought!
Oh how he fought, Astolfo; ranks of men
Falling as swathes of grass before the mower;
I could but pause to gaze at him, although,
Like the pale horseman of the Apocalypse,
Each moment brought him nearer — Yet I say,

I could but pause and gaze on him, and pray
Poland had such a warrior for her king.

 Ast. The cry of triumph on the other side
Gains ground upon us here — there's but a moment
For you, my liege, to do, for me to speak,
Who back must to the field, and what man may,
Do, to retrieve the fortunes of the day. *(Firing.)*

 Fife (falling forward, shot). Oh, Lord, have mercy on me.

 King   What a shriek —
Oh, some poor creature wounded in a cause
Perhaps not worth the loss of one poor life! —
So young too — and no soldier —

 Fife   A poor lad
Who choosing play at hide and seek with death,
Just hid where death just came to look for him;
For there's no place, I think, can keep him out,
Once he's his eye upon you. All grows dark —
You glitter finely too — Well — we are dreaming —
But when the bullet's off — Heav'n save the mark!
So tell my mister — mastress —   *(Dies.)*

 King Oh God! How this poor creature's ignorance
Confounds our so-call'd wisdom! Even now
When death has stopt his lips, the wound through which
His soul went out, still with its bloody tongue
Preaching how vain our struggle against fate!

 (Voices within.) After them! After them! This way!
  This way!
The day is ours — Down with Basilio, &c.

 Ast. Fly, sir —

 King   And slave-like flying not out-ride
The fate which better like a King abide!

Enter SEGISMUND, ROSAURA, Soldiers, &c.

 Segismund Where is the King?

 King (prostrating himself). Behold him, — by this late
Anticipation of resistless fate,
Thus underneath your feet his golden crown,
And the white head that wears it, laying down,
His fond resistance hope to expiate.

 Segismund Princes and warriors of Poland — you

That stare on this unnatural sight aghast,
Listen to one who, Heav'n-inspired to do
What in its secret wisdom Heav'n forecast,
By that same Heav'n instructed prophet-wise
To justify the present in the past.   .
What in the sapphire volume of the skies
Is writ by God's own finger misleads none,
But him whose vain and misinstructed eyes,
They mock with misinterpretation,
Or who, mistaking what he rightly read,
Ill commentary makes, or misapplies
Thinking to shirk or thwart it.   Which has done
The wisdom of this venerable head;
Who, well provided with the secret key
To that gold alphabet, himself made me,
Himself, I say, the savage he fore-read
Fate somehow should be charged with; nipp'd the growth
Of better nature in constraint and sloth,
That only bring to bear the seed of wrong,
And turn'd the stream to fury whose out-burst
Had kept his lawful channel uncoerced,
And fertilized the land he flow'd along.
Then like to some unskilful duellist,
Who having over-reach'd himself pushing too hard
His foe, or but a moment off his guard —
What odds, when Fate is one's antagonist! —
Nay, more, this royal father, self-dismay'd
At having Fate against himself array'd,
Upon himself the very sword he knew
Should wound him, down upon his bosom drew,
That might well handled, well have wrought; or, kept
Undrawn, have harmless in the scabbard slept.
But Fate shall not by human force be broke,
Nor foil'd by human feint; the Secret learn'd
Against the scholar by that master turn'd
Who to himself reserves the master-stroke.
Witness whereof this venerable Age,
Thrice crown'd as Sire, and Sovereign, and Sage,
Down to the very dust dishonour'd by
The very means he tempted to defy
The irresistible.   And shall not I,

Till now the mere dumb instrument that wrought
The battle Fate has with my father fought,
Now the mere mouth-piece of its victory —
Oh, shall not I, the champion's sword laid down,
Be yet more shamed to wear the teacher's gown,
And, blushing at the part I had to play,
Down where that honour'd head I was to lay
By this more just submission of my own,
The treason Fate has forced on me atone?

    King   Oh, Segismund, in whom I see indeed,
Out of the ashes of my self-extinction
A better self revive; if not beneath
Your feet, beneath your better wisdom bow'd,
The Sovereignty of Poland I resign,
With this its golden symbol; which if thus
Saved with its silver head inviolate,
Shall nevermore be subject to decline;
But when the head that it alights on now
Falls honour'd by the very foe that must,
As all things mortal, lay it in the dust,
Shall star-like shift to his successor's brow.

    Shouts, trumpets, &c.   God save King Segismund!
    Seg.   For what remains —
As for my own, so for my people's peace,
Astolfo's and Estrella's plighted hands
I disunite, and taking hers to mine,
His to one yet more dearly his resign.

    Shouts, &c.   God save Estrella, Queen of Poland!
    Seg. (to CLOTALDO).   You
That with unflinching duty to your King,
Till countermanded by the mightier Power,
Have held your Prince a captive in the tower,
Henceforth as strictly guard him on the throne,
No less my people's keeper than my own.[1]
You stare upon me all, amazed to hear

[1] In Calderon's drama, the Soldier who liberates Segismund
meets with even worse recompense than in the version below. I
suppose some such saving clause against prosperous treason was
necessary in the days of Philip IV., if not later.

    CAPT.   And what for him, my liege, who made you free
To honour him who held you prisoner?

The word of civil justice from such lips
As never yet seem'd tuned to such discourse.
But listen — In that same enchanted tower,
Not long ago I learn'd it from a dream
Expounded by this ancient prophet here;
And which he told me, should it come again,
How I should bear myself beneath it; not
As then with angry passion all on fire,
Arguing and making a distemper'd soul;
But ev'n with justice, mercy, self-control,
As if the dream I walk'd in were no dream,
And conscience one day to account for it.
A dream it was in which I thought myself,
And you that hail'd me now then hail'd me King,
In a brave palace that was all my own,
Within, and all without it, mine; until,
Drunk with excess of majesty and pride,
Methought I tower'd so high and swell'd so wide,
That of myself I burst the glittering bubble,
That my ambition had about me blown,
And all again was darkness.   Such a dream
As this in which I may be walking now;
Dispensing solemn justice to you shadows,
Who make believe to listen; but anon,
With all your glittering arms and equipage,
King, princes, captains, warriors, plume and steel,
Aye, ev'n with all your airy theatre,
May flit into the air you seem to rend
With acclamation, leaving me to wake
In the dark tower; or dreaming that I wake
From this that waking is; or this and that
Both waking or both dreaming; such a doubt
Confounds and clouds our mortal life about.
And, whether wake or dreaming; this I know,
How dream-wise human glories come and go;

     SEG.   By such self-proclamation self-betray'd
Less to your Prince's service or your King's
Loyal, than to the recompence it brings;
The tower he leaves I make you keeper of
For life — and, mark you, not to leave alive;
For treason may, but not the traitor, thrive.

Whose momentary tenure not to break,
Walking as one who knows he soon may wake,
So fairly carry the full cup, so well
Disorder'd insolence and passion quell,
That there be nothing after to upbraid
Dreamer or doer in the part he play'd,
Whether To-morrow's dawn shall break the spell,
Or the Last Trumpet of the eternal Day,
When Dreaming with the Night shall pass away.

DATE DUE

GAYLORD No. 2333   PRINTED IN U.S.A.

**PQ 6292 .A1 F513 2000
Calderon de la Barca,
Pedro, 1600-1681.**

University of Illinois Press
1325 South Oak Street
Champaign, IL 61820-6903
WWW.PRESS.UILLINOIS.EDU